NEW YORK REVIEW I
CLASSICS

ON WRITERS AND WRITING

HENRY JAMES (1843–1916), the younger brother of the
psychologist William James and one of the greatest of
American writers, was born in New York but lived for most
of his life in England. Among the best known of his many
stories and novels are *The Portrait of a Lady*, *The Turn of the
Screw*, and *The Wings of the Dove*. In addition to *On Writers
and Writing*, New York Review Classics has published *The
New York Stories of Henry James* and three long-unavailable
novels: *The Other House*, *The Outcry*, and *The Ivory Tower*.

MICHAEL GORRA is the author of *Portrait of a Novel:
Henry James and the Making of an American Masterpiece*, a
finalist for the Pulitzer Prize in Biography; *The Bells in Their
Silence: Travels Through Germany*; and *The Saddest Words:
William Faulkner's Civil War*. A regular contributor to *The
New York Review of Books*, he is a member of the American
Academy of Arts and Sciences. Born in New London,
Connecticut, Gorra has taught at Smith College since 1985,
where he is the Mary Augusta Jordan Professor of English.

ON WRITERS AND WRITING

HENRY JAMES

Edited and with an introduction by
MICHAEL GORRA

NEW YORK REVIEW BOOKS

New York

THIS IS A NEW YORK REVIEW BOOK
PUBLISHED BY THE NEW YORK REVIEW OF BOOKS
207 East 32nd Street, New York, NY 10016
www.nyrb.com

Library of Congress Cataloging-in-Publication Data
Names: James, Henry, 1843–1916, author. | Gorra, Michael Edward, editor.
Title: On writers and writing: selected essays / by Henry James, edited and
    with an introduction by Michael Gorra.
Identifiers: LCCN 2024046443 (print) | LCCN 2024046444 (ebook) |
    ISBN 9781681379234 (paperback) | ISBN 9781681379241 (ebook)
Subjects: LCSH: Authorship. | LCGFT: Essays.
Classification: LCC PS2120 .O5 2025 (print) | LCC PS2120 (ebook) |
    DDC 814/.4—dc23/eng/20241002
LC record available at https://lccn.loc.gov/2024046443
LC ebook record available at https://lccn.loc.gov/2024046444

ISBN 978-1-68137-923-4
Available as an electronic book; ISBN 978-1-68137-924-1

The authorized representative in the EU for product safety and
compliance is eucomply OÜ, Pärnu mnt 139b-14, 11317 Tallinn, Estonia,
hello@eucompliancepartner.com, +33 757690241.

Printed in the United States of America on acid-free paper.
10 9 8 7 6 5 4 3 2 1

CONTENTS

Introduction · vii

THE ART OF FICTION · 3

NEW NOVELS IN REVIEW
Mary Elizabeth Braddon, *Aurora Floyd* · 29
Charles Dickens, *Our Mutual Friend* · 35
Elizabeth Gaskell, *Wives and Daughters* · 41
George Eliot, *Middlemarch* · 46
Thomas Hardy, *Far from the Madding Crowd* · 55
Émile Zola, *Nana* · 61

MEMORIALS
George Sand · 71
Anthony Trollope · 98
Ivan Turgénieff · 122
The Life of George Eliot · 143
Emerson · 160
Browning in Westminster Abbey · 183

FORMS OF FICTION

Guy de Maupassant · 191

The Future of the Novel · 220

Matilde Serao · 231

Gustave Flaubert · 246

Émile Zola · 279

The Lesson of Balzac · 308

VALEDICTIONS

The Tempest · 335

Mr. and Mrs. James T. Fields · 351

Bibliographical Notes · 369

INTRODUCTION

THE NERVE HE HAD. Twenty-two years old and living with his parents in Cambridge, a law-school dropout with just two pieces of published fiction to his name: this boy sets out in the fall of 1865 to take down the most famous novelist of the day, and pretty nearly succeeds. *Our Mutual Friend*, the young Henry James suggested, stands as the poorest of Charles Dickens's novels, and "poor with the poverty not of momentary embarrassment, but of permanent exhaustion." Nobody but Dickens could have written it, and yet is that really a recommendation? For its characters are "mere bundle[s] of eccentricities" in a way that underlines his long-standing limitations, and to call him one of our greatest novelists is to commit "an offence against humanity." Weak, depressing, unprofitable, insufficient, mechanical, superficial, gratuitous, cheap, lifeless—those are the adjectives James used, in writing for a new weekly called *The Nation*, and once you've read that list you can't forget it. Because even the most devoted of Dickens's readers have felt that way at times about individual chapters or characters or maybe whole novels. James's account may be extreme and yet it isn't unfair; *Our Mutual Friend* is among my favorites, but don't ask me about *Hard Times*.

Nowadays we'd say that Dickens needs those eccentricities, that his hallucinatory power depends upon them. And probably James—an older James—would have agreed with that. His brief references to the novelist in his later essays are invariably generous, and in *A Small Boy and Others* (1913), the first volume of his memoirs, he remembers sobbing in fear and delight at hearing the "golden harvest" of the newly published *David Copperfield* read aloud. But the young writer used his sharply critical reviews of his elders to steer by. He was funny and quotable, uncowed by reputation, and a few years later he called the newly published *Middlemarch* "at once one of the strongest and one of the weakest of English novels." It is a "treasure-house of details, but ... an indifferent whole," a work that fails because it tries to tell too many stories at once. James still hadn't released a book of his own, but he could always spot the issues even if we might now disagree with his evaluation. Most readers today believe that that plenitude is part of George Eliot's special glory, and yet he was absolutely right in claiming that the book set a limit to "the old-fashioned English novel"; she made it impossible for her successors to blunder on in the belief that they were simply describing life as it was. He was more admiring in his letters, admitting the novel's power while also distinguishing it from the kind of fiction he wanted to write himself. His own work, he said, would have less brain and more form. James wasn't yet at the point of trying to create the taste by which he would be appreciated, though that would come. Nevertheless he wrote about what his predecessors got wrong in the hopes that he might someday get it right.

It didn't happen quickly. James found his voice as a critic long before he did as a novelist, and some of his friends thought, after reading his initial and rather static short stories, that this was where his real abilities lay. The first thing he published was an 1864 review of a book of essays by a forgotten writer with an unforgettable name, an English lawyer called Nassau W. Senior. James didn't like it, but he did like the fact that the *North American Review* was willing to give him twelve dollars for a few opinionated pages. He had never earned a cent before, and each greenback held the promise of a future. He turned out hundreds of pieces over the next dozen-odd years: travel sketches of Newport and Saratoga; letters from Paris that included a surprisingly shrewd analysis of the political news along with an account of the latest plays and paintings; descriptions of English castles, Swiss stagecoaches, and Roman holidays; and one book review after another. James reviewed everything. He wrote badly about Walt Whitman's *Drum-Taps* and quizzically about Charles Baudelaire, whose understanding of evil he saw as no match for Nathaniel Hawthorne's. Louisa May Alcott's *Eight Cousins*, the nature writing of John Burroughs, the now-unreadable epic poetry of William Morris, Goethe, Victor Hugo, and *A Ride to Khiva*, that minor classic of the Great Game by the English soldier Frederick Burnaby: James covered them all, a few thousand words at a time.

But sometimes he wrote at much greater length. James made his first adult trip to Europe in 1869–1870, and he returned in 1872, accompanying his sister, Alice, at the start and then staying on after she went home. He only came back to the States in 1874 under a mixture of familial and financial pressures. Much of that time abroad was spent in Florence and Rome, in the expatriate world in which he set most of his first novel, *Roderick Hudson* (1875). He went north in the summer, however, and in one of the German spa towns picked up a translation of some stories by Ivan Turgenev. Very little of the Russian writer had as yet come into English, but James had studied German as a boy and the older novelist was available in French as well. Now he read him through, and found in his work the guide that the English novel had not provided. For James, Turgenev belonged "to the limited class of very careful writers." Nothing about his fiction seemed improvised, and his characters were the result of a close, precise, and indeed "narrow observation" of the people around him. "His figures are all portraits," and Turgenev excelled in distinguishing the individual from the general class to which he or she belonged, in particularizing what made this landowner or peasant different from that one. The incidents of his plots grew directly out of and in fact served to illustrate those characters, and his tales often ended with an unanswered question, their loose ends emphatically untied.

James's essay appeared in the *North American Review* in April 1874, just before he returned to the States. He had learned in Italy that his material lay in the lives of Americans abroad, in charting the relations of the new national culture to the European past. And he had wanted to stay on, only to persuade himself that it would after all be cheaper to live in New York; he took an apartment on East Twenty-Fifth Street and told himself that he liked the "big bustling luxurious place." He wrote two articles a week, most of them for *The Nation*, and saw two more books through the press as well, a volume of stories and a collection of travel sketches to go along with *Roderick Hudson*. These were smart professional moves, but New York wasn't cheaper, it never is, and in October 1875 he left America once more, settling in Paris for a year before crossing to the London that would become his home. Yet he was no longer a beginner, and one mark of that was a letter from Turgenev himself. James's proud busybody of a father had sent the Russian writer a copy of the essay, and gotten back an invitation for the young man to call.

Henry James was a working critic for the entirety of his professional life. The essays I've chosen for this book cover a fifty-year span, going back to his early accounts of new novels and running forward to one of the very last things he wrote, his brief 1915 memoir of "Mr. and Mrs. James T. Fields," an evocation of the literary New England in which he had grown up. These essays are of many kinds: short reviews, obituaries, masterly accounts of another writer's oeuvre, and even a few statements of principle, in which he tells us both how to write and how to read. Some pieces set a task for the future, suggesting the representational limits that the novel—the Anglophone novel in particular—had yet to overcome. Others are more anecdotal, pictures of his elders and contemporaries, and built upon small nuggets of narrative; gold for biographers, and not only those of James himself. None of them stands as a panegyric. James was at once generous and strict, and invariably tells us where he thinks his favorites go wrong, where Gustave Flaubert's pages turn lifeless and Balzac strains belief. Not that he was always consistent. In "The Art of Fiction" he suggested that the critic must begin by granting each novelist his *donnée*, his givens of subject and sensibility. But late in his career he couldn't write about other people's books without trying to show how much better they might have been if only he'd written them himself, remaking work by Robert Browning and Arnold Bennett, among others, in his own image. It didn't help that he was usually right.

The body of James's criticism is so large that with the exception of "The Art of Fiction" few of the essays here selected themselves. An 1875 article on Balzac is among his best, with its observation that though "each particular episode of the 'Comédie Humaine' has its own hero and heroine . . . the great general protagonist is the twenty-franc piece." So is that early piece on Turgenev. They are among the many writers about whom he wrote repeatedly, but one of the guidelines I set for myself in making this selection was to include just a single full-length account of such figures; and in each case I preferred a later essay. There are, however, two pieces on both Émile Zola and George Eliot, a brief review of a new novel along with a retrospective survey. For another of my rules was to reprint his straight-up, one-book notices of those novels that still have some critical currency. Elizabeth Gaskell's *Wives and Daughters*, Thomas Hardy's *Far from the Madding Crowd*—any student of the Victorian novel will want to see what James said about them. And so they will too with Mary Elizabeth Braddon's *Aurora Floyd*, a page-turning bestseller that James used to particularize the crawling fear on which the sensation novel depends: not the terrors of the Gothic or the supernatural but the infinitely more frightful experiences of everyday life, those "mysteries which are at our own doors." I've always regretted the fact that he essentially stopped writing such reviews at the end of the 1870s; we can only imagine what he might have said about *The Egoist* or *Kim* or *A Hazard of New Fortunes*.

More rules. I've used only whole pieces, not excerpts. James wrote some brilliant paragraphs about both Joseph Conrad and Edith Wharton in a 1914 essay called "The New Novel," but his few pages on them are surrounded by accounts of writers who are now barely remembered even by specialists. I've skipped over his 1879 book on Hawthorne as well. No American writer had so great an influence upon him, and the way in which James's characters scrutinize themselves, canvassing their own motivations and uncertainties, owes a great deal to his introspective predecessor, a writer whose work always insists on "the doctrine of the supremacy of the individual to himself." Yet the book as a whole seems diffuse. Its great passages are widely scattered; any excerpt would be but a loose collection of favorite quotations. Finally, this volume gathers James's impressions of other writers, his account of their work and not his own. So I've included nothing from his readily available prefaces to the New York Edition, however much those essays add to our understanding of both his own artistic processes and his sense of novelistic form.

Still, those prefaces are hard to avoid, and I'll use them to bring us back to James's account of Turgenev. He composed the one for *The Portrait of a Lady* in the summer of 1906, and in it he remembered a conversation he'd had with the Russian writer some thirty years before. For Turgenev a story always began with "the vision of some person or persons, who hovered before him, soliciting him, as the active or passive figure, interesting him and appealing to him just as they were and by what they were." They were all taken, the older man said, from the people he had seen or known, and he never consciously added anything to them; he distrusted invention and believed that there was beauty and strangeness enough in the real. Plot was for him an irrelevance. The business of writing, as James himself had suggested in that 1874 essay, lay not in making his characters "do" anything but rather in discovering a situation that would allow them to reveal themselves, that would yield "the complications they would be most likely to produce and to feel." For Turgenev, that was story enough; but as he ruefully told the younger writer, it might not be for one's readers.

James's letters fill out that conversation. It was a rainy afternoon, and they met in the house that the Russian shared with the opera singer Pauline Viardot and her husband in the rue de Douai, just below the Place Pigalle. James had called on him almost immediately after he arrived in Paris in the fall of 1875, and at that first meeting they talked for two hours. Turgenev seemed never to have read a word of the young man's fiction, and yet he soon gave him a rare mark of his esteem. He introduced him to the circle of French writers with whom he gathered on Sundays at the flat of Flaubert. There James met Zola, flush with the success of *L'Assommoir*, his frank unsparing novel about the family of a Paris laundress; there too he met the then-unknown Guy de Maupassant. James was the only important writer in English to gain access to Flaubert's *cénacle*, though he never became an integral part of that circle and some of its regulars never quite caught his name. When he came back to Paris in 1884, after *Portrait* had made him famous, a few of Flaubert's old friends were startled to realize that they had already met the newly celebrated American writer. But those afternoons in the rue du Faubourg Saint-Honoré would have a decisive effect on James's fiction and his criticism alike.

He would write, and often, about the writers he met there: five essays on both Turgenev and Alphonse Daudet, four on Zola, three on Flaubert. The lessons he got in those rooms on the one hand stressed the importance of formal rigor and conscious design, and on the other showed how unflinching a novelist might be in dealing with sexual passion. By Anglo-American standards that apartment was full of aesthetic radicals, men who all denied that a book had any business in trying to teach a lesson. Art to them had no more to do with morality than it did with "astronomy or embryology," and any attempt to bring them together was the mark of a primitive mind. Flaubert's own books, with their obsessive search for the right word, the right rhythm, might appear to stress formal concerns above all, and yet in bracketing off all moral issues his aesthetic allowed a space for other kinds of freedom, and one his disciples were quick to explore. No subject matter could be excluded, and every aspect of human life had a legitimate place upon the page. James himself would not fully draw on that education until the early years of the twentieth century, in books like *The Golden Bowl* and *The Ambassadors*, novels about adultery that offer as well a minute account of consciousness itself, of how one knows what one knows. He would, moreover, always wonder why Zola's own imagination was so frequently drawn to scenes of "misery, vice and uncleanness," why he invariably depicted human life "as a combination of the cesspool and the house of prostitution," as though nature itself needed washing. But he recognized the challenge to his own inherited standards that French fiction presented, and the essays on Zola and Maupassant that I've reprinted here will show his attempt to meet it.

In that sense Turgenev's discreet conversation pieces gave him little to worry about. The Russian writer died in September 1883, when James had just returned to London from a long stay in America; his own father had died the previous December, and he had taken many months in settling the estate and attending to an exhausting series of family issues. Now the American almost immediately began to write a memorial tribute to the first great writer whom he had been able to count as a friend. It appeared in the January 1884 issue of *The Atlantic*, and begins on a rhetorical note that even for James seems high: "When the mortal remains of Ivan Turgénieff…" The piece differs from his other essays in saying almost nothing about its subject's work. The details are instead personal, evoking such things as the look of Turgenev's green sitting room in the rue de Douai, or his physical appearance, tall and broad-shouldered but with "an air of neglected strength." James recalls fragments of conversation, the raciness of Turgenev's spoken French, and their Sunday afternoons at Flaubert's; and he remembers too that the Russian had a reservoir of experience into which neither a young American nor their French colleagues could enter. The article is fond, but it's something more as well, and ends with his memory of their last meeting, in November 1882, when they shared a ride into Paris from the countryside. The older man was wracked by gout, and yet despite his suffering, his talk maintained its accustomed flow of brilliance. The coach dropped James on an outer boulevard, and he could hear the sounds of a Punch and Judy show nearby. Then "I bade him good-bye at the carriage window, and never saw him again." At that moment the essay becomes filial.

I've described this memorial sketch at length because it illustrates something important about James's career, something beyond the influence that his experience in Paris had upon him. *The Portrait of a Lady* finished its serial run and appeared in book form at the end of 1881, a novel that stands as a declaration of maturity, a self-conscious attempt to write a masterpiece. His mother died just a few months later, in January 1882, and his father followed in December. Outside of his letters and journal, James did not write about his parents until he himself was old; *A Small Boy and Others* appeared only as he turned seventy. But over the next few years he did often write about the deaths of others, working his way through a series of extraordinary obituary essays about his literary forebears. Flaubert had died in May 1880, and George Eliot that December. Emerson went in April 1882 and Trollope at the end of the year; and then at last Turgenev. James had known them all, and with the exception of Flaubert he wrote about them all in the years immediately following his parents' deaths; the French novelist had to wait until an 1893 edition of his letters, though the essay I've reprinted here dates from the early twentieth century. Some of these pieces may have begun with an editor's request, and their sheer number doubtless owes something to the accidents of death itself. James usually chose his own subjects, however, and what he chose, at this moment, was to mark the passing of his predecessors.

Over time he became an expert undertaker, fixing the terms and sealing the vault of one reputation after another. An earlier memorial essay had provided a comprehensive overview of the life and career of George Sand, and later ones looked at both Zola and Robert Browning. One of his best stories even begins with the writing of an obituary. In "Greville Fane" a journalist assigned to come up with a column on the death of a popular novelist finds it hard to fulfill his editor's charge that he "let her off easy, but not too easy." That, however is exactly what James himself did in his 1883 essay on Trollope. He got many things wrong about the most prolific of the great Victorians, but in praising his "complete appreciation of the usual" he set the terms of debate for the next century. He wrote the piece that spring in Boston, a break from the press of family business, and at the same time worked up an account of Emerson's correspondence with Thomas Carlyle. In writing the latter, James suggested that their letters belonged not only to a vanished generation but also to a vanished world. The people and things that concerned them had faded into "a past which is already remote," and those two difficult minds were now for the ages. Which meant, in a way, that they weren't for his own. That on Turgenev aside, James's obituary essays don't speak with any special reverence. Even his 1885 piece on George Eliot offers a sharp account of her limitations, and taken as a group his articles depict an era that in its passing has left him alone. The deaths of such figures as Trollope and Flaubert meant that there was no longer a great and still-present older generation to whom he could compare himself, and against whom he might be judged; the newcomer Thomas Hardy was still on the cusp of his own major work. Henry James was now forty years old, and he himself would set the standard.

In April 1884 the journeyman English novelist Walter Besant gave a lecture called "The Art of Fiction" in which he argued that fiction was indeed a fine art, something comparable to and as worthy of respect as music or poetry or sculpture. The claim is uncontroversial now and even at the time was less remarkable than most writers pretended; though Trollope, it's true, had likened the novelist to a shoemaker, a skilled craftsman and nothing more. Besant offered younger writers some advice of the kind that's still given about keeping a notebook and writing from experience, and the piece as a whole is both inoffensive and dull. It would be entirely forgotten if James hadn't taken it as the occasion for the playfully magisterial essay he published under the same title later that year.

James's own "Art of Fiction" responds to a complicated moment in the history of Anglo-American criticism, not only to Besant but also to a controversy that had arisen from an article by his friend and editor William Dean Howells. Writing in *The Century*, the glossiest New York magazine of its period, Howells had suggested that in these latter days, and with the work of James in particular, the art of fiction had become a much finer one "than it was with Dickens and Thackeray." By "fine" Howells meant "refined," but the evaluative note was inescapable, and the British critics had pounced. They saw him as claiming that both the methods and the pleasures of those English masters were obsolete, with Margaret Oliphant arguing in the conservative *Blackwood's Magazine* that American literature was now engaged in a hostile takeover of the language itself. James's response to the controversy was to float above it, and he begins his own essay with disarming modesty. He wants merely "to edge in a few words under cover" of Besant's "encouraging" work, encouraging because until recently

> it might have been supposed that the English novel was not what the French call *discutable*. It had no air of having a theory, a conviction, a consciousness of itself behind it—of being the expression of an artistic faith, the result of choice and comparison. I do not say it was necessarily the worse for that: it would take much more courage than I possess to intimate that the form of the novel as Dickens and Thackeray (for instance) saw it had any taint of incompleteness. It was, however, *naïf* . . .

James mentions neither Howells nor Oliphant, but his use of French looks mischievous, and at point after point he offers a tacit reply to his critics; it's possible to read the piece as an elaborate series of coded references, in-jokes accessible only to those who sit at a groaning board of the period's magazines. But the essay provides far more than that, and what's made it last is its air of joy. James's prose in "The Art of Fiction" is as buoyant as a Mozart serenade, sly and generous and above all confident, the voice of a writer who knows the worth of his own achievement. What he offers—what "The Art of Fiction" gave me as a student and what it gives me still—is a sense of the exhilarating complexity of form itself. Usually we talk about books in pieces: plot and character, language and theme. We pull them apart because it's easier that way, and if we're lucky we somehow manage to put them back together again. James won't let us do that. He insists that we take it whole. The critics of his day made a conventional distinction between a work's "subject" and its "treatment," but to him a novel was "a living thing, all one and continuous . . . and in proportion as it lives will it be found, I think, that in each of the parts there is something of each of the other parts."

Two moments in "The Art of Fiction" seem worth special attention, moments that in clarifying his critical principles point toward both his later essays and to what he would call "the future of the novel."

Howells had wondered whether readers would be content with what he called an "analytic study," with a novel predicated on a close account of character rather than on a densely plotted and thrilling story. But James rejects the period's customary distinction between "the novel of character and the novel of incident." The only distinction he recognizes is one between good novels and bad. For "What is character but the determination of incident? What is incident but the illustration of character?" It's an incident, James writes, for a woman to give you a particular look. At the same time, the way in which she looks will also provide an indication of her character. Plot and character in this economy are interchangeable and transitive, "all one and continuous," an equation that will forever balance. A closer examination suggests, however, that for James character always takes precedence. Character creates incident; incident merely illustrates some already existing way of being. Events reveal character, but they do not make or mold it, and the force of circumstance alone is never determinative.

Most of the novelists James admired would have agreed with that, Turgenev in particular. Begin with a character—Isabel Archer standing in a doorway at the start of *The Portrait of a Lady*—and then look for the incidents that will best display her essence. James's argument would have an incalculable effect on the future of Anglo-American fiction and criticism alike; the New Critical accounts of novelists as varied as Jane Austen and William Faulkner seem to me inconceivable without it. Nevertheless James claims too much. His aesthetic grows out of the belief that we have the ability and the freedom to act and to choose, that character in the nonliterary sense makes fate. That might work for his own kind of fiction, and certainly the modernist suspicion of story as such—Virginia Woolf had it, and E.M. Forster —dates to his own work, and to "The Art of Fiction" in particular. But he won't allow that there might be other modes of writing, and other novelists would offer a different account of the relation between character and incident. Hardy is perhaps the best example; his people often seem pursued by some external fate, by circumstances or incidents against which they are helpless.

That said, "The Art of Fiction" remains the most important English-language essay ever written about the novel, rivaled only by Woolf's "Mr. Bennett and Mrs. Brown." James did, however, recognize one particular challenge to his own ideas. He ended "The Art of Fiction" with the briefest of bows toward France in general and Zola in particular. He could never get himself to walk in the naturalist's path, but James still preferred it to the English fiction of his moment, and in the winter of 1884 wrote to Howells that the only new work he could respect was to be found in Paris. The one "duty of a novel was to be well written." So he claimed in his obituary essay for Turgenev, and a few years later Oscar Wilde would echo those words in his preface to *The Picture of Dorian Gray*, suggesting that "There is no such thing as a moral or an immoral book. Books are well written, or badly written. That is all." For James that belief can be traced back to the discussions he heard at Flaubert's, and it has a particular bearing on a second crucial moment in his great manifesto.

Madame Bovary would not be translated until 1886, but the English lawyer and journalist James Fitzjames Stephen had reviewed the French edition on its 1857 publication and found it repellent. He thought it contained passages that "no English author of reputation" would have published, but what especially troubled him was Flaubert's refusal to offer any moral condemnation of his heroine's actions. He also recognized, however, that the novelist had a lesson to teach his English peers. The British fiction of the day stopped short in dealing with sexual issues, and contained nothing "which a modest man might not, with satisfaction to himself, read aloud to a young lady." But that was a problem. Was it really desirable that the only fiction available should be that "fit for young ladies to read"? Stephen admitted that there were passages in *Othello* that he himself would not be able to read aloud to a woman, but that restriction would have blotted many of Shakespeare's best lines; and with an eye on London's streets he suggested, moreover, that such prudery had done nothing to improve English conduct.

What could the novelist allow him or herself to describe? How reticent need one be? Almost every Victorian writer had something to say about the question, and in *Our Mutual Friend* Dickens satirized

English prudery by inventing a character called Podsnap, who refuses to have any book in the house that might "bring a blush into the cheek of [a] young person." Some novelists kicked against those strictures. Others were willing to be guided by them, and Dickens may have been one of them; he almost never violated Podsnap's principles, and we now need to read his satire ironically. James himself thought they had made the whole of English fiction seem both diffident and cautious, a form unwilling "to face the difficulties with which on every side the treatment of reality bristles." Anglo-American fiction, he argued, was far too scrupulous in observing the

> traditional difference between that which people know and that which they agree to admit that they know, that which they see and that which they speak of, that which they feel to be a part of life and that which they allow to enter into literature. There is the great difference, in short, between what they talk of in conversation and what they talk of in print.... [The novel] as we find it in England today... strikes me as addressed in a large degree to "young people," and ... this in itself constitutes a presumption that it will be rather shy. There are certain things which it is generally agreed not to discuss, not even to mention, before young people. That is very well, but the absence of discussion is not a symptom of the moral passion.

James would return to that issue throughout his career, and in fact strikes that note repeatedly in the later essays I've selected for this volume, in his accounts of Maupaussant, Zola, and Matilde Serao, and also in the 1899 essay "The Future of the Novel." And as with Dickens there is, of course, an irony: this famously celibate novelist became an advocate for an honest treatment of the sexual life. In 1876 he had thought Zola a writer of "brutal indecency," but in the 1903 essay reprinted here he argued that *L'Assommoir* would have been destroyed by any shred of "timidity." Its greatness depended on Zola's willingness to soak himself in a world gone rank. James did, however, have one final reservation about the French fiction of his age. He might grant Zola and Maupassant their subjects, but he also thought that their concentration on the "carnal side of man" had limited their sense of human possibility. They saw all life in terms of lust, a matter of compulsion and desire, a struggle for existence in which people were at the mercy of forces they could neither resist nor control. That determinism was entirely at odds with his belief in the shaping force of character, in the freedom of conscious choice. In *The Portrait of a Lady* he gives young Isabel Archer a faith in the idea—the ideal—of Emersonian self-fashioning, and then proceeds to undermine it. But despite his skepticism he continued to feel the seductions of that faith himself.

In "The Future of the Novel" James suggested that Anglo-American fiction would deal with sexual questions—with what he elliptically called "the constant world-renewal"—in a different way than the French had. He wouldn't commit himself as to just how, but he did think that great changes were taking place in the condition of women. The New Woman of the 1890s was not yet a suffragette, but young people were now "older" than they used to be, they knew more than his own generation had, and things were shifting "deeply in the quiet." Such women didn't want to be protected from knowledge, and he thought that the "female elbow itself" might come to smash the windows of discretion. He suggested, moreover, that in doing so they wouldn't show much consideration for the modesty of the Podsnaps around them. A generation later Woolf would echo that sentiment in her "Professions for Women," noting that one of the difficulties in writing honestly about her own physical experience was the fact that men would be shocked; she felt "impeded by the extreme conventionality of the other sex." James was not shocked. The smashed window would need to wait for the work of Mary McCarthy and Doris Lessing, among others, but he looked forward to a fiction that might say what his own age could not.

Two of the essays I've reprinted here remain little known even by devoted Jamesians. One is his 1901 account of the Neapolitan writer

Matilde Serao. She was the first woman in Italy to edit a newspaper, running journals in both Rome and Naples, and a prolific novelist as well. Very little of her work is available in translation, but Edith Wharton also admired her and Serao's reputation is now enjoying a revival in Italy itself. For James she was something unthinkable in English—a female disciple of Zola. As such she presented a lesson to the Anglophone writers of his day, caught as they were by "a certain received canon of the 'proper.'" To Serao all subjects were "treatable," and James drew from her work the same conclusion that he did in "The Future of the Novel." Still, there was a limitation. Serao's characters may all "love indeed with fury," but they don't do anything else. Their lives are full of passion, excitement, and despair, and yet he also thought they were depicted as though they were exempt from life's "usual conditions," figures entirely without "friends, enemies, husbands, wives, children, parents, interests, occupations..." English writers ignored the physical. Serao was in danger of ignoring everything else, and in a way that made him want to lay "a clinging hand on dear old Jane Austen." And besides, he asked, with *The Ambassadors* already sprouting in his mind, doesn't passion have a comic side as well?

The other essay is of a very different kind. James T. Fields had been Hawthorne's publisher, and in his house on Boston's Charles Street *The Atlantic Monthly* "had virtually come into being." He hosted Dickens on his 1867–1868 American reading tour, and his wife, Annie, made that house into the closest thing the city had to a salon. After Fields died in 1881 his widow shared her home and her life with the novelist Sarah Orne Jewett, and James used her drawing room as a model for Olive Chancellor's in *The Bostonians*, with its view onto a Back Bay that was still all water. When Annie Fields died in 1915 he promptly produced a memoir, and perhaps it would have found a place in *The Middle Years*, the unfinished third volume of his autobiography, if he hadn't died himself the next year. James never wrote a conventional biography. His book on Hawthorne assembles the facts of the life, as they were then known, but it stands above all as an account of the work; his 1903 *William Wetmore Story and His*

Friends gives us not an individual life but a milieu, a record of the first generation of American artists to make their careers in Europe. But his essays abound in biographical moments, in sketches and vignettes and memories, and this one ends not with its subjects but with "that immemorial and inextinguishable lady Mrs. Julia Ward Howe" rising at ninety to chant her way through the "Battle Hymn of the Republic."

"The Art of Fiction" aside, James's greatest critical essays are all portraits: studies of a sensibility, pictures in which the work and the life seem fully interfused. Sometimes they are self-portraits as well. No one can read his 1907 account of *The Tempest* and not think of James's own late style, with its evocation of the writer "who plays for his own ear, his own hand, his own innermost sense, and for the bliss and capacity of his instrument." Maybe we think of him all the more because we know so little about Shakespeare's life. With George Sand we know almost everything, and what James's comprehensive account suggests above all is the inseparability of her work and her life. For which one is he describing in saying that she had "a great mind, curious about all things, open to all things, nobly accessible to experience, asking only to live, expand, respond"? But the finest of his portraits belongs to the writer he saw as the master of them all. "The Lesson of Balzac" starts slowly, almost apologetically, and bears the marks of its origin; it was one of the two lectures that he delivered on his American tour of 1904–1905, the other being an odd little thing about the need for proper pronunciation that he called "The Question of Our Speech." James spoke about Balzac in Philadelphia and Los Angeles and at many places in between; some of his audiences approached a thousand but his voice on the platform was at once conversational and perfectly audible.

The French writer was always one of his touchstones. He set the standard by which other writers might be judged, and among the things he offered was his absolute and total sincerity, his complete conviction in the importance of whatever story he happened to be telling. All novelists pretend, as James told his listeners, "and Balzac's great glory is that he pretended hardest." He believed in his characters, his people, and he put them before his readers in unrivaled detail, showing how their circumstances pressed upon them, and how they pressed back in turn. Their houses and families, their obsessions and salaries and tastes: Balzac knew everything about them, and consequently had "more to spend" in giving them to us, more even than George Eliot or Tolstoy. Nor did he stop with belief. Because he loved them too, his villains as much as the good ones, delighting in

> each seized identity, and of the sharpest and liveliest identities most. . . . The love, as we call it, the joy in their communicated and exhibited movement, in their standing on their feet and going of themselves and acting out their characters, was what rendered possible the saturation I speak of. . . . It was by loving them—as the terms of his subject and the nuggets of his mine— that he knew them; it was not by knowing them that he loved.

James is thinking here of Valérie Marneffe, the great scheming temptress of *Cousine Bette*, and suggests that as readers we need to let her seduce us. We must feel her fascination, feel what the men she ruins feel, for we need to love her in order to think our way inside her. Keats called it "negative capability," that willingness to sink yourself into another soul, to step into an experience unlike your own, and what lay behind it was a fundamental respect for the otherness of other people. All Balzac's effort went into putting himself into the "clothes, gloves . . . the very skin and bones" of the people he wanted to give us, for he knew that we cannot know anyone "unless we know their situation for themselves." Only then can we understand Valérie's soul-destroying greed, and only then may we judge her. Not in advance, and once more James hits out at his English forebears, at the a priori moral categories according to which they arraigned their characters.

One moment in "The Lesson of Balzac" has always stood out for me. In "The Art of Fiction" James had denied Walter Besant's supposition that a novel required "adventures," with its implicit claim that some subjects were more intrinsically interesting than others. For what *is* an adventure, after all? A novel's incidents might lie within, rooted in "psychological reasons" alone, and James himself suggested that it was even "an adventure—an immense one—for me to write this little article." In "The Lesson of Balzac" he went further, and in doing so left the French writer behind. For "there is no such thing in the world as an adventure pure and simple; there is only mine and yours, and his and hers—it being the greatest adventure of all, I verily think, just to *be* you or I, just to be he or she." The adventure of being *you*. Balzac respected "the liberty of the subject," but he could hardly have imagined what James and his successors would make of that freedom, of their pulse-by-pulse evocation of everyday life, their dive into the flux and flow of consciousness itself. I look over James's lines about you, and me, and I think of Woolf's Mrs. Ramsay knitting her stocking, of Hans Castorp's X-ray and Swann in love, of Addie Bundren speaking to us from beyond the grave. The modernist novel in its entirety lies in those words, and my spine chills whenever I read them.

James reminds us that Balzac died at fifty (actually fifty-one), "worn out with work and thought and passion," the passions not of the body so much as of the desire to write his world into life. It was a hard job, being him, and so it was to be Dickens as well, who lasted but a few years more, a burned cinder at fifty-eight. Each of them, as James wrote of the Frenchman, was "a figure more extraordinary than any he drew." He himself was built differently. He wrote every bit as much as they did but he still reached his seventies, and the young man's effrontery became the wise judicious authority of a master. The essays in this book are just one of the many reasons why he too stands as his own greatest creation.

—MICHAEL GORRA

ON WRITERS AND WRITING

THE ART OF FICTION

I SHOULD not have affixed so comprehensive a title to these few remarks, necessarily wanting in any completeness upon a subject the full consideration of which would carry us far, did I not seem to discover a pretext for my temerity in the interesting pamphlet lately published under this name by Mr. Walter Besant. Mr. Besant's lecture at the Royal Institution—the original form of his pamphlet—appears to indicate that many persons are interested in the art of fiction, and are not indifferent to such remarks, as those who practise it may attempt to make about it. I am therefore anxious not to lose the benefit of this favourable association, and to edge in a few words under cover of the attention which Mr. Besant is sure to have excited. There is something very encouraging in his having put into form certain of his ideas on the mystery of story-telling.

It is a proof of life and curiosity—curiosity on the part of the brotherhood of novelists as well as on the part of their readers. Only a short time ago it might have been supposed that the English novel was not what the French call *discutable*. It had no air of having a theory, a conviction, a consciousness of itself behind it—of being the expression of an artistic faith, the result of choice and comparison. I do not say it was necessarily the worse for that: it would take much more courage than I possess to intimate that the form of the novel as Dickens and Thackeray (for instance) saw it had any taint of incompleteness. It was, however, *naif* (if I may help myself out with another French word); and evidently if it be destined to suffer in any way for having lost its *naïveté* it has now an idea of making sure of the corresponding advantages. During the period I have alluded to there was a comfortable, good-humoured feeling abroad that a novel is a novel, as a pudding is a pudding, and that our only business with it could be to swallow it. But within a year or two, for some reason or other, there have been signs of returning animation—the era of discussion would appear to have been to a certain extent opened. Art lives upon discussion, upon experiment, upon curiosity, upon variety of attempt, upon the exchange of views and the comparison of stand-points; and there is a presumption that those times when no one has anything particular to say about it, and has no reason to give for practice or preference, though they may be times of honour, are not times of development—are times, possibly even, a little of dullness. The successful application of any art is a delightful spectacle, but the theory too is interesting; and though there is a great deal of the latter without the former I suspect there has never been a genuine success that has not had a latent core of conviction. Discussion, suggestion, formulation, these things are fertilising when they are frank and sincere. Mr. Besant has set an excellent example in saying what he thinks, for his part, about the way in which fiction should be written, as well as about the way in which it should be published; for his view of the "art," carried on into an appendix, covers that too. Other la-bourers in the same field will doubtless take up the argument, they will give it the light of their experience, and the effect will surely be to make our interest in the novel a little more what it had for some time threatened to fail to be—a serious, active, inquiring interest, under protection of which this delightful study may, in moments of confidence, venture to say a little more what it thinks of itself.

It must take itself seriously for the public to take it so. The old superstition about fiction being "wicked" has doubtless died out in England; but the spirit of it lingers in a certain oblique regard directed toward any story which does not more or less admit that it is only a joke. Even the most jocular novel feels in some degree the weight of the proscription that was formerly directed against literary levity: the jocularity does not always succeed in passing for orthodoxy. It is still expected, though perhaps people are ashamed to say it, that a production which is after all only a "make-believe" (for what else is a "story"?) shall be in some degree apologetic—shall renounce the pretension of attempting really to represent life. This, of course, any sensible, wide-awake story declines to do, for it quickly perceives that the tolerance granted to it on such a condition is only an attempt to stifle it disguised in the form of generosity. The old evangelical hostility to the novel, which was as explicit as it was narrow, and which regarded it as little less favourable to our immortal part than a stage-play, was in reality far less insulting. The only reason for the existence of a novel is that it does attempt to represent life. When it relinquishes this attempt, the same attempt that we see on the canvas of the painter, it will have arrived at a very strange pass. It is not expected of the picture that it will make itself humble in order to be forgiven; and the analogy between the art of the painter and the art of the novelist is, so far as I am able to see, complete. Their inspiration is the same, their process (allowing for the different quality of the vehicle), is the same, their success is the same. They may learn from each other, they may explain and sustain each other. Their cause is the same, and the honour of one is the honour of another. The Mahometans think a picture an unholy thing, but it is a long time since any Christian did, and it is therefore the more odd that in the Christian mind the traces (dissimulated though they may be) of a suspicion of the sister art should linger to this day. The only effectual way to lay it to rest is to emphasise the analogy to which I just alluded—to insist on the fact that as the picture is reality, so the novel is history. That is the only general description (which does it justice) that we may give of the novel. But history also is allowed to represent life; it is not, any more than painting, expected to apologise. The subject-matter of fiction is stored up likewise in documents and records, and if it will not give itself away, as they say in California, it must speak with assurance, with the tone of the historian. Certain accomplished novelists have a habit of giving themselves away which must often bring tears to the eyes of people who take their fiction seriously. I was lately struck, in reading over many pages of Anthony Trollope, with his want of discretion in this particular. In a digression, a parenthesis or an aside, he concedes to the reader that he and this trusting friend are only "making believe." He admits that the events he narrates have not really happened, and that he can give his narrative any turn the reader may like best. Such a betrayal of a sacred office seems to me, I confess, a terrible crime; it is what I mean by the attitude of apology, and it shocks me every whit as much in Trollope as it would have shocked me in Gibbon or Macaulay. It implies that the novelist is less occupied in looking for the truth (the truth, of course I mean, that he assumes, the premises that we must grant him, whatever they may be), than the historian, and in doing so it deprives him at a stroke of all his standing-room. To represent and illustrate the past, the actions of men, is the task of either writer, and the only difference that I can see is, in proportion as he succeeds, to the honour of the novelist, consisting as it does in his having more difficulty in collecting his evidence, which is so far from being purely literary. It seems to me to give him a great character, the fact that he has at once so much in common with the philosopher and the painter; this double analogy is a magnificent heritage.

It is of all this evidently that Mr. Besant is full when he insists upon the fact that fiction is one of the *fine* arts, deserving in its turn of all the honours and emoluments that have hitherto been reserved for the successful profession of music, poetry, painting, architecture. It is impossible to insist too much on so important a truth, and the place that Mr. Besant demands for the work of the novelist may be represented, a trifle less abstractly, by saying that he demands not only that it shall be reputed artistic, but that it shall be reputed very artistic indeed. It is excellent that he should have struck this note, for his doing so indicates that there was need of it, that his proposition may be to many people a novelty. One rubs one's eyes at the thought; but the rest of Mr. Besant's essay confirms the revelation. I suspect in truth that it would be possible to confirm it still further, and that one would not be far wrong in saying that in addition to the people to whom it has never occurred that a novel ought to be artistic, there are a great many others who, if this principle were urged upon them, would be filled with an indefinable mistrust. They would find it difficult to explain their repugnance, but it would operate strongly to put them on their guard. "Art," in our Protestant communities, where so many things have got so strangely twisted about, is supposed in certain circles to have some vaguely injurious effect upon those who make it an important consideration, who let it weigh in the balance. It is assumed to be opposed in some mysterious manner to morality, to amusement, to instruction. When it is embodied in the work of the painter (the sculptor is another affair!) you know what it is: it stands there before you, in the honesty of pink and green and a gilt frame; you can see the worst of it at a glance, and you can be on your guard. But when it is introduced into literature it becomes more insidious—there is danger of its hurting you before you know it. Literature should be either instructive or amusing, and there is in many minds an impression that these artistic preoccupations, the search for form, contribute to neither end, interfere indeed with both. They are too frivolous to be edifying, and too serious to be diverting; and they are moreover priggish and paradoxical and superfluous. That, I think, represents the manner in which the latent thought of many people who read novels as an exercise in skipping would explain itself if it were to become articulate. They would argue, of course, that a novel ought to be "good," but they would interpret this term in a fashion of their own, which indeed would vary considerably from one critic to another. One would say that being good means representing virtuous and aspiring characters, placed in prominent positions; another would say that it depends on a "happy ending," on a distribution at the last of prizes, pensions, husbands, wives, babies, millions, appended paragraphs, and cheerful remarks. Another still would say that it means being full of incident and movement, so that we shall wish to jump ahead, to see who was the mysterious stranger, and if the stolen will was ever found, and shall not be distracted from this pleasure by any tiresome analysis or "description." But they would all agree that the "artistic" idea would spoil some of their fun. One would hold it accountable for all the description, another would see it revealed in the absence of sympathy. Its hostility to a happy ending would be evident, and it might even in some cases render any ending at all impossible. The "ending" of a novel is, for many persons, like that of a good dinner, a course of dessert and ices, and the artist in fiction is regarded as a sort of meddlesome doctor who forbids agreeable aftertastes. It is therefore true that this conception of Mr. Besant's of the novel as a superior form encounters not only a negative but a positive indifference. It matters little that as a work of art it should really be as little or as much of its essence to supply happy endings, sympathetic characters, and an objective tone, as if it were a work of mechanics: the association of ideas, however incongruous, might easily be too much for it if an eloquent voice were not sometimes raised to call attention to the fact that it is at once as free and as serious a branch of literature as any other.

Certainly this might sometimes be doubted in presence of the enormous number of works of fiction that appeal to the credulity of our generation, for it might easily seem that there could be no great character in a commodity so quickly and easily produced. It must be admitted that good novels are much compromised by bad ones, and that the field at large suffers discredit from overcrowding. I think, however, that this injury is only superficial, and that the superabundance of written fiction proves nothing against the principle itself. It has been vulgarised, like all other kinds of literature, like everything else to-day, and it has proved more than some kinds accessible to vulgarisation. But there is as much difference as there ever was between a good novel and a bad one: the bad is swept with all the daubed canvases and spoiled marble into some unvisited limbo, or infinite rubbish-yard beneath the back-windows of the world, and the good subsists and emits its light and stimulates our desire for perfection. As I shall take the liberty of making but a single criticism of Mr. Besant, whose tone is so full of the love of his art, I may as well have done with it at once. He seems to me to mistake in attempting to say so definitely beforehand what sort of an affair the good novel will be. To indicate the danger of such an error as that has been the purpose of these few pages; to suggest that certain traditions on the subject, applied *a priori,* have already had much to answer for, and that the good health of an art which undertakes so immediately to reproduce life must demand that it be perfectly free. It lives upon exercise, and the very meaning of exercise is freedom. The only obligation to which in advance we may hold a novel, without incurring the accusation of being arbitrary, is that it be interesting. That general responsibility rests upon it, but it is the only one I can think of. The ways in which it is at liberty to accomplish this result (of interesting us) strike me as innumerable, and such as can only suffer from being marked out or fenced in by prescription. They are as various as the temperament of man, and they are successful in proportion as they reveal a particular mind, different from others. A novel is in its broadest definition a personal, a direct, impression of life: that, to begin with, constitutes its value, which is greater or less according to the intensity of the impression. But there will be no intensity at all, and therefore no value, unless there is freedom to feel and say. The tracing of a line to be followed, of a tone to be taken, of a form to be filled out, is a limitation of that freedom and a suppression of the very thing that we are most curious about. The form, it seems to me, is to be appreciated after the fact: then the author's choice has been made, his standard has been indicated; then we can follow lines and directions and compare tones and resemblances. Then in a word we can enjoy one of the most charming of pleasures, we can estimate quality, we can apply the test of execution. The execution belongs to the author alone; it is what is most personal to him, and we measure him by that. The advantage, the luxury, as well as the torment and responsibility of the novelist, is that there is no limit to what he may attempt as an executant—no limit to his possible experiments, efforts, discoveries, successes. Here it is especially that he works, step by step, like his brother of the brush, of whom we may always say that he has painted his picture in a manner best known to himself. His manner is his secret, not necessarily a jealous one. He cannot disclose it as a general thing if he would; he would be at a loss to teach it to others. I say this with a due recollection of having insisted on the community of method of the artist who paints a picture and the artist who writes a novel. The painter is able to teach the rudiments of his practice, and it is possible, from the study of good work (granted the aptitude), both to learn how to paint and to learn how to write. Yet it remains true, without injury to the *rapprochement,* that the literary artist would be obliged to say to his pupil much more than the other, "Ah, well, you must do it as you can!" It is a question of degree, a matter of delicacy. If there are exact sciences, there are also exact arts, and the grammar of painting is so much more definite that it makes the difference.

I ought to add, however, that if Mr. Besant says at the beginning of his essay that the "laws of fiction may be laid down and taught with as much precision and exactness as the laws of harmony, perspective, and proportion," he mitigates what might appear to be an extravagance by applying his remark to "general" laws, and by expressing most of these rules in a manner with which it would certainly be unaccommodating to disagree. That the novelist must write from his experience, that his "characters must be real and such as might be met with in actual life"; that "a young lady brought up in a quiet country village should avoid descriptions of garrison life," and "a writer whose friends and personal experiences belong to the lower middle-class should carefully avoid introducing his characters into society"; that one should enter one's notes in a common-place book; that one's figures should be clear in outline; that making them clear by some trick of speech or of carriage is a bad method, and "describing them at length" is a worse one; that English Fiction should have a "conscious moral purpose"; that "it is almost impossible to estimate too highly the value of careful workmanship—that is, of style"; that "the most important point of all is the story," that "the story is everything": these are principles with most of which it is surely impossible not to sympathise. That remark about the lower middle-class writer and his knowing his place is perhaps rather chilling; but for the rest I should find it difficult to dissent from any one of these recommendations. At the same time, I should find it difficult positively to assent to them, with the exception, perhaps, of the injunction as to entering one's notes in a common-place book. They scarcely seem to me to have the quality that Mr. Besant attributes to the rules of the novelist—the "precision and exactness" of "the laws of harmony, perspective, and proportion." They are suggestive, they are even inspiring, but they are not exact, though they are doubtless as much so as the case admits of: which is a proof of that liberty of interpretation for which I just contended. For the value of these different injunctions— so beautiful and so vague—is wholly in the meaning one attaches to them. The characters, the situation, which strike one as real will be those that touch and interest one most, but the measure of reality is very difficult to fix. The reality of Don Quixote or of Mr. Micawber is a very delicate shade; it is a reality so coloured by the author's vision that, vivid as it may be, one would hesitate to propose it as a model: one would expose one's self to some very embarrassing questions on the part of a pupil. It goes without saying that you will not write a good novel unless you possess the sense of reality; but it will be difficult to give you a recipe for calling that sense into being. Humanity is immense, and reality has a myriad forms; the most one can affirm is that some of the flowers of fiction have the odour of it, and others have not; as for telling you in advance how your nosegay should be composed, that is another affair. It is equally excellent and inconclusive to say that one must write from experience; to our supposititious aspirant such a declaration might savour of mockery. What kind of experience is intended, and where does it begin and end? Experience is never limited, and it is never complete; it is an immense sensibility, a kind of huge spider-web of the finest silken threads suspended in the chamber of consciousness, and catching every airborne particle in its tissue. It is the very atmosphere of the mind; and when the mind is imaginative—much more when it happens to be that of a man of genius—it takes to itself the faintest hints of life, it converts the very pulses of the air into revelations. The young lady living in a village has only to be a damsel upon whom nothing is lost to make it quite unfair (as it seems to me) to declare to her that she shall have nothing to say about the military. Greater miracles have been seen than that, imagination assisting, she should speak the truth about some of these gentlemen. I remember an English novelist, a woman of genius, telling me that she was much commended for the impression she had managed to give in one of her tales of the nature and way of life of the French Protestant youth. She had been asked where she learned so much about this recondite being, she had been congratulated on her peculiar opportunities. These opportunities consisted in her having once, in Paris, as she ascended a staircase, passed an open door where, in the household of a *pasteur,* some of the young Protestants were seated at table round a finished meal. The glimpse made a picture; it lasted only a moment, but that moment was experience. She had got her direct personal impression, and she turned out her type. She knew what youth was, and what Protestantism; she also had the advantage of having seen what it was to be French, so that she converted these ideas into a concrete image and produced a reality. Above all, however, she was blessed with the faculty which when you give it an inch takes an ell, and which for the artist is a much greater source of strength than any accident of residence or of place in the social scale. The power to guess the unseen from the seen, to trace the implication of things, to judge the whole piece by the pattern, the condition of feeling life in general so completely that you are well on your way to knowing any particular corner of it—this cluster of gifts may almost be said to constitute experience, and they occur in country and in town, and in the most differing stages of education. If experience consists of impressions, it may be said that impressions *are* experience, just as (have we not seen it?) they are the very air we breathe. Therefore, if I should certainly say to a novice, "'Write from experience and experience only,' I should feel that this was rather a tantalising monition if I were nor careful immediately to add, "Try to be one of the people on whom nothing is lost!"

I am far from intending by this to minimise the importance of exactness—of truth of detail. One can speak best from one's own taste, and I may therefore venture to say that the air of reality (solidity of specification) seems to me to be the supreme virtue of a novel—the merit on which all its other merits (including that conscious moral purpose of which Mr. Besant speaks) helplessly and submissively depend. If it be not there they are all as nothing, and if these be there, they owe their effect to the success with which the author has produced the illusion of life. The cultivation of this success, the study of this exquisite process, form, to my taste, the beginning and the end of the art of the novelist. They are his inspiration, his despair, his reward, his torment, his delight. It is here in very truth that he competes with life; it is here that he competes with his brother the painter in *his* attempt to render the look of things, the look that conveys their meaning, to catch the colour, the relief, the expression, the surface, the substance of the human spectacle. It is in regard to this that Mr. Besant is well inspired when he bids him take notes. He cannot possibly take too many, he cannot possibly take enough. All life solicits him, and to "render" the simplest surface, to produce the most momentary illusion, is a very complicated business.

His case would be easier, and the rule would be more exact, if Mr. Besant had been able to tell him what notes to take. But this I fear, he can never learn in any manual; it is the business of his life. He has to take a great many in order to select a few, he has to work them up as he can, and even the guides and philosophers who might have most to say to him must leave him alone when it comes to the application of precepts, as we leave the painter in communion with his palette That his characters "must be clear in outline," as Mr. Besant says—he feels that down to his boots; but how he shall make them so is a secret between his good angel and himself. It would be absurdly simple if he could be taught that a great deal of "description" would make them so, or that on the contrary the absence of description and the cultivation of dialogue, or the absence of dialogue and the multiplication of "incident," would rescue him from his difficulties. Nothing, for instance, is more possible than that he be of a turn of mind for which this odd, literal opposition of description and dialogue, incident and description, has little meaning and light. People often talk of these things as if they had a kind of internecine distinctness, instead of melting into each other at every breath, and being intimately associated parts of one general effort of expression. I cannot imagine composition existing in a series of blocks, nor conceive, in any novel worth discussing at all, of a passage of description that is not in its intention narrative, a passage of dialogue that is not in its intention descriptive, a touch of truth of any sort that does not partake of the nature of incident, or an incident that derives its interest from any other source than the general and only source of the success of a work of art—that of being illustrative. A novel is a living thing, all one and continuous, like any other organism, and in proportion as it lives will it be found, I think, that in each of the parts there is something of each of the other parts. The critic who over the close texture of a finished work shall pretend to trace a geography of items will mark some frontiers as artificial, I fear, as any that have been known to history. There is an old-fashioned distinction between the novel of character and the novel of incident which must have cost many a smile to the intending fabulist who was keen about his work. It appears to me as little to the point as the equally celebrated distinction between the novel and the romance—to answer as little to any reality. There are bad novels and good novels, as there are bad pictures and good pictures; but that is the only distinction in which I see any meaning, and I can as little imagine speaking of a novel of character as I can imagine speaking of a picture of character. When one says picture one says of character, when one says novel one says of incident, and the terms may be transposed at will. What is character but the determination of incident? What is incident but the illustration of character? What is either a picture or a novel that is *not* of character? What else do we seek in it and find in it? It is an incident for a woman to stand up with her hand resting on a table and look out at you in a certain way; or if it be not an incident I think it will be hard to say what it is. At the same time it is an expression of character. If you say you don't see it (character in *that—allons donc!*), this is exactly what the artist who has reasons of his own for thinking he *does* see it undertakes to show you. When a young man makes up his mind that he has not faith enough after all to enter the church as he intended, that is an incident, though you may not hurry to the end of the chapter to see whether perhaps he doesn't change once more. I do not say that these are extraordinary or startling incidents. I do not pretend to estimate the degree of interest proceeding from them, for this will depend upon the skill of the painter. It sounds almost puerile to say that some incidents are intrinsically much more important than others, and I need not take this precaution after having professed my sympathy for the major ones in remarking that the only classification of the novel that I can understand is into that which has life and that which has it not.

The novel and the romance, the novel of incident and that of character—these clumsy separations appear to me to have been made by critics and readers for their own convenience, and to help them out of some of their occasional queer predicaments, but to have little reality or interest for the producer, from whose point of view it is of course that we are attempting to consider the art of fiction. The case is the same with another shadowy category which Mr. Besant apparently is disposed to set up—that of the "modern English novel"; unless indeed it be that in this matter he has fallen into an accidental confusion of standpoints. It is not quite clear whether he intends the remarks in which he alludes to it to be didactic or historical. It is as difficult to suppose a person intending to write a modern English as to suppose him writing an ancient English novel: that is a label which begs the question. One writes the novel, one paints the picture of one's language and of one's time, and calling it modern English will not, alas! make the difficult task any easier. No more, unfortunately, will calling this or that work of one's fellow-artist a romance—unless it be, of course, simply for the pleasantness of the thing, as for instance when Hawthorne gave this heading to his story of *Blithedale*. The French, who have brought the theory of fiction to remarkable completeness, have but one name for the novel, and have not attempted smaller things in it, that I can see, for that I can think of no obligation to which the romancer would not be held equally with the novelist; the standard of execution is equally high for each. Of course it is of execution that we are talking—that being the only point of a novel that is open to contention. This is perhaps too often lost sight of, only to produce interminable confusions and cross-purposes. We must grant the artist his subject, his idea, his *donnée*: our criticism is applied only to what he makes of it. Naturally I do not mean that we are bound to like it or find it interesting: in case we do not our course is perfectly simple—to let it alone. We may believe that of a certain idea even the most sincere novelist can make nothing at all, and the event may perfectly justify our belief; but the failure will have been a failure to execute, and it is in the execution that the fatal weakness is recorded. If we pretend to respect the artist at all, we must allow him his freedom of choice, in the face, in particular cases, of innumerable presumptions that the choice will not fructify. Art derives a considerable part of its beneficial exercise from flying in the face of presumptions, and some of the most interesting experiments of which it is capable are hidden in the bosom of common things. Gustave Flaubert has written a story about the devotion of a servant-girl to a parrot, and the production, highly finished as it is, cannot on the whole be called a success. We are perfectly free to find it flat, but I think it might have been interesting; and I, for my part, am extremely glad he should have written it; it is a contribution to our knowledge of what can be done—or what cannot. Ivan Turgénieff has written a tale about a deaf and dumb serf and a lap-dog, and the thing is touching, loving, a little masterpiece. He struck the note of life where Gustave Flaubert missed it—he flew in the face of a presumption and achieved a victory.

Nothing, of course, will ever take the place of the good old fashion of "liking" a work of art or not liking it: the most improved criticism will not abolish that primitive, that ultimate test. I mention this to guard myself from the accusation of intimating that the idea, the subject, of a novel or a picture, does not matter. It matters, to my sense, in the highest degree, and if I might put up a prayer it would be that artists should select none but the richest. Some, as I have already hastened to admit, are much more remunerative than others, and it would be a world happily arranged in which persons intending to treat them should be exempt from confusions and mistakes. This fortunate condition will arrive only, I fear, on the same day that critics become purged from error. Meanwhile, I repeat, we do not judge the artist with fairness unless we say to him, "Oh, I grant you your starting-point, because if I did not I should seem to prescribe to you, and heaven forbid I should take that responsibility. If I pretend to tell you what you must not take, you will call upon me to tell you then what you must take; in which case I shall be prettily caught.

Moreover, it isn't till I have accepted your data that I can begin to measure you. I have the standard, the pitch; I have no right to tamper with your flute and then criticise your music. Of course I may not care for your idea at all; I may think it silly, or stale, or unclean; in which case I wash my hands of you altogether. I may content myself with believing that you will not have succeeded in being interesting, but I shall, of course, not attempt to demonstrate it, and you will be as indifferent to me as I am to you. I needn't remind you that there are all sorts of tastes: who can know it better? Some people, for excellent reasons, don't like to read about carpenters; others, for reasons even better, don't like to read about courtesans. Many object to Americans. Others (I believe they are mainly editors and publishers) won't look at Italians. Some readers don't like quiet subjects; others don't like bustling ones. Some enjoy a complete illusion, others the consciousness of large concessions. They choose their novels accordingly, and if they don't care about your idea they won't, *a fortiori,* care about your treatment."

So that it comes back very quickly, as I have said, to the liking: in spite of M. Zola, who reasons less powerfully than he represents, and who will not reconcile himself to this absoluteness of taste, thinking that there are certain things that people ought to like, and that they can be made to like. I am quite at a loss to imagine anything (at any rate in this matter of fiction) that people *ought* to like or to dislike. Selection will be sure to take care of itself, for it has a constant motive behind it. That motive is simply experience. As people feel life, so they will feel the art that is most closely related to it. This closeness of relation is what we should never forget in talking of the effort of the novel. Many people speak of it as a factitious, artificial form, a product of ingenuity, the business of which is to alter and arrange the things that surround us, to translate them into conventional, traditional moulds. This, however, is a view of the matter which carries us but a very short way, condemns the art to an eternal repetition of a few familiar *clichés,* cuts short its development, and leads us straight up to a dead wall. Catching the very note and trick, the strange irregular rhythm of life, that is the attempt whose strenuous force keeps Fiction upon her feet. In proportion as in what she offers us we see life *without* rearrangement do we feel that we are touching the truth; in proportion as we see it *with* rearrangement do we feel that we are being put off with a substitute, a compromise and convention. It is not uncommon to hear an extraordinary assurance of remark in regard to this matter of rearranging, which is often spoken of as if it were the last word of art. Mr. Besant seems to me in danger of falling into the great error with his rather unguarded talk about "selection." Art is essentially selection, but it is a selection whose main care is to be typical, to be inclusive. For many people art means rose-coloured window-panes, and selection means picking a bouquet for Mrs. Grundy. They will tell you glibly that artistic considerations have nothing to do with the disagreeable, with the ugly; they will rattle off shallow commonplaces about the province of art and the limits of art till you are moved to some wonder in return as to the province and the limits of ignorance. It appears to me that no one can ever have made a seriously artistic attempt without becoming conscious of an immense increase—a kind of revelation—of freedom. One perceives in that case—by the light of a heavenly ray—that the province of art is all life, all feeling, all observation, all vision. As Mr. Besant so justly intimates, it is all experience. That is a sufficient answer to those who maintain that it must not touch the sad things of life, who stick into its divine unconscious bosom little prohibitory inscriptions on the end of sticks, such as we see in public gardens—"It is forbidden to walk on the grass; it is forbidden to touch the flowers; it is not allowed to introduce dogs or to remain after dark; it is requested to keep to the right." The young aspirant in the line of fiction whom we continue to imagine will do nothing without taste, for in that case his freedom would be of little use to him; but the first advantage of his taste will be to reveal to him the absurdity of the little sticks and tickets. If he have taste, I must add, of course he will have ingenuity, and my disrespectful reference to that quality just now was not meant to imply that it is useless in fiction. But it is only a secondary aid; the first is a capacity for receiving straight impressions.

Mr. Besant has some remarks on the question of "the story" which

I shall not attempt to criticise, though they seem to me to contain a singular ambiguity, because I do not think I understand them. I cannot see what is meant by talking as if there were a part of a novel which is the story and part of it which for mystical reasons is not unless indeed the distinction be made in a sense in which it is difficult to suppose that any one should attempt to convey anything. "The story," if it represents anything, represents the subject, the idea, the *donnée* of the novel; and there is surely no "school"—Mr. Besant speaks of a school—which urges that a novel should be all treatment and no subject. There must assuredly be something to treat; every school is intimately conscious of that. This sense of the story being the idea, the starting-point, of the novel, is the only one that I see in which it can be spoken of as something different from its organic whole; and since in proportion as the work is successful the idea permeates and penetrates it, informs and animates it, so that every word and every punctuation-point contribute directly to the expression, in that proportion do we lose our sense of the store being a blade which may be drawn more or less out of its sheath. The store and the novel, the idea and the form, are the needle and thread, and I never heard of a guild of tailors who recommended the use of the thread without the needle, or the needle without the thread. Mr. Besant is not the only critic who may be observed to have spoken as if there were certain things in life which constitute stories, and certain others which do not. I find the same odd implication in an entertaining article in the *Pall Mall Gazette,* devoted, as it happens, to Mr. Besant's lecture. "The story is the thing!" says this graceful writer, as if with a tone of opposition to some other idea. I should think it was, as every painter who, as the time for "sending in" his picture looms in the distance, finds himself still in quest of a subject—as every belated artist not fixed about his theme will heartily agree. There are some subjects which speak to us and others which do not, but he would be a clever man who should undertake to give a rule—an index expurgatorius—by which the story and the no-story should be known apart. It is impossible (to me at least) to imagine any such rule which shall not be altogether arbitrary. The writer in the *Pall Mall* opposes the delightful (as I suppose novel) of *Margot la Balafrée* to certain tales in which "Bostonian nymphs" appear to have "rejected English dukes for psychological reasons." I am not acquainted with the romance just designated, and can scarcely forgive the *Pall Mall* critic for not mentioning the name of the author, but the title appears to refer to a lady who may have received a scar in some heroic adventure. I am inconsolable at not being acquainted with this episode, but am utterly at a loss to see why it is a story when the rejection (or acceptance) of a duke is not and why a reason, psychological or other, is not a subject when a cicatrix is. They are all particles of the multitudinous life with which the novel deals, and surely no dogma which pretends to make it lawful to touch the one and unlawful to touch the other will stand for a moment on its feet. It is the special picture that must stand or fall, according as it seems to possess truth or to lack it. Mr. Besant does not, to my sense, light up the subject by intimating that a story must, under penalty of not being a story, consist of "adventures." Why of adventures more than of green spectacles? He mentions a category of impossible things, and among them he places "fiction without adventure." Why without adventure, more than without matrimony, or celibacy, or parturition, or cholera, or hydropathy, or Jansenism? This seems to me to bring the novel back to the hapless little *rôle* of being an artificial, ingenious thing—bring it down from its large, free character of an immense and exquisite correspondence with life. And what *is* adventure, when it comes to that, and by what sign is the listening pupil to recognise it? It is an adventure—an immense one—for me to write this little article; and for a Bostonian nymph to reject an English duke is an adventure only less stirring, I should say, than for an English duke to be rejected by a Bostonian nymph. I see dramas within dramas in that, and innumerable points of view. A psychological reason is, to my imagination, an object adorably pictorial; to catch the tint of its complexion I feel as if that idea might inspire one to Titianesque efforts. There are few things more exciting to me, in short, than a psychological reason, and yet, I protest, the novel seems to me the most magnificent form of art. I have just been reading, at the same time, the delightful story of

Treasure Island, by Mr. Robert Louis Stevenson and, in a manner less consecutive, the last tale from M. Edmond de Goncourt, which is entitled *Chérie*. One of these works treats of murders, mysteries, islands of dreadful renown, hairbreadth escapes, miraculous coincidences and buried doubloons. The other treats of a little French girl who lived in a fine house in Paris, and died of wounded sensibility because no one would marry her. I call *Treasure Island* delightful, because it appears to me to have succeeded wonderfully in what it attempts; and I venture to bestow no epithet upon *Chérie*, which strikes me as having failed deplorably in what it attempts—that is in tracing the development of the moral consciousness of a child. But one of these productions strikes me as exactly as much of a novel as the other, and as having a "story" quite as much. The moral consciousness of a child is as much a part of life as the islands of the Spanish Main, and the one sort of geography seems to me to have those "surprises" of which Mr. Besant speaks quite as much as the other. For myself (since it comes back in the last resort, as I say, to the preference of the individual), the picture of the child's experience has the advantage that I can at successive steps (an immense luxury, near to the sensual pleasure of which Mr. Besant's critic in the *Pall Mall* speaks) say Yes or No, as it may be, to what the artist puts before me. I have been a child in fact, but I have been on a quest for a buried treasure only in supposition, and it is a simple accident that with M. de Goncourt I should have for the most part to say No. With George Eliot, when she painted that country with a far other intelligence, I always said Yes.

The most interesting part of Mr. Besant's lecture is unfortunately the briefest passage—his very cursory allusion to the "conscious moral purpose" of the novel. Here again it is not very clear whether he be recording a fact or laying down a principle; it is a great pity that in the latter case he should not have developed his idea. This branch of the subject is of immense importance, and Mr. Besant's few words point to considerations of the widest reach, not to be lightly disposed of. He will have treated the art of fiction but superficially who is not prepared to go every inch of the way that these considerations will carry him. It is for this reason that at the beginning of these remarks

I was careful to notify the reader that my reflections on so large a theme have no pretension to be exhaustive. Like Mr. Besant, I have left the question of the morality of the novel till the last, and at the last I find I have used up my space. It is a question surrounded with difficulties, as witness the very first that meets us, in the form of a definite question, on the threshold. Vagueness, in such a discussion, is fatal, and what is the meaning of your morality and your conscious moral purpose? Will you not define your terms and explain how (a novel being a picture) a picture can be either moral or immoral? You wish to paint a moral picture or carve a moral statue: will you not tell us how you would set about it? We are discussing the Art of Fiction; questions of art are questions (in the widest sense) of execution; questions of morality are quite another affair, and will you not let us see how it is that you find it so easy to mix them up? These things are so clear to Mr. Besant that he has deduced from them a law which he sees embodied in English Fiction, and which is "a truly admirable thing and a great cause for congratulation." It is a great cause for congratulation indeed when such thorny problems become as smooth as silk. I may add that in so far as Mr. Besant perceives that in point of fact English Fiction has addressed itself preponderantly to these delicate questions he will appear to many people to have made a vain discovery. They will have been positively struck, on the contrary, with the moral timidity of the usual English novelist; with his (or with her) aversion to face the difficulties with which on every side the treatment of reality bristles. He is apt to be extremely shy (whereas the picture that Mr. Besant draws is a picture of boldness), and the sign of his work, for the most part, is a cautious silence on certain subjects. In the English novel (by which of course I mean the American as well), more than in any other, there is a traditional difference between that which people know and that which they agree to admit that they know, that which they see and that which they speak of, that which they feel to be a part of life and that which they allow to enter into literature. There is the great difference, in short, between what they talk of in conversation and what they talk of in print. The essence of moral energy is to survey the whole field, and I should directly reverse Mr. Besant's remark and say not that the English novel has a purpose, but that it has a diffidence. To what degree a purpose in a work of art is a source of corruption I shall not attempt to inquire; the one that seems to me least dangerous is the purpose of making a perfect work. As for our novel, I may say lastly on this score that as we find it in England today it strikes me as addressed in a large degree to "young people," and that this in itself constitutes a presumption that it will be rather shy. There are certain things which it is generally agreed not to discuss, not even to mention, before young people. That is very well, but the absence of discussion is not a symptom of the moral passion. The purpose of the English novel—"a truly admirable thing, and a great cause for congratulation"—strikes me therefore as rather negative.

There is one point at which the moral sense and the artistic sense lie very near together; that is in the light of the very obvious truth that the deepest quality of a work of art will always be the quality of the mind of the producer. In proportion as that intelligence is fine will the novel, the picture, the statue partake of the substance of beauty and truth. To be constituted of such elements is, to my vision, to have purpose enough. No good novel will ever proceed from a superficial mind; that seems to me an axiom which, for the artist in fiction, will cover all needful moral ground: if the youthful aspirant take it to heart it will illuminate for him many of the mysteries of "purpose." There are many other useful things that might be said to him, but I have come to the end of my article, and can only touch them as I pass. The critic in the *Pall Mall Gazette,* whom I have already quoted, draws attention to the danger, in speaking of the art of fiction, of generalising. The danger that he has in mind is rather, I imagine, that of particularising, for there are some comprehensive remarks which, in addition to those embodied in Mr. Besant's suggestive lecture, might without fear of misleading him be addressed to the ingenuous student. I should remind him first of the magnificence of the form that is open to him, which offers to sight so few restrictions and such innumerable opportunities. The other arts, in comparison, appear confined and hampered; the various conditions under which they are exercised are so rigid and definite. But the only condition that I can think of attaching to the composition of the novel is as I have already said, that it be sincere. This freedom is a splendid privilege; and the first lesson of the young novelist is to learn to be worthy of it. "Enjoy it as it deserves," I should say to him; "take possession of it, explore it to its utmost extent, publish it, rejoice in it. All life belongs to you, and do not listen either to those who would shut you up into corners of it and tell you that it is only here and there that art inhabits, or to those who would persuade you that this heavenly messenger wings her way outside of life altogether, breathing a superfine air, and turning away her head from the truth of things There is no impression of life, no manner of seeing it and feeling it, to which the plan of the novelist may not offer a place; you have only to remember that talents so dissimilar as those of Alexandre Dumas and Jane Austen, Charles Dickens and Gustave Flaubert have worked in this field with equal glory. Do not think too much about optimism and pessimism; try and catch the colour of life itself. In France to-day we see a prodigious effort (that of Emile Zola, to whose solid and serious work no explorer of the capacity of the novel can allude without respect), we see an extraordinary effort vitiated by a spirit of pessimism on a narrow basis. M. Zola is magnificent, but he strikes an English reader as ignorant; he has an air of working in the dark; if he had as much light as energy, his results would be of the highest value. As for the aberrations of a shallow optimism, the ground (of English fiction especially) is strewn with their brittle particles as with broken glass. If you must indulge in conclusions, let them have the taste of a wide knowledge. Remember that your first duty is to be as complete as possible—to make as perfect a work. Be generous and delicate and pursue the prize."

NEW NOVELS IN REVIEW

MARY ELIZABETH BRADDON
Aurora Floyd

MISS AURORA Floyd, as half the world knows, was a young lady
who got into no end of trouble by marrying her father's groom. We
had supposed that this adventure had long ago become an old story;
but here is a new edition of her memoirs to prove that the public has
not done with her yet. We would assure those individuals who look
with regret upon this assumption by a "sensation" novel of the honors
of legitimate fiction, that the author of *Aurora Floyd* is an uncom-
monly clever person. Her works are distinguished by a quality for
which we can find no better name than "pluck"; and should not pluck
have its reward wherever found? If common report is correct, Miss
Braddon had for many years beguiled the leisure moments of an arduous profession—the dramatic profession—by the composition of
fictitious narrative. But until the publication of *Lady Audley's Secret*
she failed to make her mark. To what secret impulse or inspiration
we owe this sudden reversal of fortune it is difficult to say; but the
grim determination to succeed is so apparent in every line of *Lady
Audley's Secret*, that the critic is warranted in conjecturing that she
had at last become desperate. People talk of novels with a purpose;
and from this class of works, both by her patrons and her enemies,
Miss Braddon's tales are excluded. But what novel ever betrayed a
more resolute purpose than the production of what we may call Miss
Braddon's second manner? Her purpose was at any hazard to make
a hit, to catch the public ear. It was a difficult task, but audacity could
accomplish it. Miss Braddon accordingly resorted to extreme measures,
and created the sensation novel. It is to this audacity, this courage of
despair, as manifested in her later works, that we have given the name

of pluck. In these works it has settled down into a quiet determination not to let her public get ahead of her. A writer who has suddenly leaped into a popularity greatly disproportionate to his merit, can only retain his popularity by observing a strictly respectful attitude to his readers. This has been Miss Braddon's attitude, and she has maintained it with unwearied patience. She has been in her way a disciple as well as a teacher. She has kept up with the subtle innovations to which her art, like all others, is subject, as well as with the equally delicate fluctuations of the public taste. The result has been a very obvious improvement in her style.

She had been preceded in the same path by Mr. Wilkie Collins, whose *Woman in White*, with its diaries and letters and its general ponderosity, was a kind of nineteenth century version of *Clarissa Harlowe*. Mind, we say a nineteenth century version. To Mr. Collins belongs the credit of having introduced into fiction those most mysterious of mysteries, the mysteries which are at our own doors. This innovation gave a new impetus to the literature of horrors. It was fatal to the authority of Mrs. Radcliffe and her everlasting castle in the Apennines. What are the Apennines to us, or we to the Apennines? Instead of the terrors of *Udolpho*, we were treated to the terrors of the cheerful country-house and the busy London lodgings. And there is no doubt that these were infinitely the more terrible. Mrs. Radcliffe's mysteries were romances pure and simple; while those of Mr. Wilkie Collins were stern reality. The supernatural, which Mrs. Radcliffe constantly implies, though she generally saves her conscience, at the eleventh hour, by explaining it away, requires a powerful imagination in order to be as exciting as the natural, as Mr. Collins and Miss Braddon, without any imagination at all, know how to manage it. A good ghost-story, to be half as terrible as a good murder-story, must be connected at a hundred points with the common objects of life. The best ghost-story probably ever written—a tale published some years ago in *Blackwood's Magazine*—was constructed with an admirable understanding of this principle. Half of its force was derived from its prosaic, commonplace, daylight accessories. Less delicately terrible, perhaps, than the vagaries of departed spirits, but to the full as *interesting*, as the modern novel reader understands the word, are the numberless possible forms of human malignity. Crime, indeed, has always been a theme for dramatic poets; but with the old poets its dramatic interest lay in the fact that it compromised the criminal's moral repose. Whence else is the interest of *Orestes* and *Macbeth*? With Mr. Collins and Miss Braddon (our modern Euripides and Shakespeare) the interest of crime is in the fact that it compromises the criminal's personal safety. The play is a tragedy, not in virtue of an avenging deity, but in virtue of a preventive system of law; not through the presence of a company of fairies, but through that of an admirable organization of police detectives. Of course, the nearer the criminal and the detective are brought home to the reader, the more lively his "sensation." They are brought home to the reader by a happy choice of probable circumstances; and it is through their skill in the choice of these circumstances—their thorough-going realism—that Mr. Collins and Miss Braddon have become famous. In like manner, it is by the thorough-going realism of modern actors that the works of the most poetic of poets have been made to furnish precedent for sensational writers. There are no *circumstances* in *Macbeth*, as you read it; but as you see it played by Mr. Charles Kean or Mr. Booth it is nothing but circumstances. And we may here remark, in parentheses, that if the actors of a past generation—Garrick and Mrs. Siddons—left with their contemporaries so profound a conviction of their *greatness*, it is probably because, like the great dramatists they interpreted, they were ideal and poetic; because their effort was not to impress but to express.

We have said that although Mr. Collins anticipated Miss Braddon in the work of devising domestic mysteries adapted to the wants of a sternly prosaic age, she was yet the founder of the sensation novel. Mr. Collins's productions deserve a more respectable name. They are massive and elaborate constructions—monuments of mosaic work, for the proper mastery of which it would seem, at first, that an index and notebook were required. They are not so much works of art as works of science. To read *The Woman in White*, requires very much the same intellectual effort as to read Motley or Froude. We may say, therefore, that Mr. Collins being to Miss Braddon what Richardson is to Miss Austen, we date the novel of domestic mystery from the former lady, for the same reason that we date the novel of domestic tranquillity from the latter. Miss Braddon began by a skilful combination of bigamy, arson, murder, and insanity. These phenomena are all represented in the deeds of Lady Audley. The novelty lay in the heroine being, not a picturesque Italian of the fourteenth century, but an English gentlewoman of the current year, familiar with the use of the railway and the telegraph. The intense probability of the story is constantly reiterated. Modern England—the England of to-day's newspaper—crops up at every step. Of course Lady Audley is a nonentity, without a heart, a soul, a reason. But what we may call the small change for these facts—her eyes, her hair, her mouth, her dresses, her bedroom furniture, her little words and deeds—are so lavishly bestowed that she successfully maintains a kind of half illusion. Lady Audley was diabolically wicked; Aurora Floyd, her successor, was simply foolish, or indiscreet, or indelicate—or anything you please to say of a young lady who runs off with a hostler. But as bigamy had been the cause of Lady Audley's crimes, so it is the cause of Aurora's woes. She marries a second time, on the hypothesis of the death of the hostler. But, to paraphrase a sentence of Thackeray's in a sketch of the projected plot of *Denis Duval*, suppose, after all, it should turn out that the hostler was *not* dead? In *Aurora Floyd* the small change is more abundant than ever. Aurora's hair, in particular, alternately blue-black, purple-black, and dead-black, is made to go a great way. Since *Aurora Floyd*, Miss Braddon has published half-a-dozen more novels; each, as we have intimated, better than the previous one, and running through more editions; but each fundamentally a repetition of *Aurora Floyd*. These works are censured and ridiculed, but they are extensively read. The author has a hold upon the public. It is, assuredly, worth our while to enquire more particularly how she has obtained it.

The great public, in the first place, is made up of a vast number of little publics, very much as our Union is made up of States, and it is necessary to consider which of these publics is Miss Braddon's. We can best define it with the half of a negative. It is that public which reads nothing but novels, and yet which reads neither George Eliot, George Sand, Thackeray, nor Hawthorne. People who read nothing but novels are very poor critics of human nature. Their foremost desire is for something new. Now, we all know that human nature is very nearly as old as the hills. But *society* is for ever renewing itself. To society, accordingly, and not to life, Miss Braddon turns, and produces, not stories of passion, but stories of action. Society is a vast magazine of crime and suffering, of enormities, mysteries, and miseries of every description, of incidents, in a word. In proportion as an incident is exceptional, it is interesting to persons in search of novelty. Bigamy, murder, and arson are exceptional. Miss Braddon distributes these materials with a generous hand, and attracts the attention of her public. The next step is to hold its attention. There have been plenty of tales of crime which have not made their authors famous, nor put money in their purses. The reason can have been only that they were not well executed. Miss Braddon, accordingly, goes to work like an artist. Let not the curious public take for granted that, from a literary point of view, her works are contemptible. Miss Braddon writes neither fine English nor slovenly English; not she. She writes what we may call very knowing English. If her readers have not read George Eliot and Thackeray and all the great authorities, she assuredly has, and, like every one else, she is the better for it. With a telling subject and a knowing style she proceeds to get up her photograph. These require shrewd observation and wide experience; Miss Braddon has both. Like all women, she has a turn for color; she knows how to paint. She overloads her canvas with detail. It is the peculiar character of these details that constitute her chief force. They betray an intimate acquaintance with that disorderly half of society which becomes every day a greater object of interest to the orderly half. They intimate that, to use an irresistible vulgarism, Miss Braddon "has been there." The novelist who interprets the illegitimate world to the legitimate world, commands from the nature of his position a certain popularity. Miss Braddon deals familiarly with gamblers, and betting-men, and flashy reprobates of every description. She knows much that ladies are not accustomed to know, but that they are apparently very glad to learn. The names of drinks, the technicalities of the faro-table, the lingo of the turf, the talk natural to a crowd of fast men at supper, when there are no ladies present but Miss Braddon, the way one gentleman knocks another down—all these things—the exact local coloring of Bohemia—our sisters and daughters may learn from these works. These things are the incidents of vice; and vice, as is well-known, even modern, civilized, elegant, prosaic vice, has its romance. Of this romance Miss Braddon has taken advantage, and the secret of her success is, simply, that she has done her work better than her predecessors. That is, she has done it with a woman's *finesse* and a strict regard to morality. If one of her heroines elopes with a handsome stable-boy, she saves the proprieties by marrying him. This may be indecent if you like, but it is not immoral. If another of her heroines is ever tempted, she resists. With people who are not particular, therefore, as to the moral delicacy of their author, or as to their intellectual strength, Miss Braddon is very naturally a favorite.

CHARLES DICKENS
Our Mutual Friend

OUR MUTUAL Friend is, to our perception, the poorest of Mr. Dickens's works. And it is poor with the poverty not of momentary embarrassment, but of permanent exhaustion. It is wanting in inspiration. For the last ten years it has seemed to us that Mr. Dickens has been unmistakably forcing himself. *Bleak House* was forced; *Little Dorritt* was labored; the present work is dug out as with a spade and pickaxe. Of course—to anticipate the usual argument—who but Dickens could have written it? Who, indeed? Who else would have established a lady in business in a novel on the admirably solid basis of her always putting on gloves and tieing a handkerchief round her head in moments of grief, and of her habitually addressing her family with "Peace! hold!" It is needless to say that Mrs. Reginald Wilfer is first and last the occasion of considerable true humor. When, after conducting her daughter to Mrs. Boffin's carriage, in sight of all the envious neighbors, she is described as enjoying her triumph during the next quarter of an hour by airing herself on the door-step "in a kind of splendidly serene trance," we laugh with as uncritical a laugh as could be desired of us. We pay the same tribute to her assertions, as she narrates the glories of the society she enjoyed at her father's table, that she has known as many as three copper-plate engravers exchanging the most exquisite sallies and retorts there at one time. But when to these we have added a dozen more happy examples of the humor which was exhaled from every line of Mr. Dickens's earlier writings, we shall have closed the list of the merits of the work before us. To say that the conduct of the story, with all its complications, betrays a long-practised hand, is to pay no compliment worthy the author. If this were, indeed, a compliment, we should be inclined to carry it further, and congratulate him on his success in what we should call the manufacture of fiction; for in so doing we should express a feeling that has attended us throughout the book. Seldom, we reflected, had we read a book so intensely *written*, so little seen, known, or felt.

In all Mr. Dickens's works the fantastic has been his great resource; and while his fancy was lively and vigorous it accomplished great things. But the fantastic, when the fancy is dead, is a very poor business. The movement of Mr. Dickens's fancy in Mrs. Wilfer and Mr. Boffin and Lady Tippins, and the Lammles and Miss Wren, and even in Eugene Wrayburn, is, to our mind, a movement lifeless, forced, mechanical. It is the letter of his old humor without the spirit. It is hardly too much to say that every character here put before us is a mere bundle of eccentricities, animated by no principle of nature whatever. In former days there reigned in Mr. Dickens's extravagances a comparative consistency; they were exaggerated statements of types that really existed. We had, perhaps, never known a Newman Noggs, nor a Pecksniff, nor a Micawber; but we had known persons of whom these figures were but the strictly logical consummation. But among the grotesque creatures who occupy the pages before us, there is not one whom we can refer to as an existing type. In all Mr. Dickens's stories, indeed, the reader has been called upon, and has willingly consented, to accept a certain number of figures or creatures of pure fancy, for this was the author's poetry. He was, moreover, always repaid for his concession by a peculiar beauty or power in these exceptional characters. But he is now expected to make the same concession with a very inadequate reward. What do we get in return for accepting Miss Jenny Wren as a possible person? This young lady is the type of a certain class of characters of which Mr. Dickens has made a specialty, and with which he has been accustomed to draw alternate smiles and tears, according as he pressed one spring or another. But this is very cheap merriment and very cheap pathos. Miss Jenny Wren is a poor little dwarf, afflicted, as she constantly reiterates, with a "bad back" and "queer legs," who makes doll's dresses, and is for ever pricking at those with whom she converses, in the air, with her needle, and as-

suring them that she knows their "tricks and their manners." Like
all Mr. Dickens's pathetic characters, she is a little monster; she is
deformed, unhealthy, unnatural; she belongs to the troop of hunch-
backs, imbeciles, and precocious children who have carried on the
sentimental business in all Mr. Dickens's novels; the little Nells, the
Smikes, the Paul Dombeys.

Mr. Dickens goes as far out of the way for his wicked people as he
does for his good ones. Rogue Riderhood, indeed, in the present story,
is villanous with a sufficiently natural villany; he belongs to that
quarter of society in which the author is most at his ease. But was
there ever such wickedness as that of the Lammles and Mr. Fledgeby?
Not that people have not been as mischievous as they; but was any
one ever mischievous in that singular fashion? Did a couple of elegant
swindlers ever take such particular pains to be aggressively inhu-
man?—for we can find no other word for the gratuitous distortions
to which they are subjected. The word *humanity* strikes us as strangely
discordant, in the midst of these pages; for, let us boldly declare it,
there is no humanity here. Humanity is nearer home than the Boffins,
and the Lammles, and the Wilfers, and the Veneerings. It is in what
men have in common with each other, and not in what they have in
distinction. The people just named have nothing in common with
each other, except the fact that they have nothing in common with
mankind at large. What a world were this world if the world of *Our
Mutual Friend* were an honest reflection of it! But a community of
eccentrics is impossible. Rules alone are consistent with each other;
exceptions are inconsistent. Society is maintained by natural sense
and natural feeling. We cannot conceive a society in which these
principles are not in some manner represented. Where in these pages
are the depositaries of that intelligence without which the movement
of life would cease? Who represents nature? Accepting half of Mr.
Dickens's persons as intentionally grotesque, where are those exemplars
of sound humanity who should afford us the proper measure of their
companions' variations? We ought not, in justice to the author, to
seek them among his weaker—that is, his mere conventional—characters; in John Harmon, Lizzie Hexam, or Mortimer Lightwood;

but we assuredly cannot find them among his stronger—that is, his artificial creations. Suppose we take Eugene Wrayburn and Bradley Headstone. They occupy a halfway position between the habitual probable of nature and the habitual impossible of Mr. Dickens. A large portion of the story rests upon the enmity borne by Headstone to Wrayburn, both being in love with the same woman. Wrayburn is a gentleman, and Headstone is one of the people. Wrayburn is well-bred, careless, elegant, sceptical, and idle: Headstone is a high-tempered, hard-working, ambitious young schoolmaster. There lay in the opposition of these two characters a very good story. But the prime requisite was that they should *be* characters: Mr. Dickens, according to his usual plan, has made them simply figures, and between them the story that was to be, the story that should have been, has evaporated. Wrayburn lounges about with his hands in his pockets, smoking a cigar, and talking nonsense. Headstone strides about, clenching his fists and biting his lips and grasping his stick. There is one scene in which Wrayburn chaffs the schoolmaster with easy insolence, while the latter writhes impotently under his well-bred sarcasm. This scene is very clever, but it is very insufficient. If the majority of readers were not so very timid in the use of words we should call it vulgar. By this we do not mean to indicate the conventional impropriety of two gentlemen exchanging lively personalities; we mean to emphasize the essentially small character of these personalities. In other words, the moment, dramatically, is great, while the author's conception is weak. The friction of two *men*, of two characters, of two passions, produces stronger sparks than Wrayburn's boyish repartees and Headstone's melodramatic commonplaces. Such scenes as this are useful in fixing the limits of Mr. Dickens's insight. Insight is, perhaps, too strong a word; for we are convinced that it is one of the chief conditions of his genius not to see beneath the surface of things. If we might hazard a definition of his literary character, we should, accordingly, call him the greatest of superficial novelists. We are aware that this definition confines him to an inferior rank in the department of letters which he adorns; but we accept this consequence of our proposition. It were, in our opinion, an offence against humanity to place Mr. Dickens among the greatest novelists. For, to repeat what we have already intimated, he has created nothing but figure. He has added nothing to our understanding of human character. He is master of but two alternatives: he reconciles us to what is commonplace, and he reconciles us to what is odd. The value of the former service is questionable; and the manner in which Mr. Dickens performs it sometimes conveys a certain impression of charlatanism. The value of the latter service is incontestable, and here Mr. Dickens is an honest, an admirable artist. But what is the condition of the truly great novelist? For him there are no alternatives, for him there are no oddities, for him there is nothing outside of humanity. He cannot shirk it; it imposes itself upon him. For him alone, therefore, there is a true and a false; for him alone it is possible to be right, because it is possible to be wrong. Mr. Dickens is a great observer and a great humorist, but he is nothing of a philosopher. Some people may hereupon say, so much the better; we say, so much the worse. For a novelist very soon has need of a little philosophy. In treating of Micawber, and Boffin, and Pickwick, *et hoc genus omne*, he can, indeed, dispense with it, for this—we say it with all deference—is not serious writing. But when he comes to tell the story of a passion, a story like that of Headstone and Wrayburn, he becomes a moralist as well as an artist. He must know *man* as well as *men*, and to know man is to be a philosopher. The writer who knows men alone, if he have Mr. Dickens's humor and fancy, will give us figures and pictures for which we cannot be too grateful, for he will enlarge our knowledge of the world. But when he introduces men and women whose interest is preconceived to lie not in the poverty, the weakness, the drollery of their natures, but in their complete and unconscious subjection to ordinary and healthy human emotions, all his humor, all his fancy, will avail him nothing if, out of the fulness of his sympathy, he is unable to prosecute those generalizations in which alone consists the real greatness of a work of art. This may sound like very subtle talk about a very simple matter; it is rather very simple talk about a very subtle matter. A story based upon those elementary passions in which alone we seek the true and final manifestation of character must be told in a spirit of intellectual superiority to those passions. That is, the author must understand what he is talking about. The perusal of a story so told is one of the most elevating experiences within the reach of the human mind. The perusal of a story which is not so told is infinitely depressing and unprofitable.

ELIZABETH GASKELL
Wives and Daughters

WE CANNOT help thinking that in *Wives and Daughters* the late Mrs. Gaskell has added to the number of those works of fiction—of which we cannot perhaps count more than a score as having been produced in our time—which will outlast the duration of their novelty and continue for years to come to be read and relished for a higher order of merits. Besides being the best of the author's own tales—putting aside *Cranford*, that is, which as a work of quite other pretensions ought not to be weighed against it, and which seems to us manifestly destined in its modest way to become a classic—it is also one of the very best novels of its kind. So delicately, so elaborately, so artistically, so truthfully, and heartily is the story wrought out, that the hours given to its perusal seem like hours actually spent, in the flesh as well as the spirit, among the scenes and people described, in the atmosphere of their motives, feelings, traditions, associations. The gentle skill with which the reader is slowly involved in the tissue of the story; the delicacy of the handwork which has perfected every mesh of the net in which he finds himself ultimately entangled; the lightness of touch which, while he stands all unsuspicious of literary artifice, has stopped every issue into the real world; the admirable, inaudible, invisible exercise of creative power, in short, with which a new and arbitrary world is reared over his heedless head—a world insidiously inclusive of him (such is the *assoupissement* of his critical sense), complete in every particular, from the divine blue of the summer sky to the June-bugs in the roses, from Cynthia Kirkpatrick and her infinite revelations of human nature to old Mrs. Goodenough and her provincial bad grammar—these marvellous results, we say, are such as to compel the reader's very warmest admiration, and to make him feel, in his gratitude for this seeming accession of social and moral knowledge, as if he made but a poor return to the author in testifying, no matter how strongly, to the fact of her genius.

For Mrs. Gaskell's genius was so very composite as a quality, it was so obviously the offspring of her affections, her feelings, her associations, and (considering that, after all, it *was* genius) was so little of an intellectual matter, that it seems almost like slighting these charming facts to talk of them under a collective name, especially when that name is a term so coarsely and disrespectfully synthetic as the word genius has grown to be. But genius is of many kinds, and we are almost tempted to say that that of Mrs. Gaskell strikes us as being little else than a peculiar play of her personal character. In saying this we wish to be understood as valuing not her intellect the less, but her character the more. Were we touching upon her literary character at large, we should say that in her literary career as a whole she displayed, considering her success, a minimum of head. Her career was marked by several little literary indiscretions, which show how much writing was a matter of pure feeling with her. Her *Life of Miss Brontë*, for instance, although a very readable and delightful book, is one which a woman of strong head could not possibly have written; for, full as it is of fine qualities, of affection, of generosity, of sympathy, of imagination, it lacks the prime requisites of a good biography. It is written with a signal want of judgment and of critical power; and it has always seemed to us that it tells the reader considerably more about Mrs. Gaskell than about Miss Brontë. In the tale before us this same want of judgment, as we may still call it in the absence of a better name, presuming that the term applies to it only as it stands contrasted with richer gifts, is shown; not in the general management of the story, nor yet in the details, most of which are as good as perfect, but in the way in which, as the tale progresses, the author loses herself in its current very much as we have seen that she causes the reader to do.

The book is very long and of an interest so quiet that not a few of its readers will be sure to vote it dull. In the early portion especially the details are so numerous and so minute that even a very well-disposed reader will be tempted to lay down the book and ask himself of what possible concern to him are the clean frocks and the French lessons of little Molly Gibson. But if he will have patience awhile he will see. As an end these modest domestic facts are indeed valueless; but as a means to what the author would probably have called a "realization" of her central idea, *i.e.*, Molly Gibson, a product, to a certain extent, of clean frocks and French lessons, they hold an eminently respectable place. As he gets on in the story he is thankful for them. They have educated him to a proper degree of interest in the heroine. He feels that he knows her the better and loves her the more for a certain acquaintance with the *minutiae* of her homely *bourgeois* life. Molly Gibson, however, in spite of the almost fraternal relation which is thus established between herself and the reader—or perhaps, indeed, because of it, for if no man is a hero to his *valet de chambre*, it may be said that no young lady is a heroine to one who, if we may so express our meaning, has known her since she was "*so* high"—Molly Gibson, we repeat, commands a slighter degree of interest than the companion figure of Cynthia Kirkpatrick. Of this figure, in a note affixed to the book in apology for the absence of the final chapter, which Mrs. Gaskell did not live to write, the editor of the magazine in which the story originally appeared speaks in terms of very high praise; and yet, as it seems to us, of praise thoroughly well deserved. To describe Cynthia as she stands in Mrs. Gaskell's pages is impossible. The reader who cares to know her must trace her attentively out. She is a girl of whom, in life, any one of her friends, so challenged, would hesitate to attempt to give a general account, and yet whose specific sayings and doings and looks such a friend would probably delight to talk about. This latter has been Mrs. Gaskell's course; and if, in a certain sense, it shows her weakness, it also shows her wisdom. She had probably known a Cynthia Kirkpatrick, a résumé of whose character she had given up as hopeless; and she has here accordingly taken a generous revenge in an analysis as admirably conducted as any we remember to have read. She contents herself with a simple record of the innumerable small facts of the young girl's daily life, and leaves the reader to draw his conclusions. He draws them as he proceeds, and yet leaves them always subject to revision; and he derives from the author's own marked abdication of the authoritative generalizing tone which, when the other characters are concerned, she has used as a right, a very delightful sense of the mystery of Cynthia's nature and of those large proportions which mystery always suggests. The fact is that genius is always difficult to formulate, and that Cynthia had a genius for fascination. Her whole character subserved this end. Next after her we think her mother the best drawn character in the book. Less difficult indeed to draw than the daughter, the very nicest art was yet required to keep her from merging, in the reader's sight, into an amusing caricature—a sort of commixture of a very mild solution of Becky Sharp with an equally feeble decoction of Mrs. Nickleby. Touch by touch, under the reader's eye, she builds herself up into her selfish and silly and consummately natural completeness.

Mrs. Gaskell's men are less successful than her women, and her hero in this book, making all allowance for the type of man intended, is hardly interesting enough in juxtaposition with his vivid sweethearts. Still his defects as a masculine being are negative and not positive, which is something to be thankful for, now that lady-novelists are growing completely to eschew the use of simple and honest youths. Osborne Hamley, a much more ambitious figure than Roger, and ambitious as the figure of Cynthia is ambitious, is to our judgment less successful than either of these; and we think the praise given him in the editorial note above-mentioned is excessive. He has a place in the story, and he is delicately and even forcibly conceived, but he is practically little more than a suggestion. Mrs. Gaskell had exhausted her poetry upon Cynthia, and she could spare to Osborne's very dramatic and even romantic predicaments little more than the close prosaic handling which she had found sufficient for the more vulgar creations. Where this handling accords thoroughly with the spirit of the figures, as in the case of Doctor Gibson and Squire Hamley, the result is admirable. It is good praise of these strongly marked, masculine, middle-aged men to say that they are as forcibly drawn as if a wise masculine hand had drawn them. Perhaps the best scene in the book (as the editor remarks) is the one in which the squire smokes a pipe with one of his sons after his high words with the other. We have intimated that this scene is prosaic; but let not the reader take fright at the word. If an author can be powerful, delicate, humorous, pathetic, dramatic, within the strict limits of homely prose, we see no need of his "dropping into poetry," as Mr. Dickens says. It is Mrs. Gaskell's highest praise to have been all of this, and yet to have written "an everyday story" (as, if we mistake not, the original title of *Wives and Daughters* ran) in an everyday style.

GEORGE ELIOT
Middlemarch

MIDDLEMARCH is at once one of the strongest and one of the weakest of English novels. Its predecessors as they appeared might have been described in the same terms; *Romola*, is especially a rare masterpiece, but the least *entraînant* of masterpieces. *Romola* sins by excess of analysis; there is too much description and too little drama; too much reflection (all certainly of a highly imaginative sort) and too little creation. Movement lingers in the story, and with it attention stands still in the reader. The error in *Middlemarch* is not precisely of a similar kind, but it is equally detrimental to the total aspect of the work. We can well remember how keenly we wondered, while its earlier chapters unfolded themselves, what turn in the way of form the story would take—that of an organized, moulded, balanced composition, gratifying the reader with a sense of design and construction, or a mere chain of episodes, broken into accidental lengths and unconscious of the influence of a plan. We expected the actual result, but for the sake of English imaginative literature which, in this line is rarely in need of examples, we hoped for the other. If it had come we should have had the pleasure of reading, what certainly would have seemed to us in the immediate glow of attention, the first of English novels. But that pleasure has still to hover between prospect and retrospect. *Middlemarch* is a treasure-house of details, but it is an indifferent whole.

Our objection may seem shallow and pedantic, and may even be represented as a complaint that we have had the less given us rather than the more. Certainly the greatest minds have the defects of their qualities, and as George Eliot's mind is preëminently contemplative and analytic, nothing is more natural than that her manner should be discursive and expansive. "Concentration" would doubtless have deprived us of many of the best things in the book—of Peter Featherstone's grotesquely expectant legatees, of Lydgate's medical rivals, and of Mary Garth's delightful family. The author's purpose was to be a generous rural historian, and this very redundancy of touch, born of abundant reminiscence, is one of the greatest charms of her work. It is as if her memory was crowded with antique figures, to whom for very tenderness she must grant an appearance. Her novel is a picture—vast, swarming, deep-colored, crowded with episodes, with vivid images, with lurking master-strokes, with brilliant passages of expression; and as such we may freely accept it and enjoy it. It is not compact, doubtless; but when was a panorama compact? And yet, nominally, *Middlemarch* has a definite subject—the subject indicated in the eloquent preface. An ardent young girl was to have been the central figure, a young girl framed for a larger moral life than circumstance often affords, yearning for a motive for sustained spiritual effort and only wasting her ardor and soiling her wings against the meanness of opportunity. The author, in other words, proposed to depict the career of an obscure St. Theresa. Her success has been great, in spite of serious drawbacks. Dorothea Brooke is a genuine creation, and a most remarkable one when we consider the delicate material in which she is wrought. George Eliot's men are generally so much better than the usual trowsered offspring of the female fancy, that their merits have perhaps overshadowed those of her women. Yet her heroines have always been of an exquisite quality, and Dorothea is only that perfect flower of conception of which her predecessors were the less unfolded blossoms. An indefinable moral elevation is the sign of these admirable creatures; and of the representation of this quality in its superior degrees the author seems to have in English fiction a monopoly. To render the expression of a soul requires a cunning hand; but we seem to look straight into the unfathomable eyes of the beautiful spirit of Dorothea Brooke. She exhales a sort of aroma of spiritual sweetness, and we believe in her as in a woman we might providentially meet some fine day when we should find ourselves doubting of the immortality of the soul. By what un-erring mechanism this effect is produced—whether by fine strokes or broad ones, by description or by narration, we can hardly say; it is certainly the great achievement of the book. Dorothea's career is, however, but an episode, and though doubtless in intention, not distinctly enough in fact, the central one. The history of Lydgate's *menage*, which shares honors with it, seems rather to the reader to carry off the lion's share. This is certainly a very interesting story, but on the whole it yields in dignity to the record of Dorothea's unreso-nant woes. The "love-problem," as the author calls it, of Mary Garth, is placed on a rather higher level than the reader willingly grants it. To the end we care less about Fred Vincy than appears to be expected of us. In so far as the writer's design has been to reproduce the total sum of life in an English village forty years ago, this common-place young gentleman, with his somewhat meagre tribulations and his rather neutral egotism, has his proper place in the picture; but the author narrates his fortunes with a fulness of detail which the reader often finds irritating. The reader indeed is sometimes tempted to complain of a tendency which we are at loss exactly to express—a tendency to make light of the serious elements of the story and to sacrifice them to the more trivial ones. Is it an unconscious instinct or is it a deliberate plan? With its abundant and massive ingredients *Middlemarch* ought somehow to have depicted a weightier drama. Dorothea was altogether too superb a heroine to be wasted; yet she plays a narrower part than the imagination of the reader demands. She is of more consequence than the action of which she is the nom-inal centre. She marries enthusiastically a man whom she fancies a great thinker, and who turns out to be but an arid pedant. Here, indeed, is a disappointment with much of the dignity of tragedy; but the situation seems to us never to expand to its full capacity. It is analyzed with extraordinary penetration, but one may say of it, as of most of the situations in the book, that it is treated with too much refinement and too little breadth. It revolves too constantly on the same pivot; it abounds in fine shades, but it lacks, we think, the great dramatic *chiaroscuro*. Mr. Casaubon, Dorothea's husband (of whom more anon) embittered, on his side, by matrimonial disappointment, takes refuge in vain jealousy of his wife's relations with an interesting young cousin of his own and registers this sentiment in a codicil to his will, making the forfeiture of his property the penalty of his widow's marriage with this gentleman. Mr. Casaubon's death befalls about the middle of the story, and from this point to the close our interest in Dorothea is restricted to the question, will she or will she not marry Will Ladislaw? The question is relatively trivial and the implied struggle slightly factitious. The author has depicted the struggle with a sort of elaborate solemnity which in the interviews related in the two last books tends to become almost ludicrously excessive.

The dramatic current stagnates; it runs between hero and heroine almost a game of hair-splitting. Our dissatisfaction here is provoked in a great measure by the insubstantial character of the hero. The figure of Will Ladislaw is a beautiful attempt, with many finely-completed points; but on the whole it seems to us a failure. It is the only eminent failure in the book, and its defects are therefore the more striking. It lacks sharpness of outline and depth of color; we have not found ourselves believing in Ladislaw as we believe in Dorothea, in Mary Garth, in Rosamond, in Lydgate, in Mr. Brooke and Mr. Casaubon. He is meant, indeed, to be a light creature (with a large capacity for gravity, for he finally gets into Parliament), and a light creature certainly should not be heavily drawn. The author, who is evidently very fond of him, has found for him here and there some charming and eloquent touches; but in spite of these he remains vague and impalpable to the end. He is, we may say, the one figure which a masculine intellect of the same power as George Eliot's would not have conceived with the same complacency; he is, in short, roughly speaking, a woman's man. It strikes us as an oddity in the author's scheme that she should have chosen just this figure of Ladislaw as the creature in whom Dorothea was to find her spiritual compensations. He is really, after all, not the ideal foil to Mr. Casaubon which her soul must have imperiously demanded, and if the author of the "Key to all Mythologies" sinned by lack of order, Ladislaw too has not the concentrated fervor essential in the man chosen by so nobly strenuous a heroine. The impression once given that he is a *dilettante* is never properly removed, and there is slender poetic justice in Dorothea's marrying a *dilettante*. We are doubtless less content with Ladislaw, on account of the noble, almost sculptural, relief of the neighboring figure of Lydgate, the real hero of the story. It is an illustration of the generous scale of the author's picture and of the conscious power of her imagination that she has given us a hero and heroine of broadly distinct interests—erected, as it were, two suns in her firmament, each with its independent solar system. Lydgate is so richly successful a figure that we have regretted strongly at moments, for immediate interests' sake, that the current of his fortunes should not mingle more freely with the occasionally thin-flowing stream of Dorothea's. Toward the close, these two fine characters are brought into momentary contact so effectively as to suggest a wealth of dramatic possibility between them; but if this train had been followed we should have lost Rosamond Vincy—a rare psychological study. Lydgate is a really complete portrait of a *man*, which seems to us high praise. It is striking evidence of the altogether superior quality of George Eliot's imagination that, though elaborately represented, Lydgate should be treated so little from what we may roughly (and we trust without offence) call the sexual point of view. Perception charged with feeling has constantly guided the author's hand, and yet her strokes remain as firm, her curves as free, her whole manner as serenely impersonal, as if, on a small scale, she were emulating the creative wisdom itself. Several English romancers—notably Fielding, Thackeray, and Charles Reade—have won great praise for their figures of women: but they owe it, in reversed conditions, to a meaner sort of art, it seems to us, than George Eliot has used in the case of Lydgate; to an indefinable appeal to masculine prejudice—to a sort of titillation of the masculine sense of difference. George Eliot's manner is more philosophic—more broadly intelligent, and yet her result is as concrete or, if you please, as picturesque. We have no space to dwell on Lydgate's character; we can but repeat that he is a vividly consistent, manly figure—powerful, ambitious, sagacious, with the maximum rather than the minimum of egotism, strenuous, generous, fallible, and altogether human. A work of the liberal scope of *Middlemarch* contains a multitude of artistic intentions, some of the finest of which become clear only in the meditative after-taste of perusal. This is the case with the balanced contrast between the two histories of Lydgate and Dorothea. Each is a tale of matrimonial infelicity, but the conditions in each are so different and the circumstances so broadly opposed that the mind passes from one to the other with that supreme sense of the vastness and variety of human life, under aspects apparently similar, which it belongs only to the greatest novels to produce. The most perfectly successful passages in the book are perhaps those painful fireside scenes between Lydgate and his miserable little wife. The author's rare psychological penetration is lavished upon this veritably mulish domestic flower. There is nothing more powerfully real than these scenes in all English fiction, and nothing certainly more *intelligent*. Their impressiveness, and (as regards Lydgate) their pathos, is deepened by the constantly low key in which they are pitched. It is a tragedy based on unpaid butchers' bills, and the urgent need for small economies. The author has desired to be strictly real and to adhere to the facts of the common lot, and she has given us a powerful version of that typical human drama, the struggles of an ambitious soul with sordid disappointments and vulgar embarrassments. As to her catastrophe we hesitate to pronounce (for Lydgate's ultimate assent to his wife's worldly programme is nothing less than a catastrophe). We almost believe that some terrific explosion would have been more probable than his twenty years of smothered aspiration. Rosamond deserves almost to rank with Tito in *Romola* as a study of a gracefully vicious, or at least of a practically baleful nature. There is one point, however, of which we question the consistency. The author insists on her instincts of coquetry, which seems to us a discordant note. They would have made her better or worse—more generous or more reckless; in either case more manageable. As it is, Rosamond represents, in a measure, the fatality of British decorum.

In reading, we have marked innumerable passages for quotation and comment; but we lack space and the work is so ample that half a dozen extracts would be an ineffective illustration. There would be a great deal to say on the broad array of secondary figures, Mr. Casaubon, Mr. Brooke, Mr. Bulstrode, Mr. Farebrother, Caleb Garth, Mrs. Cadwallader, Celia Brooke. Mr. Casaubon is an excellent invention; as a dusky *repoussoir* to the luminous figure of his wife he could not have been better imagined. There is indeed something very noble in the way in which the author has apprehended his character. To depict hollow pretentiousness and mouldy egotism with so little of narrow sarcasm and so much of philosophic sympathy, is to be a rare moralist as well as a rare story-teller. The whole portrait of Mr. Casaubon has an admirably sustained greyness of tone in which the shadows are never carried to the vulgar black of coarser artists. Every stroke contributes to the unwholesome, helplessly sinister expression. Here and there perhaps (as in his habitual diction), there is a hint of exaggeration; but we confess we like fancy to be fanciful. Mr. Brooke and Mr. Garth are in their different lines supremely genial creations; they are drawn with the touch of a Dickens chastened and intellectualized. Mrs. Cadwallader is, in another walk of life, a match for Mrs. Poyser, and Celia Brooke is as pretty a fool as any of Miss Austen's. Mr. Farebrother and his delightful "womankind" belong to a large group of figures begotten of the super-abundance of the author's creative instinct. At times they seem to encumber the stage and to produce a rather ponderous mass of dialogue; but they add to the reader's impression of having walked in the Middlemarch lanes and listened to the Middlemarch accent. To but one of these accessory episodes—that of Mr. Bulstrode, with its multiplex ramifications—do we take exception. It has a slightly artificial cast, a melodramatic tinge, unfriendly to the richly natural coloring of the whole. Bulstrode himself—with the history of whose troubled conscience the author has taken great pains—is, to our sense, too diffusely treated; he never grasps the reader's attention. But the touch of genius is never idle or vain. The obscure figure of Bulstrode's comely wife emerges at the needful moment, under a few light strokes, into the happiest reality.

All these people, solid and vivid in their varying degrees, are members of a deeply human little world, the full reflection of whose antique image is the great merit of these volumes. How bravely rounded a little world the author has made it—with how dense an atmosphere of interests and passions and loves and enmities and strivings and failings, and how motley a group of great folk and small, all after their kind, she has filled it, the reader must learn for himself. No writer seems to us to have drawn from a richer stock of those long-cherished memories which one's later philosophy makes doubly tender. There are few figures in the book which do not seem to have grown mellow in the author's mind. English readers may fancy they enjoy the "atmosphere" of *Middlemarch*; but we maintain that to relish its inner essence we must—for reasons too numerous to detail—be an American. The author has commissioned herself to be real, her native tendency being that of an idealist, and the intellectual result is a very fertilizing mixture. The constant presence of thought, of generalizing instinct, of *brain*, in a word, behind her observation, gives the latter its great value and her whole manner its high superiority. It denotes a mind in which imagination is illumined by faculties rarely found in fellowship with it. In this respect—in that broad reach of vision which would make the worthy historian of solemn fact as well as wanton fiction—George Eliot seems to us among English romancers to stand alone. Fielding approaches her, but to our mind, she surpasses Fielding. Fielding was didactic—the author of *Middlemarch* is really philosophic. These great qualities imply corresponding perils. The first is the loss of simplicity. George Eliot lost hers some time since; it lies buried (in a splendid mausoleum) in *Romola*. Many of the discursive portions of *Middlemarch* are, as we may say, too clever by half. The author wishes to say too many things, and to say them too well; to recommend herself to a scientific audience. Her style, rich and flexible as it is, is apt to betray her on these transcendental flights; we find, in our copy, a dozen passages marked "obscure." *Silas Marner* has a delightful tinge of Goldsmith—we may almost call it; *Middlemarch* is too often an echo of Messrs. Darwin and Huxley. In spite of these faults—which it seems graceless to indicate with this crude rapidity—it remains a very splendid performance. It sets a limit, we think, to the development of the old-fashioned English novel. Its diffuseness, on which we have touched, makes it too copious a dose of pure fiction. If we write novels so, how shall we write History? But it is nevertheless a contribution of the first importance to the rich imaginative department of our literature.

THOMAS HARDY
Far from the Madding Crowd

MR. HARDY's novel came into the world under brilliant auspices—
such as the declaration by the London *Spectator* that either George
Eliot had written it or George Eliot had found her match. One could
make out in a manner what the *Spectator* meant. To guess, one has
only to open *Far from the Madding Crowd* at random: "Mr. Jan Coggan, who had passed the cup to Henery, was a crimson man with a
spacious countenance and a private glimmer in his eye, whose name
had appeared on the marriage register of Weatherbury and neighboring parishes as best-man and chief witness in countless unions of the
previous twenty years; he also very frequently filled the post of head
godfather in baptisms of the subtly-jovial kind." That is a very fair
imitation of George Eliot's humorous manner. Here is a specimen of
her serious one: "He fancied he had felt himself in the penumbra of
a very deep sadness when touching that slight and fragile creature.
But wisdom lies in moderating mere impressions, and Gabriel endeav-
ored to think little of this." But the *Spectator*'s theory had an even
broader base, and we may profitably quote a passage which perhaps
constituted one of its solidest blocks. The author of *Silas Marner* has
won no small part of her fame by her remarkable faculty as a reporter
of ale-house and kitchen-fire conversations among simple-minded
rustics. Mr. Hardy has also made a great effort in this direction, and
here is a specimen—a particularly favorable specimen—of his success:

> "Why, Joseph Poorgrass, you han't had a drop!" said Mr. Cog-
> gan to a very shrinking man in the background, thrusting the
> cup towards him.

"Such a shy man as he is," said Jacob Smallbury. "Why, ye've hardly had strength of eye enough to look in our young mis'ess's face, so I hear, Joseph?"

All looked at Joseph Poorgrass with pitying reproach.

"No, I've hardly looked at her at all," faltered Joseph, reducing his body smaller while talking, apparently from a meek sense of undue prominence; "and when I see'd her, it was nothing but blushes with me!"

"Poor fellow," said Mr. Clark.

"'Tis a curious nature for a man," said Jan Coggan.

"Yes," continued Joseph Poorgrass, his shyness, which was so painful as a defect, just beginning to fill him with a little complacency, now that it was regarded in the light of an interesting study. "'Twere blush, blush, blush with me every minute of the time when she was speaking to me."

"I believe ye, Joseph Poorgrass, for we all know ye to be a very bashful man."

"'Tis terrible bad for a man, poor soul!" said the maltster. "And how long have ye suffered from it, Joseph?"

"Oh, ever since I was a boy. Yes—mother was concerned to her heart about it—yes. But 'twas all naught."

"Did ye ever take anything to try and stop it, Joseph Poorgrass?"

"Oh, aye, tried all sorts. They took me to Greenhill Fair, and into a great large jerry-go-nimble show, where there were womenfolk riding round—standing up on horses, with hardly anything on but their smocks; but it didn't cure me a morsel—no, not a morsel. And then was put errand-man at the Woman's Skittle Alley at the back of the Tailor's Arms in Casterbridge. 'Twas a horrible gross situation, and altogether a very curious place for a good man. I had to stand and look at wicked people in the face from morning till night; but 'twas no use—I was just as bad as ever after all. Blushes have been in the family for generations. There, 'tis a happy providence I be no worse, so to speak it—yes, a happy thing, and I feel my few poor gratitudes."

This is extremely clever, and the author has evidently read to good purpose the low-life chapters in George Eliot's novels; he has caught very happily her trick of seeming to humor benignantly her queer people and look down at them from the heights of analytic omniscience. But we have quoted the episode because it seems to us an excellent example of the cleverness which is only cleverness, of the difference between original and imitative talent—the disparity, which it is almost unpardonable not to perceive, between first-rate talent and those inferior grades which range from second-rate downward, and as to which confusion is a more venial offence. Mr. Hardy puts his figures through a variety of comical movements; he fills their mouths with quaint turns of speech; he baptizes them with odd names ("Joseph Poorgrass" for a bashful, easily-snubbed Dissenter is excellent); he pulls the wires, in short, and produces a vast deal of sound and commotion; and his novel, at a cursory glance, has a rather promising air of life and warmth. But by critics who prefer a grain of substance to a pound of shadow it will, we think, be pronounced a decidedly delusive performance; it has a fatal lack of magic. We have found it hard to read, but its shortcomings are easier to summarize than to encounter in order. Mr. Hardy's novel is very long, but his subject is very short and simple, and the work has been distended to its rather formidable dimensions by the infusion of a large amount of conversational and descriptive padding and the use of an ingeniously verbose and redundant style. It is inordinately diffuse, and, as a piece of narrative, singularly inartistic. The author has little sense of proportion, and almost none of composition. We learn about Bathsheba and Gabriel, Farmer Boldwood and Sergeant Troy, what we can rather than what we should; for Mr. Hardy's inexhaustible faculty for spinning smart dialogue makes him forget that dialogue in a story is after all but episode, and that a novelist is after all but a historian, thoroughly possessed of certain facts, and bound in some way or other to impart them. To tell a story almost exclusively by reporting people's talks is the most difficult art in the world, and really leads, logically, to a severe economy in the use of rejoinder and repartee, and not to a lavish expenditure of them. *Far from the Madding Crowd* gives us an uncomfortable sense of being a simple "tale," pulled and stretched to make the conventional three volumes; and the author, in his long-sustained appeal to one's attention, reminds us of a person fishing with an enormous net, of which the meshes should be thrice too wide.

We are happily not subject, in this (as to minor matters) much-emancipated land, to the tyranny of the three volumes; but we confess that we are nevertheless being rapidly urged to a conviction that (since it is in the nature of fashions to revolve and recur) the day has come round again for some of the antique restrictions as to literary form. The three unities, in Aristotle's day, were inexorably imposed on Greek tragedy: why shouldn't we have something of the same sort for English fiction in the day of Mr. Hardy? Almost all novels are greatly too long, and the being too long becomes with each elapsing year a more serious offence. Mr. Hardy begins with a detailed description of his hero's smile, and proceeds thence to give a voluminous account of his large silver watch. Gabriel Oak's smile and his watch were doubtless respectable and important phenomena; but everything is relative, and daily becoming more so; and we confess that, as a hint of the pace at which the author proposed to proceed, his treatment of these facts produced upon us a deterring and depressing effect. If novels were the only books written, novels written on this scale would be all very well; but as they compete, in the esteem of sensible people, with a great many other books, and a great many other objects of interest of all kinds, we are inclined to think that, in the long run, they will be defeated in the struggle for existence unless they lighten their baggage very considerably and do battle in a more scientific equipment. Therefore, we really imagine that a few arbitrary rules—a kind of depleting process—might have a wholesome effect. It might be enjoined, for instance, that no "tale" should exceed fifty pages and no novel two hundred; that a plot should have but such and such a number of ramifications; that no ramification should have more than a certain number of persons; that no person should utter more than a given number of words; and that no description of an inanimate object should consist of more than a fixed number of lines. We should not incline to advocate this oppressive legislation as a comfortable or ideal finality for the romancer's art, but we think it might be excellent as a transitory discipline or drill. Necessity is the mother of invention, and writers with a powerful tendency to expatiation might in this temporary strait-jacket be induced to transfer their attention rather more severely from quantity to quality. The use of the strait-jacket would have cut down Mr. Hardy's novel to half its actual length and, as he is a clever man, have made the abbreviated work very ingeniously pregnant. We should have had a more occasional taste of all the barn-yard worthies—Joseph Poorgrass, Laban Tall, Matthew Moon, and the rest—and the vagaries of Miss Bathsheba would have had a more sensible consistency. Our restrictions would have been generous, however, and we should not have proscribed such a fine passage as this:

> Then there came a third flash. Manoeuvres of the most extraordinary kind were going on in the vast firmamental hollows overhead. The lightning now was the color of silver, and gleamed in the heavens like a mailed army. Rumbles became rattles. Gabriel, from his elevated position, could see over the landscape for at least half a dozen miles in front. Every hedge, bush, and tree was distinct as in a line engraving. In a paddock in the same direction was a herd of heifers, and the forms of these were visible at this moment in the act of galloping about in the wildest and maddest confusion, flinging their heels and tails high into the air, their heads to earth. A poplar in the immediate foreground was like an ink-stroke on burnished tin. Then the picture vanished, leaving a darkness so intense that Gabriel worked entirely by feeling with his hands.

Mr. Hardy describes nature with a great deal of felicity, and is evidently very much at home among rural phenomena. The most genuine thing in his book, to our sense, is a certain aroma of the meadows and lanes—a natural relish for harvestings and sheep-washings. He has laid his scene in an agricultural county, and his characters are children of the soil—unsophisticated country-folk.

Bathsheba Everdene is a rural heiress, left alone in the world, in possession of a substantial farm. Gabriel Oak is her shepherd, Farmer Boldwood is her neighbor, and Sergeant Troy is a loose young soldier who comes a-courting her. They are all in love with her, and the young lady is a flirt, and encourages them all. Finally she marries the Sergeant, who has just seduced her maid-servant. The maid-servant dies in the work-house, the Sergeant repents, leaves his wife, and is given up for drowned. But he reappears and is shot by Farmer Boldwood, who delivers himself up to justice. Bathsheba then marries Gabriel Oak, who has loved and waited in silence, and is, in our opinion, much too good for her. The chief purpose of the book is, we suppose, to represent Gabriel's dumb, devoted passion, his biding his time, his rendering unsuspected services to the woman who has scorned him, his integrity and simplicity and sturdy patience. In all this the tale is very fairly successful, and Gabriel has a certain vividness of expression. But we cannot say that we either understand or like Bathsheba. She is a young lady of the inconsequential, wilful, mettlesome type which has lately become so much the fashion for heroines, and of which Mr. Charles Reade is in a manner the inventor—the type which aims at giving one a very intimate sense of a young lady's *womanishness*. But Mr. Hardy's embodiment of it seems to us to lack reality; he puts her through the Charles Reade paces, but she remains alternately vague and coarse, and seems always artificial. This is Mr. Hardy's trouble; he rarely gets beyond ambitious artifice—the mechanical simulation of heat and depth and wisdom that are absent. Farmer Boldwood is a shadow, and Sergeant Troy an elaborate stage-figure. Everything human in the book strikes us as factitious and insubstantial; the only things we believe in are the sheep and the dogs. But, as we say, Mr. Hardy has gone astray very cleverly, and his superficial novel is a really curious imitation of something better.

ÉMILE ZOLA
Nana

M. ZOLA's new novel has been immensely talked about for the last six months; but we may doubt whether, now that we are in complete possession of it, its fame will further increase. It is a difficult book to read; we have to push our way through it very much as we did through *L'Assommoir*, with the difference that in *L'Assommoir* our perseverance, our patience, were constantly rewarded, and that in *Nana,* these qualities have to content themselves with the usual recompense of virtue, the simple sense of duty accomplished. I do not mean, indeed, by this allusion to duty that there is any moral obligation to read *Nana*; I simply mean that such an exertion may have been felt to be due to M. Zola by those who have been interested in his general attempt. His general attempt is highly interesting, and *Nana* is the latest illustration of it. It is far from being the most successful one; the obstacles to the reader's enjoyment are numerous and constant. It is true that, if we rightly understand him, enjoyment forms no part of the emotion to which M. Zola appeals; in the eyes of "naturalism" enjoyment is a frivolous, a superficial, a contemptible sentiment. It is difficult, however, to express conveniently by any other term the reader's measure of the entertainment afforded by a work of art. If we talk of interest, instead of enjoyment, the thing does not better our case—as it certainly does not better M. Zola's. The obstacles to interest in *Nana* constitute a formidable body, and the most comprehensive way to express them is to say that the work is inconceivably and inordinately dull. M. Zola (if we again understand him) will probably say that it is a privilege, or even a duty, of naturalism to be dull, and to a certain extent this is doubtless a very lawful plea. It is not an absolutely fatal defect for a novel not to be amusing, as we may see by the example of several important works. *Wilhelm Meister* is not a sprightly composition, and yet *Wilhelm Meister* stands in the front rank of novels. *Romola* is a very easy book to lay down, and yet *Romola* is full of beauty and truth. *Clarissa Harlowe* discourages the most robust persistence, and yet, paradoxical as it seems, *Clarissa Harlowe* is deeply interesting. It is obvious, therefore, that there is something to be said for dullness; and this something is perhaps, primarily, that there is dullness and dullness. That of which *Nana* is so truly a specimen, is of a peculiarly unredeemed and unleavened quality; it lacks that human savor, that finer meaning which carries it off in the productions I just mentioned. What *Nana* means it will take a very ingenious apologist to set forth. I speak, of course, of the impression it produces on English readers; into the deep mystery of the French taste in such matters it would be presumptuous for one of these to attempt to penetrate. The other element that stops the English reader's way is that monstrous uncleanness to which—to the credit of human nature in whatever degree it may seem desirable to determine—it is probably not unjust to attribute a part of the facility with which the volume before us has reached, on the day of its being offered for sale by retail, a thirty-ninth edition. M. Zola's uncleanness is not a thing to linger upon, but it is a thing to speak of, for it strikes us as an extremely curious phenomenon. In this respect *Nana* has little to envy its predecessors. The book is, perhaps, not pervaded by that ferociously bad smell which blows through *L'Assommoir* like an emanation from an open drain and makes the perusal of the history of Gervaise and Coupeau very much such an ordeal as a crossing of the Channel in a November gale; but in these matters comparisons are as difficult as they are unprofitable, and *Nana* is, in all conscience, untidy enough. To say the book is indecent, is to make use of a term which (always, if we understand him), M. Zola holds to mean nothing and to prove nothing. Decency and indecency, morality and immorality, beauty and ugliness, are conceptions with which "naturalism" has nothing to do; in M. Zola's system these distinctions are void, these allusions are idle. The only business of naturalism is to be—natural, and therefore, instead of saying of *Nana* that it contains a great deal of filth, we should simply say of it that it contains a great deal of nature. Once upon a time a rather pretentious person, whose moral tone had been corrupted by evil communications, and who lived among a set of people equally pretentious, but regrettably low-minded, being in conversation with another person, a lady of great robustness of judgment and directness of utterance, made use constantly, in a somewhat cynical and pessimistic sense, of the expression, "the world—the world." At last the distinguished listener could bear it no longer, and abruptly made reply: "My poor lady, do you call that corner of a pig-sty in which you happen to live, *the world*?" Some such answer as this we are moved to make to M. Zola's naturalism. Does he call that vision of things of which *Nana* is a representation, *nature*? The mighty mother, in her blooming richness, seems to blush from brow to chin at the insult! On what authority does M. Zola represent nature to us as a combination of the cesspool and the house of prostitution? On what authority does he represent foulness rather than fairness as the sign that we are to know her by? On the authority of his predilections alone; and this is his great trouble and the weak point of his incontestably remarkable talent. This is the point that, as we said just now, makes the singular foulness of his imagination worth touching upon, and which, we should suppose, will do much towards preserving his works for the curious contemplation of the psychologist and the historian of literature. Never was such foulness so spontaneous and so complete, and never was it united with qualities so superior to itself and intrinsically so respectable. M. Zola is an artist, and this is supposed to be a safeguard; and, indeed, never surely was any other artist so dirty as M. Zola! Other performers may have been so, but they were not artists; other such exhibitions may have taken place, but they have not taken place between the covers of a book—and especially of a book containing so much of vigorous and estimable effort. We have no space to devote to a general consideration of M. Zola's theory of the business of a novelist, or to the question of naturalism at large—much further than to say that the system on which the series of *Les Rougons-Macquart* has been written, contains, to our sense, a great deal of very solid ground. M. Zola's attempt is an extremely fine one; it deserves a great deal of respect and deference, and though his theory is constantly at odds with itself, we could, at a pinch, go a long way with it without quarreling. What we quarrel with is his application of it—is the fact that he presents us with his decoction of "nature" in a vessel unfit for the purpose, a receptacle lamentably, fatally in need of scouring (though no scouring, apparently, would be really effective), and in which no article intended for intellectual consumption should ever be served up. Reality is the object of M. Zola's efforts, and it is because we agree with him in appreciating it highly that we protest against its being discredited. In a time when literary taste has turned, to a regrettable degree, to the vulgar and the insipid, it is of high importance that realism should not be compromised. Nothing tends more to compromise it than to represent it as necessarily allied to the impure. That the pure and the impure are for M. Zola, as conditions of taste, vain words, and exploded ideas, only proves that his advocacy does more to injure an excellent cause than to serve it. It takes a very good cause to carry a *Nana* on its back, and if realism breaks down, and the conventional comes in again with a rush, we may know the reason why. The real has not a single shade more affinity with an unclean vessel than with a clean one, and M. Zola's system, carried to its utmost expression, can dispense as little with taste and tact as the floweriest mannerism of a less analytic age. Go as far as we will, so long as we abide in literature, the thing remains always a question of taste, and we can never leave taste behind without leaving behind, by the same stroke, the very grounds on which we appeal, the whole human side of the business. Taste, in its intellectual applications, is the most human faculty we possess, and as the novel may be said to be the most human form of art, it is a poor speculation to put the two things out of conceit of each other. Calling it naturalism will never make it profitable. It is perfectly easy to agree with M. Zola, who has taken his stand with more emphasis than is necessary; for the matter reduces itself to a question of application. It is impossible to see why the question of application is less urgent in naturalism than at any other point of the

scale, or why, if naturalism is, as M. Zola claims, a method of observation, it can be followed without delicacy or tact. There are all sorts
of things to be said about it; it costs us no effort whatever to admit
in the briefest terms that it is an admirable invention, and full of
promise; but we stand aghast at the want of tact it has taken to make
so unreadable a book as *Nana*.

To us English readers, I venture to think, the subject is very interesting, because it raises questions which no one apparently has the
energy or the good faith to raise among ourselves. (It is of distinctly
serious readers only that I speak, and *Nana* is to be recommended
exclusively to such as have a very robust appetite for a moral.) A
novelist with a system, a passionate conviction, a great plan—incontestable attributes of M. Zola—is not now to be easily found in
England or the United States, where the storyteller's art is almost
exclusively feminine, is mainly in the hands of timid (even when very
accomplished) women, whose acquaintance with life is severely restricted, and who are not conspicuous for general views. The novel,
moreover, among ourselves, is almost always addressed to young
unmarried ladies, or at least always assumes them to be a large part
of the novelist's public. This fact, to a French storyteller, appears, of
course, a damnable restriction, and M. Zola would probably decline
to take *au sérieux* any work produced under such unnatural conditions. Half of life is a sealed book to young unmarried ladies, and
how can a novel be worth anything that deals only with half of life?
How can a portrait be painted (in any way to be recognizable) of half
a face? It is not in one eye, but in the two eyes together that the expression resides, and it is the combination of features that constitutes
the human identity. These objections are perfectly valid, and it may
be said that our English system is a good thing for virgins and boys,
and a bad thing for the novel itself, when the novel is regarded as
something more than a simple *jeu d'esprit*, and considered as a composition that treats of life at large and helps us to *know*. But under
these unnatural conditions and insufferable restrictions a variety of
admirable works have been produced; Thackeray, Dickens, George
Eliot, have all had an eye to the innocent classes. The fact is anomalous,

and the advocates of naturalism must make the best of it. In fact, I believe they have little relish for the writers I have mentioned. They find that something or other is grievously wanting in their productions—as it most assuredly is! They complain that such writers are not serious. They are not so, certainly, as M. Zola is so; but there are many different ways of being serious. That of the author of *L'Assommoir*, of *La Conquête de Plassans*, of *La Faute de L'Abbé Mouret* may, as I say, with all its merits and defects taken together, suggest a great many things to English readers. They must admire the largeness of his attempt and the richness of his intention. They must admire, very often, the brilliancy of his execution. *L'Assommoir*, in spite of its fetid atmosphere, is full of magnificent passages and episodes, and the sustained power of the whole thing, the art of carrying a weight, is extraordinary. What will strike the English reader of M. Zola at large, however, and what will strike the English reader of *Nana*, if he have stoutness of stomach enough to advance in the book, is the extraordinary absence of humor, the dryness, the solemnity, the air of tension and effort. M. Zola disapproves greatly of wit; he thinks it is an impertinence in a novel, and he would probably disapprove of humor if he *knew* what it is. There is no indication in all his works that he has a suspicion of this; and what tricks the absence of a sense of it plays him! What a mess it has made of this admirable *Nana*! The presence of it, even in a limited degree, would have operated, to some extent, as a disinfectant, and if M. Zola had had a more genial fancy he would also have had a cleaner one. Is it not also owing to the absence of a sense of humor that this last and most violent expression of the realistic faith is extraordinarily wanting in reality? Anything less illusory than the pictures, the people, the indecencies of *Nana*, could not well be imagined. The falling-off from *L'Assommoir* in this respect can hardly be exaggerated. The human note is completely absent, the perception of character, of the way that people feel and think and act, is helplessly, hopelessly at fault; so that it becomes almost grotesque at last to see the writer trying to drive before him a herd of figures that never for an instant stand on their legs. This is what saves us in England, in spite of our artistic levity and the presence of the young ladies—this fact that we are by disposition better psychologists, that we have, as a general thing, a deeper, more delicate perception of the play of character and the state of the soul. This is what often gives an interest to works conceived on a much narrower program than those of M. Zola—makes them more touching and more real, although the apparatus and the machinery of reality may, superficially, appear to be wanting. French novelists are at bottom, with all their extra freedom, a good deal more conventional than our own; and *Nana*, with the prodigious freedom that her author has taken, never, to my sense, leaves for a moment the region of the conventional. The figure of the brutal *fille,* without a conscience or a soul, with nothing but devouring appetites and impudences, has become the stalest of the stock properties of French fiction, and M. Zola's treatment has here imparted to her no touch of superior verity. He is welcome to draw as many figures of the same type as he finds necessary, if he will only make them human; this is as good a way of making a contribution to our knowledge of ourselves as another. It is not his choice of subject that has shocked us; it is the melancholy dryness of his execution, which gives us all the bad taste of a disagreeable dish and none of the nourishment.

MEMORIALS

GEORGE SAND

AMONG the eulogies and dissertations called forth by the death of the great writer who shared with Victor Hugo the honour of literary pre-eminence in France, quite the most valuable was the short notice published in the *Journal des Débats*, by M. Taine. In this notice the apostle of the "milieu" and the "moment" very justly remarked that George Sand is an exceptionally good case for the study of the pedigree of a genius—for ascertaining the part of prior generations in forming one of those minds which shed back upon them the light of glory. What renders Madame Sand so available an example of the operation of heredity is the fact that the process went on very publicly, as one may say; that her ancestors were people of qualities at once very strongly marked and very abundantly recorded. The record has been kept in a measure by George Sand herself. When she was fifty years old she wrote her memoirs, and in this prolix and imperfect but extremely entertaining work a large space is devoted to the heroine's parents and grandparents.

It was a very picturesque pedigree—quite an ideal pedigree for a romancer. Madame Sand's great-grandfather was the Maréchal Maurice de Saxe, one of the very few generals in the service of Louis XV who tasted frequently of victory. Maurice de Saxe was a royal bastard, the son of Augustus II, surnamed the Strong, Elector of Saxony and King of Poland, and of a brilliant mistress, Aurore de Königsmark. The victories of the Maréchal de Saxe were not confined to the battle-field; one of his conquests was an agreeable actress much before the Parisian public. This lady became the mother of Madame Sand's grandmother, who was honourably brought up and married at a very early age to the Comte de Horn. The Comte de Horn shortly died, and his widow, after an interval, accepted the hand of M. Dupin de Francueil, a celebrity and a very old man. M. Dupin was one of the brilliant figures in Paris society during the period immediately preceding the Revolution. He had a large fortune, and he too was a conqueror. A sufficiently elaborate portrait of him may be found in that interesting, if disagreeable, book, the *Mémoires* of Madame d'Epinay. This clever lady had been one of his spoils of victory. Old enough to be his wife's grandfather, he survived his marriage but a few years, and died with all his illusions intact, on the eve of the Revolution, leaving to Madame Dupin an only son. His wife outweathered the tempest, which, however, swept away her fortune; though she was able to buy a small property in the country—the rustic Château de Nohant, which George Sand has so often introduced into her writings. Here she settled herself with her son, a boy of charming promise, who was in due time drawn into the ranks of Napoleon's conquering legions. Young Dupin became an ardent Bonapartist and an accomplished soldier. He won rapid promotion. In one of the so-called "glorious" Italian campaigns he met a young girl who had followed the army from Paris, from a personal interest in one of its officers; and falling very honestly in love with her he presently married her, to the extreme chagrin of his mother. This young girl, the daughter of a bird-catcher, and, as George Sand calls her, an "enfant du vieux pavé de Paris," became the mother of the great writer. She was a child of the people and a passionate democrat, and in the person of her daughter we see the confluence of a plebeian stream with a strain no less (in spite of its irregularity) than royal. On the paternal side Madame Sand was cousin (in we know not what degree) to the present Bourbon claimant of the French crown; on the other she was affiliated to the stock which, out of the "vieux pavé," makes the barricades before which Bourbons go down.

This may very properly be called a "picturesque" descent; it is in a high degree what the French term *accidenté*. Its striking feature is that each conjunction through which it proceeds is a violent or irregular one. Two are illegitimate—those of the King of Poland and his son with their respective mistresses; the other two, though they had the sanction of law, may be called in a manner irregular. It was irregular for the fresh young Comtesse de Horn to be married to a man of seventy; it was irregular in her son, young Dupin, to make a wife of another man's mistress, often as this proceeding has been reversed. If it is a fair description of Madame Sand to say that she was, during that portion of her career which established her reputation, an apostle of the rights of love *quand même*, a glance at her pedigree shows that this was a logical disposition. She was herself more sensibly the result of a series of love-affairs than most of us. In each of these cases the woman had been loved with a force that asserted itself in contradiction to propriety or to usage.

We may observe moreover, in this course of transmission, the opposition of the element of insubordination and disorder (which sufficiently translated itself in outward acts in Madame Sand's younger years) and the "official" element, the respectable, conservative, exclusive strain. Three of our author's ancestresses were light women—women at odds with society, defiant of it, and, theoretically at least, discountenanced by it. The grand-daughter of the Comtesse de Königsmark and of Mademoiselle Verrières, the daughter of Madame Dupin the younger, could hardly have been expected not to take up this hereditary quarrel. It is striking that on the feminine side of the house what is called respectability was a very relative quality. Madame Dupin the elder took it very hard when her only and passionately loved son married a *femme galante.* She did not herself belong to this category, and her opposition is easily conceivable; but the reader of *L'Histoire de ma Vie* cannot help smiling a little when he reflects that this irreconcilable mother-in-law was the offspring of two illegitimate unions, and that her mother and grandmother had each enjoyed a plurality of lovers. At the same time, if there is anything more striking in George Sand, as a literary figure, than a certain traditional Bohemianism, it is that other very different quality which we just now called official, and which is constantly interrupting and complicating her Bohemianism. "George Sand immoral?" I once heard one of her more conditional admirers exclaim. "The fault I find with her is that she is so insufferably virtuous." The military and aristocratic side of her lineage is attested by this "virtuous" property—by her constant tendency to edification and didacticism, her love of philosophizing and preaching, of smoothing and harmonizing things, and by her great literary gift, her noble and imperturbable style, the style which, if she had been a man, would have seated her in that temple of all the proprieties, the French Academy.

It is not the purpose of these few pages to recapitulate the various items of George Sand's biography. Many of these are to be found in *L'Histoire de ma Vie*, a work which, although it was thought disappointing at the time of its appearance, is very well worth reading. It was given to the world day by day, as the feuilleton of a newspaper, and, like all the author's compositions, it has the stamp of being written to meet a current engagement. It lacks plan and proportion; the book is extremely ill made. But it has a great charm, and it contains three or four of the best portraits—the only portraits, we were on the point of saying—that the author has painted. The story was begun, but was never really finished; this was the public's disappointment. It contained a great deal about Madame Sand's grandmother and her father—a large part of two volumes are given to a transcript of her father's letters (and very charming letters they are). It abounded in anecdotes of the writer's childhood, her playmates, her pet animals, her school-adventures, the nuns at the Convent des Anglaises by whom she was educated; it related the juvenile unfolding of her mind, her fits of early piety, and her first acquaintance with Montaigne and Rousseau; it contained a superabundance of philosophy, psychology, morality and harmless gossip about people unknown to the public; but it was destitute of just that which the public desired—an explicit account of the more momentous incidents of the author's maturity. When she reaches the point at which her story becomes peculiarly interesting (up to that time it has simply been agreeable and entertaining) she throws up the game and drops the curtain. In other words, she talks no scandal—a consummation devoutly to be rejoiced in.

The reader nevertheless deems himself unfairly used, and takes his revenge in seeing something very typical of the author in the

shortcomings of the work. He declares it to be a nondescript performance, which has neither the value of truth nor the illusion of fiction;
and he inquires why the writer should preface her task with such
solemn remarks upon the edifying properties of autobiography, and
adorn it with so pompous an epigraph, if she meant simply to tell
what she might tell without trouble. It may be remembered, however,
that George Sand has sometimes been compared to Goethe, and that
there is this ground for the comparison—that in form *L'Histoire de
ma Vie* greatly resembles the *Dichtung und Wahrheit*. There is the
same charming, complacent expatiation upon youthful memories,
the same arbitrary confidences and silences, the same digressions and
general judgments, the same fading away of the narrative on the
threshold of maturity. We should never look for analogies between
George Sand and Goethe; but we should say that the lady's long au-
tobiographic fragment is in fact extremely typical—the most so indeed
of all her works. It shows in the highest degree her great strength and
her great weakness—her unequalled faculty of improvisation, as it
may be called, and her peculiar want of veracity. Every one will recognise what we mean by the first of these items. People may like
George Sand or not, but they can hardly deny that she is the great
improvisatrice of literature—the writer who best answers to Shelley's
description of the skylark singing "in profuse strains of unpremedi-
tated art." No writer has produced such great effects with an equal
absence of premeditation.

On the other hand, what we have called briefly and crudely her
want of veracity requires some explanation. It is doubtless a condition
of her serene volubility; but if this latter is a great literary gift, its value
is impaired by our sense that it rests to a certain extent upon a weakness. There is something very liberal and universal in George Sand's
genius, as well as very masculine; but our final impression of her always
is that she is a woman and a Frenchwoman. Women, we are told, do
not value the truth for its own sake, but only for some personal use
they make of it. My present criticism involves an assent to this somewhat cynical dogma. Add to this that woman, if she happens to be
French, has an extraordinary taste for investing objects with a grace-

ful drapery of her own contrivance, and it will be found that George Sand's cast of mind includes both the generic and the specific idiosyncrasy. We have more than once heard her readers say (whether it was professed fact or admitted fiction that they had in hand), "It is all very well, but I can't believe a word of it!" There is something very peculiar in this inability to believe George Sand even in that relative sense in which we apply the term to novelists at large. We believe Balzac, we believe Gustave Flaubert, we believe Dickens and Thackeray and Miss Austen. Dickens is far more incredible than George Sand, and yet he produces much more illusion. In spite of her plausibility, the author of *Consuelo* always appears to be telling a fairy-tale. We say in spite of her plausibility, but we might rather say that her excessive plausibility is the reason of our want of faith. The narrative is too smooth, too fluent; the narrator has a virtuous independence that the Muse of history herself might envy her. The effect it produces is that of a witness who is eager to tell more than is asked him, the worth of whose testimony is impaired by its importunity. The thing is beautifully done, but you feel that rigid truth has come off as it could; the author has not a high standard of exactitude; she never allows facts to make her uncomfortable. *L'Histoire de ma Vie* is full of charming recollections and impressions of Madame Sand's early years, of delightful narrative, of generous and elevated sentiment; but we have constantly the feeling that it is what children call "made up." If the fictitious quality in our writer's reminiscences is very sensible, of course the fictitious quality in her fictions is still more so; and it must be said that in spite of its odd mixture of the didactic and the irresponsible, *L'Histoire de ma Vie* sails nearer to the shore than its professedly romantic companions.

The usual objection to the novels, and a very just one, is that they contain no living figures, no people who stand on their feet, and who, like so many of the creations of the other great novelists, have become part of the public fund of allusion and quotation. As portraits George Sand's figures are vague in outline, deficient in detail. Several of those, however, which occupy the foreground of her memoirs have a remarkable vividness. In the four persons associated chiefly with her childhood and youth she really makes us believe. The first of these is the great figure which appears quite to have filled up the background of her childhood—almost to the exclusion of the child herself—that of her grandmother, Madame Dupin, the daughter of the great soldier. The second is that of her father, who was killed at Nohant by a fall from his horse, while she was still a young girl. The third is that of her mother—a particularly remarkable portrait. The fourth is the grotesque but softly-lighted image of Deschartres, the old pedagogue who served as tutor to Madame Sand and her half-brother; the latter youth being the fruit of an "amourette" between the Commandant Dupin and one of his mother's maids. Madame Dupin philosophically adopted the child; she dated from the philosophers of the preceding century. It is worth noting that George Sand's other playmate—the "Caroline" of the memoirs—was a half-sister on her mother's side, a little girl whose paternity antedated the Commandant Dupin's acquaintance with his wife.

In George Sand's account of her father there is something extremely delightful; full of filial passion as it is, and yet of tender discrimination. She makes him a charming figure—the ideal "gallant" Frenchman of the old type; a passionate soldier and a delightful talker, leaving fragments of his heart on every bush; clever, tender, full of artistic feeling and of Gallic gaiety—having in fair weather and foul always the *mot pour rire*. His daughter's publication of his letters has been called a rather inexpensive mode of writing her own biography; but these letters—charming, natural notes to his mother during his boyish campaigns—were well worth bringing to the light. All George Sand is in the author's portrait of her mother; all her great merit and all her strange defects. We should recommend the perusal of the scattered passages of *L'Histoire de ma Vie* which treat of this lady to a person ignorant of Madame Sand and desiring to make her acquaintance; they are an excellent measure of her power. On one side an extraordinary familiarity with the things of the mind, the play of character, the psychological mystery, and a beautiful clearness and quietness, a beautiful instinct of justice in dealing with them; on the other side a startling absence of delicacy, of reticence, of the sense of certain spiritual sanctities and reservations. That a woman should deal in so free-handed a fashion with a female parent upon whom nature and time have enabled her to look down from an eminence, seems at first a considerable anomaly; and the woman who does it must to no slight extent have shaken herself free from the bonds of custom. We do not mean that George Sand talks scandal and tittle-tattle about her mother; but that Madame Dupin having been a light woman and an essentially irregular character, her daughter holds her up in the sunshine of her own luminous contemplation with all her imperfections on her head. At the same time it is very finely done— very intelligently and appreciatively; it is at the worst a remarkable exhibition of the disinterestedness of a great imagination.

It must be remembered also that the young Aurore Dupin "belonged" much more to her grandmother than to her mother, to whom in her childhood she was only lent, as it were, on certain occasions. There is nothing in all George Sand better than her history of the relations of these two women, united at once and divided (after the death of the son and husband) by a common grief and a common interest; full of mutual jealousies and defiances, and alternately quarrelling and "making up" over their little girl. Jealousy carried the day. One was a patrician and the other a jealous democrat, and no common ground was attainable. Among the reproaches addressed by her critics to the author of *Valentine* and *Valvèdre* is the charge of a very imperfect knowledge of family life and a tendency to strike false notes in the portrayal of it. It is apparent that both before and after her marriage her observation of family life was peculiarly restricted and perverted. Of what it must have been in the former case this figure of her mother may give us an impression; of what it was in the latter we may get an idea from the somewhat idealized *ménage* in *Lucrezia Floriani.*

George Sand's literary fame came to her very abruptly. The history of her marriage, which is briefly related in her memoirs, is sufficiently well known. The thing was done, on her behalf, by her relatives (she had a small property) and the husband of their choice, M. Dudevant, was neither appreciative nor sympathetic. His tastes were vulgar and his manners frequently brutal; and after a short period of violent dissension and the birth of two children, the young couple separated. It is safe to say, however, that even with an "appreciative" husband Madame Sand would not have accepted matrimony once for all. She represents herself as an essentially dormant, passive and shrinking nature, upon which celebrity and productiveness were forced by circumstances, and whose unconsciousness of its own powers was dissipated only by the violent breaking of a spell. There is evidently much truth in these assertions; for of all great literary people few strike us as having had a smaller measure of the more vulgar avidities and ambitions. But for all that, it is tolerably plain that even by this profoundly slumbering genius the most brilliant matrimonial associate would have been utterly overmatched.

Madame Sand, even before she had written *Indiana*, was too imperious a force, too powerful a machine, to make the limits of her activity coincide with those of wifely submissiveness. It is very possible that for her to write *Indiana* and become a woman of letters a spell had to be broken; only, the real breaking of the spell lay not in the vulgarity of a husband, but in the deepening sense, quickened by the initiations of marriage, that outside of the quiet meadows of Nohant there was a vast affair called *life,* with which she had a capacity for making acquaintance at first hand. This making acquaintance with life at first hand is, roughly speaking, the great thing that, as a woman, Madame Sand achieved; and she was predestined to achieve it. She was more masculine than any man she might have married; and what powerfully masculine person—even leaving genius apart—is content at five-and-twenty with submissiveness and renunciation? "It was a mere accident that George Sand was a woman," a person who had known her well said to the writer of these pages; and though the statement needs an ultimate corrective, it represents a great deal of truth. What was feminine in her was the quality of her genius; the *quantity* of it—its force, and mass, and energy—was masculine, and masculine were her temperament and character. All this masculinity needed to set itself free; which it proceeded to do according to its temporary light. Her separation from her husband was judicial, and assured her the custody of her children; but as, in return for this privilege, she made financial concessions, it left her without income (though in possession of the property of Nohant) and dependent upon her labours for support. She had betaken herself to Paris in quest of labour, and it was with this that her career began.

This determination to address herself to life at first hand—this personal, moral impulse, which was not at all a literary impulse—was her great inspiration, the great pivot on which her history wheeled round into the bright light of experience and fame. It is, strictly, as we said just now, the most interesting thing about her. Such a disposition was not customary, was not what is usually called womanly, was not modest nor delicate, nor, for many other persons, in any way comfortable. But it had one great merit: it was in a high degree original and active; and because it was this it constitutes the great service which George Sand rendered her sex—a service in which, we hasten to add, there was as much of fortune as of virtue. The disposition to cultivate an "acquaintance with life at first hand" might pass for an elegant way of describing the attitude of many young women who are never far to seek, and who render no service to their own sex—whatever they may render to the other. George Sand's superiority was that she looked at life from a high point of view, and that she had an extraordinary talent. She painted fans and glove-boxes to get money, and got very little. *Indiana*, however—a mere experiment— put her on her feet, and her reputation dawned. She found that she could write, and she took up her pen never to lay it down. Her early novels, all of them brilliant, and each one at that day a literary event, followed each other with extraordinary rapidity. About this sudden entrance into literature, into philosophy, into rebellion, and into a great many other matters, there are various different things to be said. Very remarkable, indeed, was the immediate development of the literary faculty in this needy young woman who lived in cheap lodgings and looked for "employment." She wrote as a bird sings; but unlike most birds, she found it unnecessary to indulge, by way of prelude, in twitterings and vocal exercises; she broke out at once with her full volume of expression. From the beginning she had a great style. *Indiana*, perhaps, is rather in falsetto, as the first attempts of young, sentimental writers are apt to be; but in *Valentine*, which immediately followed, there is proof of the highest literary instinct— an art of composition, a propriety and harmony of diction, such as belong only to the masters.

One might certainly have asked Madame Sand, as Lord Jeffrey asked Macaulay on the appearance of his first contribution to the *Edinburgh Review*, where in the world she had picked up that style. She had picked it up apparently at Nohant, among the meadows and the *traînes*—the deeply-sunken byroads among the thick, high hedges. Her language had to the end an odour of the hawthorn and the wild honeysuckle—the mark of the "climat souple et chaud," as she some-where calls it, from which she had received "l'initiation première." How completely her great literary faculty was a matter of intuition is indicated by the fact that *L'Histoire de ma Vie* contains no allusion to it, no account of how she learned to write, no record of effort or apprenticeship. She appears to have begun at a stage of the journey at which most talents arrive only when their time is up. During the five-and-forty years of her literary career, she had something to say about most things in the universe; but the thing about which she had least to say was the writer's, the inventor's, the romancer's art. She possessed it by the gift of God, but she seems never to have felt the temptation to examine the pulse of the machine.

To the cheap edition of her novels, published in 1852–'3, she prefixed a series of short prefaces, in which she relates the origin of each tale—the state of mind and the circumstances in which it was writ-ten. These prefaces are charming; they almost justify the publisher's declaration that they form the "most beautiful examination that a great mind has ever made of itself." But they all commemorate the writer's extraordinary facility and spontaneity. One of them says that on her way home from Spain she was shut up for some days at an inn, where she had her children at play in the same room with her. She found that the sight of their play quickened her imagination, and while they tumbled about the floor near her table, she produced "Gabriel"—a work which, though inspired by the presence of infancy, cannot be said to be addressed to infants. Of another story she relates that she wrote it at Fontainebleau, where she spent all her days wandering about the forest, making entomological collections, with her son. At night she came home and took up the thread of *La Dernière Aldini*, on which she had never bestowed a thought all day. Being at Venice, much depressed, in a vast dusky room in an old palace that had been turned into an inn, while the sea wind roared about her windows, and brought up the sound of the carnival as a kind of melancholy wail, she began a novel by simply looking round her and describing the room and the whistling of the mingled tumult without. She finished it in a week, and, hardly reading it over, sent it to Paris as *Léone Léoni*—a masterpiece.

In the few prefatory lines to *Isidora* I remember she says something of this kind: "It was a beautiful young woman who used to come and see me, and profess to relate her sorrows. I saw that she was attitudinizing before me, and not believing herself a word of what she said. So it is not her I described in *Isidora*." This is a happy way of saying how a hint—a mere starting point—was enough for her. Particularly charming is the preface to the beautiful tale of "André"; it is a capital proof of what one may call the author's limpidity of reminiscence, and want of space alone prevents me from quoting it. She was at Venice, and she used to hear her maidservant and her sempstress, as they sat at work together, chattering in the next room. She listened to their talk in order to accustom her ear to the Venetian dialect, and in so doing she came into possession of a large amount of local gossip. The effect of it was to remind her of the small social life of the little country town near Nohant. The women told each other just such stories as might have been told there, and indulged in just such reflections and "appreciations" as would have been there begotten. She was reminded that men and women are everywhere the same, and at the same time she felt homesick. "I recalled the dirty, dusky streets, the tumble-down houses, the poor moss-grown roofs, the shrill concerts of cocks, children and cats, of my own little town. I dreamed too of our beautiful meadows, of our perfumed hay, of our little running streams, and of the botany beloved of old which I could follow now only on the muddy mosses and the floating weeds that adhered to the sides of the gondolas. I don't know amid what vague memories of various types I set in motion the least complex and the laziest of fictions. These types belonged quite as much to Venice as to Berry. Change dress and language, sky, landscape and architecture, the outside aspect of people and things, and you will find that at the bottom of all this man is always the same, and woman still more, because of the tenacity of her instincts."

George Sand says that she found she could write for an extraordinary length of time without weariness, and this is as far as she goes in the way of analysis of her inspiration. From the time she made the discovery to the day of her death her life was an extremely laborious one. She had evidently an extraordinary physical robustness. It was her constant practice to write at night, beginning after the rest of the world had gone to sleep. Alexandre Dumas the younger described her somewhere, during her latter years, as an old lady who came out into the garden at midday in a broad-brimmed hat and sat down on a bench or wandered slowly about. So she remained for hours, looking about her, musing, contemplating. She was gathering impressions, says M. Dumas, absorbing the universe, steeping herself in nature; and at night she would give all this forth as a sort of emanation. Without using too vague epithets one may accept this term "emanation" as a good account of her manner.

If it is needless to go into biographical detail, this is because George Sand's real history, the more interesting one, is the history of her mind. The history of her mind is of course closely connected with her personal history; she is indeed a writer whose personal situation, at a particular moment, is supposed to be reflected with peculiar vividness in her work. But to speak of her consistently we must regard the events of her life as intellectual events, and its landmarks as opinions, convictions, theories. The only difficulty is that such landmarks are nearly as numerous as the trees in a forest. Some, however, are more salient than others. Madame Sand's account of herself is that her ideal of life was repose, obscurity and idleness—long days in the country spent in botany and entomology. She affirms that her natural indolence was extreme, and that the need of money alone induced her to take her pen into her hand. As this need was constant, her activity was constant; but it was a perversion of the genius of a kind, simple, friendly, motherly, profoundly unambitious woman, who would have been amply content to take care of her family, live in slippers, gossip with peasants, walk in the garden and listen to the piano. All this is certainly so far true as that no person of equal celebrity ever made fewer explicit pretensions. She philosophized upon a great many things that she did not understand, and toward the close of her life, in especial, was apt to talk metaphysics, in writing, with a mingled volubility and vagueness which might have been taken to denote an undue self-confidence. But in such things as these, as they come from George Sand's pen, there is an air as of not expecting any one in particular to read them. She never took herself too much *au sérieux*—she never postured at all as a woman of letters. She scribbled, she might have said—scribbled as well as she could; but when she was not scribbling she never thought of it; though she liked to think of all the great things that were worth scribbling about—love and religion and science and art, and man's political destiny. Her reader feels that she has no vanity, and all her contemporaries agree that her generosity was extreme.

She calls herself a *sphinx bon enfant,* or says at least that she looked like one. Judgments may differ as to what degree she was a sphinx; but her good nature is all-pervading. Some of her books are redolent of it—some of the more "objective" ones: *Consuelo, Les Maîtres Sonneurs, L'Homme de Neige, Les beaux Messieurs de Bois-Doré.* She is often passionate, but she is never rancorous; even her violent attacks upon the Church give us no impression of small acrimony. She has all a woman's loquacity, but she has never a woman's shrillness; and perhaps we can hardly indicate better the difference between great passion and small than by saying that she never is hysterical. During the last half of her career, her books went out of fashion among the new literary generation. "Realism" had been invented, or rather propagated; and in the light of *Madame Bovary* her own facile fictions began to be regarded as the work of a sort of superior Mrs. Radcliffe.

She was antiquated; she belonged to the infancy of art. She accepted this destiny with a cheerfulness which it would have savoured of vanity even to make explicit. The Realists were her personal friends; she knew that they did not, and could not, read her books; for what could Gustave Flaubert make of *Monsieur Sylvestre*, what could Ivan Turgénieff make of *Césarine Dietrich*? It made no difference; she contented herself with reading their productions, never mentioned her own, and continued to write charming, improbable romances for initiated persons of the optimistic class.

After the first few years she fell into this more and more; she wrote stories for the story's sake. Among the novels produced during a long period before her death I can think of but one, *Mademoiselle La Quintinic*, that is of a controversial cast. All her early novels, on the other hand, were controversial—if this is not too mild a description of the passionate contempt for the institution of marriage expressed in *Indiana*, *Valentine*, *Lélia*, and *Jacques*. Her own acquaintance with matrimony had been of a painful kind, and the burden of three at least of these remarkable tales (*Lélia* stands rather apart) is the misery produced by an indissoluble matrimonial knot. *Jacques* is the story of an unhappy marriage from which there is no issue but by the suicide of one of the partners; the husband throws himself into an Alpine crevasse in order to leave his wife to an undisturbed enjoyment of her lover.

It very soon became apparent that these matters were handled in a new and superior fashion. There had been plenty of tales about husbands, wives, and "third-parties," but since the *Nouvelle Héloïse* there had been none of a high value or of a philosophic tone. Madame Sand, from the first, was nothing if not philosophic; the iniquity of marriage arrangements was to her mind but one of a hundred abominations in a society which needed a complete overhauling, and to which she proceeded to propose a loftier line of conduct. The passionate eloquence of the writer in all this was only equalled by her extraordinary self-confidence. *Valentine* seems to us even now a very eloquent book, and *Jacques* is hardly less so; it is easy to imagine their having made an immense impression. The intellectual freshness, the sentimental force of *Valentine*, must have had an irresistible charm; and we say this with a full sense of what there is false and fantastical in the substance of both books. Hold them up against the light of a certain sort of ripe reason, and they seem as porous as a pair of sieves; but subject them simply to the literary test, and they hold together very bravely.

The author's philosophic predilections were at once her merit and her weakness. On the one side it was a great mind, curious about all things, open to all things, nobly accessible to experience, asking only to live, expand, respond; on the other side stood a great personal volition, making large exactions of life and society and needing constantly to justify itself—stirring up rebellion and calling down revolution in order to cover up and legitimate its own agitation. George Sand's was a French mind, and as a French mind it had to theorize; but if the positive side of its criticism of most human institutions was precipitate and ill-balanced, the error was in a great measure atoned for in later years. The last half of Madame Sand's career was a period of assent and acceptance; she had decided to make the best of those social arrangements which surrounded her—remembering, as it were, the homely native proverb which declares that when one has not got what one likes one must like what one has got. Into the phase of acceptance and serenity, the disposition to admit that even as it is society *pays,* according to the vulgar locution, our author passed at about the time that the Second Empire settled down upon France. We suspect the fact we speak of was rather a coincidence than an effect. It is very true that the Second Empire may have seemed the death-knell of "philosophy"; it may very well have appeared profitless to ask questions of a world which anticipated you with such answers as that. But we take it rather that Madame Sand was simply weary of criticism; the pendulum had swung into the opposite quarter—as it is needless to remark that it always does.

We have delayed too long to say how far it had swung in the first direction; and we have delayed from the feeling that it is difficult to say it. We have seen that George Sand was by the force of heredity projected into this field with a certain violence; she took possession of a portion of it as a conqueror, and she was never compelled to retreat. The reproach brought against her by her critics is that, as regards her particular advocacy of the claims of the heart, she has for the most part portrayed vicious love, not virtuous love. But the reply to this, from her own side, would be that she has at all events portrayed something which those who disparage her activity have not portrayed. She may claim that although she has the critics against her, the writers of her own class who represent virtuous love have not pushed her out of the field. She has the advantage that she has portrayed a *passion*, and those of the other group have the disadvantage that they have not. In English literature, which, we suppose, is more especially the region of virtuous love, we do not "go into" the matter, as the phrase is (we speak of course of English prose). We have agreed among our own confines that there is a certain point at which elucidation of it should stop short; that among the things which it is possible to say about it, the greater number had on the whole better not be said. It would be easy to make an ironical statement of the English attitude, and it would be, if not easy, at least very possible, to make a sound defence of it. The thing with us, however, is not a matter of theory; it is above all a matter of practice, and the practice has been that of the leading English novelists. Miss Austen and Sir Walter Scott, Dickens and Thackeray, Hawthorne and George Eliot, have all represented young people in love with each other; but no one of them has, to the best of our recollection, described anything that can be called a passion—put it into motion before us and shown us its various paces. To say this is to say at the same time that these writers have spared us much that we consider disagreeable, and that George Sand has not spared us; but it is to say furthermore that few persons would resort to English prose fiction for any information concerning the ardent forces of the heart—for any ideas upon them. It is George Sand's merit that she has given us ideas upon them—that she has enlarged the novel-reader's conception of them and proved herself in all that relates to them an authority. This is a great deal. From this standpoint Miss Austen, Walter Scott and Dickens will appear to have omitted the erotic sentiment altogether, and George Eliot will seem to have treated it with singular austerity. Strangely loveless, seen in this light, are those large, comprehensive fictions *Middlemarch* and *Daniel Deronda*. They seem to foreign readers, probably, like vast, cold, commodious, respectable rooms, through whose window-panes one sees a snow-covered landscape, and across whose acres of sober-hued carpet one looks in vain for a fireplace or a fire.

The distinction between virtuous and vicious love is not particu-larly insisted upon by George Sand. In her view love is always love, is always divine in its essence and ennobling in its operation. The larg-est life possible is to hold one's self open to an unlimited experience of this improving passion. This, I believe, was Madame Sand's prac-tice, as it was certainly her theory—a theory to the exposition of which one of her novels, at least, is expressly dedicated. *Lucrezia Floriani* is the history of a lady who, in the way of love, takes every-thing that comes along, and who sets forth her philosophy of the matter with infinite grace and felicity. It is probably fortunate for the world that ladies of Lucrezia Floriani's disposition have not as a general thing her argumentative brilliancy. About all this there would be much more to say than these few pages afford space for. Madame Sand's plan was to be open to *all* experience, all emotions, all convic-tions; only to keep the welfare of the human race, and especially of its humbler members, well in mind, and to trust that one's moral and intellectual life would take a form profitable to the same. One was therefore not only to extend a great hospitality to love, but to interest one's self in religion and politics. This Madame Sand did with great activity during the whole of the reign of Louis Philippe. She had broken utterly with the Church, of course, but her disposition was the reverse of sceptical. Her religious feeling, like all her feelings, was powerful and voluminous, and she had an ideal of a sort of ethereal-ized and liberated Christianity, in which unmarried but affectionate couples might find an element friendly to their "expansion." Like all her feelings, too, her religious sentiment was militant; her ideas about love were an attack upon marriage; her faith was an attack upon the Church and the clergy; her socialistic sympathies were an attack upon all present political arrangements. These things all took hold of her by turn—shook her hard, as it were, and dropped her, leaving her to be played upon by some new inspiration; then, in some cases, returned to her, took possession of her afresh and sounded another tune. M. Renan, in writing of her at the time of her death, used a fine phrase about her; he said that she was "the Aeolian harp of our time"; he spoke of her "sonorous soul." This is very just; there is nothing that belonged to her time that she had not a personal emotion about—an emotion intense enough to produce a brilliant work of art—a novel that had bloomed as rapidly and perfectly as the flower that the morning sun sees open on its stem. In her care about many things during all these years, in her expenditure of passion, reflection, and curiosity, there is something quite unprecedented. Never had philosophy and art gone so closely hand in hand. Each of them suffered a good deal; but it had appeared up to that time that their mutual concessions must be even greater. Balzac was a far superior artist; but he was incapable of a lucid reflection.

We have already said that mention has been made of George Sand's analogy with Goethe, who claimed for his lyrical poems the merit of being each the result of a particular incident in his life. It was incident too that prompted Madame Sand to write; but what it produced in her case was not a short copy of verses, but an elaborate drama, with a plot and a dozen characters. It will help us to understand this extraordinary responsiveness of mind and fertility of imagination to remember that inspiration was often embodied in a concrete form; that Madame Sand's "incidents" were usually clever, eloquent, suggestive men. "Le style c'est l'homme"—of her, it has been epigrammatically said, that is particularly true. Be this as it may, these influences were strikingly various, and they are reflected in works which may be as variously labelled: amatory tales, religious tales, political, aesthetic, pictorial, musical, theatrical, historical tales. And it is to be noticed that in whatever the author attempted, whether or no she succeeded, she appeared to lose herself. The *Lettres d'un Voyageur* read like a writer's single book. This melancholy, this desolation and weariness, might pass as the complete distillation of a soul. In the same way *Spiridion* is exclusively religious and theological. The author might, in relation to this book, have replied to such of her critics as reproach her with being too erotic, that she had performed the very rare feat of writing a novel not only containing no love save divine love, but containing not one woman's figure. We can recall but one rival to *Spiridion* in this respect—Godwin's *Caleb Williams*.

But if other things come and go with George Sand, amatory disquisition is always there. It is of all kinds, sometimes very noble and sometimes very disagreeable. Numerous specimens of the two extremes might be cited. There is to our taste a great deal too much of it; the total effect is displeasing. The author illuminates and glorifies the divine passion, but she does something which may be best expressed by saying that she cheapens it. She handles it too much; she lets it too little alone. Above all she is too positive, too explicit, too business-like; she takes too technical a view of it. Its various signs and tokens and stages, its ineffable mysteries, are all catalogued and tabulated in her mind, and she whisks out her references with the nimbleness with which the doorkeeper at an exhibition hands you back your umbrella in return for a check. In this relation, to the English mind, discretion is a great point—a virtue so absolute and indispensable that it speaks for itself and cannot be analysed away; and George Sand is judged from our point of view by one's saying that for her discretion is simply non-existent. Its place is occupied by a sort of benevolent, an almost conscientious disposition to sit down, as it were, and "talk over" the whole matter. The subject fills her with a motherly loquacity; it stimulates all her wonderful and beautiful self-sufficiency of expression—the quality that we have heard a hostile critic call her "glibness."

We can hardly open a volume of George Sand without finding an example of what we mean. We glance at a venture into *Teverino*, and we find Lady G., who has left her husband at the inn and gone out to spend a day with the more fascinating Léonce, "passing her beautiful hands over the eyes of Léonce, *peut-être par tendresse naïve,* perhaps to convince herself that it was really tears she saw shining in them." The *peut-être* here, the *tendresse naïve*, the alternatives, the impartial way in which you are given your choice, are extremely characteristic of Madame Sand. They remind us of the heroine of

Isidora, who alludes in conversation to "une de mes premières fautes."
In the list of Madame Sand's more technically amatory novels, however, there is a distinction to be made; the earlier strike us as superior
to the later. The fault of the earlier—the fact that passion is too intellectual, too pedantic, too sophistical, too much bent upon proving
itself abnegation and humility, maternity, fraternity, humanity, or
some fine thing that it really is not and that it is much simpler and
better for not pretending to be—this fault is infinitely exaggerated
in the tales written after *Lucrezia Floriani*. *Indiana*, *Valentine*, *Jacques*,
and *Mauprat* are, comparatively speaking, frankly and honestly passionate; they do not represent the love that declines to compromise
with circumstances as a sort of eating of one's cake and having it
too—an eating it as pleasure and a having it as virtue. But the stories
of the type of *Lucrezia Floriani*, which indeed is the most argumentative,*
have an indefinable falsity of tone. Madame Sand had here begun to
play with her topic intellectually; the first freshness of her interest in
it had gone, and invention had taken the place of conviction. To
acquit one's self happily of such experiments, one must certainly have
all the gifts that George Sand possessed. But one must also have two
or three that she lacked. Her sense of purity was certainly defective.
This is a brief statement, but it means a great deal, and of what it
means there are few of her novels that do not contain a number of
illustrations.

There is something very fine, for instance, about *Valentine*, in spite
of its contemptible hero; there is something very sweet and generous
in the figure of the young girl. But why, desiring to give us an impression of great purity in her heroine, should the author provide her with
a half-sister who is at once an illegitimate daughter and the mother
of a child born out of wedlock, and who, in addition, is half in love
with Valentine's lover? though George Sand thinks to better the
matter by representing this love as partly maternal. After Valentine's
marriage, a compulsory and most unhappy one, this half-sister plots

*Constance Verrier, Isidora, Pauline, Le dernier Amour, La Daniella, Francia,
Mademoiselle Merquem.*

with the doctor to place the young wife and the lover whom she has had to dismiss once more *en rapport*. She hesitates, it is true, and inquires of the physician if their scheme will not appear unlawful in the eyes of the world. But the old man reassures her, and asks, with a "sourire malin et affectueux," why she should care for the judgment of a world which has viewed so harshly her own irregularity of conduct. Madame Sand constantly strikes these false notes; we meet in her pages the most startling confusions. In *Jacques* there is the oddest table of relations between the characters. Jacques is possibly the brother of Silvia, who is probably, on another side, sister of his wife, who is the mistress of Octave, Silvia's dismissed *amant*! Add to this that if Jacques be *not* the brother of Silvia, who is an illegitimate child, he is convertible into her lover. *On s'y perd*. Silvia, a clever woman, is the guide, philosopher, and friend of this melancholy Jacques; and when his wife, who desires to become the mistress of Octave (*her* discarded lover), and yet, not finding it quite plain sailing to do so, weeps over the crookedness of her situation, she writes to the injured husband that she has been obliged to urge Fernande not to take things so hard: "je suis forcée de la consoler et de la relever à ses propres yeux." Very characteristic of Madame Sand is this fear lest the unfaithful wife should take too low a view of herself. One wonders what had become of her sense of humour. Fernande is to be "relevée" before her fall, and the operation is somehow to cover her fall prospectively.

Take another example from *Léone Léoni*. The subject of the story is the sufferings of an infatuated young girl, who follows over Europe the most faithless, unscrupulous and ignoble, but also the most irresistible of charmers. It is *Manon Lescaut*, with the incurable fickleness of Manon attributed to a man; and as in the Abbé Prévost's story the touching element is the devotion and constancy of the injured and deluded Desgrieux, so in *Léone Léoni* we are invited to feel for the too closely-clinging Juliette, who is dragged through the mire of a passion which she curses and yet which survives unnameable outrage. She tells the tale herself and yet it might have been expected that, to deepen its effect, the author would have represented her as withdrawn from the world and cured of her excessive susceptibility. But we find her living with another charmer, jewelled and perfumed; in her own words, she is a *fille entretenue*, and it is to her new lover that she relates the story of the stormy life she led with the old. The situation requires no comment beyond our saying that the author had morally no taste. Of this want of moral taste we remember another striking instance. Mademoiselle Merquem, who gives her name to one of the later novels, is a young girl of the most elevated character, beloved by a young man, the intensity of whose affection she desires to test. To do this she contrives the graceful plan of introducing into her house a mysterious infant, of whose parentage she offers an explanation so obtrusively vague, that the young man is driven regretfully to the induction that its female parent is none other than herself. We forget to what extent he is staggered, but, if we rightly remember, he withstands the test. We do not judge him, but it is permitted to judge the young lady.

We have called George Sand an *improvisatrice*, and in this character, where she deals with matters of a more "objective" cast, she is always delightful; nothing could be more charming than her tales of mystery, intrigue, and adventure. *Consuelo, L'Homme de Neige, Le Piccinino, Teverino, Le Beau Laurence* and its sequel, *Pierre qui Roule, Antonia, Tamaris, La Famille de Germandre, La Filleule, La dernière Aldini, Cadio, Flamarande*—these things have all the spontaneous inventiveness of the romances of Alexandre Dumas, his open-air quality, his pleasure in a story for a story's sake, together with an intellectual refinement, a philosophic savour, a reference to spiritual things, in which he was grotesquely deficient.

We have given, however, no full enumeration of the author's romances, and it seems needless to do so. We have lately been trying to read them over, and we frankly confess that we have found it impossible. They are excellent reading for once, but they lack that quality which makes things classical—makes them impose themselves. It has been said that what makes a book a classic is its style. We should modify this, and instead of style say *form*. Madame Sand's novels have plenty of style, but they have no form. Balzac's have not a shred of style, but they have a great deal of form. Posterity doubtless will make a selection from each list, but the few volumes of Balzac it preserves will remain with it much longer, we suspect, than those which it borrows from his great contemporary. We cannot easily imagine posterity travelling with *Valentine* or *Mauprat*, *Consuelo* or the *Marquis de Villemer* in its trunk. At the same time we can imagine that if these admirable tales fall out of fashion, such of our descendants as stray upon them in the dusty corners of old libraries will sit down on the bookcase ladder with the open volume and turn it over with surprise and enchantment. What a beautiful mind! they will say; what an extraordinary style! Why have we not known more about these things? And as, when that time comes, we suppose the world will be given over to a "realism" that we have not as yet begun faintly to foreshadow, George Sand's novels will have, for the children of the twenty-first century, something of the same charm which Spenser's *Fairy Queen* has for those of the nineteenth. For a critic of to-day to pick and choose among them seems almost pedantic; they all belong quite to the same intellectual family. They are the easy writing which makes hard reading.

In saying this we must immediately limit our meaning. All the world can read George Sand once and not find it in the least hard. But it is not easy to return to her; putting aside a number of fine descriptive pages, the reader will not be likely to resort to any volume that he has once laid down for a particular chapter, a brilliant passage, an entertaining conversation. George Sand invites reperusal less than any mind of equal eminence. Is this because after all she was a woman, and the laxity of the feminine intellect could not fail to claim its part in her? We will not attempt to say; especially as, though it may be pedantic to pick and choose among her works, we immediately think of two or three that have as little as possible of intellectual laxity. *Mauprat* is a solid, masterly, manly book; *André* and *La Mare au Diable* have an extreme perfection of form. M. Taine, whom we quoted at the beginning of these remarks, speaks of our author's rustic tales (the group to which the *Mare au Diable* belongs*) as a

François le Champi, La Petite Fadette.

signal proof of her activity and versatility of mind. Besides being charming stories, they are in fact a real study in philology—such a study as Balzac made in the *Contes Drôlatiques*, and as Thackeray made in *Henry Esmond*. George Sand's attempt to return to a more artless and archaic stage of the language which she usually handled in so modern and voluminous a fashion was quite as successful as that of her fellows. In *Les Maîtres Sonneurs* it is extremely felicitous, and the success could only have been achieved by an extraordinarily sympathetic and flexible talent. This is one of the impressions George Sand's reader—even if he have read her but once—brings away with him. His other prevailing impression will bear upon that quality which, if it must be expressed in a single word, may best be called the generosity of her genius. It is true that there are one or two things which limit this generosity. We think, for example, of Madame Sand's peculiar power of self-defence, her constant need to justify, to glorify, to place in a becoming light, to "arrange," as we said at the outset, those errors and weaknesses in which her own personal credit may be at stake. She never accepts a weakness as a weakness; she always dresses it out as a virtue; and if her heroines abandon their lovers and lie to their husbands, you may be sure it is from motives of the highest morality. Such productions as *Lucrezia Floriani* and *Elle et Lui* may be attributed to an ungenerous disposition—both of them being stories in which Madame Sand is supposed to have described her relations with distinguished men who were dead, and whose death enabled her without contradiction to portray them as monsters of selfishness, while the female protagonist appeared as the noblest of her sex. But without taking up the discussion provoked by these works, we may say that, on the face of the matter, there is a good deal of justification for their author. She poured her material into the crucible of art, and the artist's material is of necessity in a large measure his experience. Madame Sand never described the actual; this was often her artistic weakness, and as she has the reproach she should also have the credit. *Lucrezia Floriani* and *Elle et Lui* were doubtless to her imagination simply tales of what might have been.

It is hard not to feel that there is a certain high good conscience and passionate sincerity in the words in which, in one of her prefaces, she alludes to the poor novel which Alfred de Musset's brother put forth as an incriminative retort to *Elle et Lui*. Some of her friends had advised her not to notice the book; "but after reflection she judged it to be her duty to attend to it at the proper time and place. She was, however, by no means in haste. She was in Auvergne following the imaginary traces of the figures of her new novel along the scented byways, among the sweetest scenes of spring. She had brought the pamphlet with her to read it; but she did not read it. She had forgotten her herbarium, and the pages of the infamous book, used as a substitute, were purified by the contact of the wild flowers of Puy-de-Dôme and Sancy. Sweet perfumes of the things of God, who to you could prefer the memory of the foulnesses of civilization?"

It must, however, to be just all round, be farther remembered that those persons and causes which Madame Sand has been charged first and last with misrepresenting belonged to the silent, inarticulate, even defunct class. She was always the talker, the survivor, the adversary armed with a gift of expression so magical as almost to place a premium upon sophistry. To weigh everything, we imagine she really *outlived* experience, morally, to a degree which made her feel, in retrospect, as if she were dealing with the history of another person. "Où sont-ils, où sont-ils, nos amours passés?" she exclaims in one of her later novels. (What has become of the passions we have shuffled off?—into what dusky limbo are they flung away?) And she goes on to say that it is a great mistake to suppose that we die only once and at last. We die piecemeal; some part of us is always dying; it is only what is left that dies at last. As for our "amours passés," where are they indeed? Jacques Laurent and the Prince Karol may be fancied, in echo, to exclaim.

In saying that George Sand lacks truth the critic more particularly means that she lacks exactitude—lacks the method of truth. Of a certain general truthfulness she is full to overflowing; we feel that to her mind nothing human is alien. We should say of her, not that she *knew* human nature, but that she felt it. At all events she loved it and enjoyed it. She was contemplative; but she was not, in the deepest sense, observant. She was a very high order of sentimentalist, but she was not a moralist. She perceived a thousand things, but she rarely in strictness judged; so that although her books have a great deal of wisdom, they have not what is called weight. With the physical world she was as familiar as with the human, and she knew it perhaps better. She would probably at any time have said that she cared much more for botany, mineralogy and astronomy, than for sociology. "Nature," as we call it—landscape, trees and flowers, rocks and streams and clouds—plays a larger part in her novels than in any others, and in none are they described with such a grand general felicity. If Turner had written his landscapes rather than painted them he might have written as George Sand has done. If she was less truthful in dealing with men and women, says M. Taine, it is because she had too high an ideal for them; she could not bear not to represent them as better than they are. She delights in the representation of virtue, and if we sometimes feel that she has not really measured the heights on which she places her characters, that so to place them has cost little to her understanding, we are nevertheless struck with the nobleness of her imagination. M. Taine calls her an idealist; we should say, somewhat more narrowly, that she was an optimist. An optimist "lined," as the French say, with a romancer, is not the making of a moralist. George Sand's optimism, her idealism, are very beautiful, and the source of that impression of largeness, luminosity and liberality which she makes upon us. But we suspect that something even better in a novelist is that tender appreciation of actuality which makes even the application of a single coat of rose-colour seem an act of violence.

ANTHONY TROLLOPE

WHEN, a few months ago, Anthony Trollope laid down his pen for the last time, it was a sign of the complete extinction of that group of admirable writers who, in England, during the preceding half century, had done so much to elevate the art of the novelist. The author of *The Warden*, of *Barchester Towers*, of *Framley Parsonage*, does not, to our mind, stand on the very same level as Dickens, Thackeray and George Eliot; for his talent was of a quality less fine than theirs. But he belonged to the same family—he had as much to tell us about English life; he was strong, genial and abundant. He published too much; the writing of novels had ended by becoming, with him, a perceptibly mechanical process. Dickens was prolific, Thackeray produced with a freedom for which we are constantly grateful; but we feel that these writers had their periods of gestation. They took more time to look at their subject; relatively (for to-day there is not much leisure, at best, for those who undertake to entertain a hungry public), they were able to wait for inspiration. Trollope's fecundity was prodigious; there was no limit to the work he was ready to do. It is not unjust to say that he sacrificed quality to quantity. Abundance, certainly, is in itself a great merit; almost all the greatest writers have been abundant. But Trollope's fertility was gross, importunate; he himself contended, we believe, that he had given to the world a greater number of printed pages of fiction than any of his literary contemporaries. Not only did his novels follow each other without visible intermission, overlapping and treading on each other's heels, but most of these works are of extraordinary length. *Orley Farm*, *Can You Forgive Her?*, *He Knew He Was Right*, are exceedingly voluminous tales. *The Way We Live Now* is one of the longest of modern novels. Trollope produced, moreover, in the intervals of larger labour a great number of short stories, many of them charming, as well as various books of travel, and two or three biographies. He was the great *improvvisatore* of these latter years. Two distinguished story-tellers of the other sex—one in France and one in England—have shown an extraordinary facility of composition; but Trollope's pace was brisker even than that of the wonderful Madame Sand and the delightful Mrs. Oliphant. He had taught himself to keep this pace, and had reduced his admirable faculty to a system. Every day of his life he wrote a certain number of pages of his current tale, a number sacramental and invariable, independent of mood and place. It was once the fortune of the author of these lines to cross the Atlantic in his company, and he has never forgotten the magnificent example of plain persistence that it was in the power of the eminent novelist to give on that occasion. The season was unpropitious, the vessel over-crowded, the voyage detestable; but Trollope shut himself up in his cabin every morning for a purpose which, on the part of a distinguished writer who was also an invulnerable sailor, could only be communion with the muse. He drove his pen as steadily on the tumbling ocean as in Montague Square; and as his voyages were many, it was his practice before sailing to come down to the ship and confer with the carpenter, who was instructed to rig up a rough writing-table in his small sea-chamber. Trollope has been accused of being deficient in imagination, but in the face of such a fact as that the charge will scarcely seem just. The power to shut one's eyes, one's ears (to say nothing of another sense), upon the scenery of a pitching Cunarder and open them upon the loves and sorrows of Lily Dale or the conjugal embarrassments of Lady Glencora Palliser, is certainly a faculty which could take to itself wings. The imagination that Trollope possessed he had at least thoroughly at his command. I speak of all this in order to explain (in part) why it was that, with his extraordinary gift, there was always in him a certain infusion of the common. He abused his gift, overworked it, rode his horse too hard. As an artist he never took himself seriously; many people will say this was why he was so delightful. The people who take themselves seriously are prigs and bores; and Trollope, with his perpetual "story," which was the only thing he cared about, his strong good sense, hearty good nature, generous appreciation of life in all its varieties, responds in perfection to a certain English ideal. According to that ideal it is rather dangerous to be explicitly or consciously an artist—to have a system, a doctrine, a form. Trollope, from the first, went in, as they say, for having as little form as possible; it is probably safe to affirm that he had no "views" whatever on the subject of novel-writing. His whole manner is that of a man who regards the practice as one of the more delicate industries, but has never troubled his head nor clogged his pen with theories about the nature of his business. Fortunately he was not obliged to do so, for he had an easy road to success; and his honest, familiar, deliberate way of treating his readers as if he were one of them, and shared their indifference to a general view, their limitations of knowledge, their love of a comfortable ending, endeared him to many persons in England and America. It is in the name of some chosen form that, of late years, things have been made most disagreeable for the novel-reader, who has been treated by several votaries of the new experiments in fiction to unwonted and bewildering sensations. With Trollope we were always safe; there were sure to be no new experiments.

His great, his inestimable merit was a complete appreciation of the usual. This gift is not rare in the annals of English fiction; it would naturally be found in a walk of literature in which the feminine mind has laboured so fruitfully. Women are delicate and patient observers; they hold their noses close, as it were, to the texture of life. They feel and perceive the real with a kind of personal tact, and their observations are recorded in a thousand delightful volumes. Trollope, therefore, with his eyes comfortably fixed on the familiar, the actual, was far from having invented a new category; his great distinction is that in resting there his vision took in so much of the field. And then he *felt* all daily and immediate things as well as saw them; felt them in a simple, direct, salubrious way, with their sadness, their gladness, their charm, their comicality, all their obvious and measurable mean-

ANTHONY TROLLOPE · 101

ings. He never wearied of the pre-established round of English cus-
toms—never needed a respite or a change—was content to go on
indefinitely watching the life that surrounded him, and holding up
his mirror to it. Into this mirror the public, at first especially, grew
very fond of looking—for it saw itself reflected in all the most credible and supposable ways, with that curiosity that people feel to know
how they look when they are represented, "just as they are," by a
painter who does not desire to put them into an attitude, to drape
them for an effect, to arrange his light and his accessories. This exact
and on the whole becoming image, projected upon a surface without
a strong intrinsic tone, constitutes mainly the entertainment that
Trollope offered his readers. The striking thing to the critic was that
his robust and patient mind had no particular bias, his imagination
no light of its own. He saw things neither pictorially and grotesquely
like Dickens; nor with that combined disposition to satire and to
literary form which gives such "body," as they say of wine, to the
manner of Thackeray; nor with anything of the philosophic, the
transcendental cast—the desire to follow them to their remote relations—which we associate with the name of George Eliot. Trollope
had his elements of fancy, of satire, of irony; but these qualities were
not very highly developed, and he walked mainly by the light of his
good sense, his clear, direct vision of the things that lay nearest, and
his great natural kindness. There is something remarkably tender and
friendly in his feeling about all human perplexities; he takes the
good-natured, temperate, conciliatory view—the humorous view,
perhaps, for the most part, yet without a touch of pessimistic prejudice.
As he grew older, and had sometimes to go farther afield for his
subjects, he acquired a savour of bitterness and reconciled himself
sturdily to treating of the disagreeable. A more copious record of
disagreeable matters could scarcely be imagined, for instance, than
The Way We Live Now. But, in general, he has a wholesome mistrust
of morbid analysis, an aversion to inflicting pain. He has an infinite
love of detail, but his details are, for the most part, the innumerable
items of the expected. When the French are disposed to pay a compliment to the English mind they are so good as to say that there is in

it something remarkably *honnête*. If I might borrow this epithet without seeming to be patronising, I should apply it to the genius of Anthony Trollope. He represents in an eminent degree this natural decorum of the English spirit, and represents it all the better that there is not in him a grain of the mawkish or the prudish. He writes, he feels, he judges like a man, talking plainly and frankly about many things, and is by no means destitute of a certain saving grace of coarseness. But he has kept the purity of his imagination and held fast to old-fashioned reverences and preferences. He thinks it a sufficient objection to several topics to say simply that they are unclean. There was nothing in his theory of the story-teller's art that tended to convert the reader's or the writer's mind into a vessel for polluting things. He recognised the right of the vessel to protest, and would have regarded such a protest as conclusive. With a considerable turn for satire, though this perhaps is more evident in his early novels than in his later ones, he had as little as possible of the quality of irony. He never played with a subject, never juggled with the sympathies or the credulity of his reader, was never in the least paradoxical or mystifying. He sat down to his theme in a serious, business-like way, with his elbows on the table and his eye occasionally wandering to the clock.

To touch successively upon these points is to attempt a portrait, which I shall perhaps not altogether have failed to produce. The source of his success in describing the life that lay nearest to him, and describing it without any of those artistic perversions that come, as we have said, from a powerful imagination, from a cynical humour or from a desire to look, as George Eliot expresses it, for the suppressed transitions that unite all contrasts, the essence of this love of reality was his extreme interest in character. This is the fine and admirable quality in Trollope, this is what will preserve his best works in spite of those flatnesses which keep him from standing on quite the same level as the masters. Indeed this quality is so much one of the finest (to my mind at least), that it makes me wonder the more that the writer who had it so abundantly and so naturally should not have just that distinction which Trollope lacks, and which we find in his three brilliant contemporaries. If he was in any degree a man of genius (and I hold that he was), it was in virtue of this happy, instinctive perception of human varieties. His knowledge of the stuff we are made of, his observation of the common behaviour of men and women, was not reasoned nor acquired, not even particularly studied. All human doings deeply interested him. Human life, to his mind, was a perpetual story; but he never attempted to take the so-called scientific view, the view which has lately found ingenious advocates among the countrymen and successors of Balzac. He had no airs of being able to tell you *why* people in a given situation would conduct themselves in a particular way; it was enough for him that he felt their feelings and struck the right note, because he had, as it were, a good ear. If he was a knowing psychologist he was so by grace; he was just and true without apparatus and without effort. He must have had a great taste for the moral question; he evidently believed that this is the basis of the interest of fiction. We must be careful, of course, in attributing convictions and opinions to Trollope, who, as I have said, had as little as possible of the pedantry of his art, and whose occasional chance utterances in regard to the object of the novelist and his means of achieving it are of an almost startling simplicity. But we certainly do not go too far in saying that he gave his practical testimony in favour of the idea that the interest of a work of fiction is great in proportion as the people stand on their feet. His great effort was evidently to make them stand so; if he achieved this result with as little as possible of a flourish of the hand it was nevertheless the measure of his success. If he had taken sides on the droll, bemuddled opposition between novels of character and novels of plot, I can imagine him to have said (except that he never expressed himself in epigrams), that he preferred the former class, inasmuch as character in itself is plot, while plot is by no means character. It is more safe indeed to believe that his great good sense would have prevented him from taking an idle controversy seriously. Character, in any sense in which we can get at it, is action, and action is plot, and any plot which hangs together, even if it pretend to interest us only in the fashion of a Chinese puzzle, plays upon our emotion, our suspense, by means of personal references. We care what happens to people only in proportion as we know what people are. Trollope's great apprehension of the real, which was what made him so interesting, came to him through his desire to satisfy us on this point—to tell us what certain people were and what they did in consequence of being so. That is the purpose of each of his tales; and if these things produce an illusion it comes from the gradual abundance of his testimony as to the temper, the tone, the passions, the habits, the moral nature, of a certain number of contemporary Britons.

His stories, in spite of their great length, deal very little in the surprising, the exceptional, the complicated; as a general thing he has no great story to tell. The thing is not so much a story as a picture; if we hesitate to call it a picture it is because the idea of composition is not the controlling one and we feel that the author would regard the artistic, in general, as a kind of affectation. There is not even much description, in the sense which the present votaries of realism in France attach to that word. The painter lays his scene in a few deliberate, not especially pictorial strokes, and never dreams of finishing the piece for the sake of enabling the reader to hang it up. The finish, such as it is, comes later, from the slow and somewhat clumsy accumulation of small illustrations. These illustrations are sometimes of the commonest; Trollope turns them out inexhaustibly, repeats them freely, unfolds them without haste and without rest. But they are all of the most obvious sort, and they are none the worse for that. The point to be made is that they have no great spectacular interest (we beg pardon of the innumerable love-affairs that Trollope has described), like many of the incidents, say, of Walter Scott and of Alexandre Dumas: if we care to know about them (as repetitions of a usual case), it is because the writer has managed, in his candid, literal, somewhat lumbering way, to tell us that about the men and women concerned which has already excited on their behalf the impression of life. It is a marvel by what homely arts, by what imperturbable button-holing persistence, he contrives to excite this impression. Take, for example, such a work as *The Vicar of Bullhampton*. It would be difficult to state the idea of this slow but excellent story, which is a capital example of interest produced by the quietest conceivable means. The principal persons in it are a lively, jovial, high-tempered country clergyman, a young woman who is in love with her cousin, and a small, rather dull squire who is in love with the young woman. There is no connection between the affairs of the clergyman and those of the two other persons, save that these two are the Vicar's friends. The Vicar gives countenance, for Christian charity's sake, to a young countryman who is suspected (falsely, as it appears), of murder, and also to the lad's sister, who is more than suspected of leading an immoral life. Various people are shocked at his indiscretion, but in the end he is shown to have been no worse a clergyman because he is a good fellow. A cantankerous nobleman, who has a spite against him, causes a Methodist conventicle to be erected at the gates of the vicarage; but afterward, finding that he has no title to the land used for this obnoxious purpose, causes the conventicle to be pulled down, and is reconciled with the parson, who accepts an invitation to stay at the castle. Mary Lowther, the heroine of *The Vicar of Bullhampton*, is sought in marriage by Mr. Harry Gilmore, to whose passion she is unable to respond; she accepts him, however, making him understand that she does not love him, and that her affections are fixed upon her kinsman, Captain Marrable, whom she would marry (and who would marry her), if he were not too poor to support a wife. If Mr. Gilmore will take her on these terms she will become his spouse; but she gives him all sorts of warnings. They are not superfluous; for, as Captain Marrable presently inherits a fortune, she throws over Mr. Gilmore, who retires to foreign lands, heart-broken, inconsolable. This is the substance of *The Vicar of Bullhampton*; the reader will see that it is not a very tangled skein. But if the interest is gradual it is extreme and constant, and it comes altogether from excellent portraiture. It is essentially a moral, a social interest. There is something masterly in the large-fisted grip with which, in work of this kind, Trollope handles his brush. The Vicar's nature is thoroughly analysed and rendered, and his monotonous friend the Squire, a man with limitations, but possessed and consumed by a genuine passion, is equally near the truth.

Trollope has described again and again the ravages of love, and it is wonderful to see how well, in these delicate matters, his plain good sense and good taste serve him. His story is always primarily a love-story, and a love-story constructed on an inveterate system. There is a young lady who has two lovers, or a young man who has two sweet-hearts; we are treated to the innumerable forms in which this pre-dicament may present itself and the consequences, sometimes pathetic, sometimes grotesque, which spring from such false situations. Trol-lope is not what is called a colourist; still less is he a poet: he is seated on the back of heavy-footed prose. But his account of those sentiments which the poets are supposed to have made their own is apt to be as touching as demonstrations more lyrical. There is something wonder-fully vivid in the state of mind of the unfortunate Harry Gilmore, of whom I have just spoken; and his history, which has no more pretensions to style than if it were cut out of yesterday's newspaper, lodges itself in the imagination in all sorts of classic company. He is not handsome, nor clever, nor rich, nor romantic, nor distinguished in any way; he is simply rather a dense, narrow-minded, stiff, obstinate, common-place, conscientious modern Englishman, exceedingly in love and, from his own point of view, exceedingly ill-used. He is in-teresting because he suffers and because we are curious to see the form that suffering will take in that particular nature. Our good fortune, with Trollope, is that the person put before us will have, in spite of opportunities not to have it, a certain particular nature. The author has cared enough about the character of such a person to find out exactly what it is. Another particular nature in *The Vicar of Bull-hampton* is the surly, sturdy, sceptical old farmer Jacob Brattle, who doesn't want to be patronised by the parson, and in his dumb, dusky, half-brutal, half-spiritual melancholy, surrounded by domestic trou-bles, financial embarrassments and a puzzling world, declines altogether to be won over to clerical optimism. Such a figure as Jacob Brattle, purely episodical though it be, is an excellent English portrait. As thoroughly English, and the most striking thing in the book, is the combination, in the nature of Frank Fenwick—the delightful Vicar— of the patronising, conventional, clerical element with all sorts of manliness and spontaneity; the union, or to a certain extent the contradiction, of official and personal geniality. Trollope touches these points in a way that shows that he knows his man. Delicacy is not his great sign, but when it is necessary he can be as delicate as any one else.

I alighted, just now, at a venture, upon the history of Frank Fenwick; it is far from being a conspicuous work in the immense list of Trollope's novels. But to choose an example one must choose arbitrarily, for examples of almost anything that one may wish to say are numerous to embarrassment. In speaking of a writer who produced so much and produced always in the same way, there is perhaps a certain unfairness in choosing at all. As no work has higher pretensions than any other, there may be a certain unkindness in holding an individual production up to the light. "Judge me in the lump," we can imagine the author saying; "I have only undertaken to entertain the British public. I don't pretend that each of my novels is an organic whole." Trollope had no time to give his tales a classic roundness; yet there is (in spite of an extraordinary defect), something of that quality in the thing that first revealed him. *The Warden* was published in 1855. It made a great impression; and when, in 1857, *Barchester Towers* followed it, every one saw that English literature had a novelist the more. These were not the works of a young man, for Anthony Trollope had been born in 1815. It is remarkable to reflect, by the way, that his prodigious fecundity (he had published before *The Warden* three or four novels which attracted little attention), was enclosed between his fortieth and his sixty-seventh years. Trollope had lived long enough in the world to learn a good deal about it; and his maturity of feeling and evidently large knowledge of English life were for much in the effect produced by the two clerical tales. It was easy to see that he would take up room. What he had picked up, to begin with, was a comprehensive, various impression of the clergy of the Church of England and the manners and feelings that prevail in cathedral towns. This, for a while, was his speciality, and, as always happens in such cases, the public was disposed to prescribe to him that path. He knew about bishops, archdeacons, prebendaries, precentors, and about their wives and daughters; he knew what these dignitaries say to each other when they are collected together, aloof from secular ears. He even knew what sort of talk goes on between a bishop and a bishop's lady when the august couple are enshrouded in the privacy of the episcopal bedroom. This knowledge, somehow, was rare and precious. No one, as yet, had been bold enough to snatch the illuminating torch from the very summit of the altar. Trollope enlarged his field very speedily—there is, as I remember that work, as little as possible of the ecclesiastical in the tale of *The Three Clerks*, which came after *Barchester Towers*. But he always retained traces of his early divination of the clergy; he introduced them frequently, and he always did them easily and well. There is no ecclesiastical figure, however, so good as the first—no creation of this sort so happy as the admirable Mr. Harding. *The Warden* is a delightful tale, and a signal instance of Trollope's habit of offering us the spectacle of a character. A motive more delicate, more slender, as well as more charming, could scarcely be conceived. It is simply the history of an old man's conscience.

The good and gentle Mr. Harding, precentor of Barchester Cathedral, also holds the post of warden of Hiram's Hospital, an ancient charity where twelve old paupers are maintained in comfort. The office is in the gift of the bishop, and its emoluments are as handsome as the duties of the place are small. Mr. Harding has for years drawn his salary in quiet gratitude; but his moral repose is broken by hearing it at last begun to be said that the wardenship is a sinecure, that the salary is a scandal, and that a large part, at least, of his easy income ought to go to the pensioners of the hospital. He is sadly troubled and perplexed, and when the great London newspapers take up the affair he is overwhelmed with confusion and shame. He thinks the newspapers are right—he perceives that the warden is an overpaid and rather a useless functionary. The only thing he can do is to resign the place. He has no means of his own—he is only a quiet, modest, innocent old man, with a taste, a passion, for old church-music and the violon-cello. But he determines to resign, and he does resign in spite of the sharp opposition of his friends. He does what he thinks right, and goes to live in lodgings over a shop in the Barchester High

Street. That is all the story, and it has exceeding beauty. The question of Mr. Harding's resignation becomes a drama, and we anxiously wait for the catastrophe. Trollope never did anything happier than the picture of this sweet and serious little old gentleman, who on most of the occasions of life has shown a lamblike softness and compliance, but in this particular matter opposes a silent, impenetrable obstinacy to the arguments of the friends who insist on his keeping his sine-cure—fixing his mild, detached gaze on the distance, and making imaginary passes with his fiddle-bow while they demonstrate his pusillanimity. The subject of *The Warden*, exactly viewed, is the op-position of the two natures of Archdeacon Grantley and Mr. Hard-ing, and there is nothing finer in all Trollope than the vividness with which this opposition is presented. The archdeacon is as happy a portrait as the precentor—an image of the full-fed, worldly church-man, taking his stand squarely upon his rich temporalities, and re-garding the church frankly as a fat social pasturage. It required the greatest tact and temperance to make the picture of Archdeacon Grantley stop just where it does. The type, impartially considered, is detestable, but the individual may be full of amenity. Trollope allows his archdeacon all the virtues he was likely to possess, but he makes his spiritual grossness wonderfully natural. No charge of exaggeration is possible, for we are made to feel that he is conscientious as well as arrogant, and expansive as well as hard. He is one of those figures that spring into being all at once, solidifying in the author's grasp. These two capital portraits are what we carry away from *The Warden*, which some persons profess to regard as our writer's masterpiece. We remember, while it was still something of a novelty, to have heard a judicious critic say that it had much of the charm of *The Vicar of Wakefield*. Anthony Trollope would not have accepted the compli-ment, and would not have wished this little tale to pass before several of its successors. He would have said, very justly, that it gives too small a measure of his knowledge of life. It has, however, a certain classic roundness, though, as we said a moment since, there is a blemish on its fair face. The chapter on Dr. Pessimist Anticant and Mr. Sentiment would be a mistake almost inconceivable if Trollope had not in other places taken pains to show us that for certain forms of satire (the more violent, doubtless), he had absolutely no gift. Dr. Anticant is a parody of Carlyle, and Mr. Sentiment is an exposure of Dickens: and both these little *jeux d'esprit* are as infelicitous as they are misplaced. It was no less luckless an inspiration to convert Archdeacon Grantley's three sons, denominated respectively Charles James, Henry and Samuel, into little effigies of three distinguished English bishops of that period, whose well-known peculiarities are reproduced in the description of these unnatural urchins. The whole passage, as we meet it, is a sudden disillusionment; we are transported from the mellow atmosphere of an assimilated Barchester to the air of ponderous allegory.

I may take occasion to remark here upon a very curious fact—the fact that there are certain precautions in the way of producing that illusion dear to the intending novelist which Trollope not only habitually scorned to take, but really, as we may say, asking pardon for the heat of the thing, delighted wantonly to violate. He took a suicidal satisfaction in reminding the reader that the story he was telling was only, after all, a make-believe. He habitually referred to the work in hand (in the course of that work) as a novel, and to himself as a novelist, and was fond of letting the reader know that this novelist could direct the course of events according to his pleasure. Already, in *Barchester Towers*, he falls into this pernicious trick. In describing the wooing of Eleanor Bold by Mr. Arabin he has occasion to say that the lady might have acted in a much more direct and natural way than the way he attributes to her. But if she had, he adds, "where would have been my novel?" The last chapter of the same story begins with the remark, "The end of a novel, like the end of a children's dinner party, must be made up of sweetmeats and sugar-plums." These little slaps at credulity (we might give many more specimens) are very discouraging, but they are even more inexplicable; for they are deliberately inartistic, even judged from the point of view of that rather vague consideration of form which is the only canon we have a right to impose upon Trollope. It is impossible to imagine what a novelist takes himself to be unless he regard himself as an historian and his narrative as a history. It is only as an historian that he has the small-est *locus standi*. As a narrator of fictitious events he is nowhere; to insert into his attempt a back-bone of logic, he must relate events that are assumed to be real. This assumption permeates, animates all the work of the most solid story-tellers; we need only mention (to select a single instance), the magnificent historical tone of Balzac, who would as soon have thought of admitting to the reader that he was deceiving him, as Garrick or John Kemble would have thought of pulling off his disguise in front of the footlights. Therefore, when Trollope suddenly winks at us and reminds us that he is telling us an arbitrary thing, we are startled and shocked in quite the same way as if Macaulay or Motley were to drop the historic mask and intimate that William of Orange was a myth or the Duke of Alva an invention.

It is a part of this same ambiguity of mind as to what constitutes evidence that Trollope should sometimes endow his people with such fantastic names. Dr. Pessimist Anticant and Mr. Sentiment make, as we have seen, an awkward appearance in a modern novel; and Mr. Neversay Die, Mr. Stickatit, Mr. Rerechild and Mr. Fillgrave (the two last the family physicians), are scarcely more felicitous. It would be better to go back to Bunyan at once. There is a person mentioned in *The Warden* under the name of Mr. Quiverful—a poor clergyman, with a dozen children, who holds the living of Puddingdale. This name is a humorous allusion to his overflowing nursery, and it mat-ters little so long as he is not brought to the front. But in *Barchester Towers*, which carries on the history of Hiram's Hospital, Mr. Quiv-erful becomes, as a candidate for Mr. Harding's vacant place, an important element, and the reader is made proportionately unhappy by the primitive character of this satiric note. A Mr. Quiverful with fourteen children (which is the number attained in *Barchester Tow-ers*) is too difficult to believe in. We can believe in the name and we can believe in the children; but we cannot manage the combination. It is probably not unfair to say that if Trollope derived half his inspi-ration from life, he derived the other half from Thackeray; his earlier novels, in especial, suggest an honourable emulation of the author of *The Newcomes*. Thackeray's names were perfect; they always had a meaning, and (except in his absolutely jocose productions, where they were still admirable) we can imagine, even when they are most figurative, that they should have been borne by real people. But in this, as in other respects, Trollope's hand was heavier than his master's; though when he is content not to be too comical his appellations are sometimes fortunate enough. Mrs. Proudie is excellent, for Mrs. Proudie, and even the Duke of Omnium and Gatherum Castle rather minister to illusion than destroy it. Indeed, the names of houses and places, throughout Trollope, are full of colour.

I would speak in some detail of *Barchester Towers* if this did not seem to commit me to the prodigious task of appreciating each of Trollope's works in succession. Such an attempt as that is so far from being possible that I must frankly confess to not having read everything that proceeded from his pen. There came a moment in his vigorous career (it was even a good many years ago) when I renounced the effort to "keep up" with him. It ceased to seem obligatory to have read his last story; it ceased soon to be very possible to know which was his last. Before that, I had been punctual, devoted; and the memories of the earlier period are delightful. It reached, if I remember correctly, to about the publication of *He Knew He Was Right*; after which, to my recollection (oddly enough, too, for that novel was good enough to encourage a continuance of past favours, as the shopkeepers say), the picture becomes dim and blurred. The author of *Orley Farm* and *The Small House at Allington* ceased to produce individual works; his activity became a huge "serial." Here and there, in the vast fluidity, an organic particle detached itself. *The Last Chronicle of Barset*, for instance, is one of his most powerful things; it contains the sequel of the terrible history of Mr. Crawley, the starving curate—an episode full of that literally truthful pathos of which Trollope was so often a master, and which occasionally raised him quite to the level of his two immediate predecessors in the vivid treatment of English life—great artists whose pathetic effects were sometimes too visibly prepared. For the most part, however, he should be judged by the productions of the first half of his career; later the strong wine was rather too copiously watered. His practice, his acquired facility, were such that his hand went of itself, as it were, and the thing looked superficially like a fresh inspiration. But it was not fresh, it was rather stale; and though there was no appearance of effort, there was a fatal dryness of texture. It was too little of a new story and too much of an old one. Some of these ultimate compositions—*Phineas Redux* (*Phineas Finn* is much better), *The Prime Minister, John Caldigate, The American Senator, The Duke's Children*—betray the dull, impersonal rumble of the mill-wheel. What stands Trollope always in good stead (in addition to the ripe habit of writing), is his various knowledge of the English world—to say nothing of his occasionally laying under contribution the American. His American portraits, by the way (they are several in number), are always friendly; they hit it off more happily than the attempt to depict American character from the European point of view is accustomed to do: though, indeed, as we ourselves have not yet learned to represent our types very finely—are not apparently even very sure what our types are—it is perhaps not to be wondered at that transatlantic talent should miss the mark. The weakness of transatlantic talent in this particular is apt to be want of knowledge; but Trollope's knowledge has all the air of being excellent, though not intimate. Had he indeed striven to learn the way to the American heart? No less than twice, and possibly even oftener, has he rewarded the merit of a scion of the British aristocracy with the hand of an American girl. The American girl was destined sooner or later to make her entrance into British fiction, and Trollope's treatment of this complicated being is full of good humour and of that fatherly indulgence, that almost motherly sympathy, which characterises his attitude throughout toward the youthful feminine. He has not mastered all the springs of her delicate organism nor sounded all the mysteries of her conversation. Indeed, as regards these latter phenomena, he has observed a few of which he has been the sole observer. "I got to be thinking if any one of them should ask me to marry him," words attributed to Miss Boncassen, in *The Duke's Children*, have much more the note of English American than of American English. But, on the whole, in these matters Trollope does very well. His fund of acquaintance with his own country—and indeed with the world at large—was apparently inexhaustible, and it gives his novels a spacious, geographical quality which we should not know where to look for elsewhere in the same degree, and which is the sign of an extraordinary difference between such an horizon as his and the limited world-outlook, as the Germans would say, of the brilliant writers who practise the art of realistic fiction on the other side of the Channel. Trollope was familiar with all sorts and conditions of men, with the business of life, with affairs, with the great world of sport, with every component part of the ancient fabric of English society. He had travelled more than once all over the globe, and for him, therefore, the background of the human drama was a very extensive scene. He had none of the pedantry of the cosmopolite; he remained a sturdy and sensible middle-class Englishman. But his work is full of implied reference to the whole arena of modern vagrancy. He was for many years concerned in the management of the Post-Office; and we can imagine no experience more fitted to impress a man with the diversity of human relations. It is possibly from this source that he derived his fondness for transcribing the letters of his love-lorn maidens and other embarrassed persons. No contemporary story-teller deals so much in letters; the modern English epistle (very happily imitated, for the most part), is his unfailing resource.

There is perhaps little reason in it, but I find myself comparing this tone of allusion to many lands and many things, and whatever it brings us of easier respiration, with that narrow vision of humanity which accompanies the strenuous, serious work lately offered us in such abundance by the votaries of art for art who sit so long at their desks in Parisian *quatrièmes*. The contrast is complete, and it would be interesting, had we space to do so here, to see how far it goes. On one side a wide, good-humoured, superficial glance at a good many things; on the other a gimlet-like consideration of a few. Trollope's plan, as well as Zola's, was to describe the life that lay near him; but the two writers differ immensely as to what constitutes life and what constitutes nearness. For Trollope the emotions of a nursery-governess in Australia would take precedence of the adventures of a depraved *femme du monde* in Paris or London. They both undertake to do the same thing—to depict French and English manners; but the English writer (with his unsurpassed industry) is so occasional, so accidental, so full of the echoes of voices that are not the voice of the muse. Gustave Flaubert, Emile Zola, Alphonse Daudet, on the other hand, are nothing if not concentrated and sedentary. Trollope's realism is as instinctive, as inveterate as theirs; but nothing could mark more the difference between the French and English mind than the difference in the application, on one side and the other, of this system. We say system, though on Trollope's part it is none. He has no visible, certainly no explicit care for the literary part of the business; he writes easily, comfortably, and profusely, but his style has nothing in common either with the minute stippling of Daudet or the studied rhythms of Flaubert. He accepted all the common restrictions, and found that even within the barriers there was plenty of material. He attaches a preface to one of his novels—*The Vicar of Bullhampton*, before mentioned—for the express purpose of explaining why he has introduced a young woman who may, in truth, as he says, be called a "castaway"; and in relation to this episode he remarks that it is the object of the novelist's art to entertain the young people of both sexes. Writers of the French school would, of course, protest indignantly against such a formula as this, which is the only one of the kind that I remember to have encountered in Trollope's pages. It is meagre, assuredly; but Trollope's practice was really much larger than so poor a theory. And indeed any theory was good which enabled him to produce the works which he put forth between 1856 and 1869, or later. In spite of his want of doctrinal richness I think he tells us, on the whole, more about life than the "naturalists" in our sister republic. I say this with a full consciousness of the opportunities an artist loses in leaving so many corners unvisited, so many topics untouched, simply because I think his perception of character was naturally more just and liberal than that of the naturalists. This has been from the beginning the good fortune of our English providers of fiction, as compared with the French. They are inferior in audacity, in neatness, in acuteness, in intellectual vivacity, in the arrangement of material, in the art of characterising visible things. But they have been more at home in the moral world; as people say to-day they know their way about the conscience. This is the value of much of the work done by the feminine wing of the school—work which presents itself to French taste as deplorably thin and insipid. Much of it is exquisitely human, and that after all is a merit. As regards Trollope, one may perhaps characterise him best, in opposition to what I have ventured to call the sedentary school, by saying that he was a novelist who hunted the fox. Hunting was for years his most valued recreation, and I remember that when I made in his company the voyage of which I have spoken, he had timed his return from the Antipodes exactly so as to be able to avail himself of the first day on which it should be possible to ride to hounds. He "worked" the hunting-field largely; it constantly reappears in his novels; it was excellent material.

But it would be hard to say (within the circle in which he revolved) what material he neglected. I have allowed myself to be detained so long by general considerations that I have almost forfeited the opportunity to give examples. I have spoken of *The Warden* not only because it made his reputation, but because, taken in conjunction with *Barchester Towers*, it is thought by many people to be his highest flight. *Barchester Towers* is admirable; it has an almost Thackerayan richness. Archdeacon Grantley grows more and more into life, and Mr. Harding is as charming as ever. Mrs. Proudie is ushered into a world in which she was to make so great an impression. Mrs. Proudie has become classical; of all Trollope's characters she is the most often referred to. She is exceedingly true; but I do not think she is quite so good as her fame, and as several figures from the same hand that have not won so much honour. She is rather too violent, too vixenish, too sour. The truly awful female bully—the completely fatal episcopal spouse—would have, I think, a more insidious form, a greater amount of superficial padding. The Stanhope family, in *Barchester Towers*, are a real *trouvaille*, and the idea of transporting the Signora Vesey-Neroni into a cathedral-town was an inspiration. There could not be a better example of Trollope's manner of attaching himself to character than the whole picture of Bertie Stanhope. Bertie is a delightful creation; and the scene in which, at the party given by Mrs. Proudie, he puts this majestic woman to rout is one of the most amusing in all the chronicles of Barset. It is perhaps permitted to wish, by the way, that this triumph had been effected by means intellectual rather than physical; though, indeed, if Bertie had not despoiled her of her drapery we should have lost the lady's admirable "Unhand it, sir!" Mr. Arabin is charming, and the henpecked bishop has painful truth; but Mr. Slope, I think, is a little too arrant a scamp. He is rather too much the old game; he goes too coarsely to work, and his clamminess and cant are somewhat overdone. He is an interesting illustration, however, of the author's dislike (at that period at least) of the bareness of evangelical piety. In one respect *Barchester Towers* is (to the best of our recollection) unique, being the only one of Trollope's novels in which the interest does not centre more or less upon a simple maiden in her flower. The novel offers us nothing in the way of a girl; though we know that this attractive object was to lose nothing by waiting. Eleanor Bold is a charming and natural person, but Eleanor Bold is not in her flower. After this, however, Trollope settled down steadily to the English girl; he took possession of her, and turned her inside out. He never made her a subject of heartless satire, as cynical fabulists of other lands have been known to make the shining daughters of those climes; he bestowed upon her the most serious, the most patient, the most tender, the most copious consideration. He is evidently always more or less in love with her, and it is a wonder how under these circumstances he should make her so objective, plant her so well on her feet. But, as I have said, if he was a lover, he was a paternal lover; as competent as a father who has had fifty daughters. He has presented the British maiden under innumerable names, in every station and in every emergency in life, and with every combination of moral and physical qualities. She is always definite and natural. She plays her part most properly. She has always health in her cheek and gratitude in her eye. She has not a touch of the morbid, and is delightfully tender, modest and fresh. Trollope's heroines have a strong family likeness, but it is a wonder how finely he discriminates between them. One feels, as one reads him, like a man with "sets" of female cousins. Such a person is inclined at first to lump each group together; but presently he finds that even in the groups there are subtle differences. Trollope's girls, for that matter, would make delightful cousins. He has scarcely drawn, that we can remember, a disagreeable damsel. Lady Alexandrina de Courcy is disagreeable, and so is Amelia Roper, and so are various provincial (and indeed metropolitan) spinsters, who set their caps at young clergymen and government clerks. Griselda Grantley was a stick; and considering that she was intended to be attractive, Alice Vavasor does not commend herself particularly to our affections. But the young women I have mentioned had ceased to belong to the blooming season; they had entered the bristling, or else the limp, period. Not that Trollope's more mature spinsters invariably fall into these extremes. Miss Thorne of Ullathorne, Miss Dunstable, Miss Mackenzie, Rachel Ray (if she may be called mature), Miss Baker and Miss Todd, in *The Bertrams*, Lady Julia Guest, who comforts poor John Eames: these and many other amiable figures rise up to contradict the idea. A gentleman who had sojourned in many lands was once asked by a lady (neither of these persons was English), in what country he had found the women most to his taste. "Well, in England," he replied. "In England?" the lady repeated. "Oh yes," said her interlocutor; "they are so affectionate!" The remark was fatuous, but it has the merit of describing Trollope's heroines. They are so affectionate. Mary Thorne, Lucy Robarts, Adela Gauntlet, Lily Dale, Nora Rowley, Grace Crawley, have a kind of clinging tenderness, a passive sweetness, which is quite in the old English tradition. Trollope's genius is not the genius of Shakespeare, but his heroines have something of the fragrance of Imogen and Desdemona. There are two little stories to which, I believe, his name has never been affixed, but which he is known to have written, that contain an extraordinarily touching representation of the passion of love in its most sensitive form. In *Linda Tressel* and *Nina Balatka* the vehicle is plodding prose, but the effect is none the less poignant. And in regard to this I may say that in a hundred places in Trollope the extremity of pathos is reached by the homeliest means. He often achieved a conspicuous intensity of the tragical. The long, slow process of the conjugal wreck of Louis Trevelyan and his wife (in *He Knew He Was Right*), with that rather lumbering movement which is often characteristic of Trollope, arrives at last at an impressive completeness of misery. It is the history of an accidental rupture between two stiff-necked and ungracious people—"the little rift within the lute"—which widens at last into a gulf of anguish. Touch is added to touch, one small, stupid, fatal aggravation to another; and as we gaze into the widening breach we wonder at the vulgar materials of which tragedy sometimes composes itself. I have always remembered the chapter called "Casalunga," toward the close of *He Knew He Was Right*, as a powerful picture of the insanity of stiff-neckedness. Louis Trevelyan, separated from his wife, alone, haggard, suspicious, unshaven, un-dressed, living in a desolate villa on a hill-top near Siena and return-ing doggedly to his fancied wrong, which he has nursed until it becomes an hallucination, is a picture worthy of Balzac. Here and in several other places Trollope has dared to be thoroughly logical; he has not sacrificed to conventional optimism; he has not been afraid of a misery which should be too much like life. He has had the same courage in the history of the wretched Mr. Crawley and in that of the much-to-be-pitied Lady Mason. In this latter episode he found an admirable subject. A quiet, charming, tender-souled English gentlewoman who (as I remember the story of *Orley Farm*) forges a codicil to a will in order to benefit her son, a young prig who doesn't appreciate immoral heroism, and who is suspected, accused, tried, and saved from conviction only by some turn of fortune that I forget; who is furthermore an object of high-bred, respectful, old-fashioned gallantry on the part of a neighbouring baronet, so that she sees herself dishonoured in his eyes as well as condemned in those of her boy: such a personage and such a situation would be sure to yield, under Trollope's handling, the last drop of their reality.

There are many more things to say about him than I am able to add to these very general observations, the limit of which I have already passed. It would be natural, for instance, for a critic who affirms that his principal merit is the portrayal of individual character, to enumer-ate several of the figures that he has produced. I have not done this, and I must ask the reader who is not acquainted with Trollope to take my assertion on trust; the reader who knows him will easily make a list for himself. No account of him is complete in which allusion is not made to his practice of carrying certain actors from one story to another—a practice which he may be said to have inherited from Thackeray, as Thackeray may be said to have borrowed it from Balzac. It is a great mistake, however, to speak of it as an artifice which would not naturally occur to a writer proposing to himself to make a general portrait of a society. He has to construct that society, and it adds to the illusion in any given case that certain other cases correspond with it. Trollope constructed a great many things—a clergy, an aristocracy, a middle-class, an administrative class, a little replica of the political world. His political novels are distinctly dull, and I confess I have not been able to read them. He evidently took a good deal of pains with his aristocracy; it makes its first appearance, if I remember right, in *Doctor Thorne*, in the person of the Lady Arabella de Courcy. It is difficult for us in America to measure the success of that picture, which is probably, however, not absolutely to the life. There is in *Doctor Thorne* and some other works a certain crudity of reference to distinctions of rank—as if people's consciousness of this matter were, on either side, rather inflated. It suggests a general state of tension. It is true that, if Trollope's consciousness had been more flaccid he would perhaps not have given us Lady Lufton and Lady Glencora Palliser. Both of these noble persons are as living as possible, though I see Lady Lufton, with her terror of Lucy Robarts, the best. There is a touch of poetry in the figure of Lady Glencora, but I think there is a weak spot in her history. The actual woman would have made a fool of herself to the end with Burgo Fitzgerald; she would not have discovered the merits of Plantagenet Palliser—or if she had, she would not have cared about them. It is an illustration of the business-like way in which Trollope laid out his work that he always provided a sort of underplot to alternate with his main story—a strain of narrative of which the scene is usually laid in a humbler walk of life. It is to his underplot that he generally relegates his vulgar people, his disagreeable young women; and I have often admired the perseverance with which he recounts these less edifying items. Now and then, it may be said, as in *Ralph the Heir*, the story appears to be all under-plot and all vulgar people. These, however, are details. As I have already intimated, it is difficult to specify in Trollope's work, on account of the immense quantity of it; and there is sadness in the thought that this enormous mass does not present itself in a very portable form to posterity.

Trollope did not write for posterity; he wrote for the day, the moment; but these are just the writers whom posterity is apt to put into its pocket. So much of the life of his time is reflected in his novels that we must believe a part of the record will be saved; and the best parts of them are so sound and true and genial, that readers with an eye to that sort of entertainment will always be sure, in a certain proportion, to turn to them. Trollope will remain one of the most trustworthy, though not one of the most eloquent, of the writers who have helped the heart of man to know itself. The heart of man does not always desire this knowledge; it prefers sometimes to look at history in another way—to look at the manifestations without troubling about the motives. There are two kinds of taste in the appreciation of imaginative literature: the taste for emotions of surprise and the taste for emotions of recognition. It is the latter that Trollope gratifies, and he gratifies it the more that the medium of his own mind, through which we see what he shows us, gives a confident direction to our sympathy. His natural rightness and purity are so real that the good things he projects must be real. A race is fortunate when it has a good deal of the sort of imagination—of imaginative feeling—that had fallen to the share of Anthony Trollope; and in this possession our English race is not poor.

IVAN TURGÉNIEFF

WHEN THE mortal remains of Ivan Turgénieff were about to be transported from Paris for interment in his own country, a short commemorative service was held at the Gare du Nord. Ernest Renan and Edmond About, standing beside the train in which his coffin had been placed, bade farewell in the name of the French people to the illustrious stranger who for so many years had been their honoured and grateful guest. M. Renan made a beautiful speech, and M. About a very clever one, and each of them characterised, with ingenuity, the genius and the moral nature of the most touching of writers, the most lovable of men. "Turgénieff," said M. Renan, "received by the mysterious decree which marks out human vocations the gift which is noble beyond all others: he was born essentially impersonal." The passage is so eloquent that one must repeat the whole of it. "His conscience was not that of an individual to whom nature had been more or less generous: it was in some sort the conscience of a people. Before he was born he had lived for thousands of years; infinite successions of reveries had amassed themselves in the depths of his heart. No man has been as much as he the incarnation of a whole race: generations of ancestors, lost in the sleep of centuries, speechless, came through him to life and utterance."

I quote these lines for the pleasure of quoting them; for while I see what M. Renan means by calling Turgénieff impersonal, it has been my wish to devote to his delightful memory a few pages written under the impression of contact and intercourse. He seems to us impersonal, because it is from his writings almost alone that we of English, French and German speech have derived our notions—even yet, I fear, rather meagre and erroneous—of the Russian people. His genius for us is the Slav genius; his voice the voice of those vaguely-imagined multitudes whom we think of more and more to-day as waiting their turn, in the arena of civilisation, in the grey expanses of the North. There is much in his writings to encourage this view, and it is certain that he interpreted with wonderful vividness the temperament of his fellow-countrymen. Cosmopolite that he had become by the force of circumstances, his roots had never been loosened in his native soil. The ignorance with regard to Russia and the Russians which he found in abundance in the rest of Europe—and not least in the country he inhabited for ten years before his death—had indeed the effect, to a certain degree, to throw him back upon the deep feelings which so many of his companions were unable to share with him, the memories of his early years, the sense of wide Russian horizons, the joy and pride of his mother-tongue. In the collection of short pieces, so deeply interesting, written during the last few years of his life, and translated into German under the name of *Senilia*, I find a passage—it is the last in the little book—which illustrates perfectly this reactionary impulse: "In days of doubt, in days of anxious thought on the destiny of my native land, thou alone art my support and my staff, O great powerful Russian tongue, truthful and free! If it were not for thee how should man not despair at the sight of what is going on at home? But it is inconceivable that such a language has not been given to a great people." This Muscovite, home-loving note pervades his productions, though it is between the lines, as it were, that we must listen for it. None the less does it remain true that he was not a simple conduit or mouthpiece; the inspiration was his own as well as the voice. He was an individual, in other words, of the most unmistakable kind, and those who had the happiness to know him have no difficulty to-day in thinking of him as an eminent, responsible figure. This pleasure, for the writer of these lines, was as great as the pleasure of reading the admirable tales into which he put such a world of life and feeling: it was perhaps even greater, for it was not only with the pen that nature had given Turgénieff the power to express himself. He was the richest, the most delightful, of talkers, and his face, his person, his temper, the thoroughness with which he had been equipped for human intercourse, make in the memory of his friends an image which is completed, but not thrown into the shade, by his literary distinction. The whole image is tinted with sadness: partly because the element of melancholy in his nature was deep and constant—readers of his novels have no need to be told of that; and partly because, during the last years of his life, he had been condemned to suffer atrociously. Intolerable pain had been his portion for too many months before he died; his end was not a soft decline, but a deepening distress. But of brightness, of the faculty of enjoyment, he had also the large allowance usually made to first-rate men, and he was a singularly complete human being. The author of these pages had greatly admired his writings before having the fortune to make his acquaintance, and this privilege, when it presented itself, was highly illuminating. The man and the writer together occupied from that moment a very high place in his affection. Some time before knowing him I committed to print certain reflections which his tales had led me to make; and I may perhaps, therefore, without impropriety give them a supplement which shall have a more vivifying reference. It is almost irresistible to attempt to say, from one's own point of view, what manner of man he was.

It was in consequence of the article I just mentioned that I found reason to meet him, in Paris, where he was then living, in 1875. I shall never forget the impression he made upon me at that first interview. I found him adorable; I could scarcely believe that he would prove— that any man could prove—on nearer acquaintance so delightful as that. Nearer acquaintance only confirmed my hope, and he remained the most approachable, the most practicable, the least unsafe man of genius it has been my fortune to meet. He was so simple, so natural, so modest, so destitute of personal pretension and of what is called the consciousness of powers, that one almost doubted at moments whether he were a man of genius after all. Everything good and fruitful lay near to him; he was interested in everything; and he was absolutely without that eagerness of self-reference which sometimes accompanies great, and even small, reputations. He had not a particle of vanity; nothing whatever of the air of having a part to play or a reputation to keep up. His humour exercised itself as freely upon himself as upon other subjects, and he told stories at his own expense with a sweetness of hilarity which made his peculiarities really sacred in the eyes of a friend. I remember vividly the smile and tone of voice with which he once repeated to me a figurative epithet which Gustave Flaubert (of whom he was extremely fond) had applied to him—an epithet intended to characterise a certain expansive softness, a comprehensive indecision, which pervaded his nature, just as it pervades so many of the characters he has painted. He enjoyed Flaubert's use of this term, good-naturedly opprobrious, more even than Flaubert himself, and recognised perfectly the element of truth in it. He was natural to an extraordinary degree; I do not think I have ever seen his match in this respect, certainly not among people who bear, as he did, at the same time, the stamp of the highest cultivation. Like all men of a large pattern, he was composed of many different pieces; and what was always striking in him was the mixture of simplicity with the fruit of the most various observation. In the little article in which I had attempted to express my admiration for his works, I had been moved to say of him that he had the aristocratic temperament: a remark which in the light of further knowledge seemed to me singularly inane. He was not subject to any definition of that sort, and to say that he was democratic would be (though his political ideal was a democracy), to give an equally superficial account of him. He felt and understood the opposite sides of life; he was imaginative, speculative, anything but literal. He had not in his mind a grain of prejudice as large as the point of a needle, and people (there are many) who think this a defect would have missed it immensely in Ivan Serguéitch. (I give his name, without attempting the Russian orthography, as it was uttered by his friends when they addressed him in French.) Our Anglo-Saxon, Protestant, moralistic, conventional standards were far away from him, and he judged things with a freedom and spontaneity in which I found a perpetual refreshment. His sense of beauty, his love of truth and right, were the foundation of his nature; but half the charm of conversation with him was that one breathed an air in which cant phrases and arbitrary measurements simply sounded ridiculous.

I may add that it was not because I had written a laudatory article about his books that he gave me a friendly welcome; for in the first place my article could have very little importance for him, and in the second it had never been either his habit or his hope to bask in the light of criticism. Supremely modest as he was, I think he attached no great weight to what might happen to be said about him; for he felt that he was destined to encounter a very small amount of intelligent appreciation, especially in foreign countries. I never heard him even allude to any judgment which might have been passed upon his productions in England. In France he knew that he was read very moderately; the "demand" for his volumes was small, and he had no illusions whatever on the subject of his popularity. He had heard with pleasure that many intelligent persons in the United States were impatient for everything that might come from his pen; but I think he was never convinced, as one or two of the more zealous of these persons had endeavoured to convince him, that he could boast of a "public" in America. He gave me the impression of thinking of criticism as most serious workers think of it—that it is the amusement, the exercise, the subsistence of the critic (and, so far as this goes, of immense use); but that though it may often concern other readers, it does not much concern the artist himself. In comparison with all those things which the production of a considered work forces the artist little by little to say to himself, the remarks of the critic are vague and of the moment; and yet, owing to the large publicity of the proceeding, they have a power to irritate or discourage which is quite out of proportion to their use to the person criticised. It was not, moreover (if this explanation be not more gross than the spectre it is meant to conjure away), on account of any esteem which he accorded to my own productions (I used regularly to send them to him) that I found him so agreeable, for to the best of my belief he was unable to read them. As regards one of the first that I had offered him he wrote me a little note to tell me that a distinguished friend, who was his constant companion, had read three or four chapters aloud to him the evening before and that one of them was written *de main de maître!* This gave me great pleasure, but it was my first and last pleasure of the kind. I continued, as I say, to send him my fictions, because they were the only thing I had to give; but he never alluded to the rest of the work in question, which he evidently did not finish, and never gave any sign of having read its successors. Presently I quite ceased to expect this, and saw why it was (it interested me much), that my writings could not appeal to him. He cared, more than anything else, for the air of reality, and my reality was not to the purpose. I do not think my stories struck him as quite meat for men. The manner was more apparent than the matter; they were too *tarabiscoté*, as I once heard him say of the style of a book—had on the surface too many little flowers and knots of ribbon. He had read a great deal of English, and knew the language remarkably well—too well, I used often to think, for he liked to speak it with those to whom it was native, and, successful as the effort always was, it deprived him of the facility and raciness with which he expressed himself in French.

I have said that he had no prejudices, but perhaps after all he had one. I think he imagined it to be impossible to a person of English speech to converse in French with complete correctness. He knew Shakespeare thoroughly, and at one time had wandered far and wide in English literature. His opportunities for speaking English were not at all frequent, so that when the necessity (or at least the occasion) presented itself, he remembered the phrases he had encountered in books. This often gave a charming quaintness and an unexpected literary turn to what he said. "In Russia, in spring, if you enter a beechen grove"—those words come back to me from the last time I saw him. He continued to read English books and was not incapable of attacking the usual Tauchnitz novel. The English writer (of our day) of whom I remember to have heard him speak with most admiration was Dickens, of whose faults he was conscious, but whose power of presenting to the eye a vivid, salient figure he rated very high. In the young French school he was much interested; I mean, in the new votaries of realism, the grandsons of Balzac. He was a good friend of most of them, and with Gustave Flaubert, the most singular and most original of the group, he was altogether intimate. He had his reservations and discriminations, and he had, above all, the great backgarden of his Slav imagination and his Germanic culture, into which the door constantly stood open, and the grandsons of Balzac were not, I think, particularly free to accompany him. But he had much sympathy with their experiment, their general movement, and it was on the side of the careful study of life as the best line of the novelist that, as may easily be supposed, he ranged himself. For some of the manifestations of the opposite tradition he had a great contempt. This was a kind of emotion he rarely expressed, save in regard to certain public wrongs and iniquities; bitterness and denunciation seldom passed his mild lips. But I remember well the little flush of conviction, the seriousness, with which he once said, in allusion to a novel which had just been running through the *Revue des Deux Mondes*, "If I had written anything so bad as that, I should blush for it all my life."

His was not, I should say, predominantly, or even in a high degree, the artistic nature, though it was deeply, if I may make the distinction, the poetic. But during the last twelve years of his life he lived much with artists and men of letters, and he was eminently capable of kindling in the glow of discussion. He cared for questions of form, though not in the degree in which Flaubert and Edmond de Goncourt cared for them, and he had very lively sympathies. He had a great regard for Madame George Sand, the head and front of the old romantic tradition; but this was on general grounds, quite independent of her novels, which he never read, and which she never expected him, or apparently any one else, to read. He thought her character remarkably noble and sincere. He had, as I have said, a great affection for Gustave Flaubert, who returned it; and he was much interested in Flaubert's extraordinary attempts at bravery of form and of matter, knowing perfectly well when they failed. During those months which it was Flaubert's habit to spend in Paris, Turgénieff went almost regularly to see him on Sunday afternoon, and was so good as to introduce me to the author of *Madame Bovary*, in whom I saw many reasons for Turgénieff's regard. It was on these Sundays, in Flaubert's little salon, which, at the top of a house at the end of the Faubourg Saint-Honoré, looked rather bare and provisional, that, in the company of the other familiars of the spot, more than one of whom* have commemorated these occasions, Turgénieff's beautiful faculty of talk showed at its best. He was easy, natural, abundant, more than I can describe, and everything that he said was touched with the exquisite quality of his imagination. What was discussed in that little smoke-clouded room was chiefly questions of taste, questions of art and form; and the speakers, for the most part, were in aesthetic matters, radicals of the deepest dye. It would have been late in the day to propose among them any discussion of the relation of art to morality, any question as to the degree in which a novel might or might not concern itself with the teaching of a lesson. They had settled these preliminaries long ago, and it would have been primitive and incongruous to recur to them. The conviction that held them together was the conviction that art and morality are two perfectly different things, and that the former has no more to do with the latter than it has with astronomy or embryology. The only duty of a novel was to be well written; that merit included every other of which it was capable. This state of mind was never more apparent than one afternoon when *ces messieurs* delivered themselves on the subject of an incident which had just befallen one of them. *L'Assommoir* of Emile Zola had been discontinued in the journal through which it was running as a serial, in consequence of repeated protests from the subscribers. The subscriber, as a type of human imbecility, received a wonderful dressing, and the Philistine in general was roughly handled. There were gulfs of difference between Turgénieff and Zola, but Turgénieff, who, as I say, understood everything, understood Zola too, and rendered perfect justice to the high solidity of much of his work. His attitude, at such times, was admirable, and I could imagine nothing more genial or more fitted to give an idea of light, easy, human intelligence. No one could desire more than he that art should be art; always, ever, incorruptibly, art. To him this proposition would have seemed as

*Maxime Du Camp, Alphonse Daudet, Emile Zola.

little in need of proof, or susceptible of refutation, as the axiom that law should always be law or medicine always medicine. As much as any one he was prepared to take note of the fact that the demand for abdications and concessions never comes from artists themselves, but always from purchasers, editors, subscribers. I am pretty sure that his word about all this would have been that he could not quite see what was meant by the talk about novels being moral or the reverse; that a novel could no more propose to itself to be moral than a painting or a symphony, and that it was arbitrary to lay down a distinction between the numerous forms of art. He was the last man to be blind to their unity. I suspect that he would have said, in short, that distinctions were demanded in the interest of the moralists, and that the demand was indelicate, owing to their want of jurisdiction. Yet at the same time that I make this suggestion as to his state of mind I remember how little he struck me as bound by mere neatness of formula, how little there was in him of the partisan or the pleader. What he thought of the relation of art to life his stories, after all, show better than anything else. The immense variety of life was ever present to his mind, and he would never have argued the question I have just hinted at in the interest of particular liberties—the liberties that were apparently the dearest to his French *confrères*. It was this air that he carried about with him of feeling all the variety of life, of knowing strange and far-off things, of having an horizon in which the Parisian horizon—so familiar, so wanting in mystery, so perpetually *exploité*—easily lost itself, that distinguished him from these companions. He was not all there, as the phrase is; he had something behind, in reserve. It was Russia, of course, in a large measure; and, especially before the spectacle of what is going on there to-day, that was a large quantity. But so far as he was on the spot, he was an element of pure sociability.

I did not intend to go into these details immediately, for I had only begun to say what an impression of magnificent manhood he made upon me when I first knew him. That impression, indeed, always remained with me, even after it had been brought home to me how much there was in him of the quality of genius. He was a beautiful intellect, of course, but above all he was a delightful, mild, masculine figure. The combination of his deep, soft, lovable spirit, in which one felt all the tender parts of genius, with his immense, fair Russian physique, was one of the most attractive things conceivable. He had a frame which would have made it perfectly lawful, and even becoming, for him to be brutal; but there was not a grain of brutality in his composition. He had always been a passionate sportsman; to wander in the woods or the steppes, with his dog and gun, was the pleasure of his heart. Late in life he continued to shoot, and he had a friend in Cambridgeshire for the sake of whose partridges, which were famous, he used sometimes to cross the Channel. It would have been impossible to imagine a better representation of a Nimrod of the north. He was exceedingly tall, and broad and robust in proportion. His head was one of the finest, and though the line of his features was irregular, there was a great deal of beauty in his face. It was eminently of the Russian type—almost everything in it was wide. His expression had a singular sweetness, with a touch of Slav languor, and his eye, the kindest of eyes, was deep and melancholy. His hair, abundant and straight, was as white as silver, and his beard, which he wore trimmed rather short, was of the colour of his hair. In all his tall person, which was very striking wherever it appeared, there was an air of neglected strength, as if it had been a part of his modesty never to remind himself that he was strong. He used sometimes to blush like a boy of sixteen. He had very few forms and ceremonies, and almost as little manner as was possible to a man of his natural *prestance*. His noble appearance was in itself a manner; but whatever he did he did very simply, and he had not the slightest pretension to not being subject to rectification. I never saw any one receive it with less irritation. Friendly, candid, unaffectedly benignant, the impression that he produced most strongly and most generally was, I think, simply that of goodness.

When I made his acquaintance he had been living, since his removal from Baden-Baden, which took place in consequence of the Franco-Prussian war, in a large detached house on the hill of Montmartre, with his friends of many years, Madame Pauline Viardot and her husband, as his fellow-tenants. He occupied the upper floor, and I like to recall, for the sake of certain delightful talks, the aspect of his little green sitting-room, which has, in memory, the consecration of irrecoverable hours. It was almost entirely green, and the walls were not covered with paper, but draped in stuff. The *portières* were green, and there was one of those immense divans, so indispensable to Russians, which had apparently been fashioned for the great person of the master, so that smaller folk had to lie upon it rather than sit. I remember the white light of the Paris street, which came in through windows more or less blinded in their lower part, like those of a studio. It rested, during the first years that I went to see Turgénieff, upon several choice pictures of the modern French school, especially upon a very fine specimen of Théodore Rousseau, which he valued exceedingly. He had a great love of painting, and was an excellent critic of a picture. The last time I saw him—it was at his house in the country—he showed me half a dozen large copies of Italian works, made by a young Russian in whom he was interested, which he had, with characteristic kindness, taken into his own apartments in order that he might bring them to the knowledge of his friends. He thought them, as copies, remarkable; and they were so, indeed, especially when one perceived that the original work of the artist had little value. Turgénieff warmed to the work of praising them, as he was very apt to do; like all men of imagination he had frequent and zealous admirations. As a matter of course there was almost always some young Russian in whom he was interested, and refugees and pilgrims of both sexes were his natural clients. I have heard it said by persons who had known him long and well that these enthusiasms sometimes led him into error, that he was apt to *se monter la tête* on behalf of his protégés. He was prone to believe that he had discovered the coming Russian genius; he talked about his discovery for a month, and then suddenly one heard no more of it. I remember his once telling me of a young woman who had come to see him on her return from America, where she had been studying obstetrics at some medical college, and who, without means and without friends, was in want of help and of work. He accidentally learned that she had written something, and asked her to let him see it. She sent it to him, and it proved to be a tale in which certain phases of rural life were described with striking truthfulness. He perceived in the young lady a great natural talent; he sent her story off to Russia to be printed, with the conviction that it would make a great impression, and he expressed the hope of being able to introduce her to French readers. When I mentioned this to an old friend of Turgénieff he smiled, and said that we should not hear of her again, that Ivan Serguéitch had already discovered a great many surprising talents, which, as a general thing, had not borne the test. There was apparently some truth in this, and Turgénieff's liability to be deceived was too generous a weakness for me to hesitate to allude to it, even after I have insisted on the usual certainty of his taste. He was deeply interested in his young Russians; they were what interested him most in the world. They were almost always unhappy, in want and in rebellion against an order of things which he himself detested. The study of the Russian character absorbed and fascinated him, as all readers of his stories know. Rich, unformed, undeveloped, with all sorts of adumbrations, of qualities in a state of fusion, it stretched itself out as a mysterious expanse in which it was impossible as yet to perceive the relation between gifts and weaknesses. Of its weaknesses he was keenly conscious, and I once heard him express himself with an energy that did him honour and a frankness that even surprised me (considering that it was of his countrymen that he spoke), in regard to a weakness which he deemed the greatest of all—a weakness for which a man whose love of veracity was his strongest feeling would have least toleration. His young compatriots, seeking their fortune in foreign lands, touched his imagination and his pity, and it is easy to conceive that under the circumstances the impression they often made upon him may have had great intensity. The Parisian background, with its brilliant sameness, its absence of surprises (for those who have known it long), threw them into relief and made him see them as he saw the figures in his tales, in relations, in situations which brought them out. There passed before him in the course of time many wonderful Russian types. He told me once of his having been visited by a religious sect. The sect consisted of but two persons, one of whom was the object of worship and the other the worshipper. The divinity apparently was travelling about Europe in company with his prophet. They were intensely serious but it was very handy, as the term is, for each. The god had always his altar and the altar had (unlike some altars) always its god.

In his little green salon nothing was out of place; there were none of the odds and ends of the usual man of letters, which indeed Turgénieff was not; and the case was the same in his library at Bougival, of which I shall presently speak. Few books even were visible; it was as if everything had been put away. The traces of work had been carefully removed. An air of great comfort, an immeasurable divan and several valuable pictures—that was the effect of the place. I know not exactly at what hours Turgénieff did his work; I think he had no regular times and seasons, being in this respect as different as possible from Anthony Trollope, whose autobiography, with its candid revelation of intellectual economies, is so curious. It is my impression that in Paris Turgénieff wrote little; his times of production being rather those weeks of the summer that he spent at Bougival, and the period of that visit to Russia which he supposed himself to make every year. I say "supposed himself," because it was impossible to see much of him without discovering that he was a man of delays. As on the part of some other Russians whom I have known, there was something Asiatic in his faculty of procrastination. But even if one suffered from it a little one thought of it with kindness, as a part of his general mildness and want of rigidity. He went to Russia, at any rate, at intervals not infrequent, and he spoke of these visits as his best time for production. He had an estate far in the interior, and here, amid the stillness of the country and the scenes and figures which give such a charm to the *Memoirs of a Sportsman*, he drove his pen without interruption.

It is not out of place to allude to the fact that he possessed considerable fortune; this is too important in the life of a man of letters. It had been of great value to Turgénieff, and I think that much of the fine quality of his work is owing to it. He could write according to his taste and his mood; he was never pressed nor checked (putting the Russian censorship aside) by considerations foreign to his plan, and never was in danger of becoming a hack. Indeed, taking into consideration the absence of a pecuniary spur and that complicated indolence from which he was not exempt, his industry is surprising, for his tales are a long list. In Paris, at all events, he was always open to proposals for the midday breakfast. He liked to breakfast *au cabaret,* and freely consented to an appointment. It is not unkind to add that, at first, he never kept it. I may mention without reserve this idiosyncrasy of Turgénieff's, because in the first place it was so inveterate as to be very amusing—it amused not only his friends but himself; and in the second, he was as sure to come in the end as he was sure not to come in the beginning. After the appointment had been made or the invitation accepted, when the occasion was at hand, there arrived a note or a telegram in which Ivan Serguéitch excused himself, and begged that the meeting might be deferred to another date, which he usually himself proposed. For this second date still another was sometimes substituted; but if I remember no appointment that he exactly kept, I remember none that he completely missed. His friends waited for him frequently, but they never lost him. He was very fond of that wonderful Parisian *déjeûner*—fond of it I mean as a feast of reason. He was extremely temperate, and often ate no breakfast at all; but he found it a good hour for talk, and little, on general grounds, as one might be prepared to agree with him, if he was at the table one was speedily convinced. I call it wonderful, the *déjeûner* of Paris, on account of the assurance with which it plants itself in the very middle of the morning. It divides the day between rising and dinner so unequally, and opposes such barriers of repletion to any prospect of ulterior labours, that the unacclimated stranger wonders when the fertile French people do their work. Not the least wonderful part of it is that the stranger himself likes it, at last, and manages to piece together his day with the shattered fragments that survive. It was not, at any rate, when one had the good fortune to breakfast at twelve o'clock with Turgénieff that one was struck with its being an inconvenient hour. Any hour was convenient for meeting a human being who conformed so completely to one's idea of the best that human nature is capable of. There are places in Paris which I can think of only in relation to some occasion on which he was present, and when I pass them the particular things I heard him say there come back to me. There is a café in the Avenue de l'Opéra—a new, sumptuous establishment, with very deep settees, on the right as you leave the Boulevard—where I once had a talk with him, over an order singularly moderate, which was prolonged far into the afternoon, and in the course of which he was extraordinarily suggestive and interesting, so that my memory now reverts affectionately to all the circumstances. It evokes the grey damp of a Parisian December, which made the dark interior of the café look more and more rich and hospitable, while the light faded, the lamps were lit, the habitués came in to drink absinthe and play their afternoon game of dominoes, and we still lingered over our morning meal. Turgénieff talked almost exclusively about Russia, the nihilists, the remarkable figures that came to light among them, the curious visits he received, the dark prospects of his native land. When he was in the vein, no man could speak more to the imagination of his auditor. For myself, at least, at such times, there was something extraordinarily vivifying and stimulating in his talk, and I always left him in a state of "intimate" excitement, with a feeling that all sorts of valuable things had been suggested to me; the condition in which a man swings his cane as he walks, leaps lightly over gutters, and then stops, for no reason at all, to look, with an air of being struck, into a shop window where he sees nothing. I remember another symposium, at a restaurant on one of the corners of the little *place* in front of the Opéra Comique, where we were four, including Ivan Serguéitch, and the two other guests were also Russian, one of them uniting to the charm of this nationality the merit of a sex that makes the combination irresistible. The establishment had been a discovery of Turgénieff's—a discovery, at least, as far as our particular needs were concerned—and I remember that we hardly congratulated him on it. The dinner, in a low entresol, was not what it had been intended to be, but the talk was better even than our expectations. It was not about nihilism but about some more agreeable features of life, and I have no recollection of Turgénieff in a mood more spontaneous and charming. One of our friends had, when he spoke French, a peculiar way of sounding the word *adorable*, which was frequently on his lips, and I remember well his expressive prolongation of the *a* when, in speaking of the occasion afterwards, he applied this term to Ivan Serguéitch. I scarcely know, however, why I should drop into the detail of such reminiscences, and my excuse is but the desire that we all have, when a human relationship is closed, to save a little of it from the past—to make a mark which may stand for some of the happy moments of it.

Nothing that Turgénieff had to say could be more interesting than his talk about his own work, his manner of writing. What I have heard him tell of these things was worthy of the beautiful results he produced; of the deep purpose, pervading them all, to show us life itself. The germ of a story, with him, was never an affair of plot—that was the last thing he thought of: it was the representation of certain persons. The first form in which a tale appeared to him was as the figure of an individual, or a combination of individuals, whom he wished to see in action, being sure that such people must do something very special and interesting. They stood before him definite, vivid, and he wished to know, and to show, as much as possible of their nature. The first thing was to make clear to himself what he did know, to begin with; and to this end, he wrote out a sort of biography of each of his characters, and everything that they had done and that had happened to them up to the opening of the story. He had their *dossier*, as the French say, and as the police has of that of every conspicuous criminal. With this material in his hand he was able to proceed; the story all lay in the question, What shall I make them do? He always made them do things that showed them completely; but, as he said, the defect of his manner and the reproach that was made him was his want of "architecture"—in other words, of composition. The great thing, of course, is to have architecture as well as precious material, as Walter Scott had them, as Balzac had them. If one reads Turgénieff's stories with the knowledge that they were composed—or rather that they came into being—in this way, one can trace the process in every line. Story, in the conventional sense of the word—a fable constructed, like Wordsworth's phantom, "to startle and waylay"—there is as little as possible. The thing consists of the motions of a group of selected creatures, which are not the result of a preconceived action, but a consequence of the qualities of the actors. Works of art are produced from every possible point of view, and stories, and very good ones, will continue to be written in which the evolution is that of a dance—a series of steps the more complicated and lively the better, of course, determined from without and forming a figure. This figure will always, probably, find favour with many readers, because it reminds them enough, without reminding them too much, of life. On this opposition many young talents in France are ready to rend each other, for there is a numerous school on either side. We have not yet in England and America arrived at the point of treating such questions with passion, for we have not yet arrived at the point of feeling them intensely, or indeed, for that matter, of understanding them very well. It is not open to us as yet to discuss whether a novel had better be an excision from life or a structure built up of picture-cards, for we have not made up our mind as to whether life in general may be described. There is evidence of a good deal of shyness on this point—a tendency rather to put up fences than to jump over them. Among us, therefore, even a certain ridicule attaches to the consideration of such alternatives. But individuals may feel their way, and perhaps even pass unchallenged, if they remark that for them the manner in which Turgénieff worked will always seem the most fruitful. It has the immense recommendation that in relation to any human occurrence it begins, as it were, further back. It lies in its power to tell us the most about men and women. Of course it will but slenderly satisfy those numerous readers among whom the answer to this would be, "Hang it, we don't care a straw about men and women: we want a good story!"

And yet, after all, *Elena* is a good story, and *Lisa* and *Virgin Soil* are good stories. Reading over lately several of Turgénieff's novels and tales, I was struck afresh with their combination of beauty and reality. One must never forget, in speaking of him, that he was both an observer and a poet. The poetic element was constant, and it had great strangeness and power. It inspired most of the short things that he wrote during the last few years of his life, since the publication of *Virgin Soil*, things that are in the highest degree fanciful and exotic. It pervades the frequent little reveries, visions, epigrams of the *Senilia*. It was no part of my intention, here, to criticise his writings, having said my say about them, so far as possible, some years ago. But I may mention that in re-reading them I find in them all that I formerly found of two other elements—their richness and their sadness. They give one the impression of life itself, and not of an arrangement, a *réchauffé* of life. I remember Turgénieff's once saying in regard to Homais, the little Norman country apothecary, with his pedantry of "enlightened opinions," in *Madame Bovary*, that the great strength of such a portrait consisted in its being at once an individual, of the most concrete sort, and a type. This is the great strength of his own representations of character; they are so strangely, fascinatingly particular, and yet they are so recognisably general. Such a remark as that about Homais makes me wonder why it was that Turgénieff should have rated Dickens so high, the weakness of Dickens being in regard to just that point. If Dickens fail to live long, it will be because his figures are particular without being general; because they are individuals without being types; because we do not feel their continuity with the rest of humanity—see the matching of the pattern with the piece out of which all the creations of the novelist and the dramatist are cut. I often meant, but accidentally neglected, to put Turgénieff on the subject of Dickens again, and ask him to explain his opinion. I suspect that his opinion was in a large measure merely that Dickens diverted him, as well he might. That complexity of the pattern was in itself fascinating. I have mentioned Flaubert, and I will return to him simply to say that there was something very touching in the nature of the friendship that united these two men. It is much to the honour of Flaubert, to my sense, that he appreciated Ivan Turgénieff. There was a partial similarity between them. Both were large, massive men, though the Russian reached to a greater height than the Norman; both were completely honest and sincere, and both had the pessimistic element in their composition. Each had a tender regard for the other, and I think that I am neither incorrect nor indiscreet in saying that on Turgénieff's part this regard had in it a strain of compassion. There was something in Gustave Flaubert that appealed to such a feeling. He had failed, on the whole, more than he had succeeded, and the great machinery of erudition,—the great polishing process,—which he brought to bear upon his productions, was not accompanied with proportionate results. He had talent without having cleverness, and imagination without having fancy. His effort was heroic, but except in the case of *Madame Bovary*, a masterpiece, he imparted something to his works (it was as if he had covered them with metallic plates) which made them sink rather than sail. He had a passion for perfection of form and for a certain splendid suggestiveness of style. He wished to produce perfect phrases, perfectly interrelated, and as closely woven together as a suit of chain-mail. He looked at life altogether as an artist, and took his work with a seriousness that never belied itself. To write an admirable page—and his idea of what constituted an admirable page was transcendent—seemed to him something to live for. He tried it again and again, and he came very near it; more than once he touched it, for *Madame Bovary* surely will live. But there was something ungenerous in his genius. He was cold, and he would have given everything he had to be able to glow. There is nothing in his novels like the passion of Elena for Inssaroff, like the purity of Lisa, like the anguish of the parents of Bazaroff, like the hidden wound of Tatiana; and yet Flaubert yearned, with all the accumulations of his vocabulary, to touch the chord of pathos. There were some parts of his mind that did not "give," that did not render a sound. He had had too much of some sorts of experience and not enough of others. And yet this failure of an organ, as I may call it, inspired those who knew him with a kindness. If Flaubert was powerful and limited, there is something human, after all, and even rather august in a strong man who has not been able completely to express himself.

After the first year of my acquaintance with Turgénieff I saw him much less often. I was seldom in Paris, and sometimes when I was there he was absent. But I neglected no opportunity of seeing him, and fortune frequently assisted me. He came two or three times to London, for visits provokingly brief. He went to shoot in Cambridgeshire, and he passed through town in arriving and departing. He liked the English, but I am not sure that he liked London, where he had passed a lugubrious winter in 1870–71. I remember some of his impressions of that period, especially a visit that he had paid to a "bishopess" surrounded by her daughters, and a description of the cookery at the lodgings which he occupied. After 1876 I frequently saw him as an invalid. He was tormented by gout, and sometimes terribly besieged; but his account of what he suffered was as charming—I can apply no other word to it—as his description of everything else. He had so the habit of observation, that he perceived in excruciating sensations all sorts of curious images and analogies, and analysed them to an extraordinary fineness. Several times I found him at Bougival, above the Seine, in a very spacious and handsome chalet—a little unsunned, it is true—which he had built alongside of the villa occupied by the family to which, for years, his life had been devoted. The place is delightful; the two houses are midway up a long slope, which descends, with the softest inclination, to the river, and behind them the hill rises to a wooded crest. On the left, in the distance, high up and above an horizon of woods, stretches the romantic aqueduct of Marly. It is a very pretty domain. The last time I saw him, in November 1882, it was at Bougival. He had been very ill, with strange, intolerable symptoms, but he was better, and he had good hopes. They were not justified by the event. He got worse again, and the months that followed were cruel. His beautiful serene mind should not have been darkened and made acquainted with violence; it should have been able to the last to take part, as it had always done, in the decrees and mysteries of fate. At the moment I saw him, however, he was, as they say in London, in very good form, and my last impression of him was almost bright. He was to drive into Paris, not being able to bear the railway, and he gave me a seat in the carriage. For an hour and a half he constantly talked, and never better. When we got into the city I alighted on the boulevard extérieur, as we were to go in different directions. I bade him good-bye at the carriage window, and never saw him again. There was a kind of fair going on, near by, in the chill November air, beneath the denuded little trees of the Boulevard, and a Punch and Judy show, from which nasal sounds proceeded. I almost regret having accidentally to mix up so much of Paris with this perhaps too complacent enumeration of occasions, for the effect of it may be to suggest that Ivan Turgénieff had been Gallicised. But this was not the case; the French capital was an accident for him, not a necessity. It touched him at many points, but it let him alone at many others, and he had, with that great tradition of ventilation of the Russian mind, windows open into distances which stretched far beyond the *banlieue*. I have spoken of him from the limited point of view of my own acquaintance with him, and unfortunately left myself little space to allude to a matter which filled his existence a good deal more than the consideration of how a story should be written—his hopes and fears on behalf of his native land. He wrote fictions and dramas, but the great drama of his life was the struggle for a better state of things in Russia. In this drama he played a distinguished part, and the splendid obsequies that, simple and modest as he was, have unfolded themselves over his grave, sufficiently attest the recognition of it by his countrymen. His funeral, restricted and officialised, was none the less a magnificent "manifestation." I have read the accounts of it, however, with a kind of chill, a feeling in which assent to the honours paid him bore less part than it ought. All this pomp and ceremony seemed to lift him out of the range of familiar recollection, of valued reciprocity, into the majestic position of a national glory. And yet it is in the presence of this obstacle to social contact that those who knew and loved him must address their farewell to him now. After all, it is difficult to see how the obstacle can be removed. He was the most generous, the most tender, the most delightful, of men; his large nature overflowed with the love of justice: but he also was of the stuff of which glories are made.

THE LIFE OF GEORGE ELIOT

THE WRITER of these pages has observed that the first question usually asked in relation to Mr. Cross's long-expected biography is whether the reader has not been disappointed in it. The inquirer is apt to be disappointed if the question be answered in the negative. It may as well be said, therefore, at the threshold of the following remarks, that such is not the feeling with which this particular reader laid down the book. The general feeling about it will depend very much on what has been looked for; there was probably, in advance, a considerable belief that we were to be treated to "revelations." I know not exactly why it should have been, but certain it is that the announcement of a biography of George Eliot has been construed more or less as a promise that we were to be admitted behind the scenes, as it were, of her life. No such result has taken place. We look at the drama from the point of view usually allotted to the public, and the curtain is lowered whenever it suits the biographer. The most "intimate" pages in the book are those in which the great novelist notes her derangements of health and depression of spirits. This history, to my sense, is quite as interesting as it might have been; that is, it is of the deepest interest, and one misses nothing that is characteristic or essential except perhaps a few more examples of the *vis comica* which made half the fortune of *Adam Bede* and *Silas Marner*. There is little that is absent that it would have been in Mr. Cross's power to give us. George Eliot's letters and journals are only a partial expression of her spirit, but they are evidently as full an expression as it was capable of giving itself when she was not wound up to the epic pitch. They do not explain her novels; they reflect in a singularly limited degree the process of growth of these great works; but it must be added that even a superficial acquaintance with the author was sufficient to assure one that her rich and complicated mind did not overflow in idle confidences. It was benignant and receptive in the highest degree, and nothing could have been more gracious than the manner of its intercourse; but it was deeply reserved and very far from egotistical, and nothing could have been less easy or agreeable to it, I surmise, than to attempt to tell people how, for instance, the plot of *Romola* got itself constructed or the character of Grandcourt got itself observed. There are critics who refuse to the delineator of this gentleman the title of a genius; who say that she had only a great talent overloaded with a great store of knowledge. The label, the epithet, matters little, but it is certain that George Eliot had this characteristic of the mind *possessed*: that the creations which brought her renown were of the incalculable kind, shaped themselves in mystery, in some intellectual back-shop or secret crucible, and were as little as possible implied in the aspect of her life. There is nothing more singular or striking in Mr. Cross's volumes than the absence of any indication, up to the time the *Scenes from Clerical Life* were published, that Miss Evans was a likely person to have written them; unless it be the absence of any indication, after they were published, that the deeply-studious, concentrated, home-keeping Mrs. Lewes was a likely person to have produced their successors. I know very well that there is no such thing in general as the air of the novelist, which it behoves those who practise this art to put on so that they may be recognised in public places; but there is such a thing as the air of the sage, the scholar, the philosopher, the votary of abstractions and of the lore of the ages, and in this pale but rich *Life* that is the face that is presented.

The plan on which it is composed is, so far as I know, without precedent, but it is a plan that could have occurred only to an "outsider" in literature, if I may venture to apply this term to one who has executed a literary task with such tact and success. The regular *littérateur*, hampered by tradition, would, I think, have lacked the boldness, the artless artfulness, of conjoining in the same text selected

morsels of letters and journals, so as to form a continuous and mul-
tifarious *talk*, on the writer's part, punctuated only by marginal names
and dates and divisions into chapters. There is something a little violent in the system, in spite of our feeling that it has been applied with
a supple hand; but it was probably the best that Mr. Cross could have
adopted, and it served especially well his purpose of appearing only
as an arranger, or rather of not appearing at all. The modesty, the
good taste, the self-effacement of the editorial element in the book
are, in a word, complete, and the clearness and care of arrangement,
the accuracy of reference, leave nothing to be desired. The form Mr.
Cross has chosen, or invented, becomes, in the application, highly
agreeable, and his rule of omission (for we have, almost always, only
parts and passages of letters) has not prevented his volumes from
being as copious as we could wish. George Eliot was not a great letter-
writer, either in quantity or quality; she had neither the spirit, the
leisure, nor the lightness of mind to conjure with the epistolary pen,
and after her union with George Henry Lewes her disposition to play
with it was further damped by his quick activity in her service.
Letter-writing was part of the trouble he saved her; in this as in other
ways he interposed between the world and his sensitive companion.
The difference is striking between her habits in this respect and those
of Madame George Sand, whose correspondence has lately been collected into six closely-printed volumes which testify afresh to her
extraordinary energy and facility. Madame Sand, however, indefatigable producer as she was, was not a woman of study; she lived from
day to day, from hand to mouth (intellectually), as it were, and had
no general plan of life and culture. Her English compeer took the
problem of production more seriously; she distilled her very substance
into the things she gave the world. There was therefore so much the
less of it left for casual utterance.

It was not till Marian Evans was past thirty, indeed, that she became an author by profession, and it may accordingly be supposed
that her early letters are those which take us most into her confidence.
This is true of those written when she was on the threshold of wom-
anhood, which form a very full expression of her feelings at the time.

The drawback here is that the feelings themselves are rather wanting in interest—one may almost say in amiability. At the age of twenty Marian Evans was a deeply religious young woman, whose faith took the form of a narrow evangelicism. Religious, in a manner, she remained to the end of her life, in spite of her adoption of a scientific explanation of things; but in the year 1839 she thought it ungodly to go to concerts and to read novels. She writes to her former governess that she can "only sigh" when she hears of the "marrying and giving in marriage that is constantly transacted"; expresses enjoyment of Hannah More's letters ("the contemplation of so blessed a character as hers is very salutary"); wishes that she "might be more useful in her own obscure and lowly station" ("I feel myself to be a mere cumberer of the ground"), that she "might seek to be sanctified wholly." These first fragments of her correspondence, first glimpses of her mind, are very curious; they have nothing in common with the later ones but the deep seriousness of the tone. Serious, of course, George Eliot continued to be to the end; the sense of moral responsibility, of the sadness and difficulty of life, was the most inveterate part of her nature. But the provincial strain in the letters from which I have quoted is very marked: they reflect a meagreness and grayness of outward circumstance; have a tinge as of Dissent in a small English town, where there are brick chapels in back streets. This was only a moment in her development; but there is something touching in the contrast between such a state of mind and that of the woman before whom, at middle age, all the culture of the world unrolled itself, and towards whom fame and fortune, and an activity which at the earlier period she would have thought very profane, pressed with rapidity. In 1839, as I have said, she thought very meanly of the art in which she was to attain such distinction. "I venture to believe that the same causes which exist in my own breast to render novels and romances pernicious have their counterpart in every fellow-creature.... The weapons of Christian warfare were never sharpened at the forge of romance." The style of these pietistic utterances is singularly strenuous and hard; the light and familiar are absent from them, and I think it is not too much to say that they show scarcely a single premonitory ray of the genius which had *Silas Marner* in reserve. This dryness was only a phase, indeed; it was speedily dispelled by more abundant showers of emotion—by the overflow of perception. Premonitory rays are still absent, however, after her first asceticism passes away—a change apparently coincident with her removal from the country to the pleasant old town of Coventry, where all American pilgrims to midland shrines go and murmur Tennyson on the bridge. After the evangelical note began to fade it was still the desire for faith (a faith which could reconcile human affection with some of the un-amiable truths of science), still the religious idea that coloured her thought; not the love of human life as a spectacle, nor the desire to spread the wings of the artist. It must be remembered, though, that during these years, if she was not stimulating prophecy in any definite form she was inhaling those impressions which were to make her first books so full of the delightful midland quality, the air of old-fashioned provincialism. The first piece of literary work she attempted (and she brought it to the best conclusion), was a translation of Strauss's *Life of Jesus*, which she began in 1844, when she was not yet twenty-five years of age; a task which indicates not only the persistence of her religious preoccupations, as well as the higher form they took, but the fact that with the limited facilities afforded by her life at that time she had mastered one of the most difficult of foreign languages and the vocabulary of a German exegetist. In 1841 she thought it wrong to encourage novels, but in 1847 she confesses to reading George Sand with great delight. There is no exhibition in Mr. Cross's pages of the steps by which she passed over to a position of tolerant scepti-cism; but the details of the process are after all of minor importance: the essential fact is that the change was predetermined by the nature of her mind.

The great event of her life was of course her acquaintance with George Henry Lewes. I say "of course," because this relation had an importance even more controlling than the publication and success of her first attempt at fiction, inasmuch as it was in consequence of Mr. Lewes's friendly urgency that she wrote the *Scenes of Clerical Life*. She met him for the first time in London, in the autumn of 1851;

but it was not till the summer of 1854 that the connection with him began (it was marked to the world by their going to spend together several months in Germany, where he was bent on researches for his *Life of Goethe*), which was to become so much closer than many formal marriages and to last till his death in 1878. The episode of Miss Evans's life in London during these three years was already tolerably well known. She had become by this time a professional literary woman, and had regular work as assistant editor of the *Westminster Review*, to which she gave her most conscientious attention. Her accomplishments now were wide. She was a linguist, a copious reader, an earnest student of history and philosophy. She wrote much for her magazine as well as solicited articles from others, and several of her contributions are contained in the volume of essays published after her death—essays of which it is fair to say that they give but a faint intimation of her latent powers. George Henry Lewes was a versatile, hard-working journalist, with a tendency, apparently, of the drifting sort; and after having been made acquainted with each other by Mr. Herbert Spencer, the pair commingled their sympathies and their efforts. Her letters, at this season, contain constant mention of Lewes (one allusion to the effect that he "has quite won my regard, after having had a good deal of my vituperation"); she takes an interest in his health and corrects his proofs for him when he is absent. It was impossible for Mr. Lewes to marry, as he had a wife living, from whom he was separated. He had also three children, of whom the care did not devolve upon their mother. The union Miss Evans formed with him was a deliberate step, of which she accepted all the consequences. These consequences were excellent, so far as the world is at liberty to judge, save in an important particular. This particular is the fact that her false position, as we may call it, produced upon George Eliot's life a certain effect of sequestration which was not favourable to social freedom, or to freedom of observation, and which excited on the part of her companion a protecting, sheltering, fostering, precautionary attitude—the assumption that they lived in special, in abnormal conditions. It would be too much to say that George Eliot had not the courage of the situation she had embraced, but she had, at least, not the levity, the indifference; she was unable, in the premises, to be sufficiently superficial. Her deep, strenuous, much-considering mind, of which the leading mark is the capacity for a sort of luminous brooding, fed upon the idea of her irregularity with an intensity which doubtless only her magnificent intellectual activity and Lewes's brilliancy and ingenuity kept from being morbid. The fault of most of her work is the absence of spontaneity, the excess of reflection; and by her action in 1854 (which seemed superficially to be of the sort usually termed reckless), she committed herself to being nothing if not reflective, to cultivating a kind of compensatory earnestness. Her earnestness, her educated conscience, her exalted sense of responsibility, were coloured by her peculiar position; they committed her to a plan of life, of study, in which the accidental, the unexpected, were too little allowed for, and this is what I mean by speaking of her sequestration. If her relations with the world had been easier, in a word, her books would have been less difficult. Mr. Cross, very justly, merely touches upon this question of her forming a tie which was deprived of the sanction of the law; but he gives a portion of a letter written to Mrs. Bray more than a year after it had begun, which sufficiently indicates the serenity of her resolution. Repentance, of course, she never had—the success of her experiment was too rare and complete for that; and I do not mean that her attitude was ever for a moment apologetic. On the contrary, it was only too superabundantly confirmatory. Her effort was to pitch her life ever in the key of the superior wisdom that made her say to Mrs. Bray, in the letter of September 1855, "That any unwordly, unsuperstitious person who is sufficiently acquainted with the realities of life can pronounce my relation to Mr. Lewes immoral, I can only understand when I remember how subtle and complex are the influences that mould opinion." I need not attempt to project the light of criticism on this particular case of conscience; there remains ever, in the mutual relations of intelligent men and women, an element which is for themselves alone to consider. One reflection, however, forces itself upon the mind: if the connection had not taken place we should have lost the spectacle and influence of one of the most successful partnerships presented to us in the history of human affection. There has been much talk about George Eliot's "example," which is not to be deprecated so long as it is remembered that in speaking of the example of a woman of this value we can only mean example for good. Exemplary indeed in her long connection with George Henry Lewes were the qualities on which beneficent intimacy rests.

She was thirty-seven years old when the *Scenes from Clerical Life* were published, but this work opened wide for her the door of success, and fame and fortune came to her rapidly. Her union with Lewes had been a union of poverty: there is a sentence in her journal, of the year 1856, which speaks of their ascending certain cliffs called the Tors, at Ilfracombe, "only twice; for a tax of 3d. per head was demanded for this luxury, and we could not afford a sixpenny walk very frequently." The incentive to writing *Amos Barton* seems to have been mainly pecuniary. There was an urgent need to make money, and it appears to have been agreed between the pair that there was at least no harm in the lady's trying her hand at a story. Lewes professed a belief that she would really do something in this line, while she, more sceptical, reserved her judgment till after the test. The *Scenes from Clerical Life* were therefore pre-eminently an empirical work of fiction. With the sending of the first episode to the late Mr. John Blackwood for approval, there opened a relation between publisher and author which lasted to the end, and which was probably more genial and unclouded than any in the annals of literature, as well as almost unprecedentedly lucrative to both parties. This first book of George Eliot's has little of the usual air of a first book, none of the crudity of an early attempt; it was not the work of a youthful person, and one sees that the material had been long in her mind. The ripeness, the pathos, a sort of considered quality, are as striking to-day as when *Amos Barton* and *Janet's Repentance* were published, and enable us to understand that people should have asked themselves with surprise, at that time, who it was, in the midst of them, that had been taking notes so long and so wisely without giving a sign. *Adam Bede*, written rapidly, appeared in 1859, and George Eliot found herself a consummate novelist without having suspected it. The book was an immense, a brilliant success, and from this moment the author's life took its definite and final direction. She accepted the great obligations which to her mind belonged to a person who had the ear of the public, and her whole effort thenceforth was highly to respond to them— to respond to them by teaching, by vivid moral illustration and even by direct exhortation. It is striking that from the first her conception of the novelist's task is never in the least as the game of art. The most interesting passage in Mr. Cross's volumes is to my sense a simple sentence in a short entry in her journal in the year 1859, just after she had finished the first volume of *The Mill on the Floss* (the original title of which, by the way, had been *Sister Maggie*): "We have just finished reading aloud Père Goriot, a hateful book." That Balzac's masterpiece should have elicited from her only this remark, at a time, too, when her mind might have been opened to it by her own activity of composition, is significant of so many things that the few words are, in the whole *Life*, those I should have been most sorry to lose. Of course they are not all George Eliot would have had to say about Balzac, if some other occasion than a simple jotting in a diary had presented itself. Still, what even a jotting may *not* have said after a first perusal of *Le Père Goriot* is eloquent; it illuminates the author's general attitude with regard to the novel, which, for her, was not primarily a picture of life, capable of deriving a high value from its form, but a moralised fable, the last word of a philosophy endeavouring to teach by example.

This is a very noble and defensible view, and one must speak respectfully of any theory of work which would produce such fruit as *Romola* and *Middlemarch*. But it testifies to that side of George Eliot's nature which was weakest—the absence of free aesthetic life (I venture this remark in the face of a passage quoted from one of her letters in Mr. Cross's third volume); it gives the hand, as it were, to several other instances that may be found in the same pages. "My function is that of the *aesthetic*, not the doctrinal teacher; the rousing of the nobler emotions, which make mankind desire the social right, not the prescribing of special measures, concerning which the artistic mind, however strongly moved by social sympathy, is often not the best judge." That is the passage referred to in my parenthetic allusion, and it is a good general description of the manner in which George Eliot may be said to have acted on her generation; but the "artistic mind," the possession of which it implies, existed in her with limitations remarkable in a writer whose imagination was so rich. We feel in her, always, that she proceeds from the abstract to the concrete; that her figures and situations are evolved, as the phrase is, from her moral consciousness, and are only indirectly the products of observation. They are deeply studied and massively supported, but they are not *seen*, in the irresponsible plastic way. The world was, first and foremost, for George Eliot, the moral, the intellectual world; the personal spectacle came after; and lovingly humanly as she regarded it we constantly feel that she cares for the things she finds in it only so far as they are types. The philosophic door is always open, on her stage, and we are aware that the somewhat cooling draught of ethical purpose draws across it. This constitutes half the beauty of her work; the constant reference to ideas may be an excellent source of one kind of reality—for, after all, the secret of seeing a thing well is not necessarily that you see nothing else. Her preoccupation with the universe helped to make her characters strike you as also belonging to it; it raised the roof, widened the area, of her aesthetic structure. Nothing is finer, in her genius, than the combination of her love of general truth and love of the special case; without this, indeed, we should not have heard of her as a novelist, for the passion of the special case is surely the basis of the story-teller's art. All the same, that little sign of all that Balzac failed to suggest to her showed at what perils the special case got itself considered. Such dangers increased as her activity proceeded, and many judges perhaps hold that in her ultimate work, in *Middlemarch* and *Daniel Deronda* (especially the latter), it ceased to be considered at all. Such critics assure us that Gwendolen and Grandcourt, Deronda and Myra, are not concrete images, but disembodied types, pale abstractions, signs and symbols of a "great lesson." I give up Deronda and Myra to the objector, but Grandcourt and Gwendolen seem to me to have a kind of superior reality; to be, in a high degree, what one demands of a figure in a novel, planted on their legs and complete.

The truth is, perception and reflection, at the outset, divided George Eliot's great talent between them; but as time went on circumstances led the latter to develop itself at the expense of the former—one of these circumstances being apparently the influence of George Henry Lewes. Lewes was interested in science, in cosmic problems; and though his companion, thanks to the original bent of her versatile, powerful mind, needed no impulse from without to turn herself to speculation, yet the contagion of his studies pushed her further than she would otherwise have gone in the direction of scientific observation, which is but another form of what I have called reflection. Her early novels are full of natural as distinguished from systematic observation, though even in them it is less the dominant note, I think, than the love of the "moral," the reaction of thought in the face of the human comedy. They had observation sufficient, at any rate, to make their fortune, and it may well be said that that is enough for any novel. In *Silas Marner*, in *Adam Bede*, the quality seems gilded by a sort of autumn haze, an afternoon light, of meditation, which mitigates the sharpness of portraiture. I doubt very much whether the author herself had a clear vision, for instance, of the marriage of Dinah Morris to Adam, or of the rescue of Hetty from the scaffold at the eleventh hour. The reason of this may be, indeed, that her perception was a perception of nature much more than of art, and that these particular incidents do not belong to nature (to my sense at least); by which I do not mean that they belong to a very happy art. I cite them, on the contrary, as an evidence of artistic weakness; they are a very good example of the view in which a story must have marriages and rescues in the nick of time, as a matter of course. I must add, in fairness to George Eliot, that the marriage of the nun-like Dinah, which shocks the reader, who sees in it a base concession, was a *trouvaille* of Lewes's and is a small sign of that same faulty judgment in literary things which led him to throw his influence on the side of her writing verse—verse which is *all* reflection, with direct, vivifying vision, or emotion, remarkably absent.

It is a part of this same limitation of the pleasure she was capable of taking in the fact of representation for itself that the various journals and notes of her visits to the Continent are, though by no means destitute of the tempered enjoyment of foreign sights which was as near as she ever came to rapture, singularly vague in expression on the subject of the general and particular spectacle—the life and manners, the works of art. She enumerates diligently all the pictures and statues she sees, and the way she does so is a proof of her active, earnest intellectual habits; but it is rarely apparent that they have said much to her, or that what they have said is one of their deeper secrets. She is capable of writing, after coming out of the great chapel of San Lorenzo, in Florence, that "the world-famous statues of Michael Angelo on the tombs . . . remained to us as affected and exaggerated in the original as in copies and casts." That sentence startles one, on the part of the author of *Romola*, and that Mr. Cross should have printed it is a commendable proof of his impartiality.

It was in *Romola*, precisely, that the equilibrium I spoke of just now was lost, and that reflection began to weigh down the scale. *Romola* is preeminently a study of the human conscience in an historical setting which is studied almost as much, and few passages in Mr. Cross's volumes are more interesting than those relating to the production of this magnificent romance. George Eliot took all her work with a noble seriousness, but into none of it did she throw herself with more passion. It drained from her as much as she gave to it, and none of her writing ploughed into her, to use her biographer's expression, so deeply. She told him that she began it a young woman and finished it an old one. More than any of her novels it was evolved, as I have said, from her moral consciousness—a moral consciousness encircled by a prodigious amount of literary research. Her literary ideal was at all times of the highest, but in the preparation of *Romola* it placed her under a control absolutely religious. She read innumerable books, some of them bearing only remotely on her subject, and consulted without stint contemporary records and documents. She neglected nothing that would enable her to live, intellectually, in the period she had undertaken to describe. We know, for the most part, I think, the result. *Romola* is on the whole the finest thing she wrote, but its defects are almost on the scale of its beauties. The great defect is that, except in the person of Tito Melema, it does not seem positively to live. It is overladen with learning, it smells of the lamp, it tastes just perceptibly of pedantry. In spite of its want of blood, however, it assuredly will survive in men's remembrance, for the finest pages in it belong to the finest part of our literature. It is on the whole a failure, but such a failure as only a great talent can produce; and one may say of it that there are many great "hits" far less interesting than such a mistake. A twentieth part of the erudition would have sufficed, would have given us the feeling and colour of the time, if there had been more of the breath of the Florentine streets, more of the faculty of optical evocation, a greater saturation of the senses with the elements of the adorable little city. The difficulty with the book, for the most part, is that it is not Italian; it has always seemed to me the most Germanic of the author's productions. I cannot imagine a German writing (in the way of a novel) anything half so good; but if I could imagine it I should suppose *Romola* to be very much the sort of picture he would achieve—the sort of medium through which he would show us how, by the Arno-side, the fifteenth century came to an end. One of the sources of interest in the book is that, more than any of its companions, it indicates how much George Eliot proceeded by reflection and research; how little important, comparatively, she thought that same breath of the streets. It carries to a maximum the in-door quality.

The most definite impression produced, perhaps, by Mr. Cross's volumes (by the second and third) is that of simple success—success which had been the result of no external accidents (unless her union with Lewes be so denominated), but was involved in the very faculties nature had given her. All the elements of an eventual happy fortune met in her constitution. The great foundation, to begin with, was there—the magnificent mind, vigorous, luminous, and eminently sane. To her intellectual vigour, her immense facility, her exemption from cerebral lassitude, her letters and journals bear the most copious testimony. Her daily stint of arduous reading and writing was of the largest. Her ability, as one may express it in the most general way, was astonishing, and it belonged to every season of her long and fruitful career. Her passion for study encountered no impediment, but was able to make everything feed and support it. The extent and variety of her knowledge is by itself the measure of a capacity which triumphed wherever it wished. Add to this an immense special talent which, as soon as it tries its wings, is found to be adequate to the highest, longest flights and brings back great material rewards. George Eliot of course had drawbacks and difficulties, physical infirmities, constant liabilities to headache, dyspepsia, and other illness, to deep depression, to despair about her work; but these jolts of the chariot were small in proportion to the impetus acquired, and were hardly greater than was necessary for reminding her of the secret of all ambitious workers in the field of art—that effort, effort, always effort, is the only key to success. Her great furtherance was that, intensely intellectual being as she was, the life of affection and emotion was also widely open to her. She had all the initiation of knowledge and none of its dryness, all the advantages of judgment and all the luxuries of feeling. She had an imagination which enabled her to sit at home with book and pen, and yet enter into the life of other generations; project herself into Warwickshire ale-houses and Florentine symposia, reconstitute conditions utterly different from her own. Toward the end she triumphed over the great impossible; she reconciled the greatest sensibility with the highest serenity. She succeeded in guarding her pursuits from intrusion; in carrying out her habits; in sacrificing her work as little as possible; in leading, in the midst of a society united in conspiracies to interrupt and vulgarise, an independent, strenuously personal life. People who had the honour of penetrating into the sequestered precinct of the Priory—the house in London in which she lived from 1863 to 1880—remember well a kind of sanctity in the place, an atmosphere of stillness and concentration, something that suggested a literary temple.

It was part of the good fortune of which I speak that in Mr. Lewes she had found the most devoted of caretakers, the most jealous of ministers, a companion through whom all business was transacted. The one drawback of this relation was that, considering what she attempted, it limited her experience too much to itself; but for the rest it helped her in a hundred ways—it saved her nerves, it fortified her privacy, it protected her leisure, it diminished the friction of living. His admiration of her work was of the largest, though not always, I think, truly discriminating, and he surrounded her with a sort of temperate zone of independence—independence of everything except him and her own standards. Nervous, sensitive, delicate in every way in which genius is delicate (except, indeed, that she had a robust reason), it was a great thing for her to have accident made rare and exposure mitigated; and to this result Lewes, as the administrator of her fame, admirably contributed. He filtered the stream, giving her only the clearer water. The accident of reading reviews of one's productions, especially when they are bad, is, for the artist of our day, one of the most frequent; and Mr. Lewes, by keeping these things out of her way, enabled her to achieve what was perhaps the highest form of her success—an inaccessibility to the newspaper. "It is remarkable to me," she writes in 1876, "that I have entirely lost my *personal* melancholy. I often, of course, have melancholy thoughts about the destinies of my fellow creatures, but I am never in that *mood* of sadness which used to be my frequent visitant even in the midst of external happiness." Her later years, coloured by this accumulated wisdom, when she had taken her final form before the world and had come to be regarded more and more as a teacher and philosopher, are full of suggestion to the critic, but have exhausted my limited space. There is a certain coldness in them perhaps—the coldness that results from most of one's opinions being formed, one's mind made up, on many great subjects; from the degree, in a word, to which "culture" had taken the place of the more primitive processes of experience.

"Ah, les livres, ils nous débordent, ils nous étouffent—nous périssons par les livres!" That cry of a distinguished French novelist (there is no harm in mentioning M. Alphonse Daudet), which fell upon the ear of the present writer some time ago, represents as little as possible the emotion of George Eliot confronted with literatures and sciences. M. Alphonse Daudet went on to say that, to his mind, the personal impression, the effort of direct observation, was the most precious source of information for the novelist; that nothing could take its place; that the effect of books was constantly to check and pervert this effort; that a second-hand, third-hand, tenth-hand, impression was constantly tending to substitute itself for a fresh perception; that we were ending by seeing everything through literature instead of through our own senses; and that in short literature was rapidly killing literature. This view has immense truth on its side, but the case would be too simple if, on one side or the other, there were only one way of finding out. The effort of the novelist is to find out, to know, or at least to see, and no one, in the nature of things, can less afford to be indifferent to sidelights. Books are themselves, unfortunately, an expression of human passions. George Eliot had no doubts, at any rate; if impressionism, before she laid down her pen, had already begun to be talked about, it would have made no difference with her—she would have had no desire to pass for an impressionist.

There is one question we cannot help asking ourselves as we close this record of her life; it is impossible not to let our imagination wander in the direction of what turn her mind or her fortune might have taken if she had never met George Henry Lewes, or never cast her lot with his. It is safe to say that, in one way or another, in the long run, her novels would have got themselves written, and it is possible they would have been more natural, as one may call it, more familiarly and casually human. Would her development have been less systematic, more irresponsible, more personal, and should we have had more of *Adam Bede* and *Silas Marner* and less of *Romola* and *Middlemarch*? The question, after all, cannot be answered, and I do not push it, being myself very grateful for *Middlemarch* and *Romola*. It is as George Eliot does actually present herself that we must judge her—a condition that will not prevent her from striking us as one of the noblest, most beautiful minds of our time. This impression bears the reader company throughout these letters and notes. It is impossible not to feel, as we close them, that she was an admirable being. They are less brilliant, less entertaining, than we might have hoped; they contain fewer "good things" and have even a certain grayness of tone, something measured and subdued, as of a person talking without ever raising her voice. But there rises from them a kind of fragrance of moral elevation; a love of justice, truth, and light; a large, generous way of looking at things; and a constant effort to hold high the torch in the dusky spaces of man's conscience. That is how we see her during the latter years of her life: frail, delicate, shivering a little, much fatigued and considerably spent, but still meditating on what could be acquired and imparted; still living, in the intelligence, a freer, larger life than probably had ever been the portion of any woman. To her own sex her memory, her example, will remain of the highest value; those of them for whom the "development" of woman is the hope of the future ought to erect a monument to George Eliot. She helped on the cause more than any one, in proving how few limitations are of necessity implied in the feminine organism. She went so far that such a distance seems enough, and in her effort she sacrificed no tenderness, no grace. There is much talk to-day about things being "open to women"; but George Eliot showed that there is nothing that is closed. If we criticise her novels we must remember that her nature came first and her work afterwards, and that it is not remarkable they should not resemble the productions, say, of Alexandre Dumas. What *is* remarkable, extraordinary—and the process remains inscrutable and mysterious—is that this quiet, anxious, sedentary, serious, invalidical English lady, without animal spirits, without adventures or sensations, should have made us believe that nothing in the world was alien to her; should have produced such rich, deep, masterly pictures of the multiform life of man.

EMERSON

MR. ELLIOT Cabot has made a very interesting contribution to a class of books of which our literature, more than any other, offers admirable examples: he has given us a biography intelligently and carefully composed. These two volumes are a model of responsible editing—I use that term because they consist largely of letters and extracts from letters: nothing could resemble less the manner in which the mere bookmaker strings together his frequently questionable pearls and shovels the heap into the presence of the public. Mr. Cabot has selected, compared, discriminated, steered an even course between meagreness and redundancy, and managed to be constantly and happily illustrative. And his work, moreover, strikes us as the better done from the fact that it stands for one of the two things that make an absorbing memoir a good deal more than for the other. If these two things be the conscience of the writer and the career of his hero, it is not difficult to see on which side the biographer of Emerson has found himself strongest. Ralph Waldo Emerson was a man of genius, but he led for nearly eighty years a life in which the sequence of events had little of the rapidity, or the complexity, that a spectator loves. There is something we miss very much as we turn these pages—something that has a kind of accidental, inevitable presence in almost any personal record—something that may be most definitely indicated under the name of colour. We lay down the book with a singular impression of paleness—an impression that comes partly from the tone of the biographer and partly from the moral complexion of his subject, but mainly from the vacancy of the page itself. That of Emerson's personal history is condensed into the single word Concord, and all the condensation in the world will not make it look rich. It presents a most continuous surface. Mr. Matthew Arnold, in his *Discourses in America*, contests Emerson's complete right to the title of a man of letters; yet letters surely were the very texture of his history. Passions, alternations, affairs, adventures had absolutely no part in it. It stretched itself out in enviable quiet—a quiet in which we hear the jotting of the pencil in the notebook. It is the very life for literature (I mean for one's own, not that of another): fifty years of residence in the home of one's forefathers, pervaded by reading, by walking in the woods and the daily addition of sentence to sentence.

If the interest of Mr. Cabot's pencilled portrait is incontestable and yet does not spring from variety, it owes nothing either to a source from which it might have borrowed much and which it is impossible not to regret a little that he has so completely neglected: I mean a greater reference to the social conditions in which Emerson moved, the company he lived in, the moral air he breathed. If his biographer had allowed himself a little more of the ironic touch, had put himself once in a way under the protection of Sainte-Beuve and had attempted something of a general picture, we should have felt that he only went with the occasion. I may over-estimate the latent treasures of the field, but it seems to me there was distinctly an opportunity—an opportunity to make up moreover in some degree for the white tint of Emerson's career considered simply in itself. We know a man imperfectly until we know his society, and we but half know a society until we know its manners. This is especially true of a man of letters, for manners lie very close to literature. From those of the New England world in which Emerson's character formed itself Mr. Cabot almost averts his lantern, though we feel sure that there would have been delightful glimpses to be had and that he would have been in a position—that is that he has all the knowledge that would enable him—to help us to them. It is as if he could not trust himself, knowing the subject only too well. This adds to the effect of extreme discretion that we find in his volumes, but it is the cause of our not finding certain things, certain figures and scenes, evoked. What is evoked is Emerson's pure spirit, by a copious, sifted series of citations and comments. But we must read as much as possible between the lines, and the picture of the transcendental time (to mention simply one corner) has yet to be painted—the lines have yet to be bitten in. Meanwhile we are held and charmed by the image of Emerson's mind and the extreme appeal which his physiognomy makes to our art of discrimination. It is so fair, so uniform and impersonal, that its features are simply fine shades, the gradations of tone of a surface whose proper quality was of the smoothest and on which nothing was reflected with violence. It is a pleasure of the critical sense to find, with Mr. Cabot's extremely intelligent help, a notation for such delicacies.

We seem to see the circumstances of our author's origin, immediate and remote, in a kind of high, vertical moral light, the brightness of a society at once very simple and very responsible. The rare singleness that was in his nature (so that he was *all* the warning moral voice, without distraction or counter-solicitation), was also in the stock he sprang from, clerical for generations, on both sides, and clerical in the Puritan sense. His ancestors had lived long (for nearly two centuries) in the same corner of New England, and during that period had preached and studied and prayed and practised. It is impossible to imagine a spirit better prepared in advance to be exactly what it was—better educated for its office in its far-away unconscious beginnings. There is an inner satisfaction in seeing so straight, although so patient, a connection between the stem and the flower, and such a proof that when life wishes to produce something exquisite in quality she takes her measures many years in advance. A conscience like Emerson's could not have been turned off, as it were, from one generation to another: a succession of attempts, a long process of refining, was required. His perfection, in his own line, comes largely from the non-interruption of the process.

As most of us are made up of ill-assorted pieces, his reader, and Mr. Cabot's, envies him this transmitted unity, in which there was no mutual hustling or crowding of elements. It must have been a kind of luxury to be—that is to feel—so homogeneous, and it helps to account for his serenity, his power of acceptance, and that absence of personal passion which makes his private correspondence read like a series of beautiful circulars or expanded cards *pour prendre congé*. He had the equanimity of a result; nature had taken care of him and he had only to speak. He accepted himself as he accepted others, accepted everything; and his absence of eagerness, or in other words his modesty, was that of a man with whom it is not a question of success, who has nothing invested or at stake. The investment, the stake, was that of the race, of all the past Emersons and Bulkeleys and Waldos. There is much that makes us smile, to-day, in the commotion produced by his secession from the mild Unitarian pulpit: we wonder at a condition of opinion in which any utterance of his should appear to be wanting in superior piety—in the essence of good instruction. All that is changed: the great difference has become the infinitely small, and we admire a state of society in which scandal and schism took on no darker hue; but there is even yet a sort of drollery in the spectacle of a body of people among whom the author of *The American Scholar* and of the Address of 1838 at the Harvard Divinity College passed for profane, and who failed to see that he only gave his plea for the spiritual life the advantage of a brilliant expression. They were so provincial as to think that brilliancy came ill-recommended, and they were shocked at his ceasing to care for the prayer and the sermon. They might have perceived that he *was* the prayer and the sermon: not in the least a seculariser, but in his own subtle insinuating way a sanctifier.

Of the three periods into which his life divides itself, the first was (as in the case of most men) that of movement, experiment and selection—that of effort too and painful probation. Emerson had his message, but he was a good while looking for his form—the form which, as he himself would have said, he never completely found and of which it was rather characteristic of him that his later years (with their growing refusal to give him the *word*), wishing to attack him in his most vulnerable point, where his tenure was least complete, had in some degree the effect of despoiling him. It all sounds rather bare and stern, Mr. Cabot's account of his youth and early manhood, and we get an impression of a terrible paucity of alternatives. If he would be neither a farmer nor a trader he could "teach school"; that was the main resource and a part of the general educative process of the young New Englander who proposed to devote himself to the things of the mind. There was an advantage in the nudity, however, which was that, in Emerson's case at least, the things of the mind did get themselves admirably well considered. If it be his great distinction and his special sign that he had a more vivid conception of the moral life than any one else, it is probably not fanciful to say that he owed it in part to the limited way in which he saw our capacity for living illustrated. The plain, God-fearing, practical society which surrounded him was not fertile in variations: it had great intelligence and energy, but it moved altogether in the straightforward direction. On three occasions later—three journeys to Europe—he was introduced to a more complicated world; but his spirit, his moral taste, as it were, abode always within the undecorated walls of his youth. There he could dwell with that ripe unconsciousness of evil which is one of the most beautiful signs by which we know him. His early writings are full of quaint animadversion upon the vices of the place and time, but there is something charmingly vague, light and general in the arraignment. Almost the worst he can say is that these vices are negative and that his fellow-townsmen are not heroic. We feel that his first impressions were gathered in a community from which misery and extravagance, and either extreme, of any sort, were equally absent. What the life of New England fifty years ago offered to the observer was the common lot, in a kind of achromatic picture, without particular intensifications. It was from this table of the usual, the merely typical joys and sorrows that he proceeded to generalise—a fact that accounts in some degree for a certain inadequacy and thinness in his enumerations. But it helps to account also for his direct, intimate vision of the soul itself—not in its emotions, its contortions and perversions, but in its passive, exposed, yet healthy form. He knows the nature of man and the long tradition of its dangers; but we feel that whereas he can put his finger on the remedies, lying for the most part, as they do, in the deep recesses of virtue, of the spirit, he has only a kind of hearsay, uninformed acquaintance with the disorders. It would require some ingenuity, the reader may say too much, to trace closely this correspondence between his genius and the frugal, dutiful, happy but decidedly lean Boston of the past, where there was a great deal of will but very little fulcrum—like a ministry without an opposition.

The genius itself it seems to me impossible to contest—I mean the genius for seeing character as a real and supreme thing. Other writers have arrived at a more complete expression: Wordsworth and Goethe, for instance, give one a sense of having found their form, whereas with Emerson we never lose the sense that he is still seeking it. But no one has had so steady and constant, and above all so natural, a vision of what we require and what we are capable of in the way of aspiration and independence. With Emerson it is ever the special capacity for moral experience—always that and only that. We have the impression, somehow, that life had never bribed him to look at anything but the soul; and indeed in the world in which he grew up and lived the bribes and lures, the beguilements and prizes, were few. He was in an admirable position for showing, what he constantly endeavoured to show, that the prize was within. Any one who in New England at that time could do that was sure of success, of listeners and sympathy: most of all, of course, when it was a question of doing it with such a divine persuasiveness. Moreover, the way in which Emerson did it added to the charm—by word of mouth, face to face, with a rare, irresistible voice and a beautiful mild, modest authority. If Mr. Arnold is struck with the limited degree in which he was a man of letters I suppose it is because he is more struck with his having been, as it were, a man of lectures. But the lecture surely was never more purged of its grossness—the quality in it that suggests a strong light and a big brush—than as it issued from Emerson's lips; so far from being a vulgarisation, it was simply the esoteric made audible, and instead of treating the few as the many, after the usual fashion of gentlemen on platforms, he treated the many as the few. There was probably no other society at that time in which he would have got so many persons to understand that; for we think the better of his audience as we read him, and wonder where else people would have had so much moral attention to give. It is to be remembered however that during the winter of 1847–48, on the occasion of his second visit to England, he found many listeners in London and in provincial cities. Mr. Cabot's volumes are full of evidence of the satisfactions he offered, the delights and revelations he may be said to have promised, to a race which had to seek its entertainment, its rewards and consolations, almost exclusively in the moral world. But his own writings are fuller still; we find an instance almost wherever we open them.

> All these great and transcendent properties are ours.... Let us find room for this great guest in our small houses.... Where the heart is, there the muses, there the gods sojourn, and not in any geography of fame. Massachusetts, Connecticut River, and Boston Bay, you think paltry places, and the ear loves names of foreign and classic topography. But here we are, and if we will tarry a little we may come to learn that here is best.... The Jerseys were handsome enough ground for Washington to tread, and London streets for the feet of Milton.... That country is fairest which is inhabited by the noblest minds.

We feel, or suspect, that Milton is thrown in as a hint that the London streets are no such great place, and it all sounds like a sort of pleading consolation against bleakness.

The beauty of a hundred passages of this kind in Emerson's pages is that they are effective, that they do come home, that they rest upon insight and not upon ingenuity, and that if they are sometimes obscure it is never with the obscurity of paradox. We seem to see the people turning out into the snow after hearing them, glowing with a finer glow than even the climate could give and fortified for a struggle with overshoes and the east wind.

> Look to it first and only, that fashion, custom, authority, plea-sure, and money, are nothing to you, are not as bandages over your eyes, that you cannot see; but live with the privilege of the immeasurable mind. Not too anxious to visit periodically all

families and each family in your parish connection, when you meet one of these men or women be to them a divine man; be to them thought and virtue; let their timid aspirations find in you a friend; let their trampled instincts be genially tempted out in your atmosphere; let their doubts know that you have doubted, and their wonder feel that you have wondered.

When we set against an exquisite passage like that, or like the familiar sentences that open the essay on History ("He that is admitted to the right of reason is made freeman of the whole estate. What Plato has thought, he may think; what a saint has felt, he may feel; what at any time has befallen any man, he can understand"); when we compare the letters, cited by Mr. Cabot, to his wife from Springfield, Illinois (January 1853) we feel that his spiritual tact needed to be very just, but that if it was so it must have brought a blessing.

Here I am in the deep mud of the prairies, misled I fear into this bog, not by a will-of-the-wisp, such as shine in bogs, but by a young New Hampshire editor, who over-estimated the strength of both of us, and fancied I should glitter in the prairie and draw the prairie birds and waders. It rains and thaws incessantly, and if we step off the short street we go up to the shoulders, perhaps, in mud. My chamber is a cabin; my fellow-boarders are legislators.... Two or three governors or ex-governors live in the house.... I cannot command daylight and solitude for study or for more than a scrawl....

And another extract:—

A cold, raw country this, and plenty of night-travelling and arriving at four in the morning to take the last and worst bed in the tavern. Advancing day brings mercy and favour to me, but not the sleep.... Mercury 15° below zero.... I find well-disposed, kindly people among these sinewy farmers of the North, but in all that is called cultivation they are only ten years old.

He says in another letter (in 1860), "I saw Michigan and its forests and the Wolverines pretty thoroughly"; and on another page Mr. Cabot shows him as speaking of his engagements to lecture in the West as the obligation to "wade, and freeze, and ride, and run, and suffer all manner of indignities." This was not New England, but as regards the country districts throughout, at that time, it was a question of degree. Certainly never was the fine wine of philosophy carried to remoter or queerer corners: never was a more delicate diet offered to "two or three governors, or ex-governors," living in a cabin. It was Mercury, shivering in a mackintosh, bearing nectar and ambrosia to the gods whom he wished those who lived in cabins to endeavour to feel that they might be.

I have hinted that the will, in the old New England society, was a clue without a labyrinth; but it had its use, nevertheless, in helping the young talent to find its mould. There were few or none ready-made: tradition was certainly not so oppressive as might have been inferred from the fact that the air swarmed with reformers and improvers. Of the patient, philosophic manner in which Emerson groped and waited, through teaching the young and preaching to the adult, for his particular vocation, Mr. Cabot's first volume gives a full and orderly account. His passage from the Unitarian pulpit to the lecture-desk was a step which at this distance of time can hardly help appearing to us short, though he was long in making it, for even after ceasing to have a parish of his own he freely confounded the two, or willingly, at least, treated the pulpit as a platform. "The young people and the mature hint at odium and the aversion of faces, to be presently encountered in society," he writes in his journal in 1838; but in point of fact the quiet drama of his abdication was not to include the note of suffering. The Boston world might feel disapproval, but it was far too kindly to make this sentiment felt as a weight: every element of martyrdom was there but the important ones of the cause and the persecutors. Mr. Cabot marks the lightness of the penalties of dissent; if they were light in somewhat later years for the transcendentalists and fruit-eaters they could press but little on a man of Emerson's distinction, to whom, all his life, people went not to carry but to ask the right word. There was no consideration to give up, he could not have been one of the dingy if he had tried; but what he did renounce in 1838 was a material profession. He was "settled," and his indisposition to administer the communion unsettled him. He calls the whole business, in writing to Carlyle, "a tempest in our washbowl"; but it had the effect of forcing him to seek a new source of income. His wants were few and his view of life severe, and this came to him, little by little, as he was able to extend the field in which he read his discourses. In 1835, upon his second marriage, he took up his habitation at Concord, and his life fell into the shape it was, in a general way, to keep for the next half-century. It is here that we cannot help regretting that Mr. Cabot had not found it possible to treat his career a little more pictorially. Those fifty years of Concord—at least the earlier part of them—would have been a subject bringing into play many odd figures, many human incongruities: they would have abounded in illustrations of the primitive New England character, especially during the time of its queer search for something to expend itself upon. Objects and occupations have multiplied since then, and now there is no lack; but fifty years ago the expanse was wide and free, and we get the impression of a conscience gasping in the void, panting for sensations, with something of the movement of the gills of a landed fish. It would take a very fine point to sketch Emerson's benignant, patient, inscrutable countenance during the various phases of this democratic communion; but the picture, when complete, would be one of the portraits, half a revelation and half an enigma, that suggest and fascinate. Such a striking personage as old Miss Mary Emerson, our author's aunt, whose high intelligence and temper were much of an influence in his earlier years, has a kind of tormenting representative value: we want to see her from head to foot, with her frame and her background; having (for we happen to have it), an impression that she was a very remarkable specimen of the transatlantic Puritan stock, a spirit that would have dared the devil. We miss a more liberal handling, are tempted to add touches of our own, and end by convincing ourselves that Miss Mary Moody Emerson, grim intellectual virgin and daughter of a hundred ministers, with her local traditions and her combined love of empire and of speculation, would have been an inspiration for a novelist. Hardly less so the charming Mrs. Ripley, Emerson's life-long friend and neighbour, most delicate and accomplished of women, devoted to Greek and to her house, studious, simple and dainty—an admirable example of the old-fashioned New England lady. It was a freak of Miss Emerson's somewhat sardonic humour to give her once a broom-stick to carry across Boston Common (under the pretext of a "moving"), a task accepted with docility but making of the victim the most benignant witch ever equipped with that utensil.

These ladies, however, were very private persons and not in the least of the reforming tribe: there are others who would have peopled Mr. Cabot's page to whom he gives no more than a mention. We must add that it is open to him to say that their features have become faint and indistinguishable to-day without more research than the question is apt to be worth: they are embalmed—in a collective way—the apprehensible part of them, in Mr. Frothingham's clever *History of Transcendentalism in New England*. This must be admitted to be true of even so lively a "factor," as we say nowadays, as the imaginative, talkative, intelligent and finally Italianised and ship-wrecked Margaret Fuller: she is now one of the dim, one of Carlyle's "then-celebrated" at most. It seemed indeed as if Mr. Cabot rather grudged her a due place in the record of the company that Emerson kept, until we came across the delightful letter he quotes toward the end of his first volume—a letter interesting both as a specimen of inimitable, imperceptible edging away, and as an illustration of the curiously generalised way, as if with an implicit protest against personalities, in which his intercourse, epistolary and other, with his friends was conducted. There is an extract from a letter to his aunt on the occasion of the death of a deeply-loved brother (his own) which reads like a passage from some fine old chastened essay on the vanity of earthly hopes: strangely unfamiliar, considering the circumstances. Courteous and humane to the furthest possible point, to the point of an almost profligate surrender of his attention, there was no familiarity in him, no personal avidity. Even his letters to his wife are courtesies, they are not familiarities. He had only one style, one manner, and he had it for everything—even for himself, in his notes, in his journals. But he had it in perfection for Miss Fuller; he retreats, smiling and flattering, on tiptoe, as if he were advancing. "She ever seems to crave," he says in his journal, "something which I have not, or have not for her." What he had was doubtless not what she craved, but the letter in question should be read to see how the modicum was administered. It is only between the lines of such a production that we read that a part of her effect upon him was to bore him; for his system was to practise a kind of universal passive hospitality—he aimed at nothing less. It was only because he was so deferential that he could be so detached; he had polished his aloofness till it reflected the image of his solicitor. And this was not because he was an "uncommunicating egotist," though he amuses himself with saying so to Miss Fuller: egotism is the strongest of passions, and he was altogether passionless. It was because he had no personal, just as he had almost no physical wants. "Yet I plead not guilty to the malice prepense. 'Tis imbecility, not contumacy, though perhaps somewhat more odious. It seems very just, the irony with which you ask whether you may not be trusted and promise such docility. Alas, we will all promise, but the prophet loiters." He would not say even to himself that she bored him; he had denied himself the luxury of such easy and obvious short cuts. There is a passage in the lecture (1844) called "Man the Reformer," in which he hovers round and round the idea that the practice of trade, in certain conditions likely to beget an underhand competition, does not draw forth the nobler parts of character, till the reader is tempted to interrupt him with, "Say at once that it is impossible for a gentleman!"

So he remained always, reading his lectures in the winter, writing them in the summer, and at all seasons taking wood-walks and looking for hints in old books.

Delicious summer stroll through the pastures.... On the steep park of Conantum I have the old regret—is all this beauty to perish? Shall none re-make this sun and wind; the sky-blue river; the river-blue sky; the yellow meadow, spotted with sacks and sheets of cranberry-gatherers; the red bushes; the iron-gray house, just the colour of the granite rocks; the wild orchard?"

His observation of Nature was exquisite—always the direct, irresistible impression.

The hawking of the wild geese flying by night; the thin note of the companionable titmouse in the winter day; the fall of swarms of flies in autumn, from combats high in the air, pattering down on the leaves like rain; the angry hiss of the woodbirds; the pine throwing out its pollen for the benefit of the next century.... (*Literary Ethics.*)

I have said there was no familiarity in him, but he was familiar with woodland creatures and sounds. Certainly, too, he was on terms of free association with his books, which were numerous and dear to him; though Mr. Cabot says, doubtless with justice, that his dependence on them was slight and that he was not "intimate" with his authors. They did not feed him but they stimulated; they were not his meat but his wine—he took them in sips. But he needed them and liked them; he had volumes of notes from his reading, and he could not have produced his lectures without them. He liked literature as a thing to refer to, liked the very names of which it is full, and used them, especially in his later writings, for purposes of ornament, to dress the dish, sometimes with an unmeasured profusion. I open *The Conduct of Life* and find a dozen on the page. He mentions more authorities than is the fashion to-day. He can easily say, of course, that he follows a better one—that of his well-loved and irrepressibly allusive Montaigne. In his own bookishness there is a certain contradiction, just as there is a latent incompleteness in his whole literary side. Independence, the return to nature, the finding out and doing for one's self, was ever what he most highly recommended; and yet he is constantly reminding his readers of the conventional signs and consecrations—of what other men have done. This was partly because the independence that he had in his eye was an independence without ill-nature, without rudeness (though he likes that word), and full of gentle amiabilities, curiosities and tolerances; and partly it is a simple matter of form, a literary expedient, confessing its character—on the part of one who had never really mastered the art of composition—of continuous expression. Charming to many a reader, charming yet ever slightly droll, will remain Emerson's frequent invocation of the "scholar": there is such a friendly vagueness and convenience in it. It is of the scholar that he expects all the heroic and uncomfortable things, the concentrations and relinquishments, that make up the noble life. We fancy this personage looking up from his book and arm-chair a little ruefully and saying, "Ah, but why *me* always and only? Why so much of me, and is there no one else to share the responsibility?" "Neither years nor books have yet availed to extirpate a prejudice then rooted in me [when as a boy he first saw the graduates of his college assembled at their anniversary], that a scholar is the favourite of heaven and earth, the excellency of his country, the happiest of men."

In truth, by this term he means simply the cultivated man, the man who has had a liberal education, and there is a voluntary plainness in his use of it—speaking of such people as the rustic, or the vulgar, speak of those who have a tincture of books. This is characteristic of his humility—that humility which was nine-tenths a plain fact (for it is easy for persons who have at bottom a great fund of indifference to be humble), and the remaining tenth a literary habit. Moreover an American reader may be excused for finding in it a pleasant sign of that prestige, often so quaintly and indeed so extravagantly acknowledged, which a connection with literature carries with it among the people of the United States. There is no country in which it is more freely admitted to be a distinction—*the* distinction; or in which so many persons have become eminent for showing it even in a slight degree. Gentlemen and ladies are celebrated there on this ground who would not on the same ground, though they might on another, be celebrated anywhere else. Emerson's own tone is an echo of that, when he speaks of the scholar—not of the banker, the great merchant, the legislator, the artist—as the most distinguished figure in the society about him. It is because he has most to give up that he is appealed to for efforts and sacrifices. "Meantime I know that a very different estimate of the scholar's profession prevails in this country," he goes on to say in the address from which I last quoted (the *Literary Ethics*), "and the importunity with which society presses its claim upon young men tends to pervert the views of the youth in respect to the culture of the intellect." The manner in which that is said represents, surely, a serious mistake: with the estimate of the scholar's profession which then prevailed in New England Emerson could have had no quarrel; the ground of his lamentation was another side of the matter. It was not a question of estimate, but of accidental practice. In 1838 there were still so many things of prime material necessity to be done that reading was driven to the wall; but the reader was still thought the cleverest, for he found time as well as intelligence. Emerson's own situation sufficiently indicates it. In what other country, on sleety winter nights, would provincial and bucolic populations have gone forth in hundreds for the cold comfort of a literary discourse? The distillation anywhere else would certainly have appeared too thin, the appeal too special. But for many years the American people of the middle regions, outside of a few cities, had in the most rigorous seasons no other recreation. A gentleman, grave or gay, in a bare room, with a manuscript, before a desk, offered the reward of toil, the refreshment of pleasure, to the young, the middle-aged and the old of both sexes. The hour was brightest, doubtless, when the gentleman was gay, like Doctor Oliver Wendell Holmes. But Emerson's gravity never sapped his career, any more than it chilled the regard in which he was held among those who were particularly his own people. It was impossible to be more honoured and cherished, far and near, than he was during his long residence in Concord, or more looked upon as the principal gentleman in the place. This was conspicuous to the writer of these remarks on the occasion of the curious, sociable, cheerful public funeral made for him in 1883 by all the countryside, arriving, as for the last honours to the first citizen, in trains, in waggons, on foot, in multitudes. It was a popular manifestation, the most striking I have ever seen provoked by the death of a man of letters.

If a picture of that singular and very illustrative institution the old American lecture-system would have constituted a part of the filling-in of the ideal memoir of Emerson, I may further say, returning to the matter for a moment, that such a memoir would also have had a chapter for some of those Concord-haunting figures which are not so much interesting in themselves as interesting because for a season Emerson thought them so. And the pleasure of that would be partly that it would push us to inquire how interesting he did really think them. That is, it would bring up the question of his inner reserves and scepticisms, his secret ennuis and ironies, the way he sympathised for courtesy and then, with his delicacy and generosity, in a world after all given much to the literal, let his courtesy pass for adhesion— a question particularly attractive to those for whom he has, in general, a fascination. Many entertaining problems of that sort present themselves for such readers: there is something indefinable for them in the mixture of which he was made—his fidelity as an interpreter of the so-called transcendental spirit and his freedom from all wish for any personal share in the effect of his ideas. He drops them, sheds them, diffuses them, and we feel as if there would be a grossness in holding him to anything so temporal as a responsibility. He had the advantage, for many years, of having the question of application assumed for him by Thoreau, who took upon himself to be, in the concrete, the sort of person that Emerson's "scholar" was in the abstract, and who paid for it by having a shorter life than that fine adumbration. The application, with Thoreau, was violent and limited (it became a matter of prosaic detail, the non-payment of taxes, the non-wearing of a necktie, the preparation of one's food one's self, the practice of a rude sincerity—all things not of the essence), so that, though he wrote some beautiful pages, which read like a translation of Emerson into the sounds of the field and forest and which no one who has ever loved nature in New England, or indeed anywhere, can fail to love, he suffers something of the *amoindrissement* of eccentricity. His master escapes that reduction altogether. I call it an advantage to have had such a pupil as Thoreau; because for a mind so much made up of reflection as Emerson's everything comes under that head which prolongs and reanimates the process—produces the return, again and yet again, on one's impressions. Thoreau must have had this moderating and even chastening effect. It did not rest, moreover, with him alone; the advantage of which I speak was not confined to Thoreau's case. In 1837 Emerson (in his journal) pronounced Mr. Bronson Alcott the most extraordinary man and the highest genius of his time: the sequence of which was that for more than forty years after that he had the gentleman living but half a mile away. The opportunity for the return, as I have called it, was not wanting.

His detachment is shown in his whole attitude toward the transcendental movement—that remarkable outburst of Romanticism on Puritan ground, as Mr. Cabot very well names it. Nothing can be more ingenious, more sympathetic and charming, than Emerson's account and definition of the matter in his lecture (of 1842) called "The Transcendentalist"; and yet nothing is more apparent from his letters and journals than that he regarded any such label or banner as a mere tiresome flutter. He liked to taste but not to drink—least of all to become intoxicated. He liked to explain the transcendentalists but did not care at all to be explained by them: a doctrine "whereof you know I am wholly guiltless," he says to his wife in 1842, "and which is spoken of as a known and fixed element, like salt or meal. So that I have to begin with endless disclaimers and explanations: 'I am not the man you take me for.'" He was never the man any one took him for, for the simple reason that no one could possibly take him for the elusive, irreducible, merely gustatory spirit for which he took himself.

> It is a sort of maxim with me never to harp on the omnipotence of limitations. Least of all do we need any suggestion of checks and measures; as if New England were anything else.... Of so many fine people it is true that being so much they ought to be a little more, and missing that are naught. It is a sort of King Renè period; there is no doing, but rare thrilling prophecy from bands of competing minstrels.

That is his private expression about a large part of a ferment in regard to which his public judgment was that

> That indeed constitutes a new feature in their portrait, that they are the most exacting and extortionate critics.... These exacting children advertise us of our wants. There is no compliment, no smooth speech with them; they pay you only this one compliment of insatiable expectation; they aspire, they severely exact, and if they only stand fast in this watch-tower, and stand fast unto the end, and without end, then they are terrible friends, whereof poet and priest cannot but stand in awe; and what if they eat clouds and drink wind, they have not been without service to the race of man.

That was saying the best for them, as he always said it for everything; but it was the sense of their being "bands of competing minstrels" and their camp being only a "measure and check," in a society too sparse for a synthesis, that kept him from wishing to don their uniform. This was after all but a misfitting imitation of his natural wear, and what he would have liked was to put that off—he did not wish to button it tighter. He said the best for his friends of the Dial, of Fruitlands and Brook Farm, in saying that they were fastidious and critical; but he was conscious in the next breath that what there was around them to be criticised was mainly a negative. Nothing is more perceptible to-day than that their criticism produced no fruit—that it was little else than a very decent and innocent recreation—a kind of Puritan carnival. The New England world was for much the most part very busy, but the Dial and Fruitlands and Brook Farm were the amusement of the leisure-class. Extremes meet, and as in older societies that class is known principally by its connection with castles and carriages, so at Concord it came, with Thoreau and Mr. W. H. Channing, out of the cabin and the wood-lot.

Emerson was not moved to believe in their fastidiousness as a productive principle even when they directed it upon abuses which he abundantly recognised. Mr. Cabot shows that he was by no means one of the professional abolitionists or philanthropists—never an enrolled "humanitarian."

> We talk frigidly of Reform until the walls mock us. It is that of which a man should never speak, but if he have cherished it in his bosom he should steal to it in darkness, as an Indian to his bride. . . . Does he not do more to abolish slavery who works all day steadily in his own garden, than he who goes to the abolition meeting and makes a speech? He who does his own work frees a slave.

I must add that even while I transcribe these words there comes to me the recollection of the great meeting in the Boston Music Hall, on the first day of 1863, to celebrate the signing by Mr. Lincoln of the proclamation freeing the Southern slaves—of the momentousness of the occasion, the vast excited multitude, the crowded platform and the tall, spare figure of Emerson, in the midst, reading out the stanzas that were published under the name of the Boston Hymn. They are not the happiest he produced for an occasion—they do not compare with the verses on the "embattled farmers," read at Concord in 1857, and there is a certain awkwardness in some of them. But I well remember the immense effect with which his beautiful voice pronounced the lines—

> Pay ransom to the owner
> And fill the bag to the brim.
> Who is the owner? The slave is owner,
> And ever was. Pay *him*!

And Mr. Cabot chronicles the fact that the *gran' rifiuto*—the great backsliding of Mr. Webster when he cast his vote in Congress for the Fugitive Slave Law of 1850—was the one thing that ever moved him to heated denunciation. He felt Webster's apostasy as strongly as he had admired his genius. "Who has not helped to praise him? Simply he was the one American of our time whom we could produce as a finished work of nature." There is a passage in his journal (not a rough jotting, but, like most of the entries in it, a finished piece of writing), which is admirably descriptive of the wonderful orator and is moreover one of the very few portraits, or even personal sketches, yielded by Mr. Cabot's selections. It shows that he could observe the human figure and "render" it to good purpose.

> His splendid wrath, when his eyes become fire, is good to see, so intellectual it is—the wrath of the fact and the cause he espouses, and not at all personal to himself.... These village parties must be dish-water to him, yet he shows himself just good-natured, just nonchalant enough; and he has his own way, without offending any one or losing any ground.... His expensiveness seems necessary to him; were he too prudent a Yankee it would be a sad deduction from his magnificence. I only wish he would not truckle [to the slave-holders]. I do not care how much he spends.

I doubtless appear to have said more than enough, yet I have passed by many of the passages I had marked for transcription from Mr. Cabot's volumes. There is one, in the first, that makes us stare as we come upon it, to the effect that Emerson "could see nothing in Shelley, Aristophanes, Don Quixote, Miss Austen, Dickens." Mr. Cabot adds that he rarely read a novel, even the famous ones (he has a point of contact here as well as, strangely enough, on two or three other sides with that distinguished moralist M. Ernest Renan, who, like Emerson, was originally a dissident priest and cannot imagine why people should write works of fiction); and thought Dante "a man to put into a museum, but not into your house; another Zerah Colburn; a prodigy of imaginative function, executive rather than contemplative or wise." The confession of an insensibility ranging from Shelley to Dickens and from Dante to Miss Austen and taking Don Quixote and Aristophanes on the way, is a large allowance to have to make for a man of letters, and may appear to confirm but slightly any claim of intellectual hospitality and general curiosity put forth for him. The truth was that, sparely constructed as he was and formed not wastefully, not with material left over, as it were, for a special function, there were certain chords in Emerson that did not vibrate at all. I well remember my impression of this on walking with him in the autumn of 1872 through the galleries of the Louvre and, later that winter, through those of the Vatican: his perception of the objects contained in these collections was of the most general order. I was struck with the anomaly of a man so refined and intelligent being so little spoken to by works of art. It would be more exact to say that certain chords were wholly absent; the tune was played, the tune of life and literature, altogether on those that remained. They had every wish to be equal to their office, but one feels that the number was short—that some notes could not be given. Mr. Cabot makes use of a singular phrase when he says, in speaking of Hawthorne, for several years our author's neighbour at Concord and a little—a very little we gather—his companion, that Emerson was unable to read his novels—he thought them "not worthy of him." This is a judgment odd almost to fascination—we circle round it and turn it over and over; it contains so elusive an ambiguity. How highly he must have esteemed the man of whose genius *The House of the Seven Gables* and *The Scarlet Letter* gave imperfectly the measure, and how strange that he should not have been eager to read almost anything that such a gifted being might have let fall! It was a rare accident that made them live almost side by side so long in the same small New England town, each a fruit of a long Puritan stem, yet with such a difference of taste. Hawthorne's vision was all for the evil and sin of the world; a side of life as to which Emerson's eyes were thickly bandaged. There were points as to which the latter's conception of right could be violated, but he had no great sense of wrong—a strangely limited one, indeed, for a moralist—no sense of the dark, the foul, the base. There were certain complications in life which he never suspected. One asks one's self whether that is why he did not care for Dante and Shelley and Aristophanes and Dickens, their works containing a considerable reflection of human perversity. But that still leaves the indifference to Cervantes and Miss Austen unaccounted for.

It has not, however, been the ambition of these remarks to account for everything, and I have arrived at the end without even pointing to the grounds on which Emerson justifies the honours of biography, discussion and illustration. I have assumed his importance and continuance, and shall probably not be gainsaid by those who read him. Those who do not will hardly rub him out. Such a book as Mr. Cabot's subjects a reputation to a test—leads people to look it over and hold it up to the light, to see whether it is worth keeping in use or even putting away in a cabinet. Such a revision of Emerson has no relegating consequences. The result of it is once more the impression that he serves and will not wear out, and that indeed we cannot afford to drop him. His instrument makes him precious. He did something better than any one else; he had a particular faculty, which has not been surpassed, for speaking to the soul in a voice of direction and authority. There have been many spiritual voices appealing, consoling, reassuring, exhorting, or even denouncing and terrifying, but none has had just that firmness and just that purity. It penetrates further, it seems to go back to the roots of our feelings, to where conduct and manhood begin; and moreover, to us to-day, there is something in it that says that it is connected somehow with the virtue of the world, has wrought and achieved, lived in thousands of minds, produced a mass of character and life. And there is this further sign of Emerson's singular power, that he is a striking exception to the general rule that writings live in the last resort by their form; that they owe a large part of their fortune to the art with which they have been composed. It is hardly too much, or too little, to say of Emerson's writings in general that they were not composed at all. Many and many things are beautifully said; he had felicities, inspirations, unforgettable phrases; he had frequently an exquisite eloquence.

O my friends, there are resources in us on which we have not yet drawn. There are men who rise refreshed on hearing a threat;

men to whom a crisis which intimidates and paralyses the majority—demanding not the faculties of prudence and thrift, but comprehension, immovableness, the readiness of sacrifice, come graceful and beloved as a bride. . . . But these are heights that we can scarce look up to and remember without contrition and shame. Let us thank God that such things exist.

None the less we have the impression that that search for a fashion and a manner on which he was always engaged never really came to a conclusion; it draws itself out through his later writings—it drew itself out through his later lectures, like a sort of renunciation of success. It is not on these, however, but on their predecessors, that his reputation will rest. Of course the way he spoke was the way that was on the whole most convenient to him; but he differs from most men of letters of the same degree of credit in failing to strike us as having achieved a style. This achievement is, as I say, usually the bribe or toll-money on the journey to posterity; and if Emerson goes his way, as he clearly appears to be doing, on the strength of his message alone, the case will be rare, the exception striking, and the honour great.

BROWNING IN WESTMINSTER
ABBEY

THE LOVERS of a great poet are the people in the world who are most to be forgiven a little wanton fancy about him, for they have before them, in his genius and work, an irresistible example of the application of the imaginative method to a thousand subjects. Certainly, therefore, there are many confirmed admirers of Robert Browning to whom it will not have failed to occur that the consignment of his ashes to the great temple of fame of the English race was exactly one of those occasions in which his own analytic spirit would have rejoiced and his irrepressible faculty for looking at human events in all sorts of slanting colored lights have found a signal opportunity. If he had been taken with it as a subject, if it had moved him to the confused yet comprehensive utterance of which he was the great professor, we can immediately guess at some of the sparks he would have scraped from it, guess how splendidly, in the case, the pictorial sense would have intertwined itself with the metaphysical. For such an occasion would have lacked, for the author of *The Ring and the Book*, none of the complexity and convertibility that were dear to him. Passion and ingenuity, irony and solemnity, the impressive and the unexpected, would each have forced their way through; in a word, the author would have been sure to take the special, circumstantial view (the inveterate mark of all his speculation) even of so foregone a conclusion as that England should pay her greatest honor to one of her greatest poets. At any rate, as they stood in the Abbey on Tuesday last those of his admirers and mourners who were disposed to profit by his warrant for inquiring curiously, may well have let their fancy range, with its muffled step, in the direction which *his* fancy would probably not have shrunk from following, even perhaps to the dim corners where humor and the whimsical lurk. Only, we hasten to add, it would have taken Robert Browning himself to render the multifold impression.

One part of it on such an occasion is, of course, irresistible—the sense that these honors are the greatest that a generous nation has to confer, and that the emotion that accompanies them is one of the high moments of a nation's life. The attitude of the public, of the multitude, at such hours, is a great expansion, a great openness to ideas of aspiration and achievement; the pride of possession and of bestowal, especially in the case of a career so complete as Mr. Browning's, is so present as to make regret a minor matter. We possess a great man most when we begin to look at him through the glass plate of death; and it is a simple truth, though containing an apparent contradiction, that the Abbey never strikes us so benignantly as when we have a valued voice to commit to silence there. For the silence is articulate after all, and in worthy instances the preservation great. It is the other side of the question that would pull most the strings of irresponsible reflection—all those conceivable postulates and hypotheses of the poetic and satiric mind to which we owe the picture of how the bishop ordered his tomb in St. Praxed's. Macaulay's "temple of silence and reconciliation"—and none the less perhaps because he himself is now a presence there—strikes us, as we stand in it, not only as local but as social—a sort of corporate company; so thick, under its high arches, its dim transepts and chapels, is the population of its historic names and figures. They are a company in possession, with a high standard of distinction, of immortality, as it were; for there is something serenely inexpugnable even in the position of the interlopers. As they look out, in the rich dusk, from the cold eyes of statues and the careful identity of tablets, they seem, with their converging faces, to scrutinize decorously the claims of each new recumbent glory, to ask each other how he is to be judged as an accession. How difficult to banish the idea that Robert Browning would have enjoyed prefiguring and disintegrating the mystifications, the reservations, even perhaps the slight buzz of scandal in the Poets' Corner, to which his own obsequies might give rise! Would not his great relish, in so characteristic an interview with this crucible, have been his perception of the bewildering modernness, to much of the society, of the new candidate for a niche? That is the interest and the fascination, from what may be termed the inside point of view, of Mr. Browning's having received, in this direction of becoming a classic, the only official assistance that is ever conferred upon English writers.

It is as classics on one ground and another—some members of it perhaps on that of not being anything else—that the numerous assembly in the Abbey holds together, and it is as a tremendous and incomparable modern that the author of *Men and Women* takes his place in it. He introduces to his predecessors a kind of contemporary individualism which surely for many a year they had not been reminded of with any such force. The tradition of the poetic character as something high, detached, and simple, which may be assumed to have prevailed among them for a good while, is one that Browning has broken at every turn; so that we can imagine his new associates to stand about him, till they have got used to him, with rather a sense of failing measures. A good many oddities and a good many great writers have been entombed in the Abbey; but none of the odd ones have been so great and none of the great ones so odd. There are plenty of poets whose right to the title may be contested, but there is no poetic head of equal power—crowned and recrowned by almost importunate hands—from which so many people would withhold the distinctive wreath. All this will give the marble phantoms at the base of the great pillars and the definite personalities of the honorary slabs something to puzzle out until, by the quick operation of time, the mere fact of his lying there among the classified and protected makes even Robert Browning lose a portion of the bristling surface of his actuality.

For the rest, judging from the outside and with his contemporaries, we of the public can only feel that his very modernness—by which we mean the all-touching, all-trying spirit of his work, permeated with accumulations and playing with knowledge—achieves a kind of conquest, or at least of extension, of the rigid pale. We cannot enter here upon any account either of that or of any other element of his genius, though surely no literary figure of our day seems to sit more unconsciously for the painter. The very imperfections of this original are fascinating, for they never present themselves as weaknesses—they are boldnesses and overgrowths, rich roughnesses and humors—and the patient critic need not despair of digging to the primary soil from which so many disparities and contradictions spring. He may finally even put his finger on some explanation of the great mystery, the imperfect conquest of the poetic form by a genius in which the poetic passion had such volume and range. He may successfully say how it was that a poet without a lyre—for that is practically Browning's deficiency: he had the scroll, but not often the sounding strings—was nevertheless, in his best hours, wonderfully rich in the magic of his art, a magnificent master of poetic emotion. He will justify on behalf of a multitude of devotees the great position assigned to a writer of verse of which the nature or the fortune has been (in proportion to its value and quantity) to be treated rarely as quotable. He will do all this and a great deal more besides; but we need not wait for it to feel that something of our latest sympathies, our latest and most restless selves, passed the other day into the high part—the show-part, to speak vulgarly—of our literature. To speak of Mr. Browning only as he was in the last twenty years of his life, how quick such an imagination as his would have been to recognize all the latent or mystical suitabilities that, in the last resort, might link to the great Valhalla by the Thames a figure that had become so conspicuously a figure of London! He had grown to be intimately and inveterately of the London world; he was so familiar and recurrent, so responsive to all its solicitations, that, given the endless incarnations he stands for to-day, he would have been missed from the congregation of worthies whose memorials are the special pride of the Londoner. Just as his great sign to those who knew him was that he was a force of health, of temperament, of tone, so what he takes into the Abbey is an immense expression of life—of life rendered with large liberty and free experiment, with an unprejudiced intellectual eagerness to put himself in other people's place, to participate in complications and consequences—a restlessness of psychological research that might well alarm any pale company for their formal orthodoxies.

But the illustrious whom he rejoins may be reassured, as they will not fail to discover: in so far as they are representative it will clear itself up that, in spite of a surface unsuggestive of marble and a reckless individualism of form, he is quite as representative as any of them. For the great value of Browning is that at bottom, in all the deep spiritual and human essentials, he is unmistakably in the great tradition—is, with all his Italianisms and cosmopolitanisms, all his victimization by societies organized to talk about him, a magnificent example of the best and least dilettantish English spirit. That constitutes indeed the main chance for his eventual critic, who will have to solve the refreshing problem of how, if subtleties be not what the English spirit most delights in, the author of, for instance, "Any Wife to Any Husband" made them his perpetual pasture and yet remained typically of his race. He was, indeed, a wonderful mixture of the universal and the alembicated. But he played with the curious and the special, they never submerged him, and it was a sign of his robustness that he could play to the end. His voice sounds loudest, and also clearest, for the things that, as a race, we like best—the fascination of faith, the acceptance of life, the respect for its mysteries, the endurance of its charges, the vitality of the will, the validity of character, the beauty of action, the seriousness, above all, of the great human passion. If Browning had spoken for us in no other way, he ought to have been made sure of, tamed, and chained as a classic, on account of the extraordinary beauty of his treatment of the special relation between man and woman. It is a complete and splendid picture of the matter, which somehow places it at the same time in the region of conduct and responsibility. But when we talk of Robert Browning's speaking "for us," we go to the end of our privilege, we say all. With a sense of security, perhaps even a certain complacency, we leave our sophisticated modern conscience, and perhaps even our heterogeneous modern vocabulary, in his charge among the illustrious. There will possibly be moments in which these things will seem to us to have widened the allowance, made the high abode more comfortable for some of those who are yet to enter it.

FORMS OF FICTION

GUY DE MAUPASSANT

I

THE FIRST artists, in any line, are doubtless not those whose general ideas about their art are most often on their lips—those who most abound in precept, apology, and formula and can best tell us the reasons and the philosophy of things. We know the first usually by their energetic practice, the constancy with which they apply their principles, and the serenity with which they leave us to hunt for their secret in the illustration, the concrete example. None the less it often happens that a valid artist utters his mystery, flashes upon us for a moment the light by which he works, shows us the rule by which he holds it just that he should be measured. This accident is happiest, I think, when it is soonest over; the shortest explanations of the products of genius are the best, and there is many a creator of living figures whose friends, however full of faith in his inspiration, will do well to pray for him when he sallies forth into the dim wilderness of theory. The doctrine is apt to be so much less inspired than the work, the work is often so much more intelligent than the doctrine. M. Guy de Maupassant has lately traversed with a firm and rapid step a literary crisis of this kind; he has clambered safely up the bank at the further end of the morass. If he has relieved himself in the preface to *Pierre et Jean*, the last-published of his tales, he has also rendered a service to his friends; he has not only come home in a recognisable plight, escaping gross disaster with a success which even his extreme good sense was far from making in advance a matter of course, but he has expressed in intelligible terms (that by itself is a ground of felicitation) his most general idea, his own sense of his direction. He has arranged, as it were, the light in which he wishes to sit. If it is a question of attempting, under however many disadvantages, a sketch of him, the critic's business therefore is simplified: there will be no difficulty in placing him, for he himself has chosen the spot, he has made the chalk-mark on the floor.

I may as well say at once that in dissertation M. de Maupassant does not write with his best pen; the philosopher in his composition is perceptibly inferior to the story-teller. I would rather have written half a page of "Boule de Suif" than the whole of the introduction to Flaubert's *Letters to Madame Sand*; and his little disquisition on the novel in general, attached to that particular example of it which he has just put forth,* is considerably less to the point than the master-piece which it ushers in. In short, as a commentator M. de Maupassant is slightly common, while as an artist he is wonderfully rare. Of course we must, in judging a writer, take one thing with another, and if I could make up my mind that M. de Maupassant is weak in theory, it would almost make me like him better, render him more approach-able, give him the touch of softness that he lacks, and show us a human flaw. The most general quality of the author of *La Maison Tellier* and *Bel-Ami*, the impression that remains last, after the others have been accounted for, is an essential hardness—hardness of form, hardness of nature; and it would put us more at ease to find that if the fact with him (the fact of execution) is so extraordinarily definite and adequate, his explanations, after it, were a little vague and sentimen-tal. But I am not sure that he must even be held foolish to have noticed the race of critics: he is at any rate so much less foolish than several of that fraternity. He has said his say concisely and as if he were say-ing it once for all. In fine, his readers must be grateful to him for such a passage as that in which he remarks that whereas the public at large very legitimately says to a writer, "Console me, amuse me, terrify me, make me cry, make me dream, or make me think," what the sincere critic says is, "Make me something fine in the form that shall suit you

Pierre et Jean. Paris: Ollendorff, 1888.

best, according to your temperament." This seems to me to put into a nutshell the whole question of the different classes of fiction, concerning which there has recently been so much discourse. There are simply as many different kinds as there are persons practising the art, for if a picture, a tale, or a novel be a direct impression of life (and that surely constitutes its interest and value), the impression will vary according to the plate that takes it, the particular structure and mixture of the recipient.

I am not sure that I know what M. de Maupassant means when he says, "The critic shall appreciate the result only according to the nature of the effort; he has no right to concern himself with tendencies." The second clause of that observation strikes me as rather in the air, thanks to the vagueness of the last word. But our author adds to the definiteness of his contention when he goes on to say that any form of the novel is simply a vision of the world from the standpoint of a person constituted after a certain fashion, and that it is therefore absurd to say that there is, for the novelist's use, only one reality of things. This seems to me commendable, not as a flight of metaphysics, hovering over bottomless gulfs of controversy, but, on the contrary, as a just indication of the vanity of certain dogmatisms. The particular way we see the world is our particular illusion about it, says M. de Maupassant, and this illusion fits itself to our organs and senses; our receptive vessel becomes the furniture of *our* little plot of the universal consciousness.

> How childish, moreover, to believe in reality, since we each carry our own in our thought and in our organs. Our eyes, our ears, our sense of smell, of taste, differing from one person to another, create as many truths as there are men upon earth. And our minds, taking instruction from these organs, so diversely impressed, understand, analyse, judge, as if each of us belonged to a different race. Each one of us, therefore, forms for himself an illusion of the world, which is the illusion poetic, or sentimental, or joyous, or melancholy, or unclean, or dismal, according to his nature. And the writer has no other mission

than to reproduce faithfully this illusion, with all the contrivances of art that he has learned and has at his command. The illusion of beauty, which is a human convention! The illusion of ugliness, which is a changing opinion! The illusion of truth, which is never immutable! The illusion of the ignoble, which attracts so many! The great artists are those who make humanity accept their particular illusion. Let us, therefore, not get angry with any one theory, since every theory is the generalised expression of a temperament asking itself questions.

What is interesting in this is not that M. de Maupassant happens to hold that we have no universal measure of the truth, but that it is the last word on a question of art from a writer who is rich in experience and has had success in a very rare degree. It is of secondary importance that our impression should be called, or not called, an illusion; what is excellent is that our author has stated more neatly than we have lately seen it done that the value of the artist resides in the clearness with which he gives forth that impression. His particular organism constitutes a *case*, and the critic is intelligent in proportion as he apprehends and enters into that case. To quarrel with it because it is not another, which it could not possibly have been without a wholly different outfit, appears to M. de Maupassant a deplorable waste of time. If this appeal to our disinterestedness may strike some readers as chilling (through their inability to conceive of any other form than the one they like—a limitation excellent for a reader but poor for a judge), the occasion happens to be none of the best for saying so, for M. de Maupassant himself precisely presents all the symptoms of a "case" in the most striking way, and shows us how far the consideration of them may take us. Embracing such an opportunity as this, and giving ourselves to it freely, seems to me indeed to be a course more fruitful in valid conclusions, as well as in entertainment by the way, than the more common method of establishing one's own premises. To make clear to ourselves those of the author of *Pierre et Jean*—those to which he is committed by the very nature of his mind—is an attempt that will both stimulate and repay curiosity. There is no way of looking at his work less dry, less academic, for as we proceed from one of his peculiarities to another, the whole horizon widens, yet without our leaving firm ground, and we see ourselves landed, step by step, in the most general questions—those explanations of things which reside in the race, in the society. Of course there are cases and cases, and it is the salient ones that the disinterested critic is delighted to meet.

What makes M. de Maupassant salient is two facts: the first of which is that his gifts are remarkably strong and definite, and the second that he writes directly *from* them, as it were: holds the fullest, the most uninterrupted—I scarcely know what to call it—the boldest communication with them. A case is poor when the cluster of the artist's sensibilities is small, or they themselves are wanting in keenness, or else when the personage fails to admit them—either through ignorance, or diffidence, or stupidity, or the error of a false ideal—to what may be called a legitimate share in his attempt. It is, I think, among English and American writers that this latter accident is most liable to occur; more than the French we are apt to be misled by some convention or other as to the sort of feeler we *ought* to put forth, forgetting that the best one will be the one that nature happens to have given us. We have doubtless often enough the courage of our opinions (when it befalls that we have opinions), but we have not so constantly that of our perceptions. There is a whole side of our perceptive apparatus that we in fact neglect, and there are probably many among us who would erect this tendency into a duty. M. de Maupassant neglects nothing that he possesses; he cultivates his garden with admirable energy; and if there is a flower you miss from the rich parterre, you may be sure that it could not possibly have been raised, his mind not containing the soil for it. He is plainly of the opinion that the first duty of the artist, and the thing that makes him most useful to his fellow-men, is to master his instrument, whatever it may happen to be.

His own is that of the senses, and it is through them alone, or almost alone, that life appeals to him; it is almost alone by their help that he describes it, that he produces brilliant works. They render him this great assistance because they are evidently, in his constitution, extraordinarily alive; there is scarcely a page in all his twenty volumes that does not testify to their vivacity. Nothing could be further from his thought than to disavow them and to minimise their importance. He accepts them frankly, gratefully, works them, rejoices in them. If he were told that there are many English writers who would be sorry to go with him in this, he would, I imagine, staring, say that that is about what was to have been expected of the Anglo-Saxon race, or even that many of them probably could not go with him if they would. Then he would ask how our authors can be so foolish as to sacrifice such a *moyen*, how they can afford to, and exclaim, "They must be pretty works, those they produce, and give a fine, true, complete account of life, with such omissions, such lacunae!" M. de Maupassant's productions teach us, for instance, that his sense of smell is exceptionally acute—as acute as that of those animals of the field and forest whose subsistence and security depend upon it. It might be thought that he would, as a student of the human race, have found an abnormal development of this faculty embarrassing, scarcely knowing what to do with it, where to place it. But such an apprehension betrays an imperfect conception of his directness and resolution, as well as of his constant economy of means. Nothing whatever prevents him from representing the relations of men and women as largely governed by the scent of the parties. Human life in his pages (would this not be the most general description he would give of it?) appears for the most part as a sort of concert of odours, and his people are perpetually engaged, or he is engaged on their behalf, in sniffing up and distinguishing them, in some pleasant or painful exercise of the nostril. "If everything in life speaks to the nostril, why on earth shouldn't we say so?" I suppose him to inquire; "and what a proof of the empire of poor conventions and hypocrisies, *chez vous autres*, that you should pretend to describe and characterise, and yet take no note (or so little that it comes to the same thing) of that essential sign!"

Not less powerful is his visual sense, the quick, direct discrimination of his eye, which explains the singularly vivid concision of his descriptions. These are never prolonged nor analytic, have nothing of enumeration, of the quality of the observer, who counts the items to be sure he has made up the sum. His eye *selects* unerringly, unscrupulously, almost impudently—catches the particular thing in which the character of the object or the scene resides, and, by expressing it with the artful brevity of a master, leaves a convincing, original picture. If he is inveterately synthetic, he is never more so than in the way he brings this hard, short, intelligent gaze to bear. His vision of the world is for the most part a vision of ugliness, and even when it is not, there is in his easy power to generalise a certain absence of love, a sort of bird's-eye-view contempt. He has none of the superstitions of observation, none of our English indulgences, our tender and often imaginative superficialities. If he glances into a railway carriage bearing its freight into the Parisian suburbs of a summer Sunday, a dozen dreary lives map themselves out in a flash.

> There were stout ladies in farcical clothes, those middle-class goodwives of the *banlieue* who replace the distinction they don't possess by an irrelevant dignity; gentlemen weary of the office, with sallow faces and twisted bodies, and one of their shoulders a little forced up by perpetual bending at work over a table. Their anxious, joyless faces spoke moreover of domestic worries, incessant needs for money, old hopes finally shattered; for they all belonged to the army of poor threadbare devils who vegetate frugally in a mean little plaster house, with a flower-bed for a garden....

Even in a brighter picture, such as the admirable vignette of the drive of Madame Tellier and her companions, the whole thing is an impression, as painters say nowadays, in which the figures are cheap. The six women at the station clamber into a country cart and go jolting through the Norman landscape to the village.

> But presently the jerky trot of the nag shook the vehicle so terribly that the chairs began to dance, tossing up the travellers

to right, to left, with movements like puppets, scared grimaces, cries of dismay suddenly interrupted by a more violent bump. They clutched the sides of the trap, their bonnets turned over on to their backs, or upon the nose or the shoulder; and the white horse continued to go, thrusting out his head and straightening the little tail, hairless like that of a rat, with which from time to time he whisked his buttocks. Joseph Rivet, with one foot stretched upon the shaft, the other leg bent under him, and his elbows very high, held the reins and emitted from his throat every moment a kind of cluck which caused the animal to prick up his ears and quicken his pace. On either side of the road the green country stretched away. The colza, in flower, produced in spots a great carpet of undulating yellow, from which there rose a strong, wholesome smell, a smell penetrating and pleasant, carried very far by the breeze. In the tall rye the cornflowers held up their little azure heads, which the women wished to pluck; but M. Rivet refused to stop. Then, in some place, a whole field looked as if it were sprinkled with blood, it was so crowded with poppies. And in the midst of the great level, taking colour in this fashion from the flowers of the soil, the trap passed on with the jog of the white horse, seeming itself to carry a nosegay of richer hues; it disappeared behind the big trees of a farm, to come out again where the foliage stopped and parade afresh through the green and yellow crops, pricked with red or blue, its blazing cartload of women, which receded in the sunshine.

As regards the other sense, the sense *par excellence*, the sense which we scarcely mention in English fiction, and which I am not very sure I shall be allowed to mention in an English periodical, M. de Maupassant speaks for that, and of it, with extraordinary distinctness and authority. To say that it occupies the first place in his picture is to say too little; it covers in truth the whole canvas, and his work is little else but a report of its innumerable manifestations. These manifestations are not, for him, so many incidents of life; they are life itself, they represent the standing answer to any question that we may ask about it. He describes them in detail, with a familiarity and a frankness which leave nothing to be added; I should say with singular truth, if I did not consider that in regard to this article he may be taxed with a certain exaggeration. M. de Maupassant would doubtless affirm that where the empire of the sexual sense is concerned, no exaggeration is possible: nevertheless it may be said that whatever depths may be discovered by those who dig for them, the impression of the human spectacle for him who takes it as it comes has less analogy with that of the monkeys' cage than this admirable writer's account of it. I speak of the human spectacle as we Anglo-Saxons see it—as we Anglo-Saxons pretend we see it, M. de Maupassant would possibly say.

At any rate, I have perhaps touched upon this peculiarity sufficiently to explain my remark that his point of view is almost solely that of the senses. If he is a very interesting case, this makes him also an embarrassing one, embarrassing and mystifying for the moralist. I may as well admit that no writer of the day strikes me as equally so. To find M. de Maupassant a lion in the path—that may seem to some people a singular proof of want of courage; but I think the obstacle will not be made light of by those who have really taken the measure of the animal. We are accustomed to think, we of the English faith, that a cynic is a living advertisement of his errors, especially in proportion as he is a thorough-going one; and M. de Maupassant's cynicism, unrelieved as it is, will not be disposed of off-hand by a critic of a competent literary sense. Such a critic is not slow to perceive, to his no small confusion, that though, judging from usual premises, the author of *Bel-Ami* ought to be a warning, he somehow is not. His baseness, as it pervades him, ought to be written all over him; yet somehow there are there certain aspects—and those commanding, as the house-agents say—in which it is not in the least to be perceived. It is easy to exclaim that if he judges life only from the point of view of the senses, many are the noble and exquisite things that he must leave out. What he leaves out has no claim to get itself considered till after we have done justice to what he takes in. It is this positive side of M. de Maupassant that is most remarkable—the fact that his literary character is so complete and edifying. "Auteur à peu près irréprochable dans un genre qui ne l'est pas," as that excellent critic M. Jules Lemaître says of him, he disturbs us by associating a conscience and a high standard with a temper long synonymous, in our eyes, with an absence of scruples. The situation would be simpler certainly if he were a bad writer; but none the less it is possible, I think, on the whole, to circumvent him, even without attempting to prove that after all he is one.

The latter part of his introduction to *Pierre et Jean* is less felicitous than the beginning, but we learn from it—and this is interesting—that he regards the analytic fashion of telling a story, which has lately begotten in his own country some such remarkable experiments (few votaries as it has attracted among ourselves), as very much less profitable than the simple epic manner which "avoids with care all complicated explanations, all dissertations upon motives, and confines itself to making persons and events pass before our eyes." M. de Maupassant adds that in his view "psychology should be hidden in a book, as it is hidden in reality under the facts of existence. The novel conceived in this manner gains interest, movement, colour, the bustle of life." When it is a question of an artistic process, we must always mistrust very sharp distinctions, for there is surely in every method a little of every other method. It is as difficult to describe an action without glancing at its motive, its moral history, as it is to describe a motive without glancing at its practical consequence. Our history and our fiction are what we do; but it surely is not more easy to determine where what we do begins than to determine where it ends— notoriously a hopeless task. Therefore it would take a very subtle sense to draw a hard and fast line on the borderland of explanation and illustration. If psychology be hidden in life, as, according to M. de Maupassant, it should be in a book, the question immediately comes up, "From whom is it hidden?" From some people, no doubt, but very much less from others; and all depends upon the observer, the nature of one's observation, and one's curiosity. For some people motives, reasons, relations, explanations, are a part of the very surface of the drama, with the footlights beating full upon them. For me an act, an incident, an attitude, may be a sharp, detached, isolated thing, of which I give a full account in saying that in such and such a way it came off. For you it may be hung about with implications, with relations, and conditions as necessary to help you to recognise it as the clothes of your friends are to help you know them in the street. You feel that they would seem strange to you without petticoats and trousers.

M. de Maupassant would probably urge that the right thing is to know, or to guess, how events come to pass, but to say as little about it as possible. There are matters in regard to which he feels the importance of being explicit, but that is not one of them. The contention to which I allude strikes me as rather arbitrary, so difficult is it to put one's finger upon the reason why, for instance, there should be so little mystery about what happened to Christiane Andermatt, in *Mont-Oriol*, when she went to walk on the hills with Paul Brétigny, and so much, say, about the forces that formed her for that gentleman's convenience, or those lying behind any other odd collapse that our author may have related. The rule misleads, and the best rule certainly is the tact of the individual writer, which will adapt itself to the material as the material comes to him. The cause we plead is ever pretty sure to be the cause of our idiosyncrasies, and if M. de Maupassant thinks meanly of "explanations," it is, I suspect, that they come to him in no great affluence. His view of the conduct of man is so simple as scarcely to require them; and indeed so far as they are needed he *is*, virtually, explanatory. He deprecates reference to motives, but there is one, covering an immense ground in his horizon, as I have already hinted, to which he perpetually refers. If the sexual impulse be not a moral antecedent, it is none the less the wire that moves almost all M. de Maupassant's puppets, and as he has not hidden it, I cannot see that he has eliminated analysis or made a sacrifice to discretion. His pages are studded with that particular analysis; he is constantly peeping behind the curtain, telling us what he discovers there. The truth is that the admirable system of simplification which makes his tales so rapid and so concise (especially his shorter ones, for his novels in some degree, I think, suffer from it), strikes us as not in the least a conscious intellectual effort, a selective, comparative process. He tells us all he knows, all he suspects, and if these things take no account of the moral nature of man, it is because he has no window looking in that direction, and not because artistic scruples have compelled him to close it up. The very compact mansion in which he dwells presents on that side a perfectly dead wall.

This is why, if his axiom that you produce the effect of truth better by painting people from the outside than from the inside has a large utility, his example is convincing in a much higher degree. A writer is fortunate when his theory and his limitations so exactly correspond, when his curiosities may be appeased with such precision and promptitude. M. de Maupassant contends that the most that the analytic novelist can do is to put himself—his own peculiarities—into the costume of the figure analysed. This may be true, but if it applies to one manner of representing people who are not ourselves, it applies also to any other manner. It is the limitation, the difficulty of the novelist, to whatever clan or camp he may belong. M. de Maupassant is remarkably objective and impersonal, but he would go too far if he were to entertain the belief that he has kept himself out of his books. They speak of him eloquently, even if it only be to tell us how easy—how easy, given his talent of course—he has found this impersonality. Let us hasten to add that in the case of describing a character it is doubtless more difficult to convey the impression of something that is not one's self (the constant effort, however delusive at bottom, of the novelist), than in the case of describing some object more immediately visible. The operation is more delicate, but that circumstance only increases the beauty of the problem.

On the question of style our author has some excellent remarks; we may be grateful indeed for every one of them, save an odd reflection about the way to "become original" if we happen not to be so. The recipe for this transformation, it would appear, is to sit down in front of a blazing fire, or a tree in a plain, or any object we encounter in the regular way of business, and remain there until the tree, or the fire, or the object, whatever it be, become different for us from all other specimens of the same class. I doubt whether this system would always answer, for surely the resemblance is what we wish to discover, quite as much as the difference, and the best way to preserve it is not to look for something opposed to it. Is not this indication of the road to take to become, as a writer, original touched with the same fallacy as the recommendation about eschewing analysis? It is the only *naïveté* I have encountered in M. de Maupassant's many volumes. The best originality is the most unconscious, and the best way to describe a tree is the way in which it has struck us. "Ah, but we don't always know how it has struck us," the answer to that may be, "and it takes some time and ingenuity—much fasting and prayer—to find out." If we do not know, it probably has not struck us very much: so little indeed that our inquiry had better be relegated to that closed chamber of an artist's meditations, that sacred back kitchen, which no *a priori* rule can light up. The best thing the artist's adviser can do in such a case is to trust him and turn away, to let him fight the matter out with his conscience. And be this said with a full appreciation of the degree in which M. de Maupassant's observations on the whole question of a writer's style, at the point we have come to to-day, bear the stamp of intelligence and experience. His own style is of so excellent a tradition that the presumption is altogether in favour of what he may have to say.

He feels oppressively, discouragingly, as many another of his countrymen must have felt—for the French have worked their language as no other people have done—the penalty of coming at the end of three centuries of literature, the difficulty of dealing with an instrument of expression so worn by friction, of drawing new sounds from the old familiar pipe. "When we read, so saturated with French writing as we are that our whole body gives us the impression of being a paste made of words, do we ever find a line, a thought, which is not familiar to us, and of which we have not had at least a confused presentiment?" And he adds that the matter is simple enough for the writer who only seeks to amuse the public by means already known; he attempts little, and he produces "with confidence, in the candour of his mediocrity," works which answer no question and leave no trace. It is he who wants to do more than this that has less and less an easy time of it. Everything seems to him to have been done, every effect produced, every combination already made. If he be a man of genius, his trouble is lightened, for mysterious ways are revealed to him, and new combinations spring up for him even after novelty is dead. It is to the simple man of taste and talent, who has only a conscience and a will, that the situation may sometimes well appear desperate; he judges himself as he goes, and he can only go step by step over ground where every step is already a footprint.

If it be a miracle whenever there is a fresh tone, the miracle has been wrought for M. de Maupassant. Or is he simply a man of genius to whom short cuts have been disclosed in the watches of the night? At any rate he has had faith—religion has come to his aid; I mean the religion of his mother tongue, which he has loved well enough to be patient for her sake. He has arrived at the peace which passeth understanding, at a kind of conservative piety. He has taken his stand on simplicity, on a studied sobriety, being persuaded that the deepest science lies in that direction rather than in the multiplication of new terms, and on this subject he delivers himself with superlative wisdom. "There is no need of the queer, complicated, numerous, and Chinese vocabulary which is imposed on us to-day under the name of artistic writing, to fix all the shades of thought; the right way is to distinguish with an extreme clearness all those modifications of the value of a word which come from the place it occupies. Let us have fewer nouns, verbs and adjectives of an almost imperceptible sense, and more different phrases variously constructed, ingeniously cast, full of the science of sound and rhythm. Let us have an excellent general form rather than be collectors of rare terms." M. de Maupassant's practice does not fall below his exhortation (though I must confess that in the foregoing passage he makes use of the detestable expression "stylist," which I have not reproduced). Nothing can exceed the masculine firmness, the quiet force of his own style, in which every phrase is a close sequence, every epithet a paying piece, and the ground is completely cleared of the vague, the ready-made and the second-best. Less than any one to-day does he beat the air; more than any one does he hit out from the shoulder.

2

He has produced a hundred short tales and only four regular novels; but if the tales deserve the first place in any candid appreciation of his talent it is not simply because they are so much the more numerous: they are also more characteristic; they represent him best in his originality, and their brevity, extreme in some cases, does not prevent them from being a collection of masterpieces. (They are very unequal, and I speak of the best.) The little story is but scantily relished in England, where readers take their fiction rather by the volume than by the page, and the novelist's idea is apt to resemble one of those old-fashioned carriages which require a wide court to turn round. In America, where it is associated pre-eminently with Hawthorne's name, with Edgar Poe's, and with that of Mr. Bret Harte, the short tale has had a better fortune. France, however, has been the land of its great prosperity, and M. de Maupassant had from the first the advantage of addressing a public accustomed to catch on, as the modern phrase is, quickly. In some respects, it may be said, he encountered prejudices too friendly, for he found a tradition of indecency ready made to his hand. I say indecency with plainness, though my indication would perhaps please better with another word, for we suffer in English from a lack of roundabout names for the *conte leste*—that element for which the French, with their *grivois,* their *gaillard*, their *égrillard,* their *gaudriole,* have so many convenient synonyms. It is an honoured tradition in France that the little story, in verse or in prose, should be liable to be more or less obscene (I can think only of that alternative epithet), though I hasten to add that among literary forms it does not monopolise the privilege. Our uncleanness is less producible—at any rate it is less produced.

For the last ten years our author has brought forth with regularity these condensed compositions, of which, probably, to an English reader, at a first glance, the most universal sign will be their licentiousness. They really partake of this quality, however, in a very differing degree, and a second glance shows that they may be divided into numerous groups. It is not fair, I think, even to say that what they have most in common is their being extremely *lestes.* What they have most in common is their being extremely strong, and after that their being extremely brutal. A story may be obscene without being brutal, and *vice versâ,* and M. de Maupassant's contempt for those interdictions which are supposed to be made in the interest of good morals is but an incident—a very large one indeed—of his general contempt. A pessimism so great that its alliance with the love of good work, or even with the calculation of the sort of work that pays best in a country of style, is, as I have intimated, the most puzzling of anomalies (for it would seem in the light of such sentiments that nothing is worth anything), this cynical strain is the sign of such gems of narration as "La Maison Tellier," "L'Histoire d'une Fille de Ferme," "L'Ane," "Le Chien, Mademoiselle Fifi," "Monsieur Parent," "L'Heritage," "En Famille," "Le Baptême," "Le Père Amable.*"* The author fixes a hard eye on some small spot of human life, usually some ugly, dreary, shabby, sordid one, takes up the particle, and squeezes it either till it grimaces or till it bleeds. Sometimes the grimace is very droll, sometimes the wound is very horrible; but in either case the whole thing is real, observed, noted, and represented, not an invention or a castle in the air. M. de Maupassant sees human life as a terribly ugly business relieved by the comical, but even the comedy is for the most part the comedy of misery, of avidity, of ignorance, helplessness, and grossness. When his laugh is not for these things, it is for the little *saletés* (to use one of his own favourite words) of luxurious life, which are intended to be prettier, but which can scarcely be said to brighten the picture. I like "La Bête à Maître Belhomme," "La Ficelle," "Le Petit Fût," "Le Cas de Madame Luneau," "Tribunaux Rustiques," and many others of this category much better than his anecdotes of the mutual confidences of his little *marquises* and *baronnes.*

Not counting his novels for the moment, his tales may be divided into the three groups of those which deal with the Norman peasantry, those which deal with the *petit employé* and small shopkeeper, usually in Paris, and the miscellaneous, in which the upper walks of life are represented, and the fantastic, the whimsical, the weird, and even the supernatural, figure as well as the unexpurgated. These last things range from "Le Horla" (which is not a specimen of the author's best vein—the only occasion on which he has the weakness of imitation is when he strikes us as emulating Edgar Poe) to "Miss Harriet," and from "Boule de Suif" (a triumph) to that almost inconceivable little growl of Anglophobia, "Découverte"—inconceivable I mean in its irresponsibility and ill-nature on the part of a man of M. de Maupassant's distinction; passing by such little perfections as "Petit Soldat," "L'Abandonné, Le Collier" (the list is too long for complete enumeration), and such gross imperfections (for it once in a while befalls our author to go woefully astray), as "La Femme de Paul," "Châli," "Les Soeurs Rondoli." To these might almost be added as a special category the various forms in which M. de Maupassant relates adventures in railway carriages. Numerous, to his imagination, are the pretexts for enlivening fiction afforded by first, second, and third class compartments; the accidents (which have nothing to do with the conduct of the train) that occur there constitute no inconsiderable part of our earthly transit.

It is surely by his Norman peasant that his tales will live; he knows this worthy as if he had made him, understands him down to the ground, puts him on his feet with a few of the freest, most plastic touches. M. de Maupassant does not admire him, and he is such a master of the subject that it would ill become an outsider to suggest a revision of judgment. He is a part of the contemptible furniture of the world, but on the whole, it would appear, the most grotesque part of it. His caution, his canniness, his natural astuteness, his stinginess, his general grinding sordidness, are as unmistakable as that quaint and brutish dialect in which he expresses himself, and on which our author plays like a virtuoso. It would be impossible to demonstrate with a finer sense of the humour of the thing the fatuities and densities of his ignorance, the bewilderments of his opposed appetites, the overreachings of his caution. His existence has a gay side, but it is apt to be the barbarous gaiety commemorated in "Farce Normande," an anecdote which, like many of M. de Maupassant's anecdotes, it is easier to refer the reader to than to repeat. If it is most convenient to place "La Maison Tellier" among the tales of the peasantry, there is no doubt that it stands at the head of the list. It is absolutely unadapted to the perusal of ladies and young persons, but it shares this peculiarity with most of its fellows, so that to ignore it on that account would be to imply that we must forswear M. de Maupassant altogether, which is an incongruous and insupportable conclusion. Every good story is of course both a picture and an idea, and the more they are interfused the better the problem is solved. In "La Maison Tellier" they fit each other to perfection; the capacity for sudden innocent delights latent in natures which have lost their innocence is vividly illustrated by the singular scenes to which our acquaintance with Madame and her staff (little as it may be a thing to boast of), successively introduces us. The breadth, the freedom, and brightness of all this give the measure of the author's talent, and of that large, keen way of looking at life which sees the pathetic and the droll, the stuff of which the whole piece is made, in the queerest and humblest patterns. The tone of "La Maison Tellier" and the few compositions which closely resemble it, expresses M. de Maupassant's nearest approach to geniality. Even here, however, it is the geniality of the showman exhilarated by the success with which he feels that he makes his mannikins (and especially his womankins) caper and squeak, and who after the performance tosses them into their box with the irreverence of a practised hand. If the pages of the author of *Bel-Ami* may be searched almost in vain for a manifestation of the sentiment of respect, it is naturally not by Mme. Tellier and her charges that we must look most to see it called forth; but they are among the things that please him most.

Sometimes there is a sorrow, a misery, or even a little heroism, that he handles with a certain tenderness (*Une Vie* is the capital example of this), without insisting on the poor, the ridiculous, or, as he is fond of saying, the bestial side of it. Such an attempt, admirable in its sobriety and delicacy, is the sketch, in "L'Abandonné," of the old lady and gentleman, Mme. de Cadour and M. d'Apreval, who, staying with the husband of the former at a little watering-place on the Normandy coast, take a long, hot walk on a summer's day, on a straight, white road, into the interior, to catch a clandestine glimpse of a young farmer, their illegitimate son. He has been pensioned, he is ignorant of his origin, and is a commonplace and unconciliatory rustic. They look at him, in his dirty farmyard, and no sign passes between them; then they turn away and crawl back, in melancholy silence, along the dull French road. The manner in which this dreary little occurrence is related makes it as large as a chapter of history. There is tenderness in *Miss Harriet*, which sets forth how an English old maid, fantastic, hideous, sentimental, and tract-distributing, with a smell of india-rubber, fell in love with an irresistible French painter, and drowned herself in the well because she saw him kissing the maid-servant; but the figure of the lady grazes the farcical. Is it because we know Miss Harriet (if we are not mistaken in the type the author has had in his eye) that we suspect the good spinster was not so weird and desperate, addicted though her class may be, as he says, to "haunting all the *tables d'hôte* in Europe, to spoiling Italy, poisoning Switzerland, making the charming towns of the Mediterranean uninhabitable, carrying everywhere their queer little manias, their *moeurs de vestales pétrifiées*, their indescribable garments, and that odour of india-rubber which makes one think that at night they must be slipped into a case?" What would Miss Harriet have said to M. de Maupassant's friend, the hero of the "Découverte," who, having married a little Anglaise because he thought she was charming when she spoke broken French, finds she is very flat as she becomes more fluent, and has nothing more urgent than to denounce her to a gentleman he meets on the steamboat, and to relieve his wrath in ejaculations of "Sales Anglais"?

M. de Maupassant evidently knows a great deal about the army of clerks who work under government, but it is a terrible tale that he has to tell of them and of the *petit bourgeois* in general. It is true that he has treated the *petit bourgeois* in *Pierre et Jean* without holding him up to our derision, and the effort has been so fruitful, that we owe to it the work for which, on the whole, in the long list of his successes, we are most thankful. But of *Pierre et Jean,* a production neither comic nor cynical (in the degree, that is, of its predecessors), but serious and fresh, I will speak anon. In "Monsieur Parent,"

"L'Héritage," "En Famille," "Une Partie de Campagne," "Promenade," and many other pitiless little pieces, the author opens the window wide to his perception of everything mean, narrow, and sordid. The subject is ever the struggle for existence in hard conditions, lighted up simply by more or less *polissonnerie.* Nothing is more striking to an Anglo-Saxon reader than the omission of all the other lights, those with which our imagination, and I think it ought to be said our observation, is familiar, and which our own works of fiction at any rate do not permit us to forget: those of which the most general description is that they spring from a certain mixture of good-humour and piety—piety, I mean, in the civil and domestic sense quite as much as in the religious. The love of sport, the sense of decorum, the necessity for action, the habit of respect, the absence of irony, the pervasiveness of childhood, the expansive tendency of the race, are a few of the qualities (the analysis might, I think, be pushed much further) which ease us off, mitigate our tension and irritation, rescue us from the nervous exasperation which is almost the commonest element of life as depicted by M. de Maupassant. No doubt there is in our literature an immense amount of conventional blinking, and it may be questioned whether pessimistic representation in M. de Maupassant's manner do not follow his particular original more closely than our perpetual quest of pleasantness (does not Mr. Rider Haggard make even his African carnage pleasant?) adheres to the lines of the world we ourselves know.

Fierce indeed is the struggle for existence among even our pious and good-humoured millions, and it is attended with incidents as to which after all little testimony is to be extracted from our literature of fiction. It must never be forgotten that the optimism of that literature is partly the optimism of women and of spinsters; in other words the optimism of ignorance as well as of delicacy. It might be supposed that the French, with their mastery of the *arts d'agrément,* would have more consolations than we, but such is not the account of the matter given by the new generation of painters. To the French we seem superficial, and we are certainly open to the reproach; but none the less even to the infinite majority of readers of good faith there will be a wonderful want of correspondence between the general picture of *Bel-Ami*, of *Mont-Oriol*, of *Une Vie, Yvette* and "En Famille," and our own vision of reality. It is an old impression of course that the satire of the French has a very different tone from ours; but few English readers will admit that the feeling of life is less in ours than in theirs. The feeling of life is evidently, *de part et d'autre,* a very different thing. If in ours, as the novel illustrates it, there are superficialities, there are also qualities which are far from being negatives and omissions: a large imagination and (is it fatuous to say?) a large experience of the positive kind. Even those of our novelists whose manner is most ironic pity life more and hate it less than M. de Maupassant and his great initiator Flaubert. It comes back I suppose to our good-humour (which may apparently also be an artistic force); at any rate, we have reserves about our shames and our sorrows, indulgences and tolerances about our Philistinism, forbearances about our blows, and a general friendliness of conception about our possibilities, which take the cruelty from our self-derision and operate in the last resort as a sort of tribute to our freedom. There is a horrible, admirable scene in "Monsieur Parent," which is a capital example of triumphant ugliness. The harmless gentleman who gives his name to the tale has an abominable wife, one of whose offensive attributes is a lover (unsuspected by her husband), only less impudent than herself. M. Parent comes in from a walk with his little boy, at dinner-time, to encounter suddenly in his abused, dishonoured, deserted home, convincing proof of her misbehaviour. He waits and waits dinner for her, giving her the benefit of every doubt; but when at last she enters, late in the evening, accompanied by the partner of her guilt, there is a tremendous domestic concussion. It is to the peculiar vividness of this scene that I allude, the way we hear it and see it, and its most repulsive details are evoked for us: the sordid confusion, the vulgar noise, the disordered table and ruined dinner, the shrill insolence of the wife, her brazen mendacity, the scared inferiority of the lover, the mere momentary heroics of the weak husband, the scuffle and somersault, the eminently unpoetic justice with which it all ends.

When Thackeray relates how Arthur Pendennis goes home to take pot-luck with the insolvent Newcomes at Boulogne, and how the dreadful Mrs. Mackenzie receives him, and how she makes a scene, when the frugal repast is served, over the diminished mutton-bone, we feel that the notation of that order of misery goes about as far as we can bear it. But this is child's play to the history of M. and Mme. Caravan and their attempt, after the death (or supposed death) of the husband's mother, to transfer to their apartment before the arrival of the other heirs certain miserable little articles of furniture belonging to the deceased, together with the frustration of the manoeuvre not only by the grim resurrection of the old woman (which is a sufficiently fantastic item), but by the shock of battle when a married daughter and her husband appear. No one gives us like M. de Maupassant the odious words exchanged on such an occasion as that: no one depicts with so just a hand the feelings of small people about small things. These feelings are very apt to be "fury"; that word is of strikingly frequent occurrence in his pages. "L'Héritage" is a drama of private life in the little world of the Ministère de la Marine—a world, according to M. de Maupassant, of dreadful little jealousies and ineptitudes. Readers of a robust complexion should learn how the wretched M. Lesable was handled by his wife and her father on his failing to satisfy their just expectations, and how he comported himself in the singular situation thus prepared for him. The story is a model of narration, but it leaves our poor average humanity dangling like a beaten rag.

Where does M. de Maupassant find the great multitude of his detestable women? or where at least does he find the courage to represent them in such colours? Jeanne de Lamare, in *Une Vie,* receives the outrages of fate with a passive fortitude; and there is something touching in Mme. Roland's *âme tendre de caissière,* as exhibited in *Pierre et Jean.* But for the most part M. de Maupassant's heroines are a mixture of extreme sensuality and extreme mendacity. They are a large element in that general disfigurement, that *illusion de l'ignoble, qui attire tant d'êtres,* which makes the perverse or the stupid side of things the one which strikes him first, which leads him, if he glances at a group of nurses and children sunning themselves in a Parisian square, to notice primarily the *yeux de brute* of the nurses; or if he speaks of the longing for a taste of the country which haunts the shopkeeper fenced in behind his counter, to identify it as the *amour bête de la nature*; or if he has occasion to put the boulevards before us on a summer's evening, to seek his effect in these terms: "The city, as hot as a stew, seemed to sweat in the suffocating night. The drains puffed their pestilential breath from their mouths of granite, and the underground kitchens poured into the streets, through their low windows, the infamous miasmas of their dishwater and old sauces." I do not contest the truth of such indications, I only note the particular selection and their seeming to the writer the most *apropos*.

Is it because of the inadequacy of these indications when applied to the long stretch that M. de Maupassant's novels strike us as less complete, in proportion to the talent expended upon them, than his *contes* and *nouvelles*? I make this invidious distinction in spite of the fact that *Une Vie* (the first of the novels in the order of time) is a remarkably interesting experiment, and that *Pierre et Jean* is, so far as my judgment goes, a faultless production. *Bel-Ami* is full of the bustle and the crudity of life (its energy and expressiveness almost bribe one to like it), but it has the great defect that the physiological explanation of things here too visibly contracts the problem in order to meet it. The world represented is too special, too little inevitable, too much to take or to leave as we like—a world in which every man is a cad and every woman a harlot. M. de Maupassant traces the career of a finished blackguard who succeeds in life through women, and he represents him primarily as succeeding in the profession of journalism. His colleagues and his mistresses are as depraved as himself, greatly to the injury of the ironic idea, for the real force of satire would have come from seeing him engaged and victorious with natures better than his own. It may be remarked that this was the case with the nature of Mme. Walter; but the reply to that is—hardly! Moreover the author's whole treatment of the episode of Mme. Walter is the thing on which his admirers have least to congratulate him. The taste of it is so atrocious, that it is difficult to do justice to the way it is made to stand out. Such an instance as this pleads with irresistible eloquence, as it seems to me, the cause of that salutary diffidence or practical generosity which I mentioned on a preceding page. I know not the English or American novelist who could have written this portion of the history of *Bel-Ami* if he would. But I also find it impossible to conceive of a member of that fraternity who would have written it if he could. The subject of *Mont-Oriol* is full of queerness to the English mind. Here again the picture has much more importance than the idea, which is simply that a gentleman, if he happen to be a low animal, is liable to love a lady very much less if she presents him with a pledge of their affection. It need scarcely be said that the lady and gentleman who in M. de Maupassant's pages exemplify this interesting truth are not united in wedlock—that is with each other.

M. de Maupassant tells us that he has imbibed many of his principles from Gustave Flaubert, from the study of his works as well as, formerly, the enjoyment of his words. It is in *Une Vie* that Flaubert's influence is most directly traceable, for the thing has a marked analogy with *L'Education Sentimentale.* That is, it is the presentation of a simple piece of a life (in this case a long piece), a series of observations upon an episode *quelconque,* as the French say, with the minimum of arrangement of the given objects. It is an excellent example of the way the impression of truth may be conveyed by that form, but it would have been a still better one if in his search for the effect of dreariness (the effect of dreariness may be said to be the subject of *Une Vie* so far as the subject is reducible) the author had not eliminated excessively. He has arranged, as I say, as little as possible; the necessity of a "plot" has in no degree imposed itself upon him, and his effort has been to give the uncomposed, unrounded look of life, with its accidents, its broken rhythm, its queer resemblance to the famous description of "Bradshaw"—a compound of trains that start but don't arrive, and trains that arrive but don't start. It is almost an arrangement of the history of poor Mme. de Lamare to have left so many things out of it, for after all she is described in very few of the relations of life. The principal ones are there certainly; we see her as a daughter, a wife, and a mother, but there is a certain accumulation of secondary experience that marks any passage from youth to old age which is a wholly absent element in M. de Maupassant's narrative, and the suppression of which gives the thing a tinge of the arbitrary. It is in the power of this secondary experience to make a great difference, but nothing makes any difference for Jeanne de Lamare as M. de Maupassant puts her before us. Had she no other points of contact than those he describes?—no friends, no phases, no episodes, no chances, none of the miscellaneous *remplissage* of life? No doubt M. de Maupassant would say that he has had to select, that the most comprehensive enumeration is only a condensation, and that, in accordance with the very just principles enunciated in that preface to which I have perhaps too repeatedly referred, he has sacrificed what is uncharacteristic to what is characteristic. It characterises the career of this French country lady of fifty years ago that its long gray expanse should be seen as peopled with but five or six figures. The essence of the matter is that she was deceived in almost every affection, and that essence is given if the persons who deceived her are given.

The reply is doubtless adequate, and I have only intended my criticism to suggest the degree of my interest. What it really amounts to is that if the subject of this artistic experiment had been the existence of an English lady, even a very dull one, the air of verisimilitude would have demanded that she should have been placed in a denser medium. *Une Vie* may after all be only a testimony to the fact of the melancholy void of the coast of Normandy, even within a moderate drive of a great seaport, under the Restoration and Louis Philippe. It is especially to be recommended to those who are interested in the question of what constitutes a "story," offering as it does the most definite sequences at the same time that it has nothing that corresponds to the usual idea of a plot, and closing with an implication that finds us prepared. The picture again in this case is much more dominant than the idea, unless it be an idea that loneliness and grief are terrible. The picture, at any rate, is full of truthful touches, and the work has the merit and the charm that it is the most delicate of the author's productions and the least hard. In none other has he occupied himself so continuously with so innocent a figure as his soft, bruised heroine; in none other has he paid our poor blind human history the compliment (and this is remarkable, considering the flatness of so much of the particular subject) of finding it so little *bête*. He may think it, here, but comparatively he does not say it. He almost betrays a sense of moral things. Jeanne is absolutely passive, she has no moral spring, no active moral life, none of the edifying attributes of character (it costs her apparently as little as may be in the way of a shock, a complication of feeling, to discover, by letters, after her mother's death, that this lady has not been the virtuous woman she has supposed); but her chronicler has had to handle the immaterial forces of patience and renunciation, and this has given the book a certain purity, in spite of two or three "physiological" passages that come in with violence—a violence the greater as we feel it to be a result of selection. It is very much a mark of M. de Maupassant that on the most striking occasion, with a single exception, on which his picture is not a picture of libertinage it is a picture of unmitigated suffering. Would he suggest that these are the only alternatives?

The exception that I here allude to is for *Pierre et Jean*, which I have left myself small space to speak of. Is it because in this masterly little novel there is a show of those immaterial forces which I just mentioned, and because Pierre Roland is one of the few instances of operative character that can be recalled from so many volumes, that many readers will place M. de Maupassant's latest production altogether at the head of his longer ones? I am not sure, inasmuch as after all the character in question is not extraordinarily distinguished, and the moral problem not presented in much complexity. The case is only relative. Perhaps it is not of importance to fix the reasons of preference in respect to a piece of writing so essentially a work of art and of talent. *Pierre et Jean* is the best of M. de Maupassant's novels mainly because M. de Maupassant has never before been so clever. It is a pleasure to see a mature talent able to renew itself, strike another note, and appear still young. This story suggests the growth of a perception that everything has not been said about the actors on the world's stage when they are represented either as helpless victims or as mere bundles of appetites. There is an air of responsibility about Pierre Roland, the person on whose behalf the tale is mainly told, which almost constitutes a pledge. An inquisitive critic may ask why in this particular case M. de Maupassant should have stuck to the *petit bourgeois*, the circumstances not being such as to typify that class more than another. There are reasons indeed which on reflection are perceptible; it was necessary that his people should be poor, and necessary even that to attenuate Madame Roland's misbehaviour she should have had the excuse of the contracted life of a shopwoman in the Rue Montmartre. Were the inquisitive critic slightly malicious as well, he might suspect the author of a fear that he should seem to give way to the *illusion du beau* if in addition to representing the little group in *Pierre et Jean* as persons of about the normal conscience he had also represented them as of the cultivated class. If they belong to the humble life this belittles and—I am still quoting the supposedly malicious critic—M. de Maupassant *must,* in one way or the other, belittle. To the English reader it will appear, I think, that Pierre and Jean are rather more of the cultivated class than two young Englishmen in the same social position. It belongs to the drama that the struggle of the elder brother—educated, proud, and acute—should be partly with the pettiness of his opportunities. The author's choice of a *milieu*, moreover, will serve to English readers as an example of how much more democratic contemporary French fiction is than that of his own country. The greater part of it—almost all the work of Zola and of Daudet, the best of Flaubert's novels, and the best of those of the brothers De Goncourt—treat of that vast, dim section of society which, lying between those luxurious walks on whose behalf there are easy presuppositions and that darkness of misery which, in addition to being picturesque, brings philanthropy also to the writer's aid, constitutes really, in extent and expressiveness, the substance of any nation. In England, where the fashion of fiction still sets mainly to the country house and the hunting-field, and yet more novels are published than anywhere else in the world, that thick twilight of mediocrity of condition has been little explored. May it yield triumphs in the years to come!

It may seem that I have claimed little for M. de Maupassant, so far as English readers are concerned with him, in saying that after publishing twenty improper volumes he has at last published a twenty-first, which is neither indecent nor cynical. It is not this circumstance that has led me to dedicate so many pages to him, but the circumstance that in producing all the others he yet remained, for those who are interested in these matters, a writer with whom it was impossible not to reckon. This is why I called him, to begin with, so many ineffectual names: a rarity, a "case," an embarrassment, a lion in the path. He is still in the path as I conclude these observations, but I think that in making them we have discovered a legitimate way round. If he is a master of his art and it is discouraging to find what low views are compatible with mastery, there is satisfaction, on the other hand in learning on what particular condition he holds his strange success. This condition, it seems to me, is that of having totally omitted one of the items of the problem, an omission which has made the problem so much easier that it may almost be described as a short cut to a solution. The question is whether it be a fair cut. M. de Maupassant has simply skipped the whole reflective part of his men and women—that reflective part which governs conduct and produces character. He may say that he does not see it, does not know it; to which the answer is, "So much the better for you, if you wish to describe life without it. The strings you pull are by so much the less numerous, and you can therefore pull those that remain with greater promptitude, consequently with greater firmness, with a greater air of knowledge." Pierre Roland, I repeat, shows a capacity for reflection, but I cannot think who else does, among the thousand figures who compete with him—I mean for reflection addressed to anything higher than the gratification of an instinct. We have an impression that M. d'Apreval and Madame de Cadour reflect, as they trudge back from their mournful excursion, but that indication is not pushed very far. An aptitude for this exercise is a part of disciplined manhood, and disciplined manhood M. de Maupassant has simply not attempted to represent. I can remember no instance in which he sketches any considerable capacity for conduct, and his women betray that capacity as little as his men. I am much mistaken if he has once painted a gentleman, in the English sense of the term. His gentlemen, like Paul

Breétigny and Gontran de Ravenel, are guilty of the most extraordinary deflections. For those who are conscious of this element in life, look for it and like it, the gap will appear to be immense. It will lead them to say, "No wonder you have a contempt if that is the way you limit the field. No wonder you judge people roughly if that is the way you see them. Your work, on your premisses, remains the admirable thing it is, but is your 'case' not adequately explained?"

The erotic element in M. de Maupassant, about which much more might have been said, seems to me to be explained by the same limitation, and explicable in a similar way wherever else its literature occurs in excess. The carnal side of man appears the most characteristic if you look at it a great deal; and you look at it a great deal if you do not look at the other, at the side by which he reacts against his weaknesses, his defeats. The more you look at the other, the less the whole business to which French novelists have ever appeared to English readers to give a disproportionate place—the business, as I may say, of the senses—will strike you as the only typical one. Is not this the most useful reflection to make in regard to the famous question of the morality, the decency, of the novel? It is the only one, it seems to me, that will meet the case as we find the case to-day. Hard and fast rules, *a priori* restrictions, mere interdictions (you shall not speak of this, you shall not look at that), have surely served their time, and will in the nature of the case never strike an energetic talent as anything but arbitrary. A healthy, living and growing art, full of curiosity and fond of exercise, has an indefeasible mistrust of rigid prohibitions. Let us then leave this magnificent art of the novelist to itself and to its perfect freedom, in the faith that one example is as good as another, and that our fiction will always be decent enough if it be sufficiently general. Let us not be alarmed at this prodigy (though prodigies are alarming) of M. de Maupassant, who is at once so licentious and so impeccable, but gird ourselves up with the conviction that another point of view will yield another perfection.

THE FUTURE OF THE NOVEL

BEGINNINGS, as we all know, are usually small things, but continuations are not always strikingly great ones, and the place occupied in the world by the prolonged prose fable has become, in our time, among the incidents of literature, the most surprising example to be named of swift and extravagant growth, a development beyond the measure of every early appearance. It is a form that has had a fortune so little to have been foretold at its cradle. The germ of the comprehensive epic was more recognisable in the first barbaric chant than that of the novel as we know it to-day in the first anecdote retailed to amuse. It arrived, in truth, the novel, late at self-consciousness; but it has done its utmost ever since to make up for lost opportunities. The flood at present swells and swells, threatening the whole field of letters, as would often seem, with submersion. It plays, in what may be called the passive consciousness of many persons, a part that directly marches with the rapid increase of the multitude able to possess itself in one way and another of the *book*. The book, in the Anglo-Saxon world, is almost everywhere, and it is in the form of the voluminous prose fable that we see it penetrate easiest and farthest. Penetration appears really to be directly aided by mere mass and bulk. There is an immense public, if public be the name, inarticulate, but abysmally absorbent, for which, at its hours of ease, the printed volume has no other association. This public—the public that subscribes, borrows, lends, that picks up in one way and another, sometimes even by purchase—grows and grows each year, and nothing is thus more apparent than that of all the recruits it brings to the book the most numerous by far are those that it brings to the "story."

This number has gained, in our time, an augmentation from three sources in particular, the first of which, indeed, is perhaps but a comprehensive name for the two others. The diffusion of the rudiments, the multiplication of common schools, has had more and more the effect of making readers of women and of the very young. Nothing is so striking in a survey of this field, and nothing to be so much borne in mind, as that the larger part of the great multitude that sustains the teller and the publisher of tales is constituted by boys and girls; by girls in especial, if we apply the term to the later stages of the life of the innumerable women who, under modern arrangements, increasingly fail to marry—fail, apparently, even, largely, to desire to. It is not too much to say of many of these that they live in a great measure by the immediate aid of the novel—confining the question, for the moment, to the fact of consumption alone. The literature, as it may be called for convenience, of children is an industry that occupies by itself a very considerable quarter of the scene. Great fortunes, if not great reputations, are made, we learn, by writing for schoolboys, and the period during which they consume the compound artfully prepared for them appears—as they begin earlier and continue later—to add to itself at both ends. This helps to account for the fact that public libraries, especially those that are private and money-making enterprises, put into circulation more volumes of "stories" than of all other things together of which volumes can be made. The published statistics are extraordinary, and of a sort to engender many kinds of uneasiness. The sort of taste that used to be called "good" has nothing to do with the matter: we are so demonstrably in presence of millions for whom taste is but an obscure, confused, immediate instinct. In the flare of railway bookstalls, in the shop-fronts of most booksellers, especially the provincial, in the advertisements of the weekly newspapers, and in fifty places besides, this testimony to the general preference triumphs, yielding a good-natured corner at most to a bunch of treatises on athletics or sport, or a patch of theology old and new.

The case is so marked, however, that illustrations easily overflow, and there is no need of forcing doors that stand wide open. What remains is the interesting oddity or mystery—the anomaly that fairly dignifies the whole circumstance with its strangeness: the wonder, in short, that men, women, and children *should* have so much attention to spare for improvisations mainly so arbitrary and frequently so loose. That, at the first blush, fairly leaves us gaping. This great fortune then, since fortune it seems, has been reserved for mere unsupported and unguaranteed history, the *inexpensive* thing, written in the air, the record of what, in any particular case, has *not* been, the account that remains responsible, at best, to "documents" with which we are practically unable to collate it. This is the side of the whole business of fiction on which it can always be challenged, and to that degree that if the general venture had not become in such a manner the admiration of the world it might but too easily have become the derision. It has in truth, I think, never philosophically met the challenge, never found a formula to inscribe on its shield, never defended its position by any better argument than the frank, straight blow: "Why am I not so unprofitable as to be preposterous? Because I can do *that*. There!" And it throws up from time to time some purely practical masterpiece. There is nevertheless an admirable minority of intelligent persons who care not even for the masterpieces, nor see any pressing point in them, for whom the very form itself has, equally at its best and at its worst, been ever a vanity and a mockery. This class, it should be added, is beginning to be visibly augmented by a different circle altogether, the group of the formerly subject, but now estranged, the deceived and bored, those for whom the whole movement too decidedly fails to live up to its possibilities. There are people who have loved the novel, but who actually find themselves drowned in its verbiage, and for whom, even in some of its approved manifestations, it has become a terror they exert every ingenuity, every hypocrisy, to evade. The indifferent and the alienated testify, at any rate, almost as much as the omnivorous, to the reign of the great ambiguity, the enjoyment of which rests, evidently, on a primary need of the mind. The novelist can only fall back on that—on his recognition that man's constant demand for what he has to offer is simply man's general appetite for a *picture*. The novel is of all pictures the most comprehensive and the most elastic. It will stretch anywhere—it will take in absolutely anything. All it needs is a subject and a painter. But for its subject, magnificently, it has the whole human consciousness. And if we are pushed a step farther backward, and asked why the representation should be required when the object represented is itself mostly so accessible, the answer to that appears to be that man combines with his eternal desire for more experience an infinite cunning as to getting his experience as cheaply as possible. He will steal it whenever he can. He likes to live the life of others, yet is well aware of the points at which it may too intolerably resemble his own. The vivid fable, more than anything else, gives him this satisfaction on easy terms, gives him knowledge abundant yet vicarious. It enables him to select, to take and to leave; so that to feel he can afford to neglect it he must have a rare faculty, or great opportunities, for the extension of experience—by thought, by emotion, by energy—at first hand.

Yet it is doubtless not this cause alone that contributes to the contemporary deluge; other circumstances operate, and one of them is probably, in truth, if looked into, something of an abatement of the great fortune we have been called upon to admire. The high prosperity of fiction has marched, very directly, with another "sign of the times," the demoralisation, the vulgarisation of literature in general, the increasing familiarity of all such methods of communication, the making itself supremely felt, as it were, of the presence of the ladies and children—by whom I mean, in other words, the reader irreflective and uncritical. If the novel, in fine, has found itself, socially speaking, at such a rate, the book *par excellence*, so on the other hand the book has in the same degree found itself a thing of small ceremony. So many ways of producing it easily have been discovered that it is by no means the occasional prodigy, for good or for evil, that it was taken for in simpler days, and has therefore suffered a proportionate discredit. Almost any variety is thrown off and taken up, handled, admired, ignored by too many people, and this, precisely, is the point at which the question of its future becomes one with that of the future of the total swarm. How are the generations to face, at all, the monstrous multiplications? Any speculation on the further development of a particular variety is subject to the reserve that the generations may at no distant day be obliged formally to decree, and to execute, great clearings of the deck, great periodical effacements and destructions. It fills, in fact, at moments the expectant ear, as we watch the progress of the ship of civilisation—the huge splash that must mark the response to many an imperative, unanimous "Overboard!" What at least is already very plain is that practically the great majority of volumes printed within a year cease to exist as the hour passes, and give up by that circumstance all claim to a career, to being accounted or provided for. In speaking of the future of the novel we must of course, therefore, be taken as limiting the inquiry to those types that have, for criticism, a present and a past. And it is only superficially that confusion seems here to reign. The fact that in England and in the United States every specimen that sees the light may look for a "review" testifies merely to the point to which, in these countries, literary criticism has sunk. The review is in nine cases out of ten an effort of intelligence as undeveloped as the ineptitude over which it fumbles, and the critical spirit, which knows where it is concerned and where not, is not touched, is still less compromised, by the incident. There are too many reasons why newspapers must live.

So, as regards the tangible type, the end is that in its undefended, its positively exposed state, we continue to accept it, conscious even of a peculiar beauty in an appeal made from a footing so precarious. It throws itself wholly on our generosity, and very often indeed gives us, by the reception it meets, a useful measure of the quality, of the delicacy, of many minds. There is to my sense no work of literary, or of any other, art, that any human being is under the smallest positive obligation to "like." There is no woman—no matter of what loveliness—in the presence of whom it is anything but a man's unchallengeably *own* affair that he is "in love" or out of it. It is not a question of manners; vast is the margin left to individual freedom; and the trap set by the artist occupies no different ground—Robert Louis Stevenson has admirably expressed the analogy—from the offer of her charms by the lady. There only remain infatuations that we envy and emulate. When we do respond to the appeal, when we *are* caught in the trap, we are held and played upon; so that how in the world can there *not* still be a future, however late in the day, for a contrivance possessed of this precious secret? The more we consider it the more we feel that the prose picture can never be at the end of its tether until it loses the sense of what it can do. It can do simply everything, and that is its strength and its life. Its plasticity, its elasticity are infinite; there is no colour, no extension it may not take from the nature of its subject or the temper of its craftsman. It has the extraordinary advantage—a piece of luck scarcely credible—that, while capable of giving an impression of the highest perfection and the rarest finish, it moves in a luxurious independence of rules and restrictions. Think as we may, there is nothing we can mention as a consideration outside itself with which it must square, nothing we can name as one of its peculiar obligations or interdictions. It must, of course, hold our attention and reward it, it must not appeal on false pretences; but these necessities, with which, obviously, disgust and displeasure interfere, are not peculiar to it—all works of art have them in common. For the rest it has so clear a field that if it perishes this will surely be by its fault—by its superficiality, in other words, or its timidity. One almost, for the very love of it, likes to think of its appearing threatened with some such fate, in order to figure the dramatic stroke of its revival under the touch of a life-giving master. The temperament of the artist can do so much for it that our desire for some exemplary felicity fairly demands even the vision of that supreme proof. If we were to linger on this vision long enough, we should doubtless, in fact, be brought to wondering—and still for very loyalty to the form itself— whether our own prospective conditions may not before too long appear to many critics to call for some such happy *coup* on the part of a great artist yet to come.

There would at least be this excuse for such a reverie: that speculation is vain unless we confine it, and that for ourselves the most convenient branch of the question is the state of the industry that makes its appeal to readers of English. From any attempt to measure the career still open to the novel in France I may be excused, in so narrow a compass, for shrinking. The French, as a result of having ridden their horse much harder than we, are at a different stage of the journey, and we have doubtless many of their stretches and baiting-places yet to traverse. But if the range grows shorter from the moment we drop to inductions drawn only from English and American material, I am not sure that the answer comes sooner. I should have at all events—a formidably large order—to plunge into the particulars of the question of the present. If the day *is* approaching when the respite of execution for almost any book is but a matter of mercy, does the English novel of commerce tend to strike us as a production more and more equipped by its high qualities for braving the danger? It would be impossible, I think, to make one's attempt at an answer to that riddle really interesting without bringing into the field many illustrations drawn from individuals—without pointing the moral with names both conspicuous and obscure. Such a freedom would carry us, here, quite too far, and would moreover only encumber the path. There is nothing to prevent our taking for granted all sorts of happy symptoms and splendid promises—so long, of course, I mean, as we keep before us the general truth that the future of fiction is intimately bound up with the future of the society that produces and consumes it. In a society with a great and diffused literary sense the talent at play can only be a less negligible thing than in a society with a literary sense barely discernible. In a world in which criticism is acute and mature such talent will find itself trained, in order successfully to assert itself, to many more kinds of precautionary expertness than in a society in which the art I have named holds an inferior place or makes a sorry figure. A community addicted to reflection and fond of ideas will try experiments with the "story" that will be left untried in a community mainly devoted to travelling and shooting, to pushing trade and playing football. There are many judges, doubtless, who hold that experiments—queer and uncanny things at best—are not necessary to it, that its face has been, once for all, turned in one way, and that it has only to go straight before it. If that is what it is actually doing in England and America the main thing to say about its future would appear to be that this future will in very truth more and more define itself as negligible. For all the while the immense variety of life will stretch away to right and to left, and all the while there may be, on such lines, perpetuation of its great mistake of failing of intelligence. That mistake will be, ever, for the admirable art, the only one really inexcusable, because of being a mistake about, as we may say, its own soul. The form of novel that is stupid on the general question of its freedom is the single form that may, *a priori*, be unhesitatingly pronounced wrong.

The most interesting thing to-day, therefore, among ourselves is the degree in which we may count on seeing a sense of that freedom cultivated and bearing fruit. What else is this, indeed, but one of the most attaching elements in the great drama of our wide English-speaking life! As the novel is at any moment the most immediate and, as it were, admirably *treacherous* picture of actual manners—indirectly as well as directly, and by what it does not touch as well as by what it does—so its present situation, where we are most concerned with it, is exactly a reflection of our social changes and chances, of the signs and portents that lay most traps for most observers, and make up in general what is most "amusing" in the spectacle we offer. Nothing, I may say, for instance, strikes me more as meeting this description than the predicament finally arrived at, for the fictive energy, in consequence of our long and most respectable tradition of making it defer supremely, in the treatment, say, of a delicate case, to the inexperience of the young. The particular knot the coming novelist who shall prefer not simply to beg the question, will have here to untie may represent assuredly the essence of his outlook. By what it shall decide to do in respect to the "young" the great prose fable will, from any serious point of view, practically see itself stand or fall. What is clear is that it has, among us, veritably never chosen—it has, mainly, always obeyed an unreasoning instinct of avoidance in which there has often been much that was felicitous. While society was frank, was free about the incidents and accidents of the human constitution, the novel took the same robust ease as society. The young then were so very young that they were not table-high. But they began to grow, and from the moment their little chins rested on the mahogany, Richardson and Fielding began to go under it. There came into being a mistrust of any but the most guarded treatment of the great relation between men and women, the constant world-renewal, which was the conspicuous sign that whatever the prose picture of life was prepared to take upon itself, it was not prepared to take upon itself not to be superficial. Its position became very much: "There are other things, don't you know? For heaven's sake let *that* one pass!" And to this wonderful propriety of letting it pass the business has been for these so many years—with the consequences we see to-day—largely devoted. These consequences are of many sorts, not a few altogether charming. One of them has been that there is an immense omission in our fiction—which, though many critics will always judge that it has vitiated the whole, others will continue to speak of as signifying but a trifle. One can only talk for one's self, and of the English and American novelists of whom I am fond, I am so superlatively fond that I positively prefer to take them as they are. I cannot so much as imagine Dickens and Scott *without* the "love-making" left, as the phrase is, out. They were, to my perception, absolutely right—from the moment their attention to it could only be perfunctory—practically not to deal with it. In all their work it is, in spite of the number of pleasant sketches of affection gratified or crossed, the element that matters least. Why not therefore assume, it may accordingly be asked, that discriminations which have served their purpose so well in the past will continue not less successfully to meet the case? What will you have better than Scott and Dickens?

Nothing certainly *can* be, it may at least as promptly be replied, and I can imagine no more comfortable prospect than jogging along perpetually with a renewal of such blessings. The difficulty lies in the fact that two of the great conditions have changed. The novel is older, and so are the young. It would seem that everything the young can possibly do for us in the matter has been successfully done. They have kept out one thing after the other, yet there is still a certain complete-ness we lack, and the curious thing is that it appears to be they themselves who are making the grave discovery. "You have kindly taken," they seem to say to the fiction-mongers, "our education off the hands of our parents and pastors, and that, doubtless, has been very convenient for *them*, and left them free to amuse themselves. But what, all the while, pray, if it is a question of education, have you done with your own? These are directions in which you seem dreadfully untrained, and in which *can* it be as vain as it appears to apply to you for information?" The point is whether, from the moment it is a question of averting discredit, the novel can afford to take things quite so easily as it has, for a good while now, settled down into the way of doing. There are too many sources of interest neglected—whole categories of manners, whole corpuscular classes and provinces, museums of character and condition, unvisited; while it is on the other hand mistakenly taken for granted that safety lies in all the loose and thin material that keeps reappearing in forms at once ready-made and sadly the worse for wear. The simple themselves may finally turn against our simplifications; so that we need not, after all, be more royalist than the king or more childish than the children. It is certain that there is no real health for any art—I am not speaking, of course, of any mere industry—that does not move a step in advance of its farthest follower. It would be curious—really a great comedy—if the renewal were to spring just from the satiety of the very readers for whom the sacrifices have hitherto been supposed to be made. It bears on this that as nothing is more salient in English life to-day, to fresh eyes, than the revolution taking place in the position and outlook of women—and taking place much more deeply in the quiet than even the noise on the surface demonstrates—so we may very well yet see the female elbow itself, kept in increasing activity by the play of the pen, smash with final resonance the window all this time most superstitiously closed. The particular draught that has been most deprecated will in that case take care of the question of freshness. It is the opinion of some observers that when women do obtain a free hand they will not repay their long debt to the precautionary attitude of men by unlimited consideration for the natural delicacy of the latter.

To admit, then, that the great anodyne can ever totally fail to work, is to imply, in short, that this will only be by some grave fault in some high quarter. Man rejoices in an incomparable faculty for

presently mutilating and disfiguring any plaything that has helped
create for him the illusion of leisure; nevertheless, so long as life retains
its power of projecting itself upon his imagination, he will find the
novel work off the impression better than anything he knows. Anything better for the purpose has assuredly yet to be discovered. He
will give it up only when life itself too thoroughly disagrees with him.
Even then, indeed, may fiction not find a second wind, or a fiftieth,
in the very portrayal of that collapse? Till the world is an unpeopled
void there will be an image in the mirror. What need more immediately concern us, therefore, is the care of seeing that the image shall
continue various and vivid. There is much, frankly, to be said for those
who, in spite of all brave pleas, feel it to be considerably menaced, for
very little reflection will help to show us how the prospect strikes
them. They see the whole business too divorced on the one side from
observation and perception, and on the other from the art and taste.
They get too little of the first-hand impression, the effort to penetrate—
that effort for which the French have the admirable expression to
fouiller—and still less, if possible, of any science of composition, any
architecture, distribution, proportion. It is not a trifle, though indeed
it is the concomitant of an edged force, that "mystery" should, to so
many of the sharper eyes, have disappeared from the craft, and a
facile flatness be, in place of it, in acclaimed possession. But these are,
at the worst, even for such of the disconcerted, signs that the novelist,
not that the novel, has dropped. So long as there is a subject to be
treated, so long will it depend wholly on the treatment to rekindle
the fire. Only the ministrant must really approach the altar; for if the
novel *is* the treatment, it is the treatment that is essentially what I
have called the anodyne.

MATILDE SERAO

FEW ATTENTIVE readers, I take it, would deny that the English novelist—from whom, in this case, there happens to be even less occasion than usual for distinguishing the American—testifies in his art much more than his foreign comrade, from whatever quarter, to the rigour of convention. There are whole sides of life about which he has as little to say as possible, about which he observes indeed in general a silence that has visibly ended by becoming for the foreign comrade his great characteristic. He strikes the spectator as having with a misplaced humility consented once for all to be admonished as to what he shall or shall not "mention"—and to be admonished in especial by an authority altogether indefinite. He subscribes, when his turn comes round, to an agreement in the drawing-up of which he has had no hand; he sits down to his task with a certain received canon of the "proper" before his eyes. The critic I am supposing reproaches him, naturally, in this critic's way, with a marked failure ever to challenge, much less to analyse, that conception; with having never, as would appear, so much as put to himself in regard to most of the matters of which he makes his mystery the simple question "Proper to what?" How can any authority, even the most embodied, asks the exponent of other views, decide for us in advance what shall in any case be proper—with the consequent implication of impropriety—to our given subject?

The English novelist would, I imagine, even sometimes be led on to finding that he has practically had to meet such an overhauling by a further admission, though an admission still tacit and showing him not a little shy of the whole discussion—principles and formulas being in general, as we know, but little his affair. Would he not, if off his guard, have been in peril of lapsing into the doctrine—suicidal when reflected upon—that there may be also an *a priori* rule, a "Thou shalt not," if not a "Thou shalt," as to treatable subjects themselves? Then it would be that his alien foe might fairly revel in the sense of having him in a corner, laughing an evil laugh to hear him plead in explanation that it is exactly *most* as to the subject to be treated that he feels the need laid upon him to conform. What is he to do when he has an idea to embody, we might suspect him rashly to inquire, unless, frankly to ask himself in the first place of *all* if it be proper? Not indeed—we catch the reservation—that he is consciously often accessible to ideas for which that virtue may not be claimed. Naturally, however, still, such a plea only brings forth for his interlocutor a repetition of the original appeal: "Proper to what?" There is only one propriety the painter of life can ask of his morsel of material: Is it, or is it not, of the stuff of life? So, in simplified terms at any rate, I seem to hear the interchange; to which I need listen no longer than thus to have derived from it a word of support for my position. The question of our possible rejoinder to the scorn of societies otherwise affected I must leave for some other connection. The point is—if point I may expect to obtain any countenance to its being called—that, in spite of our great Dickens and, in a minor degree, of our great George Eliot, the limitations of our practice are elsewhere than among ourselves pretty well held to have put us out of court. The thing least conceded to us moreover is that we handle at all frankly—if we put forward such a claim—even our own subject-matter or in other words our own life. "Your own is all we want of you, all we should like to see. But that your system really touches your own is exactly what we deny. Never, never!" For what it really comes to is that practically we, of all people in the world, are accused of a system. Call this system a conspiracy of silence, and the whole charge is upon us.

The fact of the silence, whether or no of the system, is fortunately all that at present concerns us. Did this not happen to be the case nothing could be more interesting, I think, than to follow somewhat further several of the bearings of the matter, which would bring us face to face with some wonderful and, I hasten to add, by no means doubtless merely disconcerting truths about ourselves. It has been given us to read a good deal, in these latter days, about *l'âme Française* and *l'âme Russe*—and with the result, in all probability, of our being rather less than more penetrated with the desire, in emulation of these opportunities, to deliver ourselves upon the English or the American soul. There would appear to be nothing we are totally conscious of that we are less eager to reduce to the mere expressible, to hand over to publicity, current journalistic prose aiding, than either of these fine essences; and yet incontestably there are neighbourhoods in which we feel ourselves within scent and reach of them by something of the same sense that in thick forests serves the hunter of great game. He may not quite touch the precious presence, but he knows when it is near. So somehow we know that the "Anglo-Saxon" soul, the modern at least, is not far off when we frankly consider the practice of our race—comparatively recent though it be—in taking for granted the "innocence" of literature.

Our perhaps a trifle witless way of expressing our conception of this innocence and our desire for it is, characteristically enough, by taking refuge in another vagueness, by invoking the allowances that we understand works of imagination and of criticism to make to the "young." I know not whether it has ever officially been stated for us that, given the young, given literature, and given, under stress, the need of sacrificing one or the other party, it is not certainly by our sense of "style" that our choice would be determined: no great art in the reading of signs and symptoms is at all events required for a view of our probable instinct in such a case. That instinct, however, has too many deep things in it to be briefly or easily disposed of, and there would be no greater mistake than to attempt too simple an account of it. The account most likely to be given by a completely detached critic would be that we are as a race better equipped for action than for thought, and that to let the art of expression go by the board is through that very fact to point to the limits of what we mostly have to express. If we accept such a report we shall do so, I think, rather from a strong than from a weak sense of what may easily be made of it; but I glance at these things only as at objects almost too flooded with light, and come back after my parenthesis to what more immediately concerns me: the plain reflection that, if the element of compromise—compromise with fifty of the "facts of life"—be the common feature of the novel of English speech, so it is mainly indebted for this character to the sex comparatively without a feeling for logic.

Nothing is at any rate *a priori* more natural than to trace a connection between our general mildness, as it may conveniently be called, and the fact that we are likewise so generally feminine. Is the English novel "proper" because it is so much written by women, or is it only so much written by women because its propriety has been so firmly established? The intimate relation is on either determination all that is here pertinent—effect and cause may be left to themselves. What is further pertinent, as happens, is that on a near view the relation is not constant; by which I mean that, though the ladies are always productive, the fashion of mildness is not always the same. Convention in short has its ups and downs, and these votaries have of late years, I think, been as often seen weltering in the hollow of the wave as borne aloft on its crest. Some of them may even be held positively to have distinguished themselves most—whether or no in veils of anonymity—on the occasion of the downward movement; making us really wonder if their number might not fairly, under any steadier force of such a movement, be counted on to increase. All sorts of inquiries are suggested in truth by the sight. "Emancipations" are in the air, and may it not possibly be that we shall see two of the most striking coincide? If convention has, to the tune to which I just invited an ear, blighted our fiction, what shall we say of its admitted, its still more deprecated and in so many quarters even deplored, effect upon the great body under the special patronage of which the "output" has none the less insisted on becoming incomparably copious? Since the general inaptitude of women appears by this time triumphantly to have been proved an assumption particularly hollow, despoiled more and more each day of the last tatters of its credit, why should not the new force thus liberated really, in the connection I indicate, give something of its measure?

It is at any rate keeping within bounds to say that the novel will surely not become less free in proportion as the condition of women becomes more easy. It is more or less in deference to their constant concern with it that we have seen it, among ourselves, pick its steps so carefully; but there are indications that the future may reserve us the surprise of having to thank the very class whose supposed sensibilities have most oppressed us for teaching it not only a longer stride, but a healthy indifference to an occasional splash. It is for instance only of quite recent years that the type of fiction commonly identified as the "sexual" has achieved—for purposes of reference, so far as notices in newspapers may be held to constitute reference—a salience variously estimated. Now therefore, though it is early to say that all "imaginative work" from the female hand is subject to this description, there is assuredly none markedly so subject that is *not* from the female hand. The female mind has in fact throughout the competition carried off the prize in the familiar game, known to us all from childhood's hour, of playing at "grown-up"; finding thus its opportunity, with no small acuteness, in the more and more marked tendency of the mind of the other gender to revert, alike in the grave and the gay, to those simplicities which there would appear to be some warrant for pronouncing puerile. It is the ladies in a word who have lately done most to remind us of man's relations with himself, that is with woman. His relations with the pistol, the pirate, the police, the wild and the tame beast—are not these prevailingly what the gentlemen have given us? And does not the difference sufficiently point my moral?

Let me, however, not seem to have gone too far afield to seek it; for my reflections—general perhaps to excess—closely connect themselves with a subject to which they are quite ready to yield in interest. I have lately been giving a happy extension to an old acquaintance, dating from early in the eighties, with the striking romantic work of Matilde Serao; a writer who, apart from other successes, has the excellent effect, the sign of the stronger few, that the end of her story is, for her reader, never the end of her work. On thus recently returning to her I have found in her something much more to my present purpose than the mere appearance of power and ease. If she is interesting

largely because she is, in the light of her free, her extraordinary Neapolitan temperament, a vivid painter and a rich register of sensations
and impressions, she is still more so as an exceptionally compact and
suggestive *case*, a case exempt from interference and presenting itself
with a beautiful unconsciousness. She has had the good fortune—if
it be, after all, not the ill—to develop in an air in which convention,
in our invidious sense, has had as little to say to her as possible; and
she is accordingly a precious example of the possibilities of free exercise. The questions of the proper and the improper are comfortably
far from her; and though more than in the line of her sisters of English speech she may have to reckon with prescriptions as to form—a
burden at which in truth she snaps her fingers with an approach to
impertinence—she moves in a circle practically void of all pre-judg-
ment as to subject and matter. Conscious enough, doubtless, of a
literary law to be offended, and caring little in fact, I repeat—for it
is her weakness—what wrong it may suffer, she has not even the
agreeable incentive of an ability to calculate the "moral" shocks she
may administer.

Practically chartered then she is further happy—since they both
minister to ease—in two substantial facts: she is a daughter of the
veritable south and a product of the contemporary newspaper. A
Neapolitan by birth and a journalist by circumstance, by marriage
and in some degree doubtless also by inclination, she strikes for us
from the first the note of facility and spontaneity and the note of
initiation and practice. Concerned, through her husband, in the
conduct of a Neapolitan morning paper, of a large circulation and a
radical colour, she has, as I infer, produced her novels and tales mainly
in such snatches of time and of inspiration as have been left her by
urgent day-to-day journalism. They distinctly betray, throughout, the
conditions of their birth—so little are they to the literary sense children of maturity and leisure. On the question of style in a foreign
writer it takes many contributive lights to make us sure of our ground;
but I feel myself on the safe side in conceiving that this lady, full of
perception and vibration, can not only not figure as a purist, but must
be supposed throughout, in spite of an explosive eloquence, to pretend

but little to distinction of form: which for an Italian is a much graver predicament than for one of our shapeless selves. That, however, would perhaps pass for a small quarrel with a writer, or rather with a talker and—for it is what one must most insist on—a *feeler*, of Matilde Serao's remarkable spontaneity. Her Neapolitan nature is by itself a value, to whatever literary lapses it may minister. A torch kindled at that flame can be but freely waved, and our author's arm has a fine action. Loud, loquacious, abundant, natural, happy, with luxurious insistences on the handsome, the costly and the fleshly, the fine persons and fine clothes of her characters, their satin and velvet, their bracelets, rings, white waistcoats, general appointments and bedroom furniture, with almost as many repetitions and as free a tongue, in short, as Juliet's nurse, she reflects at every turn the wonderful mixture that surrounds her—the beauty, the misery, the history, the light and noise and dust, the prolonged paganism and the renewed reactions, the great style of the distant and the past and the generally compromised state of the immediate and the near. These things were all in the germ for the reader of her earlier novels—they have since only gathered volume and assurance—so that I well remember the impression made on me, when the book was new (my copy, apparently of the first edition, bears the date of 1885), by the rare energy, the immense *disinvoltura*, of *La Conquista di Roma*. This was my introduction to the author, in consequence of which I immediately read *Fantasia* and the *Vita e Avventure di Riccardo Joanna*, with some smaller pieces; after which, interrupted but not detached, I knew nothing more till, in the course of time, I renewed acquaintance on the ground of *Il Paese di Cuccagna*, then, however, no longer in its first freshness. That work set me straightway to reading everything else I could lay hands on, and I think therefore that, save *Il Ventre di Napoli* and two or three quite recent productions that I have not met, there is nothing from our author that I have not mastered. Such as I find her in everything, she remains above all things the signal "case."

If, however, she appears, as I am bound to note, not to have kept the full promise of her early energy, this is because it has suited her to move less in the direction—where so much might have awaited her—of *Riccardo Joanna* and *La Conquista* than in that, on the whole less happily symptomatic, of *Fantasia*. *Fantasia* is, before all else, a study of "passion," or rather of the intenser form of that mystery which the Italian *passione* better expresses; and I hasten to confess that had she not so marked herself an exponent of this specialty I should probably not now be writing of her. I conceive none the less that it would have been open to her to favour more that side of her great talent of which the so powerful *Paese di Cuccagna* is the strongest example. There is by good fortune in this large miscellaneous picture of Neapolitan life no *passione* save that of the observer curiously and pityingly intent upon it, that of the artist resolute at any cost to embrace and reproduce it. Admirably, easily, convincingly objective, the thing is a sustained panorama, a chronicle of manners finding its unity in one recurrent note, that of the consuming lottery-hunger which constitutes the joy, the curse, the obsession and the ruin, according to Matilde Serao, of her fellow-citizens. Her works are thus divided by a somewhat unequal line, those on one side of which the critic is tempted to accuse her of having not altogether happily sacrificed to those on the other. When she for the most part invokes under the name of *passione* the main explanation of the mortal lot it is to follow the windings of this clue in the upper walks of life, to haunt the aristocracy, to embrace the world of fashion, to overflow with clothes, jewels and promiscuous intercourse, all to the proportionate eclipse of her strong, full vision of the more usually vulgar. *La Conquista* is the story of a young deputy who comes up to the Chamber, from the Basilicata, with a touching candour of ambition and a perilous ignorance of the pitfalls of capitals. His dream is to conquer Rome, but it is by Rome naturally that he is conquered. He alights on his political twig with a flutter of wings, but has reckoned in his innocence without the strong taste in so many quarters for sport; and it is with a charge of shot in his breast and a drag of his pinions in the dust that he takes his way back to mediocrity, obscurity and the parent nest. It is from the ladies—as was indeed even from the first to be expected with Serao—that he receives his doom; *pas-*

sione is in these pages already at the door and soon arrives; *passione* rapidly enough passes its sponge over everything not itself.

In *Cuore Infermo*, in *Addio Amore*, in *Il Castigo*, in the two volumes of *Gli Amanti* and in various other pieces this effacement is so complete that we see the persons concerned but in the one relation, with every other circumstance, those of concurrent profession, possession, occupation, connection, interest, amusement, kinship, utterly superseded and obscured. Save in the three or four books I have named as exceptional the figures evoked are literally professional lovers, "available," as the term is, for *passione* alone: which is the striking sign, as I shall presently indicate, of the extremity in which her enjoyment of the freedom we so often have to envy has strangely landed our author. *Riccardo Joanna*, which, like *La Conquista*, has force, humour and charm, sounding with freshness the note of the general life, is such a picture of certain of the sordid conditions of Italian journalism as, if I may trust my memory without re-perusal, sharply and pathetically imposes itself. I recall *Fantasia* on the other hand as wholly *passione*—all concentration and erotics, the latter practised in this instance, as in *Addio Amore*, with extreme cruelty to the "good" heroine, the person innocent and sacrificed; yet this volume too contributes its part in the retrospect to that appearance of marked discipleship which was one of the original sources of my interest. Nothing could more have engaged one's attention in these matters at that moment than the fresh phenomenon of a lady-novelist so confessedly flushed with the influence of Émile Zola. Passing among ourselves as a lurid warning even to workers of his own sex, he drew a new grace from the candid homage—all implied and indirect, but, as I refigure my impression, not the less unmistakable—of that half of humanity which, let alone attempting to follow in his footsteps, was not supposed even to turn his pages. There is an episode in *Fantasia*—a scene in which the relations of the hero and the "bad" heroine are strangely consolidated by a visit together to a cattle-show—in which the courage of the pupil has but little to envy the breadth of the master. The hot day and hot hour, the heavy air and the strong smells, the great and small beasts, the action on the sensibilities of the lady and the gentleman of the rich animal life, the collapse indeed of the lady in the presence of the prize bull—all these are touches for which luckily our author has the warrant of a greater name. The general picture, in *Fantasia*, of the agricultural exhibition at Caserta is in fact not the worse at any point for a noticeable echo of more than one French model. Would the author have found so full an occasion in it without a fond memory of the immortal "Cornices" of *Madame Bovary*?

These, however, are minor questions—pertinent only as connecting themselves with the more serious side of her talent. We may rejoice in such a specimen of it as is offered by the too brief series of episodes of *The Romance of the Maiden*. These things, dealing mainly with the small miseries of small folk, have a palpable truth, and it is striking that, to put the matter simply, Madame Serao is at her best almost in direct proportion as her characters are poor. By poor I mean literally the reverse of rich; for directly they *are* rich and begin, as the phrase is, to keep their carriage, her taste totters and lapses, her style approximates at moments to that of the ladies who do the fashions and the letters from the watering-places in the society papers. She has acutely and she renders with excellent breadth the sense of benighted lives, of small sordid troubles, of the general unhappy youthful (on the part of her own sex at least) and the general more or less starved plebeian consciousness. The degree to which it testifies to all this is one of the great beauties of *Il Paese di Cuccagna*, even if the moral of that dire picture be simply that in respect to the gaming-passion, the madness of "numbers," no walk of life at Naples is too high or too low to be ravaged. Beautiful, in *Il Romanzo della Fanciulla*, are the exhibitions of grinding girl-life in the big telegraph office and in the State normal school. The gem of *Gli Amanti* is the tiny tale of "Vicenzella," a masterpiece in twenty small pages—the vision of what three or four afternoon hours could contain for a slip of a creature of the Naples waterside, a poor girl who picks up a living by the cookery and sale, on the edge of a parapet, of various rank dismembered polyps of the southern sea, and who is from stage to stage despoiled of the pence she patiently pockets for them by the successive

small emissaries of her artful, absent lover, constantly faithless, occupied, not too far off, in regaling a lady of his temporary preference,
and proportionately clamorous for fresh remittances. The moment
and the picture are but a scrap, yet they are as large as life.

"Canituccia," in *Piccole Anime*, may happily pair with "Vicenzella,"
Canituccia being simply the humble rustic guardian, in field and
wood—scarce more than a child—of the still more tender Ciccotto;
and Ciccotto being a fine young pink-and-white pig, an animal of
endowments that lead, after he has had time to render infatuated his
otherwise quite solitary and joyless friend, to his premature conver-
sion into bacon. She assists, helplessly silent, staring, almost idiotic,
from a corner of the cabin-yard, by night and lamplight, in the presence of gleaming knives and steaming pots and bloody tubs, at the
sacrifice that deprives her of all company, and nothing can exceed
the homely truth of the touch that finally rounds off the scene and
for which I must refer my reader to the volume. Let me further not
fail to register my admiration for the curious cluster of scenes that,
in *Il Romanzo*, bears the title of "Nella Lava." Here frankly, I take it,
we have the real principle of "naturalism"—a consistent presentment
of the famous "slice of life." The slices given us—slices of shabby
hungry maidenhood in small cockney circles—are but sketchily related
to the volcanic catastrophe we hear rumbling behind them, the un-
dertone of all the noise of Naples; but they have the real artistic importance of showing us how little "story" is required to hold us when
we get, before the object evoked and in the air created, the impression
of the real thing. Whatever thing—interesting inference—has but
effectively to *be* real to constitute in itself story enough. There is no
story without it, none that is not rank humbug; whereas with it the
very desert blooms.

This last-named phenomenon takes place, I fear, but in a minor
degree in such of our author's productions as *Cuore Infermo*, *Addio
Amore*, *Il Castigo* and the double series of *Gli Amanti*; and for a
reason that I the more promptly indicate as it not only explains, I
think, the comparative inanity of these pictures, but does more than
anything else to reward our inquiry. The very first reflection suggested

by Serao's novels of "passion" is that they perfectly meet our speculation as to what might with a little time become of our own fiction
were our particular convention suspended. We see so what, on its
actual lines, does, what *has*, become of it, and are so sated with the
vision that a little consideration of the latent other chance will surely
but refresh us. The effect then, we discover, of the undertaking to
give *passione* its whole place is that by the operation of a singular law
no place speedily appears to be left for anything else; and the effect
of that in turn is greatly to modify, first, the truth of things, and
second, with small delay, what may be left them of their beauty. We
find ourselves wondering after a little whether there may not really
be more truth in the world misrepresented according to our own
familiar fashion than in such a world as that of Madame Serao's
exuberant victims of Venus. It is not only that if Venus herself is
notoriously beautiful her altar, as happens, is by no means always
proportionately august; it is also that we draw, in the long run, small
comfort from the virtual suppression, by any painter, of whatever
skill—and the skill of this particular one fails to rise to the height—
of every relation in life but that over which Venus presides. In *Fior
di Passione* and the several others of a like connection that I have
named the suppression is really complete; the common humanities
and sociabilities are wholly absent from the picture.

The effect of this is extraordinarily to falsify the total show and
to present the particular affair—the intimacy in hand for the moment,
though the moment be but brief—as taking place in a strange false
perspective, a denuded desert which experience surely fails ever to
give us the like of and the action of which on the faculty of observation in the painter is anything but favourable. It strikes at the root,
in the impression producible and produced, of discrimination and
irony, of humour and pathos. Our present author would doubtless
contend on behalf of the works I have mentioned that pathos at least
does abound in them—the particular bitterness, the inevitable despair
that she again and again shows to be the final savour of the cup of
passione. It would be quite open to her to urge—and she would be
sure to do so with eloquence—that if we pusillanimously pant for a

moral, no moral really can have the force of her almost inveterate evocation of the absolute ravage of Venus, the dry desolation that in nine cases out of ten Venus may be perceived to leave behind her. That, however, but half meets our argument—which bears by no means merely on the desolation behind, but on the desolation before, beside and generally roundabout. It is not in short at all the moral but the fable itself that in the exclusively sexual light breaks down and fails us. Love, at Naples and in Rome, as Madame Serao exhibits it, is simply unaccompanied with any interplay of our usual conditions—with affection, with duration, with circumstances or consequences, with friends, enemies, husbands, wives, children, parents, interests, occupations, the manifestation of tastes. Who are these people, we presently ask ourselves, who love indeed with fury—though for the most part with astonishing brevity—but who are so without any suggested situation in life that they can only strike us as loving for nothing and in the void, to no gain of experience and no effect of a felt medium or a breathed air. We know them by nothing but their convulsions and spasms, and we feel once again that it is not the passion of hero and heroine that gives, that can ever give, the heroine and the hero interest, but that it is they themselves, with the ground they stand on and the objects enclosing them, who give interest to their passion. This element touches us just in proportion as we see it mixed with other things, with all the things with which it has to reckon and struggle. There is moreover another reflection with which the pathetic in this connection has to count, even though it undermine not a little the whole of the tragic effect of the agitations of *passione*. Is it, ruthlessly speaking, certain that the effect most consonant, for the spectator, with truth is half as tragic as it is something else? Should not the moral be sought in the very different quarter where the muse of comedy rather would have the last word? The ambiguity and the difficulty are, it strikes me, of a new growth, and spring from a perverse desire on the part of the erotic novelist to secure for the adventures he depicts a dignity that is not of the essence. To compass this dignity he has to cultivate the high pitch and beat the big drum, but when he has done so he has given everything the wrong accent and the whole the wrong extravagance. Why see it all, we ask him, as an extravagance of the solemn and the strained? Why make *such* an erotic a matter of tears and imprecations, and by so doing render so poor a service both to pleasure and to pain? Since by your own free showing it is pre-eminently a matter of folly, let us at least have folly with her bells, or when these must—since they must—sound knells and dirges, leave them only to the light hand of the lyric poet, who turns them at the worst to music. Matilde Serao is in this connection constantly lugubrious; even from the little so-called pastels of *Gli Amanti* she manages, with an ingenuity worthy of a better cause, to expunge the note of gaiety.

This dismal *parti pris* indeed will inevitably, it is to be feared, when all the emancipations shall have said their last word, be that of the ladies. Yet perhaps too, whatever such a probability, the tone scarce signifies—in the presence, I mean, of the fundamental mistake from which the author before us warns us off. That mistake, we gather from her warning, would be to encourage, after all, any considerable lowering of the level of our precious fund of reserve. When we come to analyse we arrive at a final impression of what we pay, as lovers of the novel, for such a chartered state as we have here a glimpse of; and we find it to be an exposure, on the intervention at least of such a literary temperament as the one before us, to a new kind of vulgarity. We have surely as it is kinds enough. The absence of the convention throws the writer back on tact, taste, delicacy, discretion, subjecting these principles to a strain from which the happy office of its presence is, in a considerable degree and for performers of the mere usual endowment, to relieve him. When we have not a very fine sense the convention appears in a manner to have it on our behalf. And how frequent to-day, in the hurrying herd of brothers and sisters of the pen, *is* a fine sense—of *any* side of their affair? Do we not approach the truth in divining that only an eminent individual here and there may be trusted for it? Here—for the case is our very lesson—is this robust and wonderful Serao who is yet not to be trusted at all. Does not the dim religious light with which we surround its shrine do more, on the whole, for the poetry of *passione* than the flood of flaring gas with which, in her pages, and at her touch, it is drenched? Does it not shrink, as a subject under treatment, from such expert recognitions and easy discussions, from its so pitiless reduction to the category of the familiar? It issues from the ordeal with the aspect with which it might escape from a noisy family party or alight from a crowded omnibus. It is at the category of the familiar that vulgarity begins. There may be a cool virtue therefore even for "art," and an appreciable distinction even for truth, in the grace of hanging back and the choice of standing off, in that shade of the superficial which we best defend by simply practising it in season. A feeling revives at last, after a timed intermission, that we may not immediately be quite able, quite assured enough, to name, but which, gradually clearing up, soon defines itself almost as a yearning. We turn round in obedience to it—unmistakably we turn round again to the opposite pole, and there before we know it have positively laid a clinging hand on dear old Jane Austen.

GUSTAVE FLAUBERT

THE FIRST thing I find to-day and on my very threshold* to say about Gustave Flaubert is that he has been reported on by M. Émile Faguet in the series of Les Grands Écrivains Français with such lucidity as may almost be taken to warn off a later critic. I desire to pay at the outset my tribute to M. Faguet's exhaustive study, which is really in its kind a model and a monument. Never can a critic have got closer to a subject of this order; never can the results of the approach have been more copious or more interesting; never in short can the master of a complex art have been more mastered in his turn, nor his art more penetrated, by the application of an earnest curiosity. That remark I have it at heart to make, so pre-eminently has the little volume I refer to not left the subject where it found it. It bounds in contributive light, and yet, I feel on reflection that it scarce wholly dazzles another contributor away. One reason of this is that, though I enter into everything M. Faguet has said, there are things—things perhaps especially of the province of the artist, the fellow-craftsman of Flaubert—that I am conscious of his not having said; another is that inevitably there are particular possibilities of reaction in our English-speaking consciousness that hold up a light of their own. Therefore I venture to follow even on a field so laboured, only paying this toll to the latest and best work because the author has made it impossible to do less.

*On the occasion of these prefatory remarks to a translation of *Madame Bovary*, appearing in A Century of French Romance, under the auspices of Mr. Edmund Gosse and Mr. William Heinemann, in 1902.

Flaubert's life is so almost exclusively the story of his literary application that to speak of his five or six fictions is pretty well to account for it all. He died in 1880 after a career of fifty-nine years singularly little marked by changes of scene, of fortune, of attitude, of occupation, of character, and above all, as may be said, of mind. He would be interesting to the race of novelists if only because, quite apart from the value of his work, he so personally gives us the example and the image, so presents the intellectual case. He was born a novelist, grew up, lived, died a novelist, breathing, feeling, thinking, speaking, performing every operation of life, only as that votary; and this though his production was to be small in amount and though it constituted all his diligence. It was not indeed perhaps primarily so much that he was born and lived a novelist as that he was born and lived literary, and that to be literary represented for him an almost overwhelming situation. No life was long enough, no courage great enough, no fortune kind enough to support a man under the burden of this character when once such a doom had been laid on him. His case was a doom because he felt of his vocation almost nothing but the difficulty. He had many strange sides, but this was the strangest, that if we argued from his difficulty to his work, the difficulty being registered for us in his letters and elsewhere, we should expect from the result but the smallest things. We should be prepared to find in it well-nigh a complete absence of the signs of a gift. We should regret that the unhappy man had not addressed himself to something he might have found at least comparatively easy. We should singularly miss the consecration supposedly given to a work of art by its having been conceived in joy. That is Flaubert's remarkable, his so far as I know unmatched distinction, that he has left works of an extraordinary art even the conception of which failed to help him to think in serenity. The chapter of execution, from the moment execution gets really into the shafts, is of course always and everywhere a troubled one—about which moreover too much has of late been written; but we frequently find Flaubert cursing his subjects themselves, wishing he had not chosen them, holding himself up to derision for having done so, and hating them in the very act of sitting down to them. He cared immensely for the medium, the task and the triumph involved, but was himself the last to be able to say why. He is sustained only by the rage and the habit of effort; the mere *love* of letters, let alone the love of life, appears at an early age to have deserted him. Certain passages in his correspondence make us even wonder if it be not hate that sustains him most. So, successively, his several supremely finished and crowned compositions came into the world, and we may feel sure that none others of the kind, none that were to have an equal fortune, had sprung from such adversity.

I insist upon this because his at once excited and baffled passion gives the key of his life and determines its outline. I must speak of him at least as I feel him and as in his very latest years I had the fortune occasionally to see him. I said just now, practically, that he is for many of our tribe at large *the* novelist, intent and typical, and so, gathered together and foreshortened, simplified and fixed, the lapse of time seems to show him. It has made him in his prolonged posture extraordinarily objective, made him even resemble one of his own productions, constituted him as a subject, determined him as a figure; the limit of his range, and above all of his reach, is after this fashion, no doubt, sufficiently indicated, and yet perhaps in the event without injury to his name. If our consideration of him cultivates a certain tenderness on the double ground that he suffered supremely in the cause and that there is endlessly much to be learned from him, we remember at the same time that, indirectly, the world at large possesses him not less than the *confrère.* He has fed and fertilised, has filtered through others, and so arrived at contact with that public from whom it was his theory that he was separated by a deep and impassable trench, the labour of his own spade. He is none the less more interesting, I repeat, as a failure however qualified than as a success however explained, and it is as so viewed that the unity of his career attaches and admonishes. Save in some degree by a condition of health (a liability to epileptic fits at times frequent, but never so frequent as to have been generally suspected,) he was not outwardly hampered as the tribe of men of letters goes an anxious brotherhood at the best; yet the fewest possible things appear to have ever succeeded in happening to him. The only son of an eminent provincial physician, he inherited a modest case and no other incumbrance than, as was the case for Balzac, an over-attentive, an importunate mother; but freedom spoke to him from behind a veil, and when we have mentioned the few apparent facts of experience that make up his landmarks over and beyond his interspaced publications we shall have completed his biography. Tall, strong, striking, he caused his friends to admire in him the elder, the florid Norman type, and he seems himself, as a man of imagination, to have found some transmission of race in his stature and presence, his light-coloured salient eyes and long tawny moustache.

The central event of his life was his journey to the East in 1849 with M. Maxime Du Camp, of which the latter has left in his *Impressions Littéraires* a singularly interesting and, as we may perhaps say, slightly treacherous report, and which prepared for Flaubert a state of nostalgia that was not only never to leave him, but that was to work in him as a motive. He had during that year, and just in sufficient quantity, his revelation, the particular appropriate disclosure to which the gods at some moment treat the artist unless they happen too perversely to conspire against him: he tasted of the knowledge by which he was subsequently to measure everything, appeal from everything, find everything flat. Never probably was an impression so assimilated, so positively transmuted to a function; he lived on it to the end and we may say that in *Salammbô* and *La Tentation de Saint-Antoine* he almost died of it. He made afterwards no other journey of the least importance save a disgusted excursion to the Rigi-Kaltbad shortly before his death. The Franco-German War was of course to him for the time as the valley of the shadow itself; but this was an ordeal, unlike most of his other ordeals, shared after all with millions. He never married—he declared, toward the end, to the most comprehending of his confidants, that he had been from the first "afraid of life"; and the friendliest element of his later time was, we judge, that admirable comfortable commerce, in her fullest maturity, with Madame George Sand, the confidant I just referred to; which has been preserved for us in the published correspondence of each. He had in Ivan Turgénieff a friend almost as valued; he spent each year a few months in Paris, where (to mention everything) he had his natural place, so far as he cared to take it, at the small literary court of the Princess Mathilde; and, lastly, he lost toward the close of his life, by no fault of his own, a considerable part of his modest fortune. It is, however, in the long security, the almost unbroken solitude of Croisset, near Rouen, that he mainly figures for us, gouging out his successive books in the wide old room, of many windows, that, with an intervening terrace, overlooked the broad Seine and the passing boats. This was virtually a monastic cell, closed to echoes and accidents; with its stillness for long periods scarce broken save by the creak of the towing-chain of the tugs across the water. When I have added that his published letters offer a view, not very refreshing, of his youthful entanglement with Madame Louise Colet—whom we name because, apparently not a shrinking person, she long ago practically named herself—I shall have catalogued his personal vicissitudes. And I may add further that the connection with Madame Colet, such as it was, rears its head for us in something like a desert of immunity from such complications.

His complications were of the spirit, of the literary vision, and though he was thoroughly profane he was yet essentially anchoretic. I perhaps miss a point, however, in not finally subjoining that he was liberally accessible to his friends during the months he regularly spent in Paris. Sensitive, passionate, perverse, not less than *immediately* sociable—for if he detested his collective contemporaries this dropped, thanks to his humanising shyness, before the individual encounter— he was in particular and superexcellently not *banal*, and he attached men perhaps more than women, inspiring a marked, a by no means colourless shade of respect; a respect not founded, as the air of it is apt to be, on the vague presumption, but addressed almost in especial to his disparities and oddities and thereby, no doubt, none too different from affection. His friends at all events were a rich and eager *cénacle,* among whom he was on occasion, by his picturesque personality, a natural and overtopping centre; partly perhaps because he was so much and so familiarly at home. He wore, up to any hour of the afternoon, that long, colloquial dressing-gown, with trousers to match, which one has always associated with literature in France—the uniform really of freedom of talk. Freedom of talk abounded by his winter fire, for the *cénacle* was made up almost wholly of the more finely distinguished among his contemporaries; of philosophers, men of letters and men of affairs belonging to his own generation and the next. He had at the time I have in mind a small perch, far aloft, at the distant, the then almost suburban, end of the Faubourg Saint-Honoré, where on Sunday afternoons, at the very top of an endless flight of stairs, were to be encountered in a cloud of conversation and smoke most of the novelists of the general Balzac tradition. Others of a different birth and complexion were markedly not of the number, were not even conceivable as present; none of those, unless I misremember, whose fictions were at that time "serialised" in the *Revue des Deux Mondes*. In spite of Renan and Taine and two or three more, the contributor to the *Revue* would indeed at no time have found in the circle in question his foot on his native heath. One could recall if one would two or three vivid allusions to him, not of the most quotable, on the lips of the most famous of "naturalists"—allusions to him as represented for instance by M. Victor Cherbuliez and M. Octave Feuillet. The author of these pages recalls a concise qualification of this last of his fellows on the lips of Émile Zola, which that absorbed auditor had too directly, too rashly asked for; but which is alas not reproducible here. There was little else but the talk, which had extreme intensity and variety; almost nothing, as I remember, but a painted and gilded idol, of considerable size, a relic and a memento, on the chimneypiece. Flaubert was huge and diffident, but florid too and resonant, and my main remembrance is of a conception of courtesy in him, an accessibility to the human relation, that only wanted to be sure of the way taken or to take. The uncertainties of the French for the determination of intercourse have often struck me as quite matching the sharpness of their certainties, as we for the most part feel these latter, which sometimes in fact throw the indeterminate into almost touching relief. I have thought of them at such times as the people in the world one may have to go more of the way to meet than to meet any other, and this, as it were, through their being seated and embedded, provided for at home, in a manner that is all their own and that has bred them to the positive preacceptance of interest on their behalf. We at least of the Anglo-American race, more abroad in the world, perching everywhere, so far as grounds of intercourse are concerned, more vaguely and superficially, as well as less intelligently, are the more ready by that fact with inexpensive accommodations, rather conscious that these themselves forbear from the claim to fascinate, and advancing with the good nature that is the mantle of our obtuseness to any point whatever where entertainment may be offered us. My recollection is at any rate simplified by the fact of the presence almost always, in the little high room of the Faubourg's end, of other persons and other voices. Flaubert's own voice is clearest to me from the uneffaced sense of a winter week-day afternoon when I found him by exception alone and when something led to his reading me aloud, in support of some judgment he had thrown off, a poem of Théophile Gautier's. He cited it as an example of verse intensely and distinctively French, and French in its melancholy, which neither Goethe nor Heine nor Leopardi, neither Pushkin nor Tennyson nor, as he said, Byron, could at all have matched in *kind*. He converted me at the moment to this perception, alike by the sense of the thing and by his large utterance of it; after which it is dreadful to have to confess not only that the poem was then new to me, but that, hunt as I will in every volume of its author, I am never able to recover it. This is perhaps after all happy, causing Flaubert's own full tone, which was the note of the occasion, to linger the more unquenched. But for the rhyme in fact I could have believed him to be spouting to me something strange and sonorous of his own. The thing really rare would have been to hear him do that—hear him *gueuler,* as he liked to call it. Verse, I felt, we had always with us, and almost any idiot of goodwill could give it a value. The value of so many a passage of *Salammbô* and of *L'Éducation* was on the other hand exactly such as gained when he allowed himself, as had by the legend ever been frequent *dans l'intimité*, to "bellow" it to its fullest effect.

One of the things that make him most exhibitional and most describable, so that if we had invented him as an illustration or a character we would exactly so have arranged him, is that he was formed intellectually of two quite distinct compartments, a sense of the real and a sense of the romantic, and that his production, for our present cognisance, thus neatly and vividly divides itself. The divisions are as marked as the sections on the back of a scarab, though their distinctness is undoubtedly but the final expression of much inward strife. M. Faguet indeed, who is admirable on this question of our author's duality, gives an account of the romanticism that found its way for him into the real and of the reality that found its way into the romantic; but he none the less strikes us as a curious splendid insect sustained on wings of a different coloration, the right a vivid red, say, and the left as frank a yellow. This duality has in its sharp operation placed *Madame Bovary* and *L'Éducation* on one side together and placed together on the other *Salammbô* and *La Tentation*. *Bouvard et Pécuchet* it can scarce be spoken of, I think, as having placed anywhere or anyhow. If it was Flaubert's way to find his subject impossible there was none he saw so much in that light as this last-named, but also none that he appears to have held so important for that very reason to pursue to the bitter end. Posterity agrees with him about the impossibility, but rather takes upon itself to break with the rest of the logic. We may perhaps, however, for symmetry, let *Bouvard et Pécuchet* figure as the tail—if scarabs ever have tails—of our analogous insect. Only in that case we should also append as the very tip the small volume of the *Trois Contes*, preponderantly of the deepest imaginative hue.

His imagination was great and splendid; in spite of which, strangely enough, his masterpiece is not his most imaginative work. *Madame Bovary,* beyond question, holds that first place, and *Madame Bovary* is concerned with the career of a country doctor's wife in a petty Norman town. The elements of the picture are of the fewest, the situation of the heroine almost of the meanest, the material for interest, considering the interest yielded, of the most unpromising; but these facts only throw into relief one of those incalculable incidents that attend the proceedings of genius. *Madame Bovary* was doomed by circumstances and causes—the freshness of comparative youth and good faith on the author's part being perhaps the chief—definitely to take its position, even though its subject was fundamentally a negation of the remote, the splendid and the strange, the stuff of his fondest and most cultivated dreams. It would have seemed very nearly to exclude the free play of the imagination, and the way this faculty on the author's part nevertheless presides is one of those accidents, manoeuvres, inspirations, we hardly know what to call them, by which masterpieces grow. He of course knew more or less what he was doing for his book in making Emma Bovary a victim of the imaginative habit, but he must have been far from designing or measuring the total effect which renders the work so general, so complete an expression of himself. His separate idiosyncrasies, his irritated sensibility to the life about him, with the power to catch it in the fact and hold it hard, and his hunger for style and history and poetry, for the rich and the rare, great reverberations, great adumbrations, are here represented together as they are not in his later writings. There is nothing of the near, of the directly observed, though there may be much of the directly perceived and the minutely detailed, either in *Salammbô* or in *Saint-Antoine*, and little enough of the extravagance of illusion in that indefinable last word of restrained evocation and cold execution *L'Éducation Sentimentale*. M. Faguet has of course excellently noted this—that the fortune and felicity of the book were assured by the stroke that made the central figure an embodiment of helpless romanticism. Flaubert himself but narrowly escaped being such an embodiment after all, and he is thus able to express the romantic mind with extraordinary truth. As to the rest of the matter he had the luck of having been in possession from the first, having begun so early to nurse and work up his plan that, familiarity and the native air, the native soil, aiding, he had finally made out to the last lurking shade the small sordid sunny dusty village picture, its emptiness constituted and peopled. It is in the background and the accessories that the real, the real of his theme, abides; and the romantic, the romantic of his theme, accordingly occupies the front. Emma Bovary's poor adventures are a tragedy for the very reason that in a world unsuspecting, unassisting, unconsoling, she has herself to distil the rich and the rare. Ignorant, unguided, undiverted, ridden by the very nature and mixture of her consciousness, she makes of the business an inordinate failure, a failure which in its turn makes for Flaubert the most pointed, the most *told* of anecdotes.

There are many things to say about *Madame Bovary,* but an old admirer of the book would be but half-hearted—so far as they represent reserves or puzzlements—were he not to note first of all the circumstances by which it is most endeared to him. To remember it from far back is to have been present all along at a process of singular interest to a literary mind, a case indeed full of comfort and cheer. The finest of Flaubert's novels is to-day, on the French shelf of fiction, one of the first of the classics; it has attained that position, slowly but steadily, before our eyes; and we seem so to follow the evolution of the fate of a classic. We see how the thing takes place; which we rarely can, for we mostly miss either the beginning or the end, especially in the case of a consecration as complete as this. The consecrations of the past are too far behind and those of the future too far in front. That the production before us *should* have come in for the heavenly crown may be a fact to offer English and American readers a mystifying side; but it is exactly our ground and a part moreover of the total interest. The author of these remarks remembers, as with a sense of the way such things happen, that when a very young person in Paris he took up from the parental table the latest number of the periodical in which Flaubert's then duly unrecognised masterpiece was in course of publication. The moment is not historic, but it was to become in the light of history, as may be said, so unforgettable that every small feature of it yet again lives for him: it rests there like the backward end of the span. The cover of the old *Revue de Paris* was yellow, if I mistake not, like that of the new, and *Madame Bovary: Moeurs de Province*, on the inside of it, was already, on the spot, as a title, mysteriously arresting, inscrutably charged. I was ignorant of what had preceded and was not to know till much later what followed; but present to me still is the act of standing there before the fire, my back

against the low beplushed and begarnished French chimneypiece and
taking in what I might of that instalment, taking it in with so surprised an interest, and perhaps as well such a stir of faint foreknowl-
edge, that the sunny little salon, the autumn day, the window ajar
and the cheerful outside clatter of the Rue Montaigne are all now for
me more or less in the story and the story more or less in them. The
story, however, was at that moment having a difficult life; its fortune
was all to make; its merit was so far from suspected that, as Maxime
Du Camp—though verily with no excess of contrition—relates, its
cloth of gold barely escaped the editorial shears. This, with much
more, contributes for us to the course of things to come. The book,
on its appearance as a volume, proved a shock to the high propriety
of the guardians of public morals under the second Empire, and
Flaubert was prosecuted as author of a work indecent to scandal. The
prosecution in the event fell to the ground, but I should perhaps have
mentioned this agitation as one of the very few, of any public order,
in his short list. *Le Candidat* fell at the Vaudeville Theatre, several
years later, with a violence indicated by its withdrawal after a performance of but two nights, the first of these marked by a deafening
uproar; only if the comedy was not to recover from this accident the
misprised lustre of the novel was entirely to reassert itself. It is strange
enough at present—so far have we travelled since then—that *Madame
Bovary* should in so comparatively recent a past have been to that
extent a cause of reprobation; and suggestive above all, in such connections, as to the large unconsciousness of superior minds. The
desire of the superior mind of the day—that is the governmental,
official, legal—to distinguish a book with such a destiny before it is
a case conceivable, but conception breaks down before its design of
making the distinction purely invidious. We can imagine its knowing
so little, however face to face with the object, what it had got hold
of; but for it to have been so urged on by a blind inward spring to
publish to posterity the extent of its ignorance, that would have been
beyond imagination, beyond everything but pity.

And yet it is not after all that the place the book has taken is so
overwhelmingly explained by its inherent dignity; for here comes in

the curiosity of the matter. Here comes in especially its fund of admonition for alien readers. The dignity of its substance is the dignity of Madame Bovary herself as a vessel of experience—a question as to which, unmistakably, I judge, we can only depart from the consensus of French critical opinion. M. Faguet for example commends the character of the heroine as one of the most living and discriminated figures of women in all literature, praises it as a field for the display of the romantic spirit that leaves nothing to be desired. Subject to an observation I shall presently make and that bears heavily in general, I think, on Flaubert as a painter of life, subject to this restriction he is right; which is a proof that a work of art may be markedly open to objection and at the same time be rare in its kind, and that when it is perfect to this point nothing else particularly matters. *Madame Bovary* has a perfection that not only stamps it, but that makes it stand almost alone; it holds itself with such a supreme unapproachable assurance as both excites and defies judgment. For it deals not in the least, as to unapproachability, with things exalted or refined; it only confers on its sufficiently vulgar elements of exhibition a final unsurpassable form. The form is in *itself* as interesting, as active, as much of the essence of the subject as the idea, and yet so close is its fit and so inseparable its life that we catch it at no moment on any errand of its own. That verily is to *be* interesting—all round; that is to be genuine and whole. The work is a classic because the thing, such as it is, is ideally *done,* and because it shows that in such doing eternal beauty may dwell. A pretty young woman who lives, socially and morally speaking, in a hole, and who is ignorant, foolish, flimsy, unhappy, takes a pair of lovers by whom she is successively deserted; in the midst of the bewilderment of which, giving up her husband and her child, letting everything go, she sinks deeper into duplicity, debt, despair, and arrives on the spot, on the small scene itself of her poor depravities, at a pitiful tragic end. In especial she does these things while remaining absorbed in romantic intention and vision, and she remains absorbed in romantic intention and vision while fairly rolling in the dust. That is the triumph of the book as the triumph stands, that Emma interests us by the nature of her consciousness and the play of her mind, thanks to the reality and beauty with which those sources are invested. It is not only that they represent *her* state; they are so true, so observed and felt, and especially so shown, that they represent the state, actual or potential, of all persons like her, persons romantically determined. Then her setting, the medium in which she struggles, becomes in its way as important, becomes eminent with the eminence of art; the tiny world in which she revolves, the contracted cage in which she flutters, is hung out in space for her, and her companions in captivity there are as true as herself.

I have said enough to show what I mean by Flaubert's having in this picture expressed something of his intimate self, given his heroine something of his own imagination: a point precisely that brings me back to the restriction at which I just now hinted, in which M. Faguet fails to indulge and yet which is immediate for the alien reader. Our complaint is that Emma Bovary, in spite of the nature of her consciousness and in spite of her reflecting so much that of her creator, is really too small an affair. This, critically speaking, is in view both of the value and the fortune of her history, a wonderful circumstance. She associates herself with Frédéric Moreau in *L'Éducation* to suggest for us a question that can be answered, I hold, only to Flaubert's detriment. Emma taken alone would possibly not so directly press it, but in her company the hero of our author's second study of the "real" drives it home. Why did Flaubert choose, as special conduits of the life he proposed to depict, such inferior and in the case of Frédéric such abject human specimens? I insist only in respect to the latter, the perfection of Madame Bovary scarce leaving one much warrant for wishing anything other. Even here, however, the general scale and size of Emma, who is small even of her sort, should be a warning to hyperbole. If I say that in the matter of Frédéric at all events the answer is inevitably detrimental I mean that it weighs heavily on our author's general credit. He wished in each case to make a picture of experience—middling experience, it is true—and of the world close to him; but if he imagined nothing better for his purpose than such a heroine and such a hero, both such limited reflectors and registers, we are forced to believe it to have been by a defect of his mind. And that sign of weakness remains even if it be objected that the images in question were addressed to his purpose better than others would have been: the purpose itself then shows as inferior. *L'Éducation Sentimentale* is a strange, an indescribable work, about which there would be many more things to say than I have space for, and all of them of the deepest interest. It is moreover, to simplify my statement, very much less satisfying a thing, less pleasing whether in its unity or its variety, than its specific predecessor. But take it as we will, for a success or a failure—M. Faguet indeed ranks it, by the measure of its quantity of intention, a failure, and I on the whole agree with him— the personage offered us as bearing the weight of the drama, and in whom we are invited to that extent to interest ourselves, leaves us mainly wondering what our entertainer could have been thinking of. He takes Frédéric Moreau on the threshold of life and conducts him to the extreme of maturity without apparently suspecting for a moment either our wonder or our protest—"Why, why *him*?" Frédéric is positively too poor for his part, too scant for his charge; and we feel with a kind of embarrassment, certainly with a kind of compassion, that it is somehow the business of a protagonist to prevent in his designer an excessive waste of faith. When I speak of the faith in Emma Bovary as proportionately wasted I reflect on M. Faguet's judgment that she is from the point of view of deep interest richly or at least roundedly representative. Representative of what? he makes us ask even while granting all the grounds of misery and tragedy involved. The plea for her is the plea made for all the figures that live without evaporation under the painter's hand—that they are not only particular persons but types of their kind, and as valid in one light as in the other. It is Emma's "kind" that I question for this responsibility, even if it be inquired of me why I then fail to question that of Charles Bovary, in its perfection, or that of the inimitable, the immortal Homais. If we express Emma's deficiency as the poverty of her consciousness for the typical function, it is certainly not, one must admit, that she is surpassed in this respect either by her platitudinous husband or by his friend the pretentious apothecary. The difference is none the less somehow in the fact that they are respectively studies but of their character and office, which function in each expresses adequately *all* they are. It may be, I concede, because Emma is the only woman in the book that she is taken by M. Faguet as *femininely* typical, typical in the larger illustrative way, whereas the others pass with him for images specifically conditioned. Emma is this same for myself, I plead; she is conditioned to such an excess of the specific, and the specific in her case leaves out so many even of the commoner elements of conceivable life in a woman when we are invited to see that life as pathetic, as dramatic agitation, that we challenge both the author's and the critic's scale of importances. The book is a picture of the middling as much as they like, but does Emma attain even to *that*? Hers is a narrow middling even for a little imaginative person whose "social" significance is small. It is greater on the whole than her capacity of consciousness, taking this all round; and so, in a word, we feel her less illustrational than she might have been not only if the world had offered her more points of contact, but if she had had more of these to give it.

We meet Frédéric first, we remain with him long, as a *moyen,* a provincial bourgeois of the mid-century, educated and not without fortune, thereby with freedom, in whom the life of his day reflects itself. Yet the life of his day, on Flaubert's showing, hangs together with the poverty of Frédéric's own inward or for that matter outward life; so that, the whole thing being, for scale, intention and extension, a sort of epic of the usual (with the Revolution of 1848 introduced indeed as an episode,) it affects us as an epic without air, without wings to lift it; reminds us in fact more than anything else of a huge balloon, all of silk pieces strongly sewn together and patiently blown up, but that absolutely refuses to leave the ground. The discrimination I here make as against our author is, however, the only one inevitable in a series of remarks so brief. What it really represents—and nothing could be more curious—is that Frédéric enjoys his position not only without the aid of a single "sympathetic" character of consequence, but even without the aid of one with whom we can directly communicate. Can we communicate with the central personage? or would we really if we could? A hundred times no, and if he himself can communicate with the people shown us as surrounding him this only proves him of their kind. Flaubert on his "real" side was in truth an ironic painter, and ironic to a tune that makes his final accepted state, his present literary dignity and "classic" peace, superficially anomalous. There is an explanation to which I shall immediately come; but I find myself feeling for a moment longer in presence of *L'Éducation* how much more interesting a writer may be on occasion by the given failure than by the given success. Successes pure and simple disconnect and dismiss him; failures—though I admit they must be a bit qualified—keep him in touch and in relation. Thus it is that as the work of a "grand écrivain" *L'Éducation,* large, laboured, immensely "written," with beautiful passages and a general emptiness, with a kind of leak in its stored sadness, moreover, by which its moral dignity escapes—thus it is that Flaubert's ill-starred novel is a curiosity for a literary museum. Thus it is also that it suggests a hundred reflections, and suggests perhaps most of them directly to the intending labourer in the same field. If in short, as I have said, Flaubert is the novelist's novelist, this performance does more than any other toward making him so.

I have to add in the same connection that I had not lost sight of Madame Arnoux, the main ornament of *L'Éducation,* in pronouncing just above on its deficiency in the sympathetic. Madame Arnoux is exactly the author's one marked attempt, here or elsewhere, to represent beauty otherwise than for the senses, beauty of character and life; and what becomes of the attempt is a matter highly significant. M. Faguet praises with justice his conception of the figure and of the relation, the relation that never bears fruit, that keeps Frédéric adoring her, through hindrance and change, from the beginning of life to the end; that keeps her, by the same constraint, forever immaculately "good," from youth to age, though deeply moved and cruelly tempted and sorely tried. Her contacts with her adorer are not even frequent, in proportion to the field of time; her conditions of fortune, of association and occupation are almost sordid, and we see them with the march of the drama, such as it is, become more and more so; besides which—I again remember that M. Faguet excellently notes it—nothing in the nature of "parts" is attributed to her; not only is she not presented as clever, she is scarce invested with a character at all. Almost nothing that she says is repeated, almost nothing that she does is shown. She is an image none the less beautiful and vague, an image of passion cherished and abjured, renouncing all sustenance and yet persisting in life. Only she has for real distinction the extreme drawback that she is offered us quite preponderantly through Frédéric's vision of her, that we see her practically in no other light. Now Flaubert unfortunately has not been able not so to discredit Frédéric's vision in general, his vision of everyone and everything, and in particular of his own life, that it makes a medium good enough to convey adequately a noble impression. Madame Arnoux is of course ever so much the best thing in his life—which is saying little; but his life is made up of such queer material that we find ourselves displeased at her being "in" it on whatever terms; all the more that she seems scarcely to affect, improve or determine it. Her creator in short never had a more awkward idea than this attempt to give us the benefit of such a conception in such a way; and even though I have still something else to say about that I may as well speak of it at once as a mistake that gravely counts against him. It is but one of three, no doubt, in all his work; but I shall not, I trust, pass for extravagant if I call it the most indicative. What makes it so is its being the least superficial; the two others are, so to speak, intellectual, while this is somehow moral. It was a mistake, as I have already hinted, to propose to register in so mean a consciousness as that of such a hero so large and so mixed a quantity of life as *L'Éducation* clearly intends; and it was a mistake of the tragic sort that is a theme mainly for silence to have embarked on *Bouvard et Pécuchet* at all, not to have given it up sooner than be given up by it. But these were at the worst not wholly compromising blunders. What *was* compromising—and the great point is that it remained so, that nothing has an equal weight against it—is the unconsciousness of error in respect to the opportunity that would have counted as his finest. We feel not so much that Flaubert misses it, for that we could bear; but that he doesn't *know* he misses it is what stamps the blunder. We do not pretend to say how he might have shown us Madame Arnoux better—that was his own affair. What is ours is that he really thought he was showing her as well as he could, or as she might be shown; at which we veil our face. For once that he had a conception quite apart, apart I mean from the array of his other conceptions and more delicate than any, he "went," as we say, and spoiled it. Let me add in all tenderness, and to make up for possibly too much insistence, that it is the only stain on his shield; let me even confess that I should not wonder if, when all is said, it is a blemish no one has ever noticed.

Perhaps no one has ever noticed either what was present to me just above as the partial makeweight there glanced at, the fact that in the midst of this general awkwardness, as I have called it, there is at the same time a danger so escaped as to entitle our author to full credit. I scarce know how to put it with little enough of the ungracious, but I think that even the true Flaubertist finds himself wondering a little that some flaw of taste, some small but unfortunate lapse by the way, *should* as a matter of fact not somehow or somewhere have waited on the demonstration of the platonic purity prevailing between this heroine and her hero—so far as we do find that image projected. It is alike difficult to indicate without offence or to ignore without unkindness a fond reader's apprehension here of a possibility of the wrong touch, the just perceptibly false note. I would not have staked my life on Flaubert's security of instinct in such a connection—as an absolutely fine and predetermined security; and yet in the event that felicity has settled, there is not so much as the lightest wrong breath (speaking of the matter in this light of tact and taste) or the shade of a crooked stroke. One exclaims at the end of the question "Dear old Flaubert after all—!" and perhaps so risks seeming to patronise for fear of not making a point. The point made for what it is worth, at any rate, I am the more free to recover the benefit of what I mean by critical "tenderness" in our general connection—expressing in it as I do our general respect, and my own particular, for our author's method and process and history, and my sense of the luxury of such a senti-ment at such a vulgar literary time. It is a respect positive and settled and the thing that has most to do with consecrating for us that loyalty to him as the novelist of the novelist—unlike as it is even the best feeling inspired by any other member of the craft. He may stand for our operative conscience or our vicarious sacrifice; animated by a sense of literary honour, attached to an ideal of perfection, incapable of lapsing in fine from a self-respect, that enable us to sit at ease, to surrender to the age, to indulge in whatever comparative meannesses (and no meanness in art is so mean as the sneaking economic,) we may find most comfortable or profitable. May it not in truth be said that we practise our industry, so many of us, at relatively little cost just *because* poor Flaubert, producing the most expensive fictions ever written, so handsomely paid for it? It is as if this put it in our power to produce cheap and thereby sell dear; as if, so expressing it, literary honour being by his example effectively secure for the firm at large and the general concern, on its whole esthetic side, floated once for all, we find our individual attention free for literary and esthetic indifference. All the while we thus lavish our indifference the spirit of the author of *Madame Bovary,* in the cross-light of the old room above the Seine, is trying to the last admiration for the thing itself. That production puts the matter into a nutshell: *Madame Bovary,* subject to whatever qualification, is absolutely the most literary of novels, so literary that it covers us with its mantle. It shows us once for all that there is no *intrinsic* call for a debasement of the type. The mantle I speak of is wrought with surpassing fineness, and we may always, under stress of whatever charge of illiteracy, frivolity, vulgarity, flaunt it as the flag of the guild. Let us therefore frankly concede that to surround Flaubert with our consideration is the least return we can make for such a privilege. The consideration moreover is idle unless it be real, unless it be intelligent enough to measure his effort and his success. Of the effort as mere effort I have already spoken, of the desperate difficulty involved for him in making his form square with his conception; and I by no means attach general importance to these secrets of the workshop, which are but as the contortions of the fastidious muse who is the servant of the oracle. They are really rather secrets of the kitchen and contortions of the priestess of *that* tripod—they are not an upstairs matter. It is of their specially distinctive importance I am now speaking, of the light shed on them by the results before us.

They all represent the pursuit of a style, of the ideally right one for its relations, and would still be interesting if the style had not been achieved. *Madame Bovary, Salammbô, Saint-Antoine, L'Éducation* are so written and so composed (though the last-named in a minor degree) that the more we look at them the more we find in them, under this head, a beauty of intention and of effect; the more they figure in the too often dreary desert of fictional prose a class by themselves and a little living oasis. So far as that desert is of the complexion of our own English speech it supplies with remarkable rarity this particular source of refreshment. So strikingly is that the case, so scant for the most part any dream of a scheme of beauty in these connections, that a critic betrayed at artless moments into a plea for composition may find himself as blankly met as if his plea were for trigonometry. He makes inevitably his reflections, which are numerous enough; one of them being that if we turn our back so squarely, so universally to this order of considerations it is because the novel is so preponderantly cultivated among us by women, in other words by a sex ever gracefully, comfortably, enviably unconscious (it would be too much to call them even suspicious,) of the requirements of form. The case is at any rate sharply enough made for us, or against us, by the circumstance that women are held to have achieved on all our ground, in spite of this weakness and others, as great results as any. The judgment is undoubtedly founded: Jane Austen was instinctive and charming, and the other recognitions—even over the heads of the ladies, some of them, from Fielding to Pater—are obvious; without, however, in the least touching my contention. For signal examples of what composition, distribution, arrangement can do, of how they intensify the life of a work of art, we have to go elsewhere; and the value of Flaubert for us is that he admirably points the moral. This is the explanation of the "classic" fortune of *Madame Bovary* in especial, though I may add that also of Hérodias and Saint-Julien l'Hospitalier in the *Trois Contes*, as well as an aspect of these works endlessly suggestive. I spoke just now of the small field of the picture in the longest of them, the small capacity, as I called it, of the vessel; yet the way the thing is done not only triumphs over the question of value but in respect to it fairly misleads and confounds us. Where else shall we find in anything proportionately so small such an air of dignity of size? Flaubert *made* things big—it was his way, his ambition and his necessity; and I say this while remembering that in *L'Éducation* (in proportion I mean again,) the effect has not been produced. The subject of *L'Éducation* is in spite of Frédéric large, but an indefinable shrinkage has overtaken it in the execution. The exception so marked, however, is single; *Salammbô* and *Saint-Antoine* are both at once very "heavy" conceptions and very consistently and splendidly high applications of a manner.

It is in this assured manner that the lesson sits aloft, that the spell for the critical reader resides; and if the conviction under which Flaubert labours is more and more grossly discredited among us his compact mass is but the greater. He regarded the work of art as *existing* but by its expression, and defied us to name any other measure of its life that is not a stultification. He held style to be accordingly an indefeasible part of it, and found beauty, interest and distinction as dependent on it for emergence as a letter committed to the post-office is dependent on an addressed envelope. Strange enough it may well appear to us to have to apologise for such notions as eccentric. There are persons who consider that style comes of itself—we see and hear at present, I think, enough of them; and to whom he would doubtless have remarked that it goes, of itself, still faster. The thing naturally differs in fact with the nature of the imagination; the question is one of proprieties and affinities, sympathy and proportion. The sympathy of the author of *Salammbô* was all with the magnificent, his imagination for the phrase as variously noble or ignoble in itself, contributive or destructive, adapted and harmonious or casual and common. The worse among such possibilities have been multiplied by the infection of bad writing, and he denied that the better ever do anything so obliging as to come of themselves. They scarcely indeed for Flaubert "came" at all; their arrival was determined only by fasting and prayer or by patience of pursuit, the arts of the chase, long waits and watches, figuratively speaking, among the peaks or by the waters. The production of a book was of course made inordinately slow by the fatigue of these measures; in illustration of which his letters often record that it has taken him three days* to arrive at one right sentence, tested by the pitch of his ideal of the right for the suggestion aimed at. His difficulties drew from the author, as I have mentioned, much resounding complaint; but those voices have ceased to trouble us and the final voice remains. No feature of the whole business is more edifying than the fact that he in the first place never misses style and in the second never appears to have beaten about for it. That betrayal is of course the worst betrayal of all, and I think the way he has escaped it the happiest form of the peace that has finally visited him. It was truly a wonderful success to be so the devotee of the phrase and yet never its victim. Fine as he inveterately desired it should be he still never lost sight of the question Fine for what? It is always so related and associated, so properly part of something else that is in turn part of something other, part of a reference, a tone, a passage, a page, that the simple may enjoy it for its least bearing and the initiated for its greatest. That surely is to be a writer of the first order, to resemble when in the hand and however closely viewed a shapely crystal box, and yet to be seen when placed on the table and opened to contain innumerable compartments, springs and tricks. One is ornamental either way, but one is in the second way precious too.

The crystal box then figures the style of *Salammbô* and *Saint-Antoine* in a greater degree than that of *Bovary*, because, as the two former express the writer's romantic side, he had in them, while

---

*It was true, delightfully true, that, extravagance in this province of his life, though apparently in no other, being Flaubert's necessity and law, he deliberated and hung fire, wrestled, retreated and returned, indulged generally in a tragi-comedy of waste; which I recall a charming expression of on the lips of Edmond de Goncourt, who quite recognised the heroic legend, but prettily qualified it: "Il faut vous dire qu'il y avait là-dedans beaucoup de coucheries et d'école buissonnière." And he related how on the occasion of a stay with his friend under the roof of the Princess Mathilde, the friend, missed during the middle hours of a fine afternoon, was found to have undressed himself and gone to bed to think!

equally covering his tracks, still further to fare and still more to hunt. Beyond this allusion to their completing his duality I shall not attempt closely to characterise them; though I admit that in not insisting on them I press most lightly on the scale into which he had in his own view cast his greatest pressure. He lamented the doom that drove him so oddly, so ruefully, to choose his subjects, but he lamented it least when these subjects were most pompous and most exotic, feeling as he did that they had then after all most affinity with his special eloquence. In dealing with the near, the directly perceived, he had to keep down his tone, to make the eloquence small; though with the consequence, as we have seen, that in spite of such precautions the whole thing mostly insists on being ample. The familiar, that is, under his touch, took on character, importance, extension, one scarce knows what to call it, in order to carry the style or perhaps rather, as we may say, sit with proper ease in the vehicle, and there was accordingly a limit to its smallness; whereas in the romantic books, the preferred world of Flaubert's imagination, there was practically no need of compromise. The compromise gave him throughout endless trouble, and nothing would be more to the point than to show, had I space, why in particular it distressed him. It was obviously his strange predicament that the only spectacle open to him by experience and direct knowledge was the bourgeois, which on that ground imposed on him successively his three so intensely bourgeois themes. He was obliged to treat these themes, which he hated, because his experience left him no alternative; his only alternative was given by history, geography, philosophy, fancy, the world of erudition and of imagination, the world especially of this last. In the bourgeois sphere his ideal of expression laboured under protest; in the other, the imagined, the projected, his need for facts, for matter, and his pursuit of them, sat no less heavily. But as his style all the while required a certain exercise of pride he was on the whole more at home in the exotic than in the familiar; he escaped above all in the former connection the associations, the disparities he detested. He could be frankly noble in *Salammbô* and *Saint-Antoine*, whereas in *Bovary* and *L'Éducation* he could be but circuitously and insidiously so. He could in the one case cut his coat according to his cloth—if we mean by his cloth his predetermined tone, while in the other he had to take it already cut. Singular enough in his life the situation so constituted: the comparatively meagre human consciousness—for we must come back to that in him—struggling with the absolutely large artistic; and the large artistic half wreaking itself on the meagre human and half seeking a refuge from it, as well as a revenge against it, in something quite different.

Flaubert had in fact command of two refuges which he worked in turn. The first of these was the attitude of irony, so constant in him that *L'Éducation* bristles and hardens with it and *Bouvard et Pécuchet*—strangest of "poetic" justices—is made as dry as sand and as heavy as lead; the second only was, by processes, by journeys the most expensive, to get away altogether. And we inevitably ask ourselves whether, eschewing the policy of flight, he might not after all have fought out his case a little more on the spot. Might he not have addressed himself to the human still otherwise than in *L'Éducation* and in *Bouvard*? When one thinks of the view of the life of his country, of the vast French community and its constituent creatures, offered in these productions, one declines to believe it could make up the *whole* vision of a man of his quality. Or when all was said and done was he absolutely and exclusively condemned to irony? The second refuge I speak of, the getting away from the human, the congruously and measurably human, altogether, perhaps becomes in the light of this possibility but an irony the more. Carthage and the Thebaid, Salammbô, Spendius, Matho, Hannon, Saint Anthony, Hilarion, the Paternians, the Marcosians and the Carpocratians, what are all these, inviting because queer, but a confession of supreme impatience with the actual and the near, often queer enough too, no doubt, but not consolingly, not transcendently? Last remains the question whether, even if our author's immediate as distinguished from his remote view had had more reach, the particular gift we claim for him, the perfection of arrangement and form, would have had in certain directions the acquired flexibility. States of mind, states of soul, of the simpler kind, the kinds supposable in the Emma Bovarys, the Frédérics, the Bouvards and the Pécuchets, to say nothing of the

Carthaginians and the Eremites—for Flaubert's eremites are eminently
artless—these conditions represent, I think, his proved psychological
range. And that throws us back remarkably, almost confoundingly,
upon another face of the general anomaly. The "gift" was of the greatest, a force in itself, in virtue of which he is a consummate writer;
and yet there are whole sides of life to which it was never addressed
and which it apparently quite failed to suspect as a field of exercise.
If he never approached the complicated character in man or woman—
Emma Bovary is not the least little bit complicated—or the really
furnished, the finely civilised, was this because, surprisingly, he could
not? *L'âme française* at all events shows in him but ill.

This undoubtedly marks a limit, but limits are for the critic familiar country, and he may mostly well feel the prospect wide enough
when he finds something positively well enough done. By disposition
or by obligation Flaubert selected, and though his selection was in
some respects narrow he stops not too short to have left us three really
"cast" works and a fourth of several perfect parts, to say nothing of
the element of perfection, of the superlative for the size, in his three
nouvelles. What he attempted he attempted in a spirit that gives an
extension to the idea of the achievable and the achieved in a literary
thing, and it is by this that we contentedly gauge the matter. As success goes in this world of the approximate it may pass for success of
the greatest. If I am unable to pursue the proof of my remark in
Salammbô and *Saint-Antoine* it is because I have also had to select
and have found the questions connected with their two companions
more interesting. There are numerous judges, I hasten to mention,
who, showing the opposite preference, lose themselves with rapture
in the strange bristling archaeological picture—yet all amazingly
vivified and co-ordinated—of the Carthaginian mercenaries in revolt
and the sacred veil of the great goddess profaned and stolen; as well
in the still more peopled panorama of the ancient sects, superstitions
and mythologies that swim in the desert before the fevered eyes of
the Saint. One may be able, however, at once to breathe more freely
in *Bovary* than in *Salammbô* and yet to hope that there is no intention of the latter that one has missed. The great intention certainly,

and little as we may be sweetly beguiled, holds us fast; which is simply the author's indomitable purpose of fully pervading his field. There are countries beyond the sea in which tracts are allowed to settlers on condition that they will really, not nominally, cultivate them. Flaubert is on his romantic ground like one of these settlers; he makes good with all his might his title to his tract, and in a way that shows how it is not only for him a question of safety but a question of honour. Honour demands that he shall set up his home and his faith there in such a way that every inch of the surface be planted or paved. He would have been ashamed merely to encamp and, after the fashion of most other adventurers, knock up a log hut among charred stumps. This was not what would have been for him taking artistic possession, it was not what would have been for him even personal honour, let alone literary; and yet the general lapse from integrity was a thing that, wherever he looked, he saw not only condoned but acclaimed and rewarded. He lived, as he felt, in an age of mean production and cheap criticism, the practical upshot of which took on for him a name that was often on his lips. He called it the hatred of literature, a hatred in the midst of which, the most literary of men, he found himself appointed to suffer. I may not, however, follow him in that direction—which would take us far; and the less that he was for himself after all, in spite of groans and imprecations, a man of resources and remedies, and that there was always his possibility of building himself in.

This he did equally in all his books—built himself into literature by means of a material put together with extraordinary art; but it leads me again to the question of what such a stiff ideal imposed on him for the element of exactitude. This element, in the romantic, was his merciless law; it was perhaps even in the romantic that—if there could indeed be degrees for him in such matters—he most despised the loose and the more-or-less. To be intensely definite and perfectly positive, to know so well what he meant that he could at every point strikingly and conclusively verify it, was the first of his needs; and if in addition to being thus synthetically final he could be strange and sad and terrible, and leave the cause of these effects inscrutable, success then had for him its highest savour. We feel the inscrutability in those memorable few words that put before us Frederic Moreau's start upon his vain course of travel, "Il connût alors la mélancholic des paquebots"; an image to the last degree comprehensive and embracing, but which haunts us, in its droll pathos, without our quite knowing why. But he was really never so pleased as when he could be both rare and precise about the dreadful. His own sense of all this, as I have already indicated, was that beauty comes with expression, that expression is creation, that it *makes* the reality, and only in the degree in which it *is*, exquisitely, expression; and that we move in literature through a world of different values and relations, a blest world in which we know nothing except by style, but in which also everything is saved by it, and in which the image is thus always superior to the thing itself. This quest and multiplication of the image, the image tested and warranted and consecrated for the occasion, was accordingly his high elegance, to which he too much sacrificed and to which *Salammbô* and partly *Saint-Antoine* are monstrous monuments. Old cruelties and perversities, old wonders and errors and terrors, endlessly appealed to him; they constitute the unhuman side of his work, and if we have not the bribe of curiosity, of a lively interest in method, or rather in evocation just *as* evocation, we tread our way among them, especially in *Salammbô*, with a reserve too dry for our pleasure. To my own view the curiosity and the literary interest are equal in dealing with the non-romantic books, and the world presented, the aspects and agents, are less deterrent and more amenable both to our own social and expressional terms. Style itself moreover, with all respect to Flaubert, never *totally* beguiles; since even when we are so queerly constituted as to be ninety-nine parts literary we are still a hundredth part something else. This hundredth part may, once we possess the book—or the book possesses us—make us imperfect as readers, and yet without it should we want or get the book at all? The curiosity at any rate, to repeat, is even greatest for me in *Madame Bovary,* say, for here I can measure, can more directly appreciate, the terms. The aspects and impressions being of an experience conceivable to me I am more touched by the beauty; my interest gets more of the benefit of the beauty even though this be not intrinsically greater. Which brings back our appreciation inevitably at last to the question of our author's lucidity.

I have sufficiently remarked that I speak from the point of view of his interest to a reader of his own craft, the point of view of his extraordinary technical wealth—though indeed when I think of the general power of *Madame Bovary* I find myself desiring not to narrow the ground of the lesson, not to connect the lesson, to its prejudice, with that idea of the "technical," that question of the way a thing is done, so abhorrent, as a call upon attention, in whatever art, to the wondrous Anglo-Saxon mind. Without proposing Flaubert as the type of the newspaper novelist, or as an easy alternative to golf or the bicycle, we should do him less than justice in failing to insist that a masterpiece like *Madame Bovary* may benefit even with the simple-minded by the way it has been done. It derives from its firm roundness that sign of all rare works that there is something in it for every one. It may be read ever so attentively, ever so freely, without a suspicion of how it is written, to say nothing of put together; it may equally be read under the excitement of these perceptions alone, one of the greatest known to the reader who is fully open to them. Both readers will have been transported, which is all any can ask. Leaving the first of them, however that may be, to state the case for himself, I state it yet again for the second, if only on this final ground. The book and its companions represent for us a practical solution, Flaubert's own troubled but settled one, of the eternal dilemma of the painter of life. From the moment this rash adventurer deals with his mysterious matter at all directly his desire is not to deal with it stintedly. It at the same time remains true that from the moment he desires to produce forms in which it shall be preserved, he desires that these forms, things of *his* creation, shall not be, as testifying to his way with them, weak or ignoble. He must make them complete and beautiful, of satisfactory production, intrinsically interesting, under peril of disgrace with those who know. Those who don't know of course don't count for him, and it neither helps nor hinders him to say that every one knows about life. Every one does not—it is distinctly the case of the few; and if it were in fact the case of the many the knowledge still might exist, on the evidence around us, even in an age of unprecedented printing, without attesting itself by a multiplication of masterpieces. The question for the artist can only be of doing the artistic utmost, and thereby of *seeing* the general task. When it is seen with the intensity with which it presented itself to Flaubert a lifetime is none too much for fairly tackling it. It must either be left alone or be dealt with, and to leave it alone is a comparatively simple matter.

To deal with it is on the other hand to produce a certain number of finished works; there being no other known method; and the quantity of life depicted will depend on this array. What will this array, however, depend on, and what will condition the number of pieces of which it is composed? The "finish," evidently, that the formula so glibly postulates and for which the novelist is thus so handsomely responsible. He has on the one side to feel his subject and on the other side to render it, and there are undoubtedly two ways in which his situation may be expressed, especially perhaps by himself. The more he feels his subject the more he *can* render it—that is the first way. The more he renders it the more he *can* feel it—that is the second way. This second way was unmistakeably Flaubert's, and if the result of it for him was a bar to abundant production he could only accept such an incident as part of the game. He probably for that matter would have challenged any easy definition of "abundance," contested the application of it to the repetition, however frequent, of the thing not "done." What but the "doing" makes the thing, he would have asked, and how can a positive result from a mere iteration of negatives, or wealth proceed from the simple addition of so many instances of penury? We should here, in closer communion with him, have got into his highly characteristic and suggestive view of the fertilisation of subject by form, penetration of the sense, ever, by the expression— the latter reacting creatively on the former; a conviction in the light of which he appears to have wrought with real consistency and which borrows from him thus its high measure of credit. It would undoubtedly have suffered if his books had been things of a loose logic, whereas we refer to it not only without shame but with an encouraged confidence by their showing of a logic so close. Let the phrase, the form that the whole is at the given moment staked on, be beautiful and related, and the rest will take care of itself—such is a rough indication of Flaubert's faith; which has the importance that it was a faith sincere, active and inspiring. I hasten to add indeed that we must most of all remember how in these matters everything hangs on definitions. The "beautiful," with our author, covered for the phrase a great deal of ground, and when every sort of propriety had been gathered in under it and every relation, in a complexity of such, protected, the idea itself, the presiding thought, ended surely by being pretty well provided for.

These, however, are subordinate notes, and the plain question, in the connection I have touched upon, is of whether we would really wish him to have written more books, say either of the type of *Bovary* or of the type of *Salammbô*, and not have written them so well. When the production of a great artist who has lived a length of years has been small there is always the regret; but there is seldom, any more than here, the conceivable remedy. For the case is doubtless predetermined by the particular kind of great artist a writer happens to be, and this even if when we come to the conflict, to the historic case, deliberation and delay may not all have been imposed by temperament. The admirable George Sand, Flaubert's beneficent friend and correspondent, is exactly the happiest example we could find of the genius constitutionally incapable of worry, the genius for whom style "came," for whom the sought effect was ever quickly and easily struck off, the book freely and swiftly written, and who consequently is represented for us by upwards of ninety volumes. If the comparison were with this lady's great contemporary the elder Dumas the disparity would be quadrupled, but that ambiguous genius, somehow never really caught by us in the *fact* of composition, is out of our concern here: the issue is of those developments of expression which involve a style, and as Dumas never so much as once grazed one in all his long career, there was not even enough of that grace in him for a fillip of the finger-nail. Flaubert is at any rate represented by six books, so that he may on that estimate figure as poor, while Madame Sand, falling so little short of a hundred, figures as rich; and yet the fact remains that I can refer the congenial mind to him with confidence and can do nothing of the sort for it in respect to Madame Sand. She is loose and liquid and iridescent, as iridescent as we may undertake to find her; but I can imagine compositions quite without virtue—the virtue I mean, of sticking together—begotten by the impulse to emulate her. She had undoubtedly herself the benefit of her facility, but are we not left wondering to what extent *we* have it? There is too little in her, by the literary connection, for the critical mind, weary of much wandering, to rest upon. Flaubert himself wandered, wandered far, went much roundabout and sometimes lost himself by the way, but how handsomely he provided for our present repose! He found the French language inconceivably difficult to write with elegance and was confronted with the equal truths that elegance is the last thing that languages, even as they most mature, seem to concern themselves with, and that at the same time taste, asserting rights, insists on it, to the effect of showing us in a boundless circumjacent waste of effort what the absence of it may mean. He saw the less of this desert of death come back to that—that everything at all saved from it for us since the beginning had been saved by a soul of elegance within, or in other words by the last refinement of selection, by the indifference on the part of the very idiom, huge quite other than "composing" agent, to the individual pretension. Recognising thus that to carry through the individual pretension is at the best a battle, he adored a hard surface and detested a soft one—much more a muddled; regarded a style without rhythm and harmony as in a work of pretended beauty no style at all. He considered that the failure of complete expression so registered made of the work of pretended beauty a work of achieved barbarity. It would take us far to glance even at his fewest discriminations; but rhythm and harmony were for example most menaced in his scheme by repetition—when repetition had not a positive grace; and were above all most at the mercy of the bristling particles of which our modern tongues are mainly composed and which make of the desired surface a texture pricked through, from beneath, even to destruction, as by innumerable thorns.

On these lines production was of course slow work for him—especially as he met the difficulty, met it with an inveteracy which shows how it *can* be met; and full of interest for readers of English speech is the reflection he causes us to make as to the possibility of success at all comparable among ourselves. I have spoken of his groans and imprecations, his interminable waits and deep despairs; but what would these things have been, what would have become of him and what of his wrought residuum, had he been condemned to deal with a form of speech consisting, like ours, as to one part, of "that" and "which"; as to a second part, of the blest "it," which an English sentence may repeat in three or four opposed references without in the least losing caste; as to a third face of all the "tos" of the infinitive and the preposition; as to a fourth of our precious auxiliaries "be" and "do"; and as to a fifth, of whatever survives in the language for the precious art of pleasing? Whether or no the fact that the painter of "life" among us has to contend with a medium intrinsically indocile, on certain sides, like our own, whether this drawback accounts for his having failed, in our time, to treat us, arrested and charmed, to a single case of crowned classicism, there is at any rate no doubt that we in some degree owe Flaubert's counterweight for that deficiency to *his* having, on his own ground, more happily triumphed. By which I do not mean that *Madame Bovary* is a classic because the "thats," the "its" and the "tos" are made to march as Orpheus and his lute made the beasts, but because the element of order and harmony works as a symbol of everything else that is preserved for us by the history of the book. The history of the book remains the lesson and the important, the delightful thing, remains above all the drama that moves slowly to its climax. It is what we come back to for the sake of what it shows us. We see—from the present to the past indeed, never alas from the present to the future—how a classic almost inveterately grows. Unimportant, unnoticed, or, so far as noticed, contested, unrelated, alien, it has a cradle round which the fairies but scantly flock and is waited on in general by scarce a hint of significance. The significance comes by a process slow and small, the fact only that one perceptive private reader after another discovers at his convenience that the book is rare. The addition of the perceptive private readers

is no quick affair, and would doubtless be a vain one did they not—
while plenty of other much more remarkable books come and go—ac-
cumulate and count. They count by their quality and continuity of
attention; so they have gathered for *Madame Bovary,* and so they are
held. That is really once more the great circumstance. It is always in
order for us to feel yet again what it is we are held by. Such is my
reason, definitely, for speaking of Flaubert as the novelist's novelist.
Are we not moreover—and let it pass this time as a happy hope!—
pretty well all novelists now?

ÉMILE ZOLA

IF IT BE true that the critical spirit to-day, in presence of the rising tide of prose fiction, a watery waste out of which old standards and landmarks are seen barely to emerge, like chimneys and the tops of trees in a country under flood—if it be true that the anxious observer, with the water up to his chin, finds himself asking for the *reason* of the strange phenomenon, for its warrant and title, so we likewise make out that these credentials rather fail to float on the surface. We live in a world of wanton and importunate fable, we breathe its air and consume its fruits; yet who shall say that we are able, when invited, to account for our preferring it so largely to the world of fact? To do so would be to make some adequate statement of the good the product in question does us. What does it do for our life, our mind, our manners, our morals—what does it do that history, poetry, philosophy may not do, as well or better, to warn, to comfort and command the countless thousands for whom and by whom it comes into being? We seem too often left with our riddle on our hands. The lame conclusion on which we retreat is that "stories" are multiplied, circulated, paid for, on the scale of the present hour, simply because people "like" them. As to why people *should* like anything so loose and mean as the preponderant mass of the "output," so little indebted for the magic of its action to any mystery in the making, is more than the actual state of our perceptions enables us to say.

This bewilderment might be our last word if it were not for the occasional occurrence of accidents especially appointed to straighten out a little our tangle. We are reminded that if the unnatural prosperity of the wanton fable cannot be adequately explained, it can at least be illustrated with a sharpness that is practically an argument. An abstract solution failing we encounter it in the concrete. We catch in short a new impression or, to speak more truly, recover an old one. It was always there to be had, but we ourselves throw off an oblivion, an indifference for which there are plenty of excuses. We become conscious, for our profit, of a *case*, and we see that our mystification came from the way cases had appeared for so long to fail us. None of the shapeless forms about us for the time had attained to the dignity of one. The one I am now conceiving as suddenly effective—for which I fear I must have been regarding it as somewhat in eclipse—is that of Émile Zola, whom, as a manifestation of the sort we are considering, three or four striking facts have lately combined to render more objective and, so to speak, more massive. His close connection with the most resounding of recent public quarrels; his premature and disastrous death; above all, at the moment I write, the appearance of his last-finished novel, bequeathed to his huge public from beyond the grave—these rapid events have thrust him forward and made him loom abruptly larger; much as if our pedestrian critic, treading the dusty highway, had turned a sharp corner.

It is not assuredly that Zola has ever been veiled or unapparent; he had, on the contrary been digging his field these thirty years, and for all passers to see, with an industry that kept him, after the fashion of one of the grand grim sowers or reapers of his brother of the brush, or at least of the canvas, Jean-François Millet, duskily outlined against the sky. He was there in the landscape of labour—he had always been; but he was there as a big natural or pictorial feature, a spreading tree, a battered tower, a lumpish round-shouldered useful hayrick, confounded with the air and the weather, the rain and the shine, the day and the dusk, merged more or less, as it were, in the play of the elements themselves. We had got used to him, and, thanks in a measure just to this stoutness of his presence, to the long regularity of his performance, had come to notice him hardly more than the dwellers in the marketplace notice the quarters struck by the town-clock. On top of all accordingly, for our skeptical mood, the sense of his work— a sense determined afresh by the strange climax of his personal history—rings out almost with violence as a reply to our wonder. It is as if an earthquake or some other rude interference had shaken from the town-clock a note of such unusual depth as to compel attention. We therefore once more give heed, and the result of this is that we feel ourselves after a little probably as much enlightened as we can hope ever to be. We have worked round to the so marked and impressive anomaly of the adoption of the futile art by one of the stoutest minds and stoutest characters of our time. This extraordinarily robust worker has found it good enough for him, and if the fact is, as I say, anomalous, we are doubtless helped to conclude that by its anomalies, in future, the bankrupt business, as we are so often moved to pronounce it, will most recover credit.

What is at all events striking for us, critically speaking, is that, in the midst of the dishonour it has gradually harvested by triumphant vulgarity of practice, its pliancy and applicability can still plead for themselves. The curious contradiction stands forth for our relief—the circumstance that thirty years ago a young man of extraordinary brain and indomitable purpose, wishing to give the measure of these endowments in a piece of work supremely solid, conceived and sat down to Les Rougon-Macquart rather than to an equal task in physics, mathematics, politics or economics. He saw his undertaking, thanks to his patience and courage, practically to a close; so that it is exactly neither of the so-called constructive sciences that happens to have had the benefit, intellectually speaking, of one of the few most constructive achievements of our time. There then, provisionally at least, we touch bottom; we get a glimpse of the pliancy and variety, the ideal of vividness, on behalf of which our equivocal form may appeal to a strong head. In the name of what ideal on its own side, however, does the strong head yield to the appeal? What is the logic of its so deeply committing itself? Zola's case seems to tell us, as it tells us other things. The logic is in its huge freedom of adjustment to the temperament of the worker, which it carries, so to say, as no other vehicle can do. It expresses fully and directly the whole man, and big as he may be it can still be big enough for him without becoming false to its type. We see this truth made strong from beginning to end, in Zola's work; we see the temperament, we see the whole man, with his size and all his marks, stored and packed away in the huge hold of Les Rougon-Macquart as a cargo is packed away on a ship. His personality is the thing that finally pervades and prevails, just as so often on a vessel the presence of the cargo makes itself felt for the assaulted senses. What has most come home to me in reading him over is that a scheme of fiction so conducted is in fact a capacious vessel. It can carry anything—with art and force in the stowage; nothing in this case will sink it. And it is the only form for which such a claim can be made. All others have to confess to a smaller scope—to selection, to exclusion, to the danger of distortion, explosion, combustion. The novel has nothing to fear but sailing too light. It will take aboard all we bring in good faith to the dock.

An intense vision of this truth must have been Zola's comfort from the earliest time—the years, immediately following the crash of the Empire, during which he settled himself to the tremendous task he had mapped out. No finer act of courage and confidence, I think, is recorded in the history of letters. The critic in sympathy with him returns again and again to the great wonder of it, in which something so strange is mixed with something so august. Entertained and carried out almost from the threshold of manhood, the high project, the work of a lifetime, announces beforehand its inevitable weakness and yet speaks in the same voice for its admirable, its almost unimaginable strength. The strength was in the young man's very person—in his character, his will, his passion, his fighting temper, his aggressive lips, his squared shoulders (when he "sat up") and overweening confidence; his weakness was in that inexperience of life from which he proposed not to suffer, from which he in fact suffered on the surface remarkably little, and from which he was never to suspect, I judge, that he had suffered at all. I may mention for the interest of it that, meeting him during his first short visit to London—made several years before his stay in England during the Dreyfus trial—I received a direct impression of him that was more informing than any previous study. I had seen him a little, in Paris, years before that, when this impression was a perceptible promise, and I was now to perceive how time had made it good. It consisted, simply stated, in his fairly bristling with the betrayal that nothing whatever had happened to him in life but to write Les Rougon-Macquart. It was even for that matter almost more as if Les Rougon-Macquart had written *him,* written him as he stood and sat, as he looked and spoke, as the long, concentrated, merciless effort had made and stamped and left him. Something very fundamental was to happen to him in due course, it is true, shaking him to his base; fate was not wholly to cheat him of an independent evolution. Recalling him from this London hour one strongly felt during the famous "Affair" that his outbreak in connection with it was the act of a man with arrears of personal history to make up, the act of a spirit for which life, or for which at any rate freedom, had been too much postponed, treating itself at last to a luxury of experience.

I welcomed the general impression at all events—I intimately entertained it; it represented so many things, it suggested, just as it was, such a lesson. You could neither have everything nor be everything—you had to choose; you could not at once sit firm at your job and wander through space inviting initiations. The author of Les Rougon-Macquart had had all those, certainly, that this wonderful company could bring him; but I can scarce express how it was implied in him that his time had been fruitfully passed with *them* alone. His artistic evolution struck one thus as, in spite of its magnitude, singularly simple, and evidence of the simplicity seems further offered by his last production, of which we have just come into possession. *Vérité* truly does give the measure, makes the author's high maturity join hands with his youth, marks the rigid straightness of his course from point to point. He had seen his horizon and his fixed goal from the first, and no cross-scent, no new distance, no blue gap in the hills to right or to left ever tempted him to stray. *Vérité,* of which I shall have more to say, is in fact, as a moral finality and the crown of an edifice, one of the strangest possible performances. Machine-minted and made good by an immense expertness, it yet makes us ask how, for disinterested observation and perception, the writer had used so much time and so much acquisition, and how he can all along have handled so much material without some larger subjective consequence. We really rub our eyes in other words to see so great an intellectual adventure as Les Rougon-Macquart come to its end in deep desert sand. Difficult truly to read, because showing him at last almost completely a prey to the danger that had for a long time more and more dogged his steps, the danger of the mechanical all confident and triumphant, the book is nevertheless full of interest for a reader desirous to penetrate. It speaks with more distinctness of the author's temperament, tone and manner than if, like several of his volumes, it achieved or enjoyed a successful life of its own. Its heavy completeness, with all this, as of some prodigiously neat, strong and complicated scaffolding constructed by a firm of builders for the erection of a house whose foundations refuse to bear it and that is unable therefore to rise—its very betrayal of a method and a habit more than adequate, on past occasions, to similar ends, carries us back to the original rare exhibition, the grand assurance and grand patience with which the system was launched.

If it topples over, the system, by its own weight in these last applications of it, that only makes the history of its prolonged success the more curious and, speaking for myself, the spectacle of its origin more attaching. Readers of my generation will remember well the publication of *La Conquête de Plassans* and the portent, indefinable but irresistible, after perusal of the volume, conveyed in the general rubric under which it was a first instalment, Natural and Social History of a Family under the Second Empire. It squared itself there at its ease, the announcement, from the first, and we were to learn promptly enough what a fund of life it masked. It was like the mouth of a cave with a signboard hung above, or better still perhaps like the big booth at a fair with the name of the show across the flapping canvas. One strange animal after another stepped forth into the light, each in its way a monster bristling and spotted, each a curiosity of that "natural history" in the name of which we were addressed, though it was doubtless not till the issue of *L'Assommoir* that the true type of the monstrous seemed to be reached. The enterprise, for those who had attention, was even at a distance impressive, and the nearer the critic gets to it retrospectively the more so it becomes. The pyramid had been planned and the site staked out, but the young builder stood there, in his sturdy strength, with no equipment save his two hands and, as we may say, his wheelbarrow and his trowel. His pile of material—of stone, brick and rubble or whatever—was of the smallest, but this he apparently felt as the least of his difficulties. Poor, uninstructed, unacquainted, unintroduced, he set up his subject wholly from the outside, proposing to himself wonderfully to get into it, into its depths, as he went.

If we imagine him asking himself what he knew of the "social" life of the second Empire to start with, we imagine him also answering in all honesty: "I have my eyes and my ears—I have all my senses: I have what I've seen and heard, what I've smelled and tasted and touched. And then I've my curiosity and my pertinacity; I've libraries, books, newspapers, witnesses, the material, from step to step, of an *enquête*. And then I've my genius—that is, my imagination, my passion, my sensibility to life. Lastly I've my method, and that will be half the battle. Best of all perhaps even, I've plentiful lack of doubt." Of the absence in him of a doubt, indeed of his inability, once his direction taken, to entertain so much as the shadow of one, *Vérité* is a positive monument—which again represents in this way the unity of his tone and the meeting of his extremes. If we remember that his design was nothing if not architectural, that a "majestic whole," a great balanced façade, with all its orders and parts, that a singleness of mass and a unity of effect, in fine, were before him from the first, his notion of picking up his bricks as he proceeded becomes, in operation, heroic. It is not in the least as a record of failure for him that I note this particular fact of the growth of the long series as on the whole the liveliest interest it has to offer. "I don't know my subject, but I must live into it; I don't know life, but I must learn it as I work"—that attitude and programme represent, to my sense, a drama more intense on the worker's own part than any of the dramas he was to invent and put before us.

It was the fortune, it was in a manner the doom, of Les Rougon-Macquart to deal with things almost always in gregarious form, to be a picture of *numbers*, of classes, crowds, confusions, movements, industries—and this for a reason of which it will be interesting to attempt some account. The individual life is, if not wholly absent, reflected in coarse and common, in generalised terms; whereby we arrive precisely at the oddity just named, the circumstance that, looking out somewhere, and often woefully athirst, for the taste of fineness, we find it not in the fruits of our author's fancy, but in a different matter altogether. We get it in the very history of his effort, the image itself of his lifelong process, comparatively so personal, so spiritual even, and, through all its patience and pain, of a quality so much more distinguished than the qualities he succeeds in attributing to his figures even when he most aims at distinction. There can be no question in these narrow limits of my taking the successive volumes one by one—all the more that our sense of the exhibition is as little as possible an impression of parts and books, of particular "plots" and persons. It produces the effect of a mass of imagery in which shades are sacrificed, the effect of character and passion in the lump or by the ton. The fullest, the most characteristic episodes affect us like a sounding chorus or procession, as with a hubbub of voices and a multitudinous tread of feet. The setter of the mass into motion, he himself, in the crowd, figures best, with whatever queer idiosyncrasies, excrescences and gaps, a being of a substance akin to our own. Taking him as we must, I repeat, for quite heroic, the interest of detail in him is the interest of his struggle at every point with his problem.

The sense for crowds and processions, for the gross and the general, was largely the *result* of this predicament, of the disproportion between his scheme and his material—though it was certainly also in part an effect of his particular turn of mind. What the reader easily discerns in him is the sturdy resolution with which breadth and energy supply the place of penetration. He rests to his utmost on his documents, devours and assimilates them, makes them yield him extraordinary appearances of life; but in his way he too improvises in the grand manner, the manner of Walter Scott and of Dumas the elder. We feel that he *has* to improvise for his moral and social world, the world as to which vision and opportunity must come, if they are to come at

all, unhurried and unhustled—must take their own time, helped
undoubtedly more or less by blue-books, reports and interviews, by
inquiries "on the spot," but never wholly replaced by such substitutes
without a general disfigurement. Vision and opportunity reside in a
personal sense and a personal history, and no short cut to them in
the interest of plausible fiction has ever been discovered. The short
cut, it is not too much to say, was with Zola the subject of constant
ingenious experiment, and it is largely to this source, I surmise, that
we owe the celebrated element of his grossness. He was *obliged* to be
gross, on his system, or neglect to his cost an invaluable aid to representation, as well as one that apparently struck him as lying close at
hand; and I cannot withhold my frank admiration from the courage
and consistency with which he faced his need.

His general subject in the last analysis was the nature of man; in
dealing with which he took up, obviously, the harp of most numerous
strings. His business was to make these strings sound true, and there
were none that he did not, so far as his general economy permitted,
persistently try. What happened then was that many—say about half,
and these, as I have noted, the most silvered, the most golden—refused
to give out their music. They would only sound false, since (as with
all his earnestness he must have felt) he could command them, through
want of skill, of practice, of ear, to none of the right harmony. What
therefore was more natural than that, still splendidly bent on producing his illusion, he should throw himself on the strings he might
thump with effect, and should work them, as our phrase is, for all
they were worth? The nature of man, he had plentiful warrant for
holding, is an extraordinary mixture, but the great thing was to
represent a sufficient part of it to show that it was solidly, palpably,
commonly the nature. With this preoccupation he doubtless fell into
extravagance—there was clearly so much to lead him on. The coarser
side of his subject, based on the community of all the instincts, was
for instance the more practicable side, a sphere the vision of which
required but the general human, scarcely more than the plain physical, initiation, and dispensed thereby conveniently enough with special introductions or revelations. A free entry into this sphere was

undoubtedly compatible with a youthful career as hampered right and left even as Zola's own.

He was in prompt possession thus of the range of sympathy that he *could* cultivate, though it must be added that the complete exercise of that sympathy might have encountered an obstacle that would somewhat undermine his advantage. Our friend might have found himself able, in other words, to pay to the instinctive, as I have called it, only such tribute as protesting taste (his own dose of it) permitted. Yet there it was again that fortune and his temperament served him. Taste as he knew it, taste as his own constitution supplied it, proved to have nothing to say to the matter. His own dose of the precious elixir had no perceptible regulating power. Paradoxical as the remark may sound, this accident was positively to operate as one of his greatest felicities. There are parts of his work, those dealing with romantic or poetic elements, in which the inactivity of the principle in question is sufficiently hurtful; but it surely should not be described as hurtful to such pictures as *Le Ventre de Paris*, as *L'Assommoir*, as *Germinal*. The conception on which each of these productions rests is that of a world with which taste has nothing to do, and though the act of representation may be justly held, as an artistic act, to involve its presence, the discrimination would probably have been in fact, given the particular illusion sought, more detrimental than the deficiency. There was a great outcry, as we all remember, over the rank materialism of *L'Assommoir*, but who cannot see to-day how much a milder infusion of it would have told against the close embrace of the subject aimed at? *L'Assommoir* is the nature of man—but not his finer, nobler, cleaner or more cultivated nature; it is the image of his free instincts, the better and the worse, the better struggling as they can, gasping for light and air, the worse making themselves at home in darkness, ignorance and poverty. The whole handling makes for emphasis and scale, and it is not to be measured how, as a picture of conditions, the thing would have suffered from timidity. The qualification of the painter was precisely his stoutness of stomach, and we scarce exceed in saying that to have taken in and given out again less of the infected air would, with such a resource, have meant the waste of a faculty.

I may add in this connection moreover that refinement of intention did on occasion and after a fashion of its own unmistakably
preside at these experiments; making the remark in order to have
done once for all with a feature of Zola's literary physiognomy that
appears to have attached the gaze of many persons to the exclusion
of every other. There are judges in these matters so perversely preoc-
cupied that for them to see anywhere the "improper" is for them
straightway to cease to see anything else. The said improper, looming
supremely large and casting all the varieties of the proper quite into
the shade, suffers thus in their consciousness a much greater extension
than it ever claimed, and this consciousness becomes, for the edification of many and the information of a few, a colossal reflector and
record of it. Much may be said, in relation to some of the possibilities
of the nature of man, of the nature in especial of the "people," on the
defect of our author's sense of proportion. But the sense of proportion
of many of those he has scandalised would take us further yet. I recall
at all events as relevant—for it comes under a very attaching general
head—two occasions of long ago, two Sunday afternoons in Paris,
on which I found the question of intention very curiously lighted.
Several men of letters of a group in which almost every member either
had arrived at renown or was well on his way to it, were assembled
under the roof of the most distinguished of their number, where they
exchanged free confidences on current work, on plans and ambitions,
in a manner full of interest for one never previously privileged to see
artistic conviction, artistic passion (at least on the literary ground)
so systematic and so articulate. "Well, I on my side," I remember
Zola's saying, "am engaged on a book, a study of the *moeurs* of the
people, for which I am making a collection of all the 'bad words,' the
gros mots, of the language, those with which the vocabulary of the
people, those with which their familiar talk, bristles." I was struck
with the tone in which he made the announcement—without bravado
and without apology, as an interesting idea that had come to him
and that he was working, really to arrive at character and particular
truth, with all his conscience; just as I was struck with the unqualified
interest that his plan excited. It was *on* a plan that he was working—

formidably, almost grimly, as his fatigued face showed; and the whole consideration of this interesting element partook of the general seriousness.

But there comes back to me also as a companion-piece to this another day, after some interval, on which the interest was excited by the fact that the work for love of which the brave license had been taken was actually under the ban of the daily newspaper that had engaged to "serialise" it. Publication had definitively ceased. The thing had run a part of its course, but it had outrun the courage of editors and the curiosity of subscribers—that stout curiosity to which it had evidently in such good faith been addressed. The chorus of contempt for the ways of such people, their pusillanimity, their superficiality, vulgarity, intellectual platitude, was the striking note on this occasion; for the journal impugned had declined to proceed and the serial, broken off, been obliged, if I am not mistaken, to seek the hospitality of other columns, secured indeed with no great difficulty. The composition so qualified for future fame was none other, as I was later to learn, than *L'Assommoir*; and my reminiscence has perhaps no greater point than in connecting itself with a matter always dear to the critical spirit, especially when the latter has not too completely elbowed out the romantic—the matter of the "origins," the early consciousness, early steps, early tribulations, early obscurity, as so often happens, of productions finally crowned by time.

Their greatness is for the most part a thing that has originally begun so small; and this impression is particularly strong when we have been in any degree present, so to speak, at the birth. The course of the matter is apt to tend preponderantly in that case to enrich our stores of irony. In the eventual conquest of consideration by an abused book we recognise, in other terms, a drama of romantic interest, a drama often with large comic no less than with fine pathetic interweavings. It may of course be said in this particular connection that *L'Assommoir* had not been one of the literary things that creep humbly into the world. Its "success" may be cited as almost insolently prompt, and the fact remains true if the idea of success be restricted, after the inveterate fashion, to the idea of circulation. What remains truer still, however, is that for the critical spirit circulation mostly matters not the least little bit, and it is of the success with which the history of Gervaise and Coupeau nestles in *that* capacious bosom, even as the just man sleeps in Abraham's, that I here speak. But it is a point I may better refer to a moment hence.

Though a summary study of Zola need not too anxiously concern itself with book after book—always with a partial exception from this remark for *L'Assommoir*—groups and varieties none the less exist in the huge series, aids to discrimination without which no measure of the presiding genius is possible. These divisions range themselves to my sight, roughly speaking, however, as scarce more than three in number—I mean if the ten volumes of the Œuvres Critiques and the Théâtre be left out of account. The critical volumes in especial abound in the characteristic, as they were also a wondrous addition to his sum of achievement during his most strenuous years. But I am forced not to consider them. The two groups constituted after the close of Les Rougon-Macquart—Les Trois Villes and the incomplete Quatre Évangiles—distribute themselves easily among the three types, or, to speak more exactly, stand together under one of the three. This one, so comprehensive as to be the author's main exhibition, includes to my sense all his best volumes—to the point in fact of producing an effect of distinct inferiority for those outside of it, which are, luckily for his general credit, the less numerous. It is so inveterately pointed out in any allusion to him that one shrinks, in repeating it, from sounding flat; but as he was admirably equipped from the start for the evocation of number and quantity, so those of his social pictures that most easily surpass the others are those in which appearances, the appearances familiar to him, are at once most magnified and most multiplied.

To make his characters swarm, and to make the great central thing they swarm about "as large as life," portentously, heroically big, that was the task he set himself very nearly from the first, that was the secret he triumphantly mastered. Add that the big central thing was always some highly representative institution or industry of the France of his time, some seated Moloch of custom, of commerce, of faith, lending itself to portrayal through its abuses and excesses, its idol-face and great devouring mouth, and we embrace the main lines of his attack. In *Le Ventre de Paris* he had dealt with the life of the huge Halles, the general markets and their supply, the personal forces, personal situations, passions, involved in (strangest of all subjects) the alimentation of the monstrous city, the city whose victualling occupies so inordinately much of its consciousness. Paris richly gorged, Paris sublime and indifferent in her assurance (so all unlike poor Oliver's) of "more," figures here the theme itself, lies across the scene like some vast ruminant creature breathing in a cloud of parasites. The book was the first of the long series to show the full freedom of the author's hand, though *La Curée* had already been symptomatic. This freedom, after an interval, broke out on a much bigger scale in *L'Assommoir*, in *Au Bonheur des Dames*, in *Germinal*, in *La Bête Humaine*, in *L'Argent*, in *La Débacle*, and then again, though more mechanically and with much of the glory gone, in the more or less wasted energy of *Lourdes*, *Rome*, *Paris*, of *Fécondité*, *Travail* and *Vérité*.

Au Bonheur des Dames handles the colossal modern shop, traces the growth of such an organisation as the Bon Marché or the Magasin-du-Louvre, sounds the abysses of its inner life, marshals its population, its hierarchy of clerks, counters, departments, divisions and sub-divisions, plunges into the labyrinth of the mutual relations of its staff, and above all traces its ravage amid the smaller fry of the trade, of all the trades, pictures these latter gasping for breath in an air pumped clean by its mighty lungs. *Germinal* revolves about the coal-mines of Flemish France, with the subterranean world of the pits for its central presence, just as *La Bête Humaine* has for its protagonist a great railway and *L'Argent* presents in terms of human passion—mainly of human baseness—the fury of the Bourse and the monster of Credit. *La Débacle* takes up with extraordinary breadth the first act of the Franco-Prussian war, the collapse at Sedan, and the titles of the six volumes of The Three Cities and the Four Gospels sufficiently explain them. I may mention, however, for the last lucidity, that among these *Fécondité* manipulates, with an amazing misapprehension of means to ends, of remedies to ills, no less thickly peopled a theme than that of the decline in the French birth-rate, and that *Vérité* presents a fictive equivalent of the Dreyfus case, with a vast and elaborate picture of the battle in France between lay and clerical instruction. I may even further mention, to clear the ground, that with the close of Les Rougon-Macquart the diminution of freshness in the author's energy, the diminution of intensity and, in short, of quality, becomes such as to render sadly difficult a happy life with some of the later volumes. Happiness of the purest strain never indeed, in old absorptions of Zola, quite sat at the feast; but there was mostly a measure of coercion, a spell without a charm. From these last-named productions of the climax everything strikes me as absent but quantity (*Vérité,* for instance, is, with the possible exception of *Nana*, the longest of the list); though indeed there is something impressive in the way his quantity represents his patience.

There are efforts here at stout perusal that, frankly, I have been unable to carry through, and I should verily like, in connection with the vanity of these, to dispose on the spot of the sufficiently strange phenomenon constituted by what I have called the climax. It embodies in fact an immense anomaly; it casts back over Zola's prime and his middle years the queerest grey light of eclipse. Nothing moreover—nothing "literary"—was ever so odd as in this matter the whole turn of the case, the consummation so logical yet so unexpected. Writers have grown old and withered and failed; they have grown weak and sad; they have lost heart, lost ability, yielded in one way or another—the possible ways being so numerous—to the cruelty of time. But the singular doom of this genius, and which began to multiply its symptoms ten years before his death, was to find, with life, at fifty, still rich in him, strength only to undermine all the "authority" he had gathered. He had not grown old and he had not grown feeble; he had only grown all too wrongly insistent, setting himself to wreck, poetically, his so massive identity—to wreck it in the very waters in which he had formally arrayed his victorious fleet. (I say "poetically" on purpose to give him the just benefit of all the beauty of his power.) The process of the disaster, so full of the effect, though so without the intention, of perversity, is difficult to trace in a few words; it may best be indicated by an example or two of its action.

The example that perhaps most comes home to me is again connected with a personal reminiscence. In the course of some talk that I had with him during his first visit to England I happened to ask him what opportunity to travel (if any) his immense application had ever left him, and whether in particular he had been able to see Italy, a country from which I had either just returned or which I was luckily—not having the Natural History of a Family on my hands—about to revisit. "All I've done, alas," he replied, "was, the other year, in the course of a little journey to the south, to my own *pays*—all that has been possible was then to make a little dash as far as Genoa, a matter of only a few days." *Le Docteur Pascal*, the conclusion of Les Rougon-Macquart, had appeared shortly before, and it further befell that I asked him what plans he had for the future, now that, still *dans la force de l'âge,* he had so cleared the ground. I shall never forget the fine promptitude of his answer—"Oh, I shall begin at once Les Trois Villes." "And which cities are they to be?" The reply was finer still— "Lourdes, Paris, Rome."

It was splendid for confidence and cheer, but it left me, I fear, more or less gaping, and it was to give me afterwards the key, critically speaking, to many a mystery. It struck me as breathing to an almost tragic degree the fatuity of those in whom the gods stimulate that vice to their ruin. He was an honest man—he had always bristled with it at every pore; but no artistic reverse was inconceivable for an adventurer who, stating in one breath that his knowledge of Italy consisted of a few days spent at Genoa, was ready to declare in the next that he had planned, on a scale, a picture of Rome. It flooded his career, to my sense, with light; it showed how he had marched from subject to subject and had "got up" each in turn—showing also how consummately he had reduced such getting-up to an artifice. He had success and a rare impunity behind him, but nothing would now be so interesting as to see if he could again play the trick. One would leave him, and welcome, Lourdes and Paris—he had already dealt, on a scale, with his own country and people. But was the adored Rome also to be his on such terms, the Rome he was already giving away before possessing an inch of it? One thought of one's own frequentations, saturations—a history of long years, and of how the effect of them had somehow been but to make the subject too august. Was *he* to find it easy through a visit of a month or two with "introductions" and a Baedeker?

It was not indeed that the Baedeker and the introductions didn't show, to my sense, at that hour, as extremely suggestive; they were positively a part of the light struck out by his announcement. They defined the system on which he had brought Les Rougon-Macquart safely into port. He had had his Baedeker and his introductions for *Germinal*, for *L'Assommoir*, for *L'Argent*, for *La Débâcle*, for *Au Bonheur des Dames*; which advantages, which researches, had clearly been all the more in character for being documentary, extractive, a matter of *renseignements*, published or private, even when most mixed with personal impressions snatched, with *enquêtes sur les lieux*, with facts obtained from the best authorities, proud and happy to co-operate in so famous a connection. That was, as we say, all right, all the more that the process, to my imagination, became vivid and was wonderfully reflected back from its fruits. There *were* the fruits—so it hadn't been presumptuous. Presumption, however, was now to begin, and what omen mightn't there be in its beginning with such complacency? Well, time would show—as time in due course effectually did. *Rome*, as the second volume of The Three Cities, appeared with high punctuality a year or two later; and the interesting question, an occasion really for the moralist, was by that time not to recognise in it the mere triumph of a mechanical art, a "receipt" applied with the skill of long practice, but to do much more than this—that is really to give a name to the particular shade of blindness that could constitute a trap for so great an artistic intelligence. The presumptuous volume, without sweetness, without antecedents, superficial and violent, has the minimum instead of the maximum of *value*; so that it betrayed or "gave away" just in this degree the state of mind on the author's part responsible for its inflated hollowness. To put one's finger on the state of mind was to find out accordingly what was, as we say, the matter with him.

It seemed to me, I remember, that I found out as never before when, in its turn, *Fécondité* began the work of crowning the edifice. *Fécondité* is physiological, whereas "Rome" is not, whereas *Vérité* likewise is not; yet these three productions joined hands at a given moment to fit into the lock of the mystery the key of my meditation. They came to the same thing, to the extent of permitting me to read into them together the same precious lesson. This lesson may not, barely stated, sound remarkable; yet without being in possession of it I should have ventured on none of these remarks. "The matter with" Zola then, so far as it goes, was that, as the imagination of the artist is in the best cases not only clarified but intensified by his equal possession of Taste (deserving here if ever the old-fashioned honour of a capital) so when he has lucklessly never inherited that auxiliary blessing the imagination itself inevitably breaks down as a consequence. There is simply no limit, in fine, to the misfortune of being tasteless; it does not merely disfigure the surface and the fringe of your performance—it eats back into the very heart and enfeebles the sources of life. When you have no taste you have no discretion, which is the conscience of taste, and when you have no discretion you perpetrate books like *Rome*, which are without intellectual modesty, books like *Fécondité*, which are without a sense of the ridiculous, books like *Vérité*, which are without the finer vision of human experience.

It is marked that in each of these examples the deficiency has been directly fatal. No stranger doom was ever appointed for a man so plainly desiring only to be just than the absurdity of not resting till he had buried the felicity of his past, such as it was, under a great flat leaden slab. *Vérité* is a plea for science, as science, to Zola, is *all* truth, the mention of any other kind being mere imbecility; and the simplification of the human picture to which his negations and exasperations have here conducted him was not, even when all had been said, credible in advance. The result is amazing when we consider that the finer observation is the supposed basis of all such work. It is not that even here the author has not a queer idealism of his own; this idealism is on the contrary so present as to show positively for the falsest of his simplifications. In *Fécondité* it becomes grotesque, makes of the book the most muscular mistake of *sense* probably ever committed. Where was the judgment of which experience is supposed to be the guarantee when the perpetrator could persuade himself that the lesson he wished in these pages to convey could be made immediate and direct, chalked, with loud taps and a still louder commentary, the sexes and generations all convoked, on the blackboard of the "family sentiment"?

I have mentioned, however, all this time but one of his categories. The second consists of such things as *La Fortune des Rougon* and *La Curée*, as *Eugène Rougon* and even *Nana*, as *Pot-Bouille*, as *L'Œuvre* and *La Joie de Vivre*. These volumes may rank as social pictures in the narrowest sense, studies, comprehensively speaking, of the manners, the morals, the miseries—for it mainly comes to that—of a bourgeoisie grossly materialised. They deal with the life of individuals in the liberal professions and with that of political and social adventures, and offer the personal character and career, more or less detached, as the centre of interest. *La Curée* is an evocation, violent and "romantic," of the extravagant appetites, the fever of the senses, supposedly fostered, for its ruin, by the hapless second Empire, upon which general ills and turpitudes at large were at one time so freely and conveniently fathered. *Eugène Rougon* carries out this view in the high colour of a political portrait, not other than scandalous, for which one of the ministerial *âmes damnées* of Napoleon III., M. Rouher, is reputed, I know not how justly, to have sat. *Nana*, attaching itself by a hundred strings to a prearranged table of kinships, heredities, transmissions, is the vast crowded *epos* of the daughter of the people filled with poisoned blood and sacrificed as well as sacrificing on the altar of luxury and lust; the panorama of such a "progress" as Hogarth would more definitely have named—the progress across the high plateau of "pleasure" and down the facile descent on the other side. *Nana* is truly a monument to Zola's patience; the subject being so ungrateful, so formidably special, that the multiplication of illustrative detail, the plunge into pestilent depths, represents a kind of technical intrepidity.

There are other plunges, into different sorts of darkness; of which the esthetic, even the scientific, even the ironic motive fairly escapes us—explorations of stagnant pools like that of *La Joie de Vivre*, as to which, granting the nature of the curiosity and the substance laboured in, the patience is again prodigious, but which make us wonder what pearl of philosophy, of suggestion or just of homely recognition, the general picture, as of rats dying in a hole, has to offer. Our various senses, sight, smell, sound, touch, are, as with Zola always, more or less convinced; but when the particular effect upon each of these is added to the effect upon the others the mind still remains bewilderedly unconscious of any use for the total. I am not sure indeed that the case is in this respect better with the productions of the third order— *La Faute de l'Abbé Mouret, Une Page d'Amour, Le Rêve, Le Docteur Pascal*—in which the appeal is more directly, is in fact quite earnestly, to the moral vision; so much, on such ground, was to depend precisely on those discriminations in which the writer is least at home. The volumes whose names I have just quoted are his express tribute to the "ideal," to the select and the charming—fair fruits of invention intended to remove from the mouth so far as possible the bitterness of the ugly things in which so much of the rest of his work had been condemned to consist. The subjects in question then are "idyllic" and the treatment poetic, concerned essentially to please on the largest lines and involving at every turn that salutary need. They are matters of conscious delicacy, and nothing might interest us more than to see what, in the shock of the potent forces enlisted, becomes of this shy element. Nothing might interest us more, literally, and might positively affect us more, even very nearly to tears, though indeed sometimes also to smiles, than to see the constructor of Les Rougon-Macquart trying, "for all he is worth," to be fine with fineness, finely tender, finely true—trying to be, as it is called, distinguished—in face of constitutional hindrance.

The effort is admirably honest, the tug at his subject splendidly strong; but the consequences remain of the strangest, and we get the impression that—as representing discriminations unattainable—they are somehow the price he paid. *Le Docteur Pascal*, for instance, which winds up the long chronicle on the romantic note, on the note of invoked beauty, in order to sweeten, as it were, the total draught—*Le Docteur Pascal*, treating of the erotic ardour entertained for each other by an uncle and his niece, leaves us amazed at such a conception of beauty, such an application of romance, such an estimate of sweetness, a sacrifice to poetry and passion so little in order. Of course, we definitely remind ourselves, the whole long chronicle is explicitly a scheme, solidly set up and intricately worked out, lighted, according to the author's pretension, by "science," high, dry and clear, and with each part involved and necessitated in all the other parts, each block of the edifice, each "morceau de vie," *physiologically* determined by previous combinations. "How can I help it," we hear the builder of the pyramid ask, "if experience (by which alone I proceed) shows me certain plain results—if, holding up the torch of my famous 'experimental method,' I find it stare me in the face that the union of certain types, the conflux of certain strains of blood, the intermarriage, in a word, of certain families, produces nervous conditions, conditions temperamental, psychical and pathological, in which nieces *have* to fall in love with uncles and uncles with nieces? Observation and imagination, for any picture of life," he as audibly adds, "know no light but science, and are false to all intellectual decency, false to their own honour, when they fear it, dodge it, darken it. To pretend to any other guide or law is mere base humbug."

That is very well, and the value, in a hundred ways, of a mass of production conceived in such a spirit can never (when robust execution has followed) be small. But the formula really sees us no further. It offers a definition which is no definition. "Science" is soon said— the whole thing depends on the ground so covered. Science accepts surely *all* our consciousness of life; even, rather, the latter closes maternally round it—so that, becoming thus a force within us, not a force outside, it exists, it illuminates only as we apply it. We do emphatically apply it in art. But Zola would apparently hold that it much more applies *us.* On the showing of many of his volumes then it makes but a dim use of us, and this we should still consider the case even were we sure that the article offered us in the majestic name is absolutely at one with its own pretension. This confidence we can on too many grounds never have. The matter is one of appreciation, and when an artist answers for science who answers for the artist—who at the least answers for art? Thus it is with the mistakes that affect us, I say, as Zola's penalties. We are reminded by them that the game of art has, as the phrase is, to be played. It may not with any sure felicity for the result be both taken and left. If you insist on the common you must submit to the common; if you discriminate, on the contrary, you must, however invidious your discriminations may be called, trust to them to see you through.

To the common then Zola, often with splendid results, inordinately sacrifices, and this fact of its overwhelming him is what I have called his paying for it. In *L'Assommoir,* in *Germinal*, in *La Débâcle*, productions in which he must most survive, the sacrifice is ordered and fruitful, for the subject and the treatment harmonise and work together. He describes what he best feels, and feels it more and more as it naturally comes to him—quite, if I may allow myself the image, as we zoologically see some mighty animal, a beast of a corrugated hide and a portentous snout, soaking with joy in the warm ooze of an African riverside. In these cases everything matches, and "science," we may be permitted to believe, has had little hand in the business. The author's perceptions go straight, and the subject, grateful and responsive, gives itself wholly up. It is no longer a case of an uncertain smoky torch, but of a personal vision, the vision of genius, springing from an inward source. Of this genius *L'Assommoir* is the most extraordinary record. It contains, with the two companions I have given it, all the best of Zola, and the three books together are solid ground—or would be could I now so take them—for a study of the particulars of his power. His strongest marks and features abound in them; *L'Assommoir* above all is (not least in respect to its bold free linguistic reach, already glanced at) completely genial, while his misadventures, his unequipped and delusive pursuit of the life of the spirit and the tone of culture, are almost completely absent.

It is a singular sight enough this of a producer of illusions whose interest for us is so independent of our pleasure or at least of our complacency—who touches us deeply even while he most "puts us off," who makes us care for his ugliness and yet himself at the same time pitilessly (pitilessly, that is, for *us*) makes a mock of it, who fills us with a sense of the rich which is none the less never the rare. Gervaise, the most immediately "felt," I cannot but think, of all his characters, is a lame washerwoman, loose and gluttonous, without will, without any principle of cohesion, the sport of every wind that assaults her exposed life, and who, rolling from one gross mistake to another, finds her end in misery, drink and despair. But her career, as presented, has fairly the largeness that, throughout the chronicle, we feel as epic, and the intensity of her creator's vision of it and of the dense sordid life hanging about it is one of the great things the modern novel has been able to do. It has done nothing more completely constitutive and of a tone so rich and full and sustained. The tone of *L'Assommoir* is, for mere "keeping up," unsurpassable, a vast deep steady tide on which every object represented is triumphantly borne. It never shrinks nor flows thin, and nothing for an instant drops, dips or catches; the high-water mark of sincerity, of the genial, as I have called it, is unfailingly kept.

For the artist in the same general "line" such a production has an interest almost inexpressible, a mystery as to origin and growth over which he fondly but rather vainly bends. How after all does it so get itself *done*?—the "done" being admirably the sign and crown of it. The light of the richer mind has been elsewhere, as I have sufficiently hinted, frequent enough, but nothing truly in all fiction was ever built so strong or made so dense as here. Needless to say there are a thousand things with more charm in their truth, with more beguilement of every sort, more prettiness of pathos, more innocence of drollery, for the spectator's sense of truth. But I doubt if there has ever been a more totally *represented* world, anything more founded and established, more provided for all round, more organised and carried on. It is a world practically workable, with every part as functional as every other, and with the parts all chosen for direct mutual aid. Let it not be said either that the equal constitution of parts makes for repletion or excess; the air circulates and the subject blooms;

deadness comes in these matters only when the right parts are absent and there is vain beating of the air in their place—the refuge of the fumbler incapable of the thing "done" at all.

The mystery I speak of, for the reader who reflects as he goes, is the wonder of the scale and energy of Zola's assimilations. This wonder besets us above all throughout the three books I have placed first. How, all sedentary and "scientific," did he get so *near*? By what art, inscrutable, immeasurable, indefatigable, did he arrange to make of his documents, in these connections, a use so vivified? Say he was "near" the subject of *L'Assommoir* in imagination, in more or less familiar impression, in temperament and humour, he could not after all have been near it in personal experience, and the copious personalism of the picture, not to say its frank animalism, yet remains its note and its strength. When the note had been struck in a thousand forms we had, by multiplication, as a kind of cumulative consequence, the finished and rounded book; just as we had the same result by the same process in *Germinal*. It is not of course that multiplication and accumulation, the extraordinary pair of legs on which he walks, are easily or directly consistent with his projecting himself morally; this immense diffusion, with its appropriation of everything it meets, affects us on the contrary as perpetually delaying access to what we may call the private world, the world of the individual. Yet since the individual—for it so happens—is simple and shallow our author's dealings with him, as met and measured, maintain their resemblance to those of the lusty bee who succeeds in plumping for an instant, of a summer morning, into every flower-cup of the garden.

Grant—and the generalisation may be emphatic—that the shallow and the simple are *all* the population of his richest and most crowded pictures, and that his "psychology," in a psychologic age, remains thereby comparatively coarse, grant this and we but get another view of the miracle. We see enough of the superficial among novelists at large, assuredly, without deriving from it, as we derive from Zola at his best, the concomitant impression of the solid. It is in general—I mean among the novelists at large—the impression of the *cheap,* which the author of Les Rougon-Macquart, honest man, never faithless for a moment to his own stiff standard, manages to spare us even in the prolonged sandstorm of *Vérité*. The Common is another matter; it is one of the forms of the superficial—pervading and consecrating all things in such a book as *Germinal*—and it only adds to the number of our critical questions. How in the world is it made, this deplorable democratic malodorous Common, so strange and so interesting? How is it taught to receive into its loins the stuff of the epic and still, in spite of that association with poetry, never depart from its nature? It is in the great lusty game he plays with the shallow and the simple that Zola's mastery resides, and we see of course that when values are small it takes innumerable items and combinations to make up the sum. In *L'Assommoir* and in *Germinal*, to some extent even in *La Débâcle*, the values are all, morally, personally, of the lowest—the highest is poor Gervaise herself, richly human in her generosities and follies—yet each is as distinct as a brass-headed nail.

What we come back to accordingly is the unprecedented case of such a combination of parts. Painters, of great schools, often of great talent, have responded liberally on canvas to the appeal of ugly things, of Spanish beggars, squalid and dusty-footed, of martyred saints or other convulsed sufferers, tortured and bleeding, of boors and louts soaking a Dutch proboscis in perpetual beer; but we had never before had to reckon with so literary a treatment of the mean and vulgar. When we others of the Anglo-Saxon race are vulgar we are, handsomely and with the best conscience in the world, vulgar all through, too vulgar to be in any degree literary, and too much so therefore to be critically reckoned with at all. The French are different—they separate their sympathies, multiply their possibilities, observe their shades, remain more or less outside of their worst disasters. They mostly contrive to get the *idea,* in however dead a faint, down into the lifeboat. They may lose sight of the stars, but they save in some such fashion as that their intellectual souls. Zola's own reply to all puzzlements would have been, at any rate, I take it, a straight summary of his inveterate professional habits. "It is all very simple—I produce, roughly speaking, a volume a year, and of this time some five months go to preparation, to special study. In the other months, with all my *cadres* established, I write the book. And I can hardly say which part of the job is stiffest."

The story was not more wonderful for him than that, nor the job more complex; which is why we must say of his whole process and its results that they constitute together perhaps the most extraordinary *imitation* of observation that we possess. Balzac appealed to "science" and proceeded by her aid; Balzac had *cadres* enough and a tabulated world, rubrics, relationships and genealogies; but Balzac affects us in spite of everything as personally overtaken by life, as fairly hunted and run to earth by it. He strikes us as struggling and all but submerged, as beating over the scene such a pair of wings as were not soon again to be wielded by any visitor of his general air and as had not at all events attached themselves to Zola's rounded shoulders. His bequest is in consequence immeasurably more interesting, yet who shall declare that his adventure was in its greatness more successful? Zola "pulled it off," as we say, supremely, in that he never but once found himself obliged to quit, to our vision, his magnificent treadmill of the pigeonholed and documented—the region we may qualify as that of experience by imitation. His splendid economy saw him through, he laboured to the end within sight of his notes and his charts.

The extraordinary thing, however, is that on the single occasion when, publicly—as his whole manifestation was public—life did swoop down on him, the effect of the visitation was quite perversely other than might have been looked for. His courage in the Dreyfus connection testified admirably to his ability to live for himself and out of the order of his volumes—little indeed as living at all might have seemed a question for one exposed, when his crisis was at its height and he was found guilty of "insulting" the powers that were, to be literally torn to pieces in the precincts of the Palace of Justice. Our point is that nothing was ever so odd as that these great moments should appear to have been wasted, when all was said, for his creative intelligence. *Vérité,* as I have intimated, the production in which they might most have been reflected, is a production unrenewed and unrefreshed by them, spreads before us as somehow flatter and greyer, not richer and more relieved, by reason of them. They really arrived, I surmise, too late in the day; the imagination they might have vivified was already fatigued and spent.

I must not moreover appear to say that the power to evoke and present has not even on the dead level of *Vérité* its occasional minor revenges. There are passages, whole pages, of the old full-bodied sort, pictures that elsewhere in the series would in all likelihood have seemed abundantly convincing. Their misfortune is to have been discounted by our intensified, our finally fatal sense of the *procédé*. Quarrelling with all conventions, defiant of them in general, Zola was yet inevitably to set up his own group of them—as, for that matter, without a sufficient collection, without their aid in simplifying and making possible, how could he ever have seen his big ship into port? Art welcomes them, feeds upon them always; no sort of form is practicable without them. It is only a question of what particular ones we use—to wage war on certain others and to arrive at particular forms. The convention of the blameless being, the thoroughly "scientific" creature possessed impeccably of all truth and serving as the mouthpiece of it and of the author's highest complacencies, this character is for instance a convention inveterate and indispensable, without whom the "sympathetic" side of the work could never have been achieved. Marc in *Vérité,* Pierre Froment in *Lourdes* and in *Rome*, the wondrous representatives of the principle of reproduction in *Fécondité*, the exemplary painter of *L'Œuvre*, sublime in his modernity and paternity, the patient Jean Macquart of *La Débâcle*, whose patience is as guaranteed as the exactitude of a well-made watch, the supremely enlightened Docteur Pascal even, as I recall him, all amorous nepotism but all virtue too and all beauty of life—such figures show us the reasonable and the good not merely in the white light of the old George Sand novel and its improved moralities, but almost in that of our childhood's nursery and school-room, that of the moral tale of Miss Edgeworth and Mr. Thomas Day.

Yet let not these restrictions be my last word. I had intended, under the effect of a reperusal of *La Débâcle*, *Germinal* and *L'Assommoir*, to make no discriminations that should not be in our hero's favour.

The long-drawn incident of the marriage of Gervaise and Cadet-Cassis and that of the Homeric birthday feast later on in the laundress's workshop, each treated from beginning to end and in every item of their coarse comedy and humanity, still show the unprecedented breadth by which they originally made us stare, still abound in the particular kind and degree of vividness that helped them, when they appeared, to mark a date in the portrayal of manners. Nothing had then been so sustained and at every moment of its grotesque and pitiful existence lived into as the nuptial day of the Coupeau pair in especial, their fantastic processional pilgrimage through the streets of Paris in the rain, their bedraggled exploration of the halls of the Louvre museum, lost as in the labyrinth of Crete, and their arrival at last, ravenous and exasperated, at the *guinguette* where they sup at so much a head, each paying, and where we sit down with them in the grease and the perspiration and succumb, half in sympathy, half in shame, to their monstrous pleasantries, acerbities and miseries. I have said enough of the mechanical in Zola; here in truth is, given the elements, almost insupportably the sense of life. That effect is equally in the historic chapter of the strike of the miners in *Germinal*, another of those illustrative episodes, viewed as great passages to be "rendered," for which our author established altogether a new measure and standard of handling, a new energy and veracity, something since which the old trivialities and poverties of treatment of such aspects have become incompatible, for the novelist, with either rudimentary intelligence or rudimentary self-respect.

As for *La Débâcle*, finally, it takes its place with Tolstoi's very much more universal but very much less composed and condensed epic as an incomparably human picture of war. I have been re-reading it, I confess, with a certain timidity, the dread of perhaps impairing the deep impression received at the time of its appearance. I recall the effect it then produced on me as a really luxurious act of submission. It was early in the summer; I was in an old Italian town; the heat was oppressive, and one could but recline, in the lightest garments, in a great dim room and give one's self up. I like to think of the conditions and the emotion, which melt for me together into the memory I fear to imperil. I remember that in the glow of my admiration there was not a reserve I had ever made that I was not ready to take back. As an application of the author's system and his supreme faculty, as a triumph of what these things could do for him, how could such a performance be surpassed? The long, complex, horrific, pathetic battle, embraced, mastered, with every crash of its squadrons, every pulse of its thunder and blood resolved for us, by reflection, by communication from two of the humblest and obscurest of the military units, into immediate vision and contact, into deep human thrills of terror and pity—this bristling centre of the book was such a piece of "doing" (to come back to our word) as could only shut our mouths. That doubtless is why a generous critic, nursing the sensation, may desire to drop for a farewell no term into the other scale. That our author was clearly great at congruous subjects—this may well be our conclusion. If the others, subjects of the private and intimate order, gave him more or less inevitably "away," they yet left him the great distinction that the more he could be promiscuous and collective, the more even he could (to repeat my imputation) illustrate our large natural allowance of health, heartiness and grossness, the more he could strike us as penetrating and true. It was a distinction not easy to win and that his name is not likely soon to lose.

THE LESSON OF BALZAC

I HAVE found it necessary, at the eleventh hour, to sacrifice to the terrible question of time a very beautiful and majestic approach that I had prepared to the subject on which I have the honor of addressing you. I recognize it as impossible to ask you to linger with me on that pillared portico—paved with marble, I beg you to believe, and over-twined with charming flowers. I must invite you to pass straight into the house and bear with me there as if I had already succeeded in beginning to interest you. Let us assume, therefore, that we have exchanged some ideas on the question of the beneficent play of criticism, and that I have even ingeniously struck it off that criticism is the only gate of appreciation, just as appreciation is, in regard to a work of art, the only gate of enjoyment. You may wonder perhaps why I speak as if we were possessed, in our conditions, of a literary court of appeal, and I hasten to say that the appeal I think of is precisely from the general judgment, and not to it; is to the particular judgment altogether: by which I mean to that quantity of opinion, very small at all times, but at all times infinitely precious, that is capable of giving some intelligible account of itself. Where, among us, at this time of day, this element of the lucid report of impressions received, of estimates formed, of intentions understood, of values attached, is exactly to be looked for—that is another branch of the question, to which I am afraid I should have to devote quite another

Delivered for the first time before the Contemporary Club of Philadelphia, January 12, 1905, and repeated on various occasions elsewhere. Several passages omitted in delivery—one of considerable length—have been restored.

discourse. I do not propose for a moment to invite you to blink the fact that our huge Anglo-Saxon array of producers and readers—and especially our vast cis-Atlantic multitude—presents production uncontrolled, production untouched by criticism, unguided, unlighted, uninstructed, unashamed, on a scale that is really a new thing in the world. It is all the complete reversal of any proportion, between the elements, that was ever seen before. It is the biggest flock straying without shepherds, making its music without a sight of the classic crook, beribboned or other, without a sound of the sheepdog's bark— wholesome note, once in a way—that has ever found room for pasture. The very opposite has happened from what might have been expected to happen. The shepherds have diminished as the flock has increased— quite as if number and quantity had got beyond them, or even as if their charge had turned, by some uncanny process, to a pack of ravening wolves. Let us none the less assume that we may still find two or three of the fraternity hiding under a hedge or astride of some upper limb of a tree; let us even assume that if we set rightly, if we set tactfully about it, we may establish again some friendly connection with them.

Putting, on this basis, then, all our heads together, we may become aware of an intelligent gratitude, deep within our breasts, to any author who consents to fit with a certain fulness of presence and squareness of solidity into one of the conscious categories of our attention. There are literary figures in plenty that scarce fill out even the smaller of these critical receptacles; there are others, on the contrary, that almost strain the larger to breaking. It is to these latter that interested contemplation most fondly attaches itself—to that degree, really, that there seems, on any good occasion, more and more about them to be said. They have the great sign that their immediate presence causes our ideas, whether about life in general or about the art they have exemplified in particular, to revive and breathe again, to multiply, more or less to swarm. I must profess that no Novelist—since we are by common consent confining our attention to that great Company— no Novelist, to my sense, so rewards consideration as he or she (and I emphasize the liberality of my "she") who offers the critical spirit this opportunity for a certain intensity of educative practice. The lesson of Balzac, whom we thus march straight up to, is that he offers it as no other members of the company can pretend to do.

For there are members of the company who scarce produce the effect in question at all. Take, to begin with, close at Balzac's side, his illustrious contemporary Madame George Sand, so suggestive, so affirmative, so instructive, as a dealer with life, as an eloquent exponent of her own, as what we call today a Personality equipped and armed, but of an artistic complexion so comparatively smooth and simple, so happily harmonious, that her work, taken together, presents about as few pegs for analysis to hang upon as if it were a large, polished, gilded Easter egg, the pride of a sweet-shop if not the treasure of a museum. Let me add, further—so far as it is a question of the nameable sisterhood too—that Jane Austen, with all her light felicity, leaves us hardly more curious of her process, or of the experience in her that fed it, than the brown thrush who tells his story from the garden bough; and this, I freely confess, in spite of her being one of those of the shelved and safe, for all time, of whom I should have liked to begin by talking; one of those in whose favor discrimination has long since practically operated. She is in fact a signal instance of the way it does, with all its embarrassments, at last infallibly operate. A sharp short cut, one of the sharpest and shortest achieved, in this field, by the general judgment, came out, betimes, straight at her feet. Practically overlooked for thirty or forty years after her death, she perhaps really stands there for us as the prettiest possible example of that rectification of estimate, brought about by some slow clearance of stupidity, the half-century or so is capable of working round to. This tide has risen high on the opposite shore, the shore of appreciation—risen rather higher, I think, than the high-water mark, the highest, of her intrinsic merit and interest; though I grant indeed—as a point to be made—that we are dealing here in some degree with the tides so freely driven up, beyond their mere logical reach, by the stiff breeze of the commercial, in other words of the special bookselling spirit; an eager, active, interfering force which has a great many confusions of apparent value, a great many wild and wandering estimates, to answer for. For these distinctively mechanical and overdone reactions, of course, the critical spirit, even in its most relaxed mood, is not responsible. Responsible, rather, is the body of publishers, editors, illustrators, producers of the pleasant twaddle of magazines; who have found their "dear," our dear, everybody's dear, Jane so infinitely to their material purpose, so amenable to pretty reproduction in every variety of what is called tasteful, and in what seemingly proves to be saleable, form.

I do not, naturally, mean that she would be saleable if we had not more or less—beginning with Macaulay, her first slightly ponderous amoroso—lost our hearts to her; but I cannot help seeing her, a good deal, as in the same lucky box as the Brontés—lucky for the ultimate guerdon; a case of popularity (that in especial of the Yorkshire sisters), a beguiled infatuation, a sentimentalized vision, determined largely by the accidents and circumstances originally surrounding the manifestation of the genius—only with the reasons for the sentiment, in this latter connection, turned the other way. The key to Jane Austen's fortune with posterity has been in part the extraordinary grace of her facility, in fact of her unconsciousness: as if, at the most, for difficulty, for embarrassment, she sometimes, over her work-basket, her tapestry flowers, in the spare, cool drawing-room of other days, fell a-musing, lapsed too metaphorically, as one may say, into wool-gathering, and her dropped stitches, of these pardonable, of these precious moments, were afterwards picked up as little touches of human truth, little glimpses of steady vision, little master-strokes of imagination. The romantic tradition of the Brontés, with posterity, has been still more essentially helped, I think, by a force independent of any one of their applied faculties—by the attendant image of their dreary, their tragic history, their loneliness and poverty of life. That picture has been made to hang before us as insistently as the vividest page of *Jane Eyre* or of *Wuthering Heights*. If these things were "stories," as we say, and stories of a lively interest, the medium from which they sprang was above all in itself a story, such a story as has fairly elbowed out the rights of appreciation, as has come at last to impose itself as an expression of the power concerned. The personal position of the three sisters, of the two in particular, had been marked, in short, with so sharp an accent that this accent has become for us the very tone of their united production. It covers and supplants their matter, their spirit, their style, their talent, their taste; it embodies, really, the most complete intellectual muddle, if the term be not extravagant, ever achieved, on a literary question, by our wonderful public. The question has scarce indeed been accepted as belonging to literature at all. Literature is an objective, a projected result; it is life that is the unconscious, the agitated, the struggling, floundering cause. But the fashion has been, in looking at the Brontés, so to confound the cause with the result that we cease to know, in the presence of such ecstasies, what we have hold of or what we are talking about. They represent, the ecstasies, the highwater mark of sentimental judgment.

These are but glimmering lanterns, however, you will say, to hang in the great dusky and deserted avenue that leads up to the seated statue of Balzac; and you are so far right, I am bound to admit, as that I place them there, no doubt, in a great measure, just to render the darkness visible. We do, collectively, with all our dimness of view, arrive at rough discriminations, and by one of the roughest of these the author of the Comédie Humaine has in a manner profited; we have for many a year taken his greatness for granted; but in the graceless and nerveless fashion of those who edge away from a classic or a bore. "Oh, yes, he is as 'great' as you like—so let us not talk of him!" My purpose has been to "talk" of him, and I find this form of greeting, therefore, and still more this form of parting, not at all adequate; failing as I do to point my moral unless I show that a really paying acquaintance with a writer can never take place if our recognition remains perfunctory. Our indolence and our ignorance may prefer the empty form; but the penalty and the humiliation come for us with the perception that when the consecration really takes place we have been excluded, so to speak, from the fun. I see no better proof that the great interesting art of which Balzac remains the greatest master is practically, round about us, a bankrupt and discredited art (discredited, of course I mean, for any directed and motived attention), than this very fact that we are so ready to beg off from knowing anything about him. Perfunctory rites, even, at present, are seldom rendered; and, amid the flood of verbiage for which the thousand new novels of the season find themselves a pretext in the newspapers, the name of the man who is really the father of us all, as we stand, is scarcely more mentioned than if he were not of the family.

I may at once intimate that the family strikes me as likely to recover its wasted heritage, and pull itself together for another chance, on condition only of shutting itself up, for an hour of wholesome heart-searching, with the image of its founder. He labors, I know, under the drawback of not being presentable as a classic—which is precisely why there would have seemed to be the less furtherance for regarding him as a bore. His situation in this respect is all his own: it was not given him to flower, for our convenience, into a single supreme felicity. His "successes" hang so together that analysis is almost baffled by his consistency, by his density. Even *Eugénie Grandet* is not a supreme felicity in the sense that this particular bloom is detachable from the cluster. The cluster is too thick, the stem too tough; before we know it, when we begin to pull, we have the whole branch about our heads—or it would indeed be more just to say we have the whole tree, if not the whole forest. It tells against a great worker, for free reference, that we must take his work in the mass; for, unfortunately, the circumstance that nothing of it surpassingly stands forth to represent the rest, to symbolize the whole, suggests a striking resemblance to work of other sorts. Of the mediocrities, and the bunglers too is it true that *they* do not supremely flower—as well as, further, of certain happy geniuses who have flowed in an uncontrolled, an undirected, above all in an unfiltered, current.

But the difference is that, for the most part, these loose and easy producers, the great resounding improvisatori, have not, in general, ended by imposing themselves; when we deal with them conclusively and, as I have said, for clearance of the slate, we deal with them by simplification, by elimination: which may very well be the revenge that time takes upon them to make up for the amount of space they happened immediately to occupy. They are still there, evidently; but they are there under this condition, which enters into account, at every instant, in any pious inquiry about them, and which is attached, intimately, to the appearance they finally wear for us, that the looseness and ease showing as their main sign in the time of their freshness is now a quality still more striking and often still more disconcerting. The weak sides in an artist are weakened with time, and the strong sides strengthened; so that it is never amiss, for duration, to have as many strong sides as possible. It is the only way we have yet made out—even in this age of superlative study of the cheap and easy—not to have so many weak ones as will eventually betray us. Balzac stands almost alone as an extemporizer achieving closeness and weight, and whom closeness and weight have preserved. My reason for speaking of him as an extemporizer I shall presently mention; but let me meanwhile frankly say that I speak of him, and can only speak, as a man of his own craft, an emulous fellow-worker, who has learned from him more of the lessons of the engaging mystery of fiction than from any one else, and who is conscious of so large a debt to repay that it has had positively to be discharged in instalments, as if one could never have at once all the required cash in hand.

When I am tempted, on occasion, to ask myself why we should, after all, so much as talk about the Novel, the wanton fable, against which, in so many ways, so showy an indictment may be drawn, I seem to see that the simplest plea is not to be sought in any attempted philosophy, in any abstract reason for our perversity or our levity. The real gloss upon these things is reflected from some great practitioner, some concrete instance of the art, some ample cloak under which we may gratefully crawl. It comes back, of course, to the example and the analogy of the Poet—with the abatement, however, that the Poet is most the Poet when he is preponderantly lyrical, when he speaks, laughing or crying, most directly from his individual heart, which throbs under the impressions of life. It is not the *image* of life that he thus expresses, so much as life itself, in its sources—so much as his own intimate, essential states and feelings. By the time he has begun to collect anecdotes, to tell stories, to represent scenes, to concern himself, that is, with the states and feelings of others, he is well on the way not to be the Poet pure and simple. The lyrical element, all the same, abides in him, and it is by this element that he is connected with what is most splendid in his expression. The lyrical instinct and tradition are immense in Shakespeare; which is why, great story-teller, great dramatist and painter, great lover, in short, of the image of life though he was, we need not press the case of his example. The lyrical element is not great, is in fact not present at all, in Balzac, in Scott (the Scott of the voluminous prose), nor in Thackeray, nor in Dickens—which is precisely why they are so essentially novelists, so almost exclusively lovers of the image of life. It *is* great, or it is at all events largely present, in such a writer as George Sand— which is doubtless why we take her for a novelist in a much looser sense than the others we have named. It is considerable in that bright particular genius of our own day, George Meredith, who so strikes us as hitching winged horses to the chariot of his prose—steeds who prance and dance and caracole, who strain the traces, attempt to quit the ground, and yearn for the upper air. Balzac, with huge feet fairly ploughing the sand of our desert, is on the other hand the very type and model of the projector and creator; so that when I think, either with envy or with terror, of the nature and the effort of the Novelist, I think of something that reaches its highest expression in him. That is why those of us who, as fellow-craftsmen, have once caught a glimpse of this value in him, can never quite rest from hanging about him; that is why he seems to have all that the others have to tell us, with more, besides, that is all his own. He lived and breathed in his medium, and the fact that he was able to achieve in it, as man and as artist, so crowded a career, remains for us one of the most puzzling problems— I scarce know whether to say of literature or of life. He is himself a figure more extraordinary than any he drew, and the fascination may still be endless of all the questions he puts to us and of the answers for which we feel ourselves helpless.

He died, as we sufficiently remember, at fifty—worn out with work and thought and passion; the passion, I mean, that he had put into his mighty plan and that had ridden him like an infliction of the gods. He began, a friendless and penniless young provincial, to write early, and to write very badly, and it was not till well toward his thirtieth year, with the conception of the Comédie Humaine, as we all again remember, that he found his right ground, found his feet and his voice. This huge distributed, divided and sub-divided picture of the life of France in his time, a picture bristling with imagination and information, with fancies and facts and figures, a world of special and general insight, a rank tropical forest of detail and specification, but with the strong breath of genius forever circulating through it and shaking the treetops to a mighty murmur, got itself hung before us in the space of twenty short years. The achievement remains one of the most inscrutable, one of the unfathomable, final facts in the history of art, and if, as I have said, the author himself has his own surpassing objectivity, it is just because of this challenge his figure constitutes for any other painter of life, inflamed with ingenuity, who should feel the temptation to represent or explain him. How represent, how explain him, as a concrete active energy? How depict him, we ask ourselves, *at* his huge conceived and accepted task, how reconcile such dissemination with such intensity, the collection and possession of so vast a number of facts with so rich a presentation of each? The elements of the world he set up before us, with all its insistent particulars, these elements were not, for him, a direct revelation—of so large a part of life is it true that we can know it only by living, and that living is the process that, in our mortal span, makes the largest demand on our time. How could a man have lived at large so much if, in the service of art, he had so much abstracted and condensed himself? How could he have so much abstracted and condensed himself if, in the service of life, he had felt and fought and acted, had labored and suffered, so much as a private in the ranks? The wealth and strength of his temperament indeed partly answer the question and partly obscure it. He could so extend his existence partly because he vibrated to so many kinds of contact and curiosity. To vibrate intellectually was his motive, but it magnified, all the while, it multiplied his experience. He could live at large, in short, because he was always living in the particular necessary, the particular intended connection—was always astride of his imagination, always charging, with his heavy, his heroic lance in rest, at every object that sprang up in his path. But as he was at the same time always fencing himself in against the personal adventure, the personal experience, in order to preserve himself for converting it into history, how did experience, in the immediate sense, still get itself saved?—or, to put it as simply as possible, where, with so strenuous a conception of the use of material, was material itself so strenuously quarried? Out of what mines, by what innumerable tortuous channels, in what endless winding procession of laden chariots and tugging teams and marching elephants, did the immense consignments required for his work reach him?

The point at which the emulous admirer, however diminished by comparison, may most closely approach him is, it seems to me, through the low portal of envy, so irresistibly do we lose ourselves in the vision of the quantity of life with which his imagination communicated. Quantity and intensity are at once and together his sign; the truth being that his energy did not press hard in some places only to press lightly in others, did not lay it on thick here or there to lay it on thin elsewhere, did not seek the appearance of extent and number by faintness of evocation, by shallow soundings, or by the mere sketchiness of suggestion that dispenses, for reference and verification, with the book, the total collection of human documents, with what we call "chapter and verse." He never throws dust in our eyes, save only the fine gold-dust through the haze of which his own romantic vision operates; never does it, I mean, when he is pretending not to do it, pretending to give us the full statement of his ease, to deal with the facts of the spectacle surrounding him. Then he goes in, as we say, for a portentous clearness, a reproduction of the real on the scale of the real—with a definiteness actually proportionate; though a clearness that in truth sometimes fails (like the sight of the forest of the adage, which fails for the presence of the trees), through the positive monstrosity of his effort. He sees and presents too many facts—facts of history, of property, of genealogy, of topography, of sociology, and has too many ideas and images about them; their value is thus threatened with submersion by the flood of general reference in which they float, by their quantity of indicated relation to other facts, which break against them like waves of a high tide. He may thus at times become obscure from his very habit of striking too many matches; or we may at least say of him, out of our wondering loyalty, that the light he produces is, beyond that of any other corner of the great planted garden of romance, thick and rich and heavy—interesting, so to speak, on its own account.

There would be much to say, I think, had we only a little more time, on this question of the projected light of the individual strong temperament in fiction—the color of the air with which this, that or the other painter of life (as we call them all), more or less unconsciously suffuses his picture. I say unconsciously because I speak here of an effect of atmosphere largely, if not wholly, distinct from the effect sought on behalf of the special subject to be treated; something that proceeds from the contemplative mind itself, the very complexion of the mirror in which the material is reflected. This is of the nature of the man himself—an emanation of his spirit, temper, history; it springs from his very presence, his spiritual presence, in his work, and is, in so far, not a matter of calculation and artistry. All a matter of his own, in a word, for each seer of visions, the particular tone of the medium in which each vision, each clustered group of persons and places and objects, is bathed. Just how, accordingly, does the light of the world, the projected, painted, peopled, poetized, realized world, the furnished and fitted world into which we are beguiled for the holiday excursions, cheap trips or dear, of the eternally amusable, eternally dupeable voyaging mind—just how does this strike us as different in Fielding and in Richardson, in Scott and in Dumas, in Dickens and in Thackeray, in Hawthorne and in Meredith, in George Eliot and in George Sand, in Jane Austen and in Charlotte Brontë? Do we not feel the general landscape evoked by each of the more or less magical wands to which I have given name, not to open itself under the same sun that hangs over the neighboring scene, not to receive the solar rays at the same angle, not to exhibit its shadows with the same intensity or the same sharpness; not, in short, to seem to belong to the same time of day or same state of the weather? Why is it that the life that overflows in Dickens seems to me always to go on in the morning, or in the very earliest hours of the afternoon at most, and in a vast apartment that appears to have windows, large, uncurtained and rather unwashed windows, on all sides at once? Why is it that in George Eliot the sun sinks forever to the west, and the shadows are long, and the afternoon wanes, and the trees vaguely rustic, and the color of the day is much inclined to yellow? Why is it that in Charlotte Brontë we move through an endless autumn? Why is it that in Jane Austen we sit quite resigned in an arrested spring? Why does Hawthorne give us the afternoon hour later than any one else?—oh, late, late, quite uncannily late, and as if it were always winter outside? But I am wasting the very minutes I pretended, at the start, to cherish, and am only sustained through my levity by seeing you watch for the time of day or season of the year or state of the weather that I shall fasten upon the complicated clock-face of Thackeray. I do, I think, see his light also—see it very much as the light (a different thing from the mere dull dusk) of rainy days in "residential" streets; but we are not, after all, talking of him, and, though Balzac's waiting power has proved itself, this half-century, immense, I must not too much presume upon it.

The question of the color of Balzac's air and the time of *his* day would indeed here easily solicit our ingenuity—were I at liberty to say more than one thing about it. It is rich and thick, the mixture of sun and shade diffused through the Comédie Humaine—a mixture richer and thicker, and representing an absolutely greater quantity of "atmosphere," than we shall find prevailing within the compass of any other suspended frame. That is how we see him, living in his garden, and it is by reason of the restless energy with which he circulated there that I hold his fortune and his privilege, in spite of the burden of his toil and the brevity of his immediate reward, to have been before any others enviable. It is strange enough, but what most abides with us, as we follow his steps, is a sense of the intellectual luxury he enjoyed. To focus him at all, for a single occasion, we have to simplify, and this wealth of his vicarious experience forms the side, moreover, on which he is most attaching for those who take an interest in the real play of the imagination. From the moment our imagination plays at all, of course, and from the moment we try to catch and preserve the pictures it throws off, from that moment we too, in our comparatively feeble way, live vicariously—succeed in opening a series of dusky passages in which, with a more or less childlike ingenuity, we can romp to and fro. Our passages are mainly short and dark, however; we soon come to the end of them—dead walls, without resonance, in presence of which the candle goes out and the game stops, and we have only to retrace our steps. Balzac's luxury, as I call it, was in the extraordinary number and length of his radiating and ramifying corridors—the labyrinth in which he finally lost himself. What it comes back to, in other words, is the intensity with which we live—and his intensity is recorded for us on every page of his work.

It is a question, you see, of *penetrating* into a subject; his corridors always went further and further and further; which is but another way of expressing his inordinate passion for detail. It matters nothing—nothing for my present contention—that this extravagance is also his great fault; in spite, too, of its all being detail vivified and related, characteristic and constructive, essentially prescribed by the terms of his plan. The relations of parts to each other are at moments multiplied almost to madness—which is at the same time just why they give us the measure of his hallucination, make up the greatness of his intellectual adventure. His plan was to handle, primarily, not a world of ideas, animated by figures representing these ideas; but the packed and constituted, the palpable, proveable world before him, by the study of which ideas would inevitably find themselves thrown up. If the happy fate is accordingly to *partake* of life, actively, assertively, not passively, narrowly, in mere sensibility and sufferance, the happiness has been greatest when the faculty employed has been largest. We employ different faculties—some of us only our arms and our legs and our stomach; Balzac employed most what he possessed in largest quantity. This is where his work ceases in a manner to mystify us—this is where we make out how he did quarry his material: it is the sole solution to an otherwise baffling problem. He collected his experience within himself: no other economy explains his achievement; this thrift alone, remarkable yet thinkable, embodies the necessary miracle. His system of cellular confinement, in the interest of the miracle, was positively that of a Benedictine monk leading his life within the four walls of his convent and bent, the year round, over the smooth parchment on which, with wondrous illumination and enhancement of gold and crimson and blue, he inscribes the glories of the faith and the legends of the saints. Balzac's view of himself was indeed in a manner the monkish one; he was most at ease, while he wrought, in the white gown and cowl—an image of him that the friendly art of his time has handed down to us. Only, as happened, his subject of illumination was the legends not merely of the saints, but of the much more numerous uncanonized strugglers and sinners, an acquaintance with whose attributes was not all to be gathered in the place of piety itself; not even from the faintest ink of old records, the mild lips of old brothers, or the painted glass of church windows.

This is where envy does follow him, for to have so many other human cases, so many other personal predicaments to get into, up to one's chin, is verily to be able to get out of one's own box. And it was up to his chin, constantly, that he sank in his illusion—not, as the weak and timid in this line do, only up to his ankles or his knees. The figures he sees begin immediately to bristle with all their characteristics. Every mark and sign, outward and inward, that they possess; every virtue and every vice, every strength and every weakness, every passion and every habit, the sound of their voices, the expression of their eyes, the tricks of feature and limb, the buttons on their clothes, the food on their plates, the money in their pockets, the furniture in their houses, the secrets in their breasts, are all things that interest, that concern, that command him, and that have, for the picture, significance, relation and value. It is a prodigious multiplication of values, and thereby a prodigious entertainment of the vision—on the condition the vision can bear it. Bearing it—that is *our* bearing it— is a serious matter; for the appeal is truly to that faculty of attention out of which we are educating ourselves as hard as we possibly can; educating ourselves with such complacency, with such boisterous high spirits, that we may already be said to have practically lost it— with the consequence that any work of art or of criticism making a demand on it is by that fact essentially discredited. It takes attention not only to thread the labyrinth of the Comédie Humaine, but to keep our author himself in view, in the relations in which we thus image him. But if we can muster it, as I say, in sufficient quantity, we thus walk with him in the great glazed gallery of his thought; the long, lighted and pictured ambulatory where the endless series of windows, on one side, hangs over his revolutionized, ravaged, yet partly restored and reinstated garden of France, and where, on the other, the figures and the portraits we fancy stepping down to meet him climb back into their frames, larger and smaller, and take up position and expression as he desired they shall look out and compose.

We have lately had a literary case of the same general family as the case of Balzac, and in presence of which some of the same speculations come up: I had occasion, not long since, after the death of Émile Zola, to attempt an appreciation of *his* extraordinary performance—his series of the Rougon-Macquart constituting in fact, in the library of the fiction that can hope in some degree to live, a monument to the idea of plenitude, of comprehension and variety, second only to the Comédie Humaine. The question presented itself, in respect to Zola's ability and Zola's career, with a different proportion and value, I quite recognize, and wearing a much less distinguished face; but it was there to be met, none the less, on the very threshold, and all the more because this was just where he himself had placed it. His idea had been, from the first, in a word, to lose no time—as if one could have experience, even the mere amount requisite for showing others as having it, *without* losing time!—and yet the degree in which he too, so handicapped, has achieved valid expression is such as still to stagger us. He had had inordinately to simplify—had had to leave out the life of the soul, practically, and confine himself to the life of the instincts, of the more immediate passions, such as can be easily and promptly caught in the fact. He had had, in a word, to confine himself almost entirely to the impulses and agitations that men and women are possessed by in common, and to take them as exhibited in mass and number, so that, being writ larger, they might likewise be more easily read. He met and solved, in this manner, his difficulty—the difficulty of knowing, and of showing, of life, only what his "notes" would account for. But it is in the *waste,* I think, much rather—the waste of time, of passion, of curiosity, of contact—that true initiation resides; so that the most wonderful adventures of the artist's spirit are those, immensely quickening for his "authority," that are yet not reducible to his notes. It is exactly here that we get the difference between such a solid, square, symmetrical structure as Les Rougon-Macquart, vitiated, in a high degree, by its mechanical side, and the monument left by Balzac—without the example of which, I surmise, Zola's work would not have existed. The mystic process of the crucible, the transformation of the material under aesthetic heat, is, in the Comédie Humaine, thanks to an intenser and more sub-missive fusion, completer, and also finer; for if the commoner and more wayside passions and conditions are, in the various episodes there, at no time gathered into so large and so thick an illustrative bunch, yet on the other hand they are shown much more freely at play in the individual case—and the individual case it is that permits of supreme fineness. It is hard to say where Zola is fine; whereas it is often, for pages together, hard to say where Balzac is, even under the weight of his too ponderous personality, not. The most fundamental and general sign of the novel, from one desperate experiment to an-other, is its being everywhere an effort at *representation*—this is the beginning and the end of it: wherefore it was that one could say at last, with account taken of everything, that Zola's performance, on his immense scale, was an extraordinary show of representation imitated. The imitation in places—notably and admirably, for instance, in *L'Assommoir*—breaks through into something that we take for reality; but, for the most part, the separating rift, the determining difference, holds its course straight, prevents the attempted process from becoming the sound, straight, whole thing that is given us by those who have really *bought* their information. This is where Balzac remains unshaken—in our feeling that, with all his faults of pedantry, ponderosity, pretentiousness, bad taste and charmless form, his spirit has somehow paid for its knowledge. His subject is again and again the complicated human creature or human condition; and it is with these complications as if he knew them, as Shakespeare knew them, by his charged consciousness, by the history of his soul and the direct exposure of his sensibility. This source of supply he found, forever—and one may indeed say he mostly left—sitting at his fireside; where it constituted the company with which I see him shut up and his practical intimacy with which, during such orgies and debauches of intellectual passion, might earn itself that name of high personal good fortune that I have applied.

Let me say, definitely, that I hold several of his faults to be grave, and that if there were any question of time for it I should like to speak of them; but let me add, as promptly, that they are faults, on the whole, of execution, flaws in the casting, accidents of the process: they never come back to that fault in the artist, in the novelist, that amounts most completely to a failure of dignity, the absence of saturation with his idea. When saturation fails no other presence really avails; as when, on the other hand, it operates, no failure of method fatally interferes. There is never in Balzac that damning interference which consists of the painter's not seeing, not possessing, his image; not having fixed his creature and his creature's conditions. "Balzac aime sa Valérie," says Taine, in his great essay—so much the finest thing ever written on our author—speaking of the way in which the awful little Madame Marneffe of *Les Parents Pauvres* is drawn, and of the long rope, for her acting herself out, that her creator's participation in her reality assures her. He has been contrasting her, as it happens, with Thackeray's Becky Sharp or rather with Thackeray's attitude toward Becky, and the marked jealousy of her freedom that Thackeray exhibits from the first. I remember reading at the time of the publication of Taine's study—though it was long, long ago—a phrase in an English review of the volume which seemed to my limited perception, even in extreme youth, to deserve the highest prize ever bestowed on critical stupidity undisguised. If Balzac loved his Valérie, said this commentator, that only showed Balzac's extraordinary taste; the truth being really, throughout, that it was just through this love of each seized identity, and of the sharpest and liveliest identities most, that Madame Marneffe's creator was able to marshal his array at all. The love, as we call it, the joy in their communicated and exhibited movement, in their standing on their feet and going of themselves and acting out their characters, was what rendered possible the saturation I speak of; what supplied him, through the inevitable gaps of his preparation and the crevices of his prison, his long prison of labor, a short cut to the knowledge he required. It was by loving them—as the terms of his subject and the nuggets of his mine—that he knew them; it was not by knowing them that he loved.

He at all events robustly loved the sense of another explored, assumed, assimilated identity—enjoyed it as the hand enjoys the glove when the glove ideally fits. My image indeed is loose; for what he liked was absolutely to get into the constituted consciousness, into all the clothes, gloves and whatever else, into the very skin and bones, of the habited, featured, colored, articulated form of life that he desired to present. How do we know given persons, for any purpose of demonstration, unless we know their situation for themselves, unless we see it from their point of vision, that is from their point of pressing consciousness or sensation?—without our allowing for which there is no appreciation. Balzac loved his Valérie then as Thackeray did not love his Becky, or his Blanche Amory in *Pendennis*. But his prompting was not to expose her; it could only be, on the contrary— intensely aware as he was of all the lengths she might go, and paternally, maternally alarmed about them—to cover her up and protect her, in the interest of her special genius and freedom. All his impulse was to *la faire valoir*, to give her all her value, just as Thackeray's attitude was the opposite one, a desire positively to expose and desecrate poor Becky—to follow her up, catch her in the act and bring her to shame: though with a mitigation, an admiration, an inconsequence, now and then wrested from him by an instinct finer, in his mind, than the so-called "moral" eagerness. The English writer wants to make sure, first of all, of your moral judgment; the French is willing, while it waits a little, to risk, for the sake of his subject and its interest, your spiritual salvation. Madame Marneffe, detrimental, fatal as she is, is "exposed," so far as anything in life, or in art, may be, by the working-out of the situation and the subject themselves; so that when they have done what they would, what they logically had to, with her, we are ready to take it from them. We do not feel, very irritatedly, very lecturedly, in other words with superfluous edification, that she has been sacrificed. Who can say, on the contrary, that Blanche Amory, in *Pendennis*, with the author's lash about her little bare white back from the first—who can feel that she has *not* been sacrificed, or that her little bareness and whiteness, and all the rest of her, have been, by such a process, presented as they had a right to demand?

It all comes back, in fine, to that respect for the liberty of the subject which I should be willing to name as *the* great sign of the painter of the first order. Such a witness to the human comedy fairly holds his breath for fear of arresting or diverting that natural license; the witness who begins to breathe so uneasily in presence of it that his respiration not only warns off the little prowling or playing creature he is supposed to be studying, but drowns, for our ears, the ingenuous sounds of the animal, as well as the general, truthful hum of the human scene at large—this demonstrator has no sufficient warrant for his task. And if such an induction as this is largely the moral of our renewed glance at Balzac, there is a lesson, of a more essential sort, I think, folded still deeper within—the lesson that there is no convincing art that is not ruinously expensive. I am unwilling to say, in the presence of such of his successors as George Eliot and Tolstoi and Zola (to name, for convenience, only three of them), that he was the last of the novelists to do the thing handsomely; but I will say that we get the impression at least of his having had more to spend. Many of those who have followed him affect us as doing it, in the vulgar phrase, "on the cheap"; by reason mainly, no doubt, of their having been, all helplessly, foredoomed to cheapness. Nothing counts, of course, in art, but the excellent; nothing exists, however briefly, for estimation, for appreciation, but the superlative—always in its kind; and who shall declare that the severe economy of the vast majority of those apparently emulous of the attempt to "render" the human subject and the human scene proceeds from anything worse than the consciousness of a limited capital? This flourishing frugality operates happily, no doubt—given all the circumstances—for the novelist; but it has had terrible results for the novel, so far as the novel is a form with which criticism may be moved to concern itself. Its misfortune, its discredit, what I have called its bankrupt state among us, is the not unnatural consequence of its having ceased, for the most part, to be artistically interesting. It has become an object of easy manufacture, showing on every side the stamp of the machine; it has become the article of commerce, produced in quantity, and as we so see it we inevitably turn from it, under the rare visitations of the critical impulse, to compare it with those more precious products of the same general nature that we used to think of as belonging to the class of the handmade.

The lesson of Balzac, under this comparison, is extremely various, and I should prepare myself much too large a task were I to attempt a list of the separate truths he brings home. I have to choose among them, and I choose the most important; the three or four that more or less include the others. In reading him over, in opening him almost anywhere to-day, what immediately strikes us is the part assigned by him, in any picture, to the *conditions* of the creatures with whom he is concerned. Contrasted with him other prose painters of life scarce seem to see the conditions at all. He clearly held pretended portrayal as nothing, as less than nothing, as a most vain thing, unless it should be, in spirit and intention, the art of complete representation. "Complete" is of course a great word, and there is no art at all, we are often reminded, that is not on too many sides an abject compromise. The element of compromise is always there; it is of the essence; we live with it, and it may serve to keep us humble. The formula of the whole matter is sufficiently expressed perhaps in a reply I found myself once making to an inspired but discouraged friend, a fellow-craftsman who had declared in his despair that there was no use trying, that it was a form, the novel, absolutely too difficult. "Too difficult indeed; yet there is one way to master it—which is to pretend consistently that it isn't." We are all of us, all the while, pretending—as consistently as we can—that it isn't, and Balzac's great glory is that he pretended hardest. He never had to pretend so hard as when he addressed himself to that evocation of the medium, that distillation of the natural and social air, of which I speak, the things that most require on the part of the painter preliminary possession—so definitely require it that, terrified at the requisition when conscious of it, many a painter prefers to beg the whole question. He has thus, this ingenious person, to invent some *other* way of making his characters interesting—some other way, that is, than the arduous way, demanding so much consideration, of presenting them to us. They are interesting, in fact, as subjects of fate, the figures round whom a situation closes, in proportion as, sharing their existence, we feel where fate comes in and just how it gets at them. In the void they are not interesting—and Balzac, like Nature herself, abhorred a vacuum. Their situation takes hold of us because it is theirs, not because it is somebody's, any one's, that of creatures unidentified. Therefore it is not superfluous that their identity shall first be established for us, and their adventures, in that measure, have a relation to it, and therewith an appreciability. There is no such thing in the world as an adventure pure and simple; there is only mine and yours, and his and hers—it being the greatest adventure of all, I verily think, just to *be* you or I, just to be he or she. To Balzac's imagination that was indeed in itself an immense adventure—and nothing appealed to him more than to show *how* we all are, and how we are placed and built-in for being so. What befalls us is but another name for the way our circumstances press upon us—so that an account of what befalls us is an account of our circumstances.

Add to this, then, that the fusion of all the elements of the picture, under his hand, is complete—of what people are with what they do, of what they do with what they are, of the action with the agents, of the medium with the action, of all the parts of the drama with each other. Such a production as *Le Père Goriot* for example, or as *Eugènie Grandet*, or as *Le Curé de Village*, has, in respect to this fusion, a kind of inscrutable perfection. The situation sits shrouded in its circumstances, and then, by its inner expansive force, emerges from them, the action marches, to the rich rustle of this great tragic and ironic train, the embroidered heroic mantle, with an art of keeping together that makes of *Le Père Goriot* in especial a supreme case of composition, a model of that high virtue that we know as economy of effect, economy of line and touch. An inveterate sense of proportion was not, in general, Balzac's distinguishing mark; but with great talents one has great surprises, and the effect of this large handling of the conditions was more often than not to make the work, whatever it might be, appear admirably composed. Of all the costly charms of a "story" this interest derived from composition is the costliest—and there is perhaps no better proof of our present penury than the fact that, in general, when one makes a plea for it, the plea might seemingly (for all it is understood!) be for trigonometry or osteology. "Composition?—what may that happen to *be* and, whatever it is, what has it to do with the matter?" I shall take for granted here that every one perfectly knows, for without that assumption I shall not be able to wind up, as I must immediately do. The presence of the conditions, when really presented, when made vivid, provides for the action—which is, from step to step, constantly implied in them; whereas the process of suspending the action in the void and dressing it there with the tinkling bells of what is called dialogue only makes no provision at all for the other interest. There are two elements of the art of the novelist which, as they present, I think, the greatest difficulty, tend thereby most to fascinate us: in the first place that mystery of the foreshortened procession of facts and figures, of appearances of whatever sort, which is in some lights but another name for the picture governed by the principle of composition, and which has at any rate as little as possible in common with the method now usual among us, the juxtaposition of items emulating the column of numbers of a schoolboy's sum in addition. It is the art of the brush, I know, as opposed to the art of the slate-pencil; but to the art of the brush the novel must return, I hold, to recover whatever may be still recoverable of its sacrificed honor.

The second difficulty that I commend for its fascination, at all events, the most attaching when met and the most rewarding when triumphantly met—though I hasten to add that it also strikes me as not only the least "met," in general, but the least suspected—this second difficulty is that of representing, to put it simply, the lapse of time, the duration of the subject: representing it, that is, more subtly than by a blank space, or a row of stars, on the historic page. With the blank space and the row of stars Balzac's genius had no affinity, and he is therefore as unlike as possible those narrators—so numerous, all round us, it would appear, to-day in especial—the succession of whose steps and stages, the development of whose action, in the given case, affects us as occupying but a week or two. No one begins, to my sense, to handle the time-element and produce the time-effect with the authority of Balzac in his amplest sweeps—by which I am far from meaning in his longest passages. That study of the foreshortened image, of the neglect of which I suggest the ill consequence, is precisely the enemy of the tiresome procession of would-be narrative items, seen all in profile, like the rail-heads of a fence; a substitute for the baser device of accounting for the time-quantity by mere quantity of statement. Quality and manner of statement account for it in a finer way—always assuming, as I say, that unless it is accounted for nothing else really is. The fashion of our day is to account for it almost exclusively by an inordinate abuse of the colloquial resource, of the report, from page to page, from chapter to chapter, from beginning to end, of the talk, between the persons involved, in which situation and action may be conceived as registered. Talk between persons is perhaps, of all the parts of the novelist's plan, the part that Balzac most scrupulously weighed and measured and kept in its place; judging it, I think—though he perhaps even had an undue suspicion of its possible cheapness, as feeling it the thing that can least afford to be cheap—a precious and supreme resource, the very flower of illustration of the subject and thereby not to be inconsiderately discounted. It was his view, discernibly, that the flower must keep its bloom, or in other words not be too much handled, in order to have a fragrance when nothing but its fragrance will serve.

It was his view indeed positively that there is a *law* in these things, and that, admirable for illustration, functional for illustration, dialogue has its function perverted, and therewith its life destroyed, when forced, all clumsily, into the constructive office. It is in the drama, of course, that it is constructive; but the drama lives by a law so different, verily, that everything that is right for it seems wrong for the prose picture, and everything that is right for the prose picture addressed directly, in turn, to the betrayal of the "play." These are questions, however, that bore deep—if I have successfully braved the danger that they absolutely do bore; so that I must content myself, as a glance at this point, with the claim for the author of *Le Père Goriot* that colloquial illustration, in his work, suffers less, on the whole, than in any other I know, from its attendant, its besetting and haunting penalty of springing, unless watched, a leak in its effect. It is as if the master of the ship were keeping his eye on the pump; the pump, I mean, of relief and alternation, the pump that keeps the vessel free of too much water. We must always remember that, save in the cases where "dialogue" is organic, is the very law of the game— in which case, as I say, the game is another business altogether—it is essentially the fluid element: as, for instance (to cite, conveniently, Balzac's most eminent prose contemporary), was strikingly its character in the elder Dumas; just as its character in the younger, the dramatist, illustrates supremely what I call the other game. The current, in old Dumas, the large, loose, facile flood of talked movement, talked interest, as much as you will, is, in virtue of this fluidity, a current indeed, with so little of wrought texture that we float and splash in it; feeling it thus resemble much more some capacious tepid tank than the figured tapestry, all overscored with objects in fine perspective, which symbolizes to me (if one may have a symbol) the last word of the achieved fable. Such a tapestry, with its wealth of expression of its subject, with its myriad ordered stitches, its harmonies of tone and felicities of taste, is a work, above all, of closeness—and therefore the more pertinent image here as it is in the name of closeness that I am inviting you to let Balzac once more appeal to you.

It will strike you perhaps that I speak as if we all, as if you all, without exception were novelists, haunting the back shop, the laboratory, or, more nobly expressed, the inner shrine of the temple; but such assumptions, in this age of print—if I may not say this age of poetry—are perhaps never too wide of the mark, and I have at any rate taken your interest sufficiently for granted to ask you to close up with me for an hour at the feet of the master of us all. Many of us may stray, but he always remains—he is fixed by virtue of his weight. Do not look too knowing at that—as a hint that you were already conscious he is heavy, and that if this is what I have mainly to suggest my lesson might have been spared. He is, I grant, too heavy to be moved; many of us may stray and straggle, as I say—since we have not his inaptitude largely to circulate. There is none the less such an odd condition as circulating without motion, and I am not so sure that even in our own way we do move. We do not, at any rate, get away from him; he is behind us, at the worst, when he is not before, and I feel that any course about the country we explore is ever best held by keeping him, through the trees of the forest, in sight. So far as we do move, we move round him; every road comes back to him; he sits there, in spite of us, so massively, for orientation. "Heavy" therefore if we like, but heavy because weighted with his fortune; the extraordinary fortune that has survived all the extravagance of his career, his twenty years of royal intellectual spending, and that has done so by reason of the rare value of the original property—the high, prime genius so tied-up from him that that was safe. And "that," through all that has come and gone, has steadily, has enormously appreciated. Let us then also, if we see him, in the sacred grove, as our towering idol, see him as gilded thick, with so much gold—plated and burnished and bright, in the manner of towering idols. It is for the lighter and looser and poorer among us to be gilded thin!

VALEDICTIONS

THE TEMPEST

If the effect of the Plays and Poems, taken in their mass, be most of all to appear often to mock our persistent ignorance of so many of the conditions of their birth, and thereby to place on the rack again our strained and aching wonder, this character has always struck me as more particularly kept up for them by *The Tempest*; the production, of the long series, in which the Questions, as the critical reader of Shakespeare must ever comprehensively and ruefully call them and more or less resignedly live with them, hover before us in their most tormenting form. It may seem no very philosophic state of mind, the merely baffled and exasperated view of one of the supreme works of all literature; though I feel, for myself, that to confess to it now and then, by way of relief, is no unworthy tribute to the work. It is not, certainly, the tribute most frequently paid, for the large body of comment and criticism of which this play alone has been the theme abounds much rather in affirmed conclusions, complacencies of conviction, full apprehensions of the meaning and triumphant pointings of the moral. The Questions, in the light of all this wisdom, convert themselves, with comparatively small difficulty, into smooth and definite answers; the innumerable dim ghosts that flit, like started game at eventide, through the deep dusk of our speculation, with just form enough to quicken it and no other charity for us at all, bench themselves along the vista as solidly as Falstaff and as vividly as Hotspur. Everything has thus been attributed to the piece before us, and every attribution so made has been in turn brushed away; merely to glance at such a monument to the interest inspired is to recognise a battleground of opposed factions, not a little enveloped in sound and smoke. Of these copious elements, produced for the most part to the best intention, we remain accordingly conscious; so that to approach the general bone of contention, as we can but familiarly name it, for whatever purpose, we have to cross the scene of action at a mortal risk, making the fewest steps of it and trusting to the probable calm at the centre of the storm. There in fact, though there only, we find that serenity; find the subject itself intact and unconscious, seated as unwinking and inscrutable as a divinity in a temple, save for that vague flicker of derision, the only response to our interpretative heat, which adds the last beauty to its face. The divinity never relents—never, like the image of life in *The Winter's Tale*, steps down from its pedestal; it simply leaves us to stare on through the ages, with this fact indeed of having crossed the circle of fire, and so got into the real and right relation to it, for our one comfort.

The position of privilege of *The Tempest* as the latest example, to all appearance, of the author's rarer work, with its distance from us in time thereby shortened to the extent of the precious step or two, was certain to expose it, at whatever final cost, we easily see, to any amount of interpretative zeal. With its first recorded performance that of February 1613, when it was given in honour of the marriage of the Princess Elizabeth, its finished state cannot have preceded his death by more than three years, and we accordingly take it as the finest flower of his experience. Here indeed, as on so many of the Questions, judgments sharply differ, and this use of it as an ornament to the nuptials of the daughter of James I. and the young Elector Palatine may have been but a repetition of previous performances; though it is not in such a case supposable that these can have been numerous. They would antedate the play, at the most, by a year or two, and so not throw it essentially further back from us. *The Tempest* speaks to us, somehow, convincingly, as a *pièce de circonstance*, and the suggestion that it was addressed, in its brevity, its rich simplicity, and its free elegance, to court-production, and above all to providing, with a string of other dramas, for the "intellectual" splendour of a wedding-feast, is, when once entertained, not easily dislodged. A few things fail to fit, but more fit strikingly. I like therefore to think of the piece as of 1613. To refer it, as it is referred by other reckonings, to 1611 is but to thicken that impenetrability of silence in which Shakespeare's latest years enfold him. Written as it must have been on the earlier calculation, before the age of forty-seven, it has that rare value of the richly mature note of a genius who, by our present measure of growth and fulness, was still young enough to have had in him a world of life: we feel behind it the immense procession of its predecessors, while we yet stare wistfully at the plenitude and the majesty, the expression as of something broad-based and ultimate, that were not, in any but a strained sense, to borrow their warrant from the weight of years. Nothing so enlarges the wonder of the whole time-question in Shakespeare's career as the fact of this date, in easy middle life, of his time-climax; which, if we knew less, otherwise, than we do about him, might affect us as attempt, on the part of treacherous History, to pass him off as one of those monsters of precocity who, fortunately for their probable reputation, the too likely betrayal of short-windedness, are cut off in their comparative prime. The transmuted young rustic who, after a look over London, brief at the best, was ready at the age of thirty to produce *The Merchant of Venice* and *A Midsummer Night's Dream* (and this after the half-dozen splendid prelusive things that had included, at twenty-eight, *Romeo and Juliet*), had been indeed a monster of precocity—which all geniuses of the first order are not; but the day of his paying for it had neither arrived nor, however faintly, announced itself, and the fathomless strangeness of his story, the abrupt stoppage of his pulse after *The Tempest*, is not, in charity, lighted for us by a glimmer of explanation. The explanation by some interposing accident is as absent as any symptom of "declining powers."

His powers declined, that is—but declined merely to obey the spring we should have supposed inherent in them; and their possessor's case derives from this, I think, half the secret of its so inestimably mystifying us. He died, for a nature so organized, too lamentably soon; but who knows where we should have been with him if he had not lived long enough so to affirm, with many other mysteries, the mystery of his abrupt and complete cessation? There is that in *The Tempest*, specifically, though almost all indefinably, which seems to show us the artist consciously tasting of the first and rarest of his gifts, that of imaged creative Expression, the instant sense of some copious equivalent of thought for every grain of the grossness of reality; to show him as unresistingly aware, in the depths of his genius, that nothing like it had ever been known, or probably would ever be again known, on earth, and as so given up, more than on other occasions, to the joy of sovereign *science*. There are so many sides from which any page that shows his stamp may be looked at that a handful of reflections can hope for no coherency, in the chain of association immediately formed, unless they happen to bear upon some single truth. Such a truth then, for me, is this comparative—by which one can really but mean this superlative—artistic value of the play seen in the meagre circle of the items of our knowledge about it. Let me say that our knowledge, in the whole connection, is a quantity that shifts, surprisingly, with the measure of a felt need; appearing to some of us, on some sides, adequate, various, large, and appearing to others, on whatever side, a scant beggar's portion. We are concerned, it must be remembered, here—that is for getting *generally* near our author—not only with the number of the mustered facts, but with the kind of fact that each may strike us as being: never unmindful that such matters, when they are few, may go far for us if they be individually but ample and significant; and when they are numerous, on the other hand, may easily fall short enough to break our hearts if they be at the same time but individually small and poor. Three or four stepping-stones across a stream will serve if they are broad slabs, but it will take more than may be counted if they are only pebbles. Beyond all gainsaying then, by many an estimate, is the penury in which even the most advantageous array of the Shakespearean facts still leaves us: strung together with whatever ingenuity they remain, for our discomfiture, as the pebbles across the stream.

To balance, for our occasion, this light scale, however, *The Tempest* affects us, taking its complexity and its perfection together, as the rarest of all examples of literary art. There may be other things as exquisite, other single exhalations of beauty reaching as high a mark and sustained there for a moment, just as there are other deep wells of poetry from which cupfuls as crystalline may, in repeated dips, be drawn; but nothing, surely, of equal length and variety lives so happily and radiantly as a whole: no poetic birth ever took place under a star appointed to blaze upon it so steadily. The felicity enjoyed is enjoyed longer and more intensely, and the art involved, completely revealed, as I suggest, to the master, holds the securest revel. The man himself, in the Plays, we directly touch, to my consciousness, positively nowhere: we are dealing too perpetually with the artist, the monster and magician of a thousand masks, not one of which we feel him drop long enough to gratify with the breath of the interval that strained attention in us which would be yet, so quickened, ready to become deeper still. Here at last the artist is, comparatively speaking, so generalised, so consummate and typical, so frankly amused with himself, that is with his art, with his power, with his theme, that it is as if he came to meet us more than his usual half-way, and as if, thereby, in meeting *him*, and touching him, we were nearer to meeting and touching the man. The man everywhere, in Shakespeare's work, is so effectually locked up and imprisoned in the artist that we but hover at the base of thick walls for a sense of him; while, in addition, the artist is so steeped in the abysmal objectivity of his characters and situations that the great billows of the medium itself play with him, to our vision, very much as, over a ship's side, in certain waters, we catch, through transparent tides, the flash of strange sea-creatures. What we are present at in this fashion is a series of incalculable plunges—the series of those that have taken effect, I mean, after the great primary plunge, made once for all, of the man into the artist: the successive plunges of the artist himself into Romeo and into Juliet, into Shylock, Hamlet, Macbeth, Coriolanus, Cleopatra, Antony, Lear, Othello, Falstaff, Hotspur; immersions during which, though he always ultimately finds his feet, the very violence of the movements involved troubles and distracts our sight. In *The Tempest*, by the supreme felicity I speak of, is no violence; he sinks as deep as we like, but what he sinks into, beyond all else, is the lucid stillness of his style.

One can speak, in these matters, but from the impression determined by one's own inevitable standpoint; again and again, at any
rate, such a masterpiece puts before me the very act of the momentous
conjunction taking place for the poet, at a given hour, between his
charged inspiration and his clarified experience: or, as I should perhaps
better express it, between his human curiosity and his aesthetic passion. Then, if he happens to have been, all his career, with his equipment for it, more or less the victim and the slave of the former, he
yields, by way of a change, to the impulse of allowing the latter, for
a magnificent moment, the upper hand. The human curiosity, as I
call it, is always there—with no more need of making provision for
it than use in taking precautions against it; the surrender to the
luxury of expertness may therefore go forward on its own conditions.
I can offer no better description of *The Tempest* as fresh re-perusal
lights it for me than as such a surrender, sublimely enjoyed; and I may
frankly say that, under this impression of it, there is no refinement
of the artistic consciousness that I do not see my way—or feel it,
better, perhaps, since we but grope, at the best, in our darkness—to
attribute to the author. It is a way that one follows to the end, because
it is a road, I repeat, on which one least misses some glimpse of him
face to face. If it be true that the thing was concocted to meet a particular demand, that of the master of the King's revels, with his
prescription of date, form, tone and length, this, so far from interfering with the Poet's perception of a charming opportunity to taste for
himself, for himself above all, and as he had almost never so tasted,
not even in *A Midsummer Night's Dream*, of the quality of his mind
and the virtue of his skill, would have exceedingly favoured the happy
case. Innumerable one may always suppose these delicate debates and
intimate understandings of an artist with himself. "How much *taste*,
in the world, may I conceive that I have?—and what a charming idea
to snatch a moment for finding out! What moment could be better
than this—a bridal evening before the Court, with extra candles and
the handsomest company—if I can but put my hand on the right
'scenario'?" We can catch, across the ages, the searching sigh and the
look about; we receive the stirred breath of the ripe, amused genius;

and, stretching, as I admit I do at least, for a still closer conception of the beautiful crisis, I find it pictured for me in some such present-ment as that of a divine musician who, alone in his room, preludes or improvises at close of day. He sits at the harpsichord, by the open window, in the summer dusk; his hands wander over the keys. They stray far, for his motive, but at last he finds and holds it; then he lets himself go, embroidering and refining: it is the thing for the hour and his mood. The neighbours may gather in the garden, the night-ingale be hushed on the bough; it is none the less a private occasion, a concert of one, both performer and auditor, who plays for his own ear, his own hand, his own innermost sense, and for the bliss and capacity of his instrument. Such are the only hours at which the art-ist *may*, by any measure of his own (too many things, at others, make heavily against it); and their challenge to him is irresistible if he has known, all along, too much compromise and too much sacrifice.

The face that beyond any other, however, I seem to see *The Tempest* turn to us is the side on which it so superlatively speaks of that en-dowment for Expression, expression as a primary force, a consuming, an independent passion, which was the greatest ever laid upon man. It is for Shakespeare's power of constitutive speech quite as if he had swum into our ken with it from another planet, gathering it up there, in its wealth, as something antecedent to the occasion and the need, and if possible quite in excess of them; something that was to make of our poor world a great flat table for receiving the glitter and clink of outpoured treasure. The idea and the motive are more often than not so smothered in it that they scarce know themselves, and the resources of such a style, the provision of images, emblems, ener-gies of every sort, laid up in advance, affects us as the storehouse of a king before a famine or a siege—which not only, by its scale, braves depletion or exhaustion, but bursts, through mere excess of quantity or presence, out of all doors and windows. It renders the poverties and obscurities of our world, as I say, in the dazzling terms of a richer and better. It constitutes, by a miracle, more than half the author's material; so much more usually does it happen, for the painter or the poet, that life itself, in its appealing, overwhelming crudity, offers itself as the paste to be kneaded. Such a personage works in general in the very elements of experience; whereas we see Shakespeare working predominantly in the terms of expression, *all* in the terms of the artist's specific vision and genius; with a thicker cloud of images to attest his approach, at any point, than the comparatively meagre given case ever has to attest its own identity. He points for us as no one else the relation of style to meaning and of manner to motive; a matter on which, right and left, we hear such rank ineptitudes uttered. Unless it be true that these things, on either hand, are inseparable; unless it be true that the phrase, the cluster and order of terms, *is* the object and the sense, in as close a compression as that of body and soul, so that any consideration of them as distinct, from the moment style is an active, applied force, becomes a gross stupidity: unless we recognise this reality the author of *The Tempest* has no lesson for us. It is by his expression of it exactly as the expression stands that the particular thing is created, created as interesting, as beautiful, as strange, droll or terrible—as related, in short, to our understanding or our sensibility; in consequence of which we reduce it to naught when we begin to talk of either of its presented parts as matters by themselves.

All of which considerations indeed take us too far; what it is important to note being simply our Poet's high testimony to this independent, absolute value of Style, and to its need thoroughly to project and seat itself. It had been, as so seating itself, the very home of his mind, for his all too few twenty years; it had been the supreme source to him of the joy of life. It had been in fine his material, his plastic clay; since the more subtly he applied it the more secrets it had to give him, and the more these secrets might appear to him, at every point, one with the lights and shades of the human picture, one with the myriad pulses of the spirit of man. Thus it was that, as he passed from one application of it to another, tone became, for all its suggestions, more and more sovereign to him, and the subtlety of its secrets an exquisite interest. If I see him, at the last, over *The Tempest*, as the composer, at the harpsichord or the violin, extemporising in the summer twilight, it is exactly that he is feeling there for tone and, by the same token, finding it—finding it as *The Tempest*, beyond any register of ours, immortally gives it. This surrender to the highest sincerity of virtuosity, as we nowadays call it, is to my perception *all The Tempest*; with no possible depth or delicacy in it that such an imputed character does not cover and provide for. The subject to be treated was the simple fact (if one may call anything in the matter simple) that refinement, selection, economy, the economy not of poverty, but of wealth a little weary of congestion—the very air of the lone island and the very law of the Court celebration—were here implied and imperative things. Anything was a subject, always, that offered to sight an aperture of size enough for expression and its train to pass in and deploy themselves. If they filled up all the space, none the worse; they occupied it as nothing else could do. The subjects of the Comedies are, without exception, old wives' tales—which we are not too insufferably aware of only because the iridescent veil so perverts their proportions. The subjects of the Histories are no subjects at all; each is but a row of pegs for the hanging of the cloth of gold that is to muffle them. Such a thing as *The Merchant of Venice* declines, for very shame, to be reduced to its elements of witless "story"; such things as the two Parts of *Henry the Fourth* form no more than a straight convenient channel for the procession of evoked images that is to pour through it like a torrent. Each of these productions is none the less of incomparable splendour; by which splendour we are bewildered till we see how it comes. Then we see that every inch of it is personal tone, or in other words brooding expression raised to the highest energy. Push such energy far enough—far enough if you can!—and, being what it is, it then inevitably provides for Character. Thus we see character, in every form of which the "story" gives the thinnest hint, marching through the pieces I have named in its habit as it lives, and so filling out the scene that nothing is missed. The "story" in *The Tempest* is a thing of naught, for any story will provide a remote island, a shipwreck and a coincidence. Prospero and Miranda, awaiting their relatives, are, in the present case, *for* the relatives, the coincidence—just as the relatives are the coincidence for them. Ariel and Caliban, and the island-airs and island-scents, and all the rest of the charm and magic and the ineffable delicacy (a delicacy positively at its highest in the conception and execution of Caliban) are the style handed over to its last disciplined passion of curiosity; a curiosity which flowers, at this pitch, into the freshness of each of the characters.

There are judges for whom the piece is a tissue of symbols; symbols of the facts of State then apparent, of the lights of philosophic and political truth, of the "deeper meanings of life," above all, of a high crisis in its author's career. At this most relevant of its mystic values only we may glance; the consecrated estimate of Prospero's surrender of his magic robe and staff as a figure for Shakespeare's own self-de-spoilment, his considered purpose, at this date, of future silence. Dr. George Brandes works out in detail that analogy; the production becomes, on such a supposition, Shakespeare's "farewell to the stage"; his retirement to Stratford, to end his days in the care of his property and in oblivion of the theatre, was a course for which his arrangements had already been made. The simplest way to put it, since I have likened him to the musician at the piano, is to say that he had decided upon the complete closing of this instrument, and that in fact he was to proceed to lock it with the sharp click that has reverberated through the ages, and to spend what remained to him of life in walking about a small, squalid country-town with his hands in his pockets and an ear for no music now but the chink of the coin they might turn over there. This is indeed in general the accepted, the imposed view of the position he had gained: this freedom to "elect," as we say, to cease, intellectually, to exist: this ability, exercised at the zenith of his splendour, to shut down the lid, from one day to another, on the most potent aptitude for vivid reflection ever lodged in a human frame and to conduct himself thereafter, in all ease and comfort, not only as if it were not, but as if it had never been. I speak of our "accepting" the prodigy, but by the established record we have no choice whatever; which is why it is imposed, as I say, on our bewildered credulity. With the impossibility of proving that the author of *The Tempest* did, after the date of that production, ever again press the spring of his fountain, ever again reach for the sacred key or break his heart for an hour over his inconceivable act of sacrifice, we are reduced to behaving as if we understood the strange case; so that any rubbing of our eyes, as under the obsession of a wild dream, has been held a gesture that, for common decency, must mainly take place in private. If I state that my small contribution to any renewed study of the matter can amount, accordingly, but to little more than an irresistible need to rub mine in public, I shall have done the most that the condition of our knowledge admits of. We can "accept," but we can accept only in stupefaction—a stupefaction that, in presence of *The Tempest*, and of the intimate meaning so imputed to it, must despair of ever subsiding. These things leave us in darkness—in gross darkness about the Man; the case of which they are the warrant is so difficult to embrace. None ever appealed so sharply to some light of knowledge, and nothing could render our actual knowledge more contemptible. What manner of human being was it who *could* so, at a given moment, announce his intention of capping his divine flame with a twopenny extinguisher, and who then, the announcement made, could serenely succeed in carrying it out? Were it a question of a flame spent or burning thin, we might feel a little more possessed of matter for comprehension; the fact being, on the contrary, one can only repeat, that the value of *The Tempest* is, exquisitely, in its refinement of power, its renewed artistic freshness and roundness, its mark as of a distinction unequalled, on the whole (though I admit that we here must take subtle measures), in any predecessor. Prospero has simply waited, to cast his magic ring into the sea, till the jewel set in it shall have begun to burn as never before.

So it is then; and it puts into a nutshell the eternal mystery, the most insoluble that ever was, the complete rupture, for our understanding, between the Poet and the Man. There are moments, I admit, in this age of sound and fury, of connections, in every sense, too maddeningly multiplied, when we are willing to let it pass as a mystery, the most soothing, cooling, consoling too perhaps, that ever was. But there are others when, speaking for myself, its power to torment us intellectually seems scarcely to be borne; and we know these moments best when we hear it proclaimed that a comfortable clearness reigns.

I have been for instance reading over Mr. Halliwell-Phillipps, and I find him apparently of the opinion that it is all our fault if everything in our author's story, and above all in this last chapter of it, be not of a primitive simplicity. The complexity arises from our suffering our imagination to meddle with the Man at all; who is quite sufficiently presented to us on the face of the record. For critics of this writer's complexion the only facts we are urgently concerned with are the facts of the Poet, which are abundantly constituted by the Plays and the Sonnets. The Poet is *there*, and the Man is outside: the Man is for instance in such a perfectly definite circumstance as that he could never miss, after *The Tempest*, the key of his piano, as I have called it, since he could play so freely with the key of his cash-box. The supreme master of expression had made, before fifty, all the money he wanted; therefore what was there more to express? This view is admirable if you can get your mind to consent to it. It must ignore any impulse, in presence of Play or Sonnet (whatever vague stir behind either may momentarily act as provocation) to try for a lunge at the figured arras. In front of the tapestry sits the immitigably respectable person whom our little slateful of gathered and numbered items, heaven knows, does amply account for, since there is nothing in him to explain; while the undetermined figure, on the other hand—undetermined whether in the sense of respectability or of anything else—the figure who supremely interests us, remains as unseen of us as our Ariel, on the enchanted island, remains of the bewildered visitors. Mr. Halliwell-Phillipps's theory, as I understand it—and I refer to it but as an advertisement of a hundred others—is that we too are but bewildered visitors, and that the state of mind of the Duke of Naples and his companions is our proper critical portion.

If our knowledge of the greatest of men consists therefore but of the neat and "proved" addition of two or three dozen common particulars, the rebuke to a morbid and monstrous curiosity is no more than just. We know enough, by such an implication, when we admire enough, and as difficulties would appear to abound on our attempting to push further, this is an obvious lesson to us to stand as still as possible. Not difficulties—those of penetration, exploration, inter-

pretation, those, in the word that says everything, of appreciation—
are the approved field of criticism, but the very forefront of the
obvious and the palpable, where we may go round and round, like
holiday-makers on hobby-horses, at the turning of a crank. Differences
of estimate, in this relation, come back, too clearly, let us accordingly
say, to differences of view of the character of genius in general—if
not, in truth, more exactly stated, to that strangest of all fallacies, the
idea of the separateness of a great man's parts. His genius places itself,
under this fallacy, on one side of the line and the rest of his identity
on the other; the line being that, for instance, which, to Mr. Halliwell-
Phillipps's view, divides the author of *Hamlet* and *The Tempest* from
the man of exemplary business-method whom alone we may propose
to approach at all intimately. The stumbling-block here is that the
boundary exists only in the vision of those able to content themselves
with arbitrary marks. A mark becomes arbitrary from the moment
we have no authoritative sign of where to place it, no sign of higher
warrant than that it smoothes and simplifies the ground. But though
smoothing and simplifying, on such terms, may, by restricting our
freedom of attention and speculation, make, on behalf of our treatment of the subject, for a livelier effect of business—that business as
to a zealous care for which we seem taught that our author must above
all serve as our model—it will see us little further on any longer road.
The fullest appreciation possible is the high tribute we must offer to
greatness, and to make it worthy of its office we must surely know
where we are with it. In greatness as much as in mediocrity the man
is, under examination, *one*, and the elements of character melt into
each other. The genius is a part of the mind, and the mind a part of
the behaviour; so that, for the attitude of inquiry, without which
appreciation means nothing, where does one of these provinces end
and the other begin? We may take the genius first or the behaviour
first, but we inevitably proceed from the one to the other; we inevitably encamp, as it were, on the high central table-land that they have
in common. How are we to arrive at a relation with the object to be
penetrated if we are thus forever met by a locked door flanked with
a sentinel who merely invites us to take it for edifying? We take it

ourselves for attaching—which is the very essence of mysteries—and profess ourselves doomed forever to hang yearningly about it. An obscurity endured, in fine, one inch further, or one hour longer, than our necessity truly holds us to, strikes us but as an artificial spectre, a muffled object with waving arms, set up to keep appreciation down.

For it is never to be forgotten that we are here in presence of the human character the most magnificently endowed, in all time, with the sense of the life of man, and with the apparatus for recording it; so that of *him*, inevitably, it goes hardest of all with us to be told that we have nothing, or next to nothing, to do with the effect in him of this gift. If it does not satisfy us that the effect was to make him write *King Lear* and *Othello*, we are verily difficult to please: so it is, meanwhile, that the case for the obscurity is argued. That is sovereign, we reply, so far as it goes; but it tells us nothing of the effect on him of being *able* to write *Lear* and *Othello*. No scrap of testimony of what this may have been is offered us; it is the quarter in which our blankness is most blank, and in which we are yet most officiously put off. It is true of the poet in general—in nine examples out of ten—that his life is mainly inward, that its events and revolutions are his great impressions and deep vibrations, and that his "personality" is all pictured in the publication of his verse. Shakespeare, we essentially feel, is the tenth, is the millionth example; not the sleek bachelor of music, the sensitive harp set once for all in the window to catch the air, but the spirit in hungry quest of every possible experience and adventure of the spirit, and which, betimes, with the boldest of all intellectual movements, was to leap from the window into the street. We are in the street, as it were, for admiration and wonder, when the incarnation alights, and it is of no edification to shrug shoulders at the felt impulse (when made manifest) to follow, to pursue, all breathlessly to track it on its quickly-taken way. Such a quest of imaginative experience, we can only feel, has itself constituted one of the greatest observed adventures of mankind; so that no point of the history of it, however far back seized, is premature for our fond attention. Half our connection with it is our desire to "assist" at it; so how can we fail of curiosity and sympathy? The answer to which is doubtless again that these impulses are very well, but that as the case stands they can move but in one channel. We are free to assist in the Plays themselves—to assist at whatever we like; so long, that is, as, after the fashion I have noted, we rigidly limit our inductions from them. It is put to us once more that we can make no bricks without straw, and that, rage as we may against our barrier, it none the less stubbornly exists. Granted on behalf of the vaulting spirit all that we claim for it, it still, in the street, as we say—and in spite of the effect we see it as acrobatically producing there—absolutely defies pursuit. Beyond recovery, beyond curiosity, it was to lose itself in the crowd. The crowd, for that matter, the witnesses we must take as astonished and dazzled, has, though itself surviving but in a dozen or two dim, scarce articulate ghosts, been interrogated to the last man and the last distinguishable echo. This has practically elicited nothing—nothing, that is, of a nature to gratify the indiscreetly, the morbidly inquisitive; since we find ourselves not rarely reminded that morbidity may easily become a vice. *He* was notoriously not morbid; he stuck to his business—save when he so strangely gave it up; wherefore his own common sense about things in general is a model for the tone he should properly inspire. "You speak of his career as a transcendent 'adventure,' as *the* conspicuously transcendent adventure—even to the sight of his contemporaries—of the mind of man; but no glimmer of any such story, of any such figure or 'presence,' to use your ambiguous word, as you desire to read into the situation, can be discerned in any quarter. So what is it you propose we should do? What evidence do you suggest that, with this absence of material, we should put together? We have what we have; we are not concerned with what we have not."

In some such terms as that, one makes out, does the best attainable "appreciation" appear to invite us to let our great personage, the mighty adventurer, slink past. He slunk past in life: that was good enough for him, the contention appears to be. Why therefore should he not slink past in immortality? One's reply can indeed only be that he evidently must; yet I profess that, even while saying so, our poor point, for which *The Tempest* once more gives occasion, strikes me as still, as always, in its desperate way, worth the making. The question, I hold, will eternally interest the student of letters and of the human understanding, and the envied privilege of our play in particular will be always to keep it before him. *How* did the faculty so radiant there contrive, in such perfection, the arrest of its divine flight? By what inscrutable process was the extinguisher applied and, when once applied, kept in its place to the end? What became of the checked torrent, as a latent, bewildered presence and energy, in the life across which the dam was constructed? What other mills did it set itself turning, or what contiguous country did it—rather indeed did it *not*, in default of these—inevitably ravage? We are referred, for an account of the matter, to recorded circumstances which are only not supremely vulgar because they are supremely dim and few; in which character they but mock, and as if all consciously, as I have said, at our unrest. The one at all large indication they give is that our hero may have died—since he died so soon—of his unnatural effort. Their quality, however, redeems them a little by having for its effect that they throw us back on the work itself with a rebellious renewal of appetite and yearning. The secret that baffles us being the secret of the Man, we know, as I have granted, that we shall never touch the Man *directly* in the Artist. We stake our hopes thus on indirectness, which may contain possibilities; we take that very truth for our counsel of despair, try to look at it as helpful for the Criticism of the future. That of the past has been too often infantile; one has asked one's self how it *could*, on such lines, get at him. The figured tapestry, the long arras that hides him, is always there, with its immensity of surface and its proportionate underside. May it not then be but a question, for the fulness of time, of the finer weapon, the sharper point, the stronger arm, the more extended lunge?

MR. AND MRS. JAMES T. FIELDS

IF AT SUCH a time as this a man of my generation finds himself on occasion revert to our ancient peace in some soreness of confusion between envy and pity, I know well how best to clear up the matter for myself at least and to recover a workable relation with the blessing in eclipse. I recover it in some degree with pity, as I say, by reason of the deep illusions and fallacies in which the great glare of the present seems to show us as then steeped; there being always, we can scarce not feel, something pathetic in the recoil from fond fatuities. When these are general enough, however, they make their own law and impose their own scheme; they go on, with their fine earnestness, to their utmost limit, and the best of course are those that go on longest. When I think that the innocent confidence cultivated over a considerable part of the earth, over all the parts most offered to my own view, was to last well-nigh my whole lifetime, I cannot deny myself a large respect for it, cannot but see that if our illusion was complete we were at least insidiously and artfully beguiled. What we had taken so actively to believing in was to bring us out at the brink of the abyss, yet as I look back I see nothing but our excuses; I cherish at any rate the image of their bright plausibility. We really, we nobly, we insanely (as it can only now strike us) held ourselves comfortably clear of the worst horror that in the past had attended the life of nations, and to the grounds of this conviction we could point with lively assurance. They all come back, one now recognizes, to a single supporting proposition, to the question when in the world peace had so prodigiously flourished. It had been broken, and was again briefly broken, within our view, but only as if to show with what force and authority it could freshly assert itself; whereby it grew to look too increasingly big, positively too massive even in its blandness, for interruptions not to be afraid of it.

It is in the light of this memory, I confess, that I bend fondly over the age—so prolonged, I have noted, as to yield ample space for the exercise—in which any challenge to our faith fell below the sweet serenity of it. I see that by any measure I might personally have applied, the American, or at least the Northern, state of mind and of life that began to develop just after the Civil War formed the headspring of our assumption. Odd enough might it have indeed appeared that this conception should need four years of free carnage to launch it; yet what did that mean, after all, in New York and Boston, into which places remembrance reads the complacency soon to be the most established—what did that mean unless that we had exactly *shed* the bad possibilities, were publicly purged of the dreadful disease which had come within an inch of being fatal to us, and were by that token warranted sound forever, superlatively safe?—as we could see that during the previous existence of the country we had been but comparatively so. The breathless campaign of Sadowa, which occurred but a year after our own sublime conclusion had been sealed by Lee's surrender, enlarged the prospect much rather than ruffled it; and though we had to confess that the siege of Paris, four years later, was a false note, it was drowned in the solidification of Germany, so true, so resounding and, for all we then suspected to the contrary, so portentously pacific a one. How could peace not flourish, moreover, when wars either took only seven weeks or lasted but a summer and scarce more than a long-drawn autumn?—the siege of Paris dragging out, to our pitying sense, at the time, but raised before all the rest of us, preparing food-succor, could well turn round, and with the splendid recovery of France to follow so close on her amputation that violence fairly struck us as moving away confounded. So it was that our faith was confirmed—violence sitting down again with averted face, and the conquests we felt the truly golden ones spreading and spreading behind its back.

*

It was not perhaps in the purest gold of the matter that we pretended to deal in the New York and the Boston to which I have referred; but if I wish to catch again the silver tinkle at least, straining my ear for it through the sounds of to-day, I have but to recall the dawn of those associations that seemed then to promise everything, and the last declining ray of which rests, just long enough to be caught, on the benign figure of Mrs. Fields, of the latter city, recently deceased and leaving behind her much of the material out of which legend obligingly grows. She herself had the good fortune to assist, during all her later years, at an excellent case of such growth, for which nature not less than circumstance had perfectly fitted her—she was so intrinsically charming a link with the past and abounded so in the pleasure of reference and the grace of fidelity. She helped the present, that of her own actuality, to think well of her producing conditions, to think better of them than of many of those that open for our wonderment to-day: what a note of distinction *they* were able to contribute, she moved us to remark, what a quality of refinement they appeared to have encouraged, what a minor form of the monstrous modern noise they seemed to have been consistent with!

The truth was of course very decidedly that the seed I speak of, the seed that has flowered into legend, and with the thick growth of which her domestic scene was quite embowered, had been sown in soil peculiarly grateful and favored by pleasing accidents. The personal beauty of her younger years, long retained and not even at the end of such a stretch of life quite lost; the exquisite native tone and mode of appeal, which anciently we perhaps thought a little 'precious,' but from which the distinctive and the preservative were in time to be snatched, a greater extravagance supervening; the signal sweetness of temper and lightness of tact, in fine, were things that prepared together the easy and infallible exercise of what I have called her references. It adds greatly to one's own measure of the accumulated years to have seen her reach the age at which she could appear to the younger world about her to "go back" wonderfully far, to be almost the only person extant who did, and to owe much of her value to this delicate aroma of antiquity.

My title for thus speaking of her is that of being myself still extant enough to have known by ocular and other observational evidence what it was she went back to and why the connection should consecrate her. Every society that amounts, as we say, to anything has it own annals, and luckless any to which this cultivation of the sense of a golden age that has left a precious deposit happens to be closed. A local present of proper pretensions has in fact to invent a set of antecedents, something in the nature of an epoch either of giants or of fairies, when literal history may in this respect have failed it, in order to look other temporal claims of a like complexion in the face. Boston, all letterless and unashamed as she verily seems to-day, needs luckily, for recovery of self-respect, no resort to such make-believes— to legend, that is, before the fact; all her legend is well after it, absolutely upon it, the large, firm fact, and to the point of covering, and covering yet again, every discernible inch of it. I felt myself during the half-dozen years of my younger time spent thereabouts just a little late for history perhaps, though well before, or at least well abreast of, poetry; whereas now it all densely foreshortens, it positively all melts beautifully together, and I square myself in the state of mind of an authority not to be questioned. In other words, my impression of the golden age was a first-hand one, not a second or a third; and since those with whom I shared it have dropped off one by one,—I can think of but two or three of the distinguished, the intelligent and participant, that is, as left,—I fear there is no arrogance of authority that I am not capable of taking on.

James T. Fields must have had about him when I first knew him much of the freshness of the season, but I remember thinking him invested with a stately past; this as an effect of the spell cast from an early, or at least from *my* early, time by the "Ticknor, Reed and Fields" at the bottom of every title-page of the period that conveyed, however shyly, one of the finer presumptions. I look back with wonder to what would seem a precocious interest in title-pages, and above all into the mysterious or behind-the-scenes world suggested by publishers' names—which, in their various collocations, had a color and a character beyond even those of authors, even those of books themselves;

an anomaly that I seek not now to fathom, but which the brilliant Mr. Fields, as I aspiringly saw him, had the full benefit of, not less when I first came to know him than before. Mr. Reed, Mr. Ticknor, were never at all to materialize for me; the former was soon to forfeit any pertinence, and the latter, so far as I was concerned, never so much as peeped round the titular screen. Mr. Fields, on the other hand, planted himself well before that expanse; not only had he shone betimes with the reflected light of Longfellow and Lowell, of Emerson and Hawthorne and Whittier, but to meet him was, for an ingenuous young mind, to find that he was understood to return with interest any borrowed glory and to keep the social, or I should perhaps rather say the sentimental, account straight with each of his stars. What he truly shed back, of course, was a prompt sympathy and conversability; it was in this social and personal color that he emerged from the mere imprint, and was alone, I gather, among the American publishers of the time in emerging. He had a conception of possibilities of relation with his authors and contributors that I judge no other member of his body in all the land to have had; and one easily makes out for that matter that his firm was all but alone in improving, to this effect of amenity, on the crude relation—crude, I mean, on the part of the author. Few were our native authors, and the friendly Boston house had gathered them in almost all: the other, the New York and Phila-delphia houses (practically all we had) were friendly, I make out at this distance of time, to the public in particular, whose appetite they met to abundance with cheap reprints of the products of the London press, but were doomed to represent in a lower, sometimes indeed in the very lowest, degree the element of consideration for the British original. The British original had during that age been reduced to the solatium of publicity pure and simple; knowing, or at least presuming, that he was read in America by the fact of his being appropriated, he could himself appropriate but the complacency of this consciousness.

To the Boston constellation then almost exclusively belonged the higher complacency, as one may surely call it, of being able to measure with some closeness the good purpose to which they glittered. The Fieldses could imagine so much happier a scene that the fond fancy they brought to it seems to flush it all, as I look back, with the richest tints. I so describe the sweet influence because by the time I found myself taking more direct notice the singularly graceful young wife had become, so to speak, a highly noticeable feature; her beautiful head and hair and smile and voice (we wonder if a social circle worth naming was ever ruled by a voice without charm of quality) were so many happy items in a general array. Childless, what is vulgarly called unencumbered, addicted to every hospitality and every benevolence, addicted to the cultivation of talk and wit and to the ingenious multiplication of such ties as could link the upper half of the title-page with the lower, their vivacity, their curiosity, their mobility, the felicity of their instinct for any manner of gathered relic, remnant or tribute, conspired to their helping the "literary world" roundabout to a self-consciousness more fluttered, no doubt, yet also more romantically resolute.

To turn attention from any present hour to a past that has become distant is always to have to look through overgrowths and reckon with perversions; but even so the domestic, the waterside museum of the Fieldses hangs there clear to me; their salon positively, so far as salons were in the old Puritan city dreamed of—by which I mean allowing for a couple of exceptions not here to be lingered on. We knew in those days little of collectors; the name of the class, however, already much impressed us, and in that long and narrow drawing-room of odd dimensions—unfortunately somewhat sacrificed, I frankly confess, as American drawing-rooms are apt to be, to its main aperture or command of outward resonance—one learned for the first time how vivid a collection might be. Nothing would reconcile me at this hour to any attempt to resolve back into its elements the brave effect of the exhibition, in which the inclusive range of "old" portrait and letter, of old pictorial and literal autograph and other material gage or illustration, of old original edition or still more authentically consecrated current copy, disposed itself over against the cool sea-presence of the innermost great basin of Boston's port. Most does it come to me, I think, that the enviable pair went abroad with freedom and frequency, and that the inscribed and figured walls

were a record of delightful adventure, a display as of votive objects
attached by restored and grateful mariners to the nearest shrine. To
go abroad, to *be* abroad (for the return thence was to the advantage,
after all, only of those who could not so proceed) represented success
in life, and our couple were immensely successful.

Dickens at that time went a great way with us, the best of him
falling after this fashion well within the compass of our life; and
Thackeray, for my own circle, went, I think, a greater way still, even
if already, at the season I recall, to a more ghostly effect and as a presence definitely immortalized. The register of his two American visits
was piously, though without the least solemnity, kept in Charles
Street; which assisted, however, at Dickens's second visit to the States
and a comparatively profane contemporaneity. I was not to see him
there; I was, save for a brief moment elsewhere, but to hear him and
to wonder at his strange histrionic force in public; nevertheless the
waterside museum never ceased to retain, for my earnest recognition,
certain fine vibrations and dying echoes of all that episode. I liked to
think of the house, I couldn't do without thinking of it, as the great
man's safest harborage through the tremendous gale of those even
more leave-taking appearances, as fate was to appoint, than we then
understood; and this was a fact about it, to my taste, which made all
sorts of other, much more prolonged and reiterated, facts comparatively
subordinate and flat. The single drawback was that the intimacies
and privileges it witnessed for in that most precious connection
seemed scarce credible; the inimitable presence was anecdotically
enough attested, but I somehow rather missed the evidential sample,
"a feather, an eagle's feather," as Browning says, which I should, ideally speaking, have picked up on the stairs.

I doubtless meanwhile found it the most salient of all the circumstances that the *Atlantic Monthly* had at no ancient date virtually
come into being under the fostering roof, and that a charm, or at least
a felt soft weight, attached to one's thinking of its full-flushed earlier
form as very much edited from there. There its contributors, or many
of them, dined and supped and went to tea, and there above all, in
many a case, was almost gloriously revealed to them the possible

relation between such amenities and hospitalities and the due degree of inspiration. It would take me too far to say how I dispose of J. R. Lowell in this reconstruction, the very first editor as he was, if I mistake not, of the supremely sympathetic light miscellany that I figure; but though I have here to pick woefully among my reminiscences I must spare a word or two for another presence too intimately associated with the scene, and too constantly predominant there, to be overlooked.

The *Atlantic* was for years practically the sole organ of that admirable writer and wit, that master of almost every form of observational, of meditational, and of humorous ingenuity, the author of *The Autocrat of the Breakfast Table* and of *Elsie Venner*. Dr. Oliver Wendell Holmes had been from the first the great "card" of the new *recueil*, and this with due deference to the fact that Emerson and Longfellow and Whittier, that Lowell himself and Hawthorne and Francis Parkman, were prone to figure in no other periodical (speaking thus of course but of the worthies originally drawn upon). Mr. Longfellow was frequent and remarkably even, neither rising above nor falling below a level ruled as straight as a line for a copybook; Emerson, on the other hand, was rare, but, to make up for it, sometimes surprising; and when ask myself what best distinction the magazine owed to our remaining hands I of course remember that it put forth the whole later array of *The Biglow Papers*, and that the impressions and reminiscences of England gathered up by Hawthorne into *Our Old Home* had enjoyed their first bloom of publicity from month to month under Fields's protection. These things drew themselves out in delightful progression, to say nothing of other cognate felicities—everything that either Lowell or Hawthorne published in those days making its first appearance, inveterately, in the *Atlantic* pages. Lowell's serious as well as his hilarious, that is his broadly satiric, verse was pressed into their service; though of his literary criticism, I recall, the magazine was less avid—little indeed, at the same time, as it could emulate in advance its American-born fellows of to-day in apparent dread of that insidious appeal to attention. Which remarks, as I make them, but throw into relief for me the admirable vivacity and liberality of Dr. Holmes's *Atlantic* career, quite warranting, as they again flicker and glow, no matter what easy talk about a golden age. *The Autocrat of the Breakfast Table*, the American contribution to literature, that I can recall, most nearly meeting the conditions and enjoying the fortune of a classic, quite sufficiently accounts, I think, for our sense not only at the time, but during a long stretch of the subsequent, that we had there the most precious of the metals in the very finest fusion. Such perhaps was not entirely the air in which we saw *Elsie Venner* bathed—since if this too was a case of the shining substance of the author's mind, so extraordinarily agile within its own circle of content, the application of the admirable engine was yet not perhaps so happy; in spite of all of which nothing would induce me now to lower our then claim for this fiction as the charmingest of the "old" American group, the romances of Hawthorne of course always excepted.

The new American novel—for that was preparing—had at the season I refer to scarce glimmered into view; but its first seeds were to be sown very exactly in *Atlantic* soil, where my super-excellent friend and confrère W. D. Howells soon began editorially to cultivate them. I should find myself crossing in this reference the edge of a later period, were I moved here at all to stiff discriminations; which I am so far from being that I absolutely *like* to remember, pressing out elated irony in it, that the magazine seemed pleased to profit by Howells, whether as wise editor or delightful writer, only up to the verge of his broadening out into mastership. He broadened gradually, and far-away back numbers exhibit the tentative light footprints that were to become such firm and confident steps; but affectionate appreciation quite consciously assisted at a process in which it could mark and measure each stage—up to the time, that is, when the process quite outgrew, as who should say, the walls of the drill-ground itself.

By this time many things, as was inevitable,—things not of the earlier tradition,—had come to pass; not the least of these being that J. T. Fields, faithfully fathering man, had fallen for always out of the circle. What was to follow his death made for itself other connections, many of which indeed had already begun; but what I think of in particular, as his beguiled loose chronicler straightening out a little—though I would not for the world overmuch—the confusion of old and doubtless, in some cases, rather shrunken importances, what especially run to earth is that there were forms of increase which the "original" organ might have seemed to grow rather weak in the knees for carrying. I pin my remembrance, however, only to the Fieldses—that is, above all, to *his* active relation to the affair, and to the image left with me of guiding and nursing pleasure shown always as the intensity of personal pleasure. No confident proprietor can ever have drawn more happiness from a cherished and computed value than he drew from Dr. Holmes's success, which likewise provided so blest a medium for the Autocrat's own expansive spirit that I see the whole commerce and inspiration in the cheerful waterside light.

I find myself couple together the two Charles Street houses, though even with most weight of consideration for that where *The Autocrat, The Professor, Elsie Venner*, and the long and bright succession of the unsurpassed Boston *pièces de circonstance* in verse, to say nothing of all the eagerest and easiest and funniest, all the most winged and kept-up, most illustrational and suggestional, table-talk that ever was, sprang smiling to life. Ineffaceably present to me is all *that* atmosphere, though I enjoyed it of course at the time but as the most wonderstruck and most indulged of extreme juniors; and in the mere ghostly breath of it old unspeakable vibrations revive. I find innumerable such for instance between the faded leaves of *Soundings from the Atlantic*, and in one of the papers there reprinted, "My Hunt for the Captain," in especial, the recital of the author's search among the Virginia battle-fields for his gallant wounded son; which, with its companions, evokes for me also at this end of time, and mere fond memory aiding, a greater group of sacred images than I may begin to name, as well as the charm and community of that overlooking of the wide inlet which so corrected the towniness. The Autocrat's insuperable instinct for the double sense of words, when the drollery of the collocation was pointed enough, has its note in the title of the volume I have just mentioned (where innumerable other neglected notes would respond

again, I imagine, to the ear a bit earnestly applied); but the clue that
has lengthened out so far is primarily attached, no doubt, to the eloquence of the final passage of the paper, in which the rejoicing father,
back from his anxious quest, sees Boston bristle again on his lifelong
horizon, the immemorial signs multiply, the great dome of the State
House rise not a whit less high than before, and the Bunker Hill
obelisk point as sharply as ever its beveled capstone against the sky.

The charm I thus rake out of the period, and the aspect of the
Fieldses as bathed in that soft medium—*so* soft after the long internecine harshness—gloss over to my present view every troubled face
of my young relation with the *Atlantic*; the poor pathetic faces, as
they now pass before me, being troubled for more reasons than I can
recall, but above all, I think, because from the first I found "writing
for the magazines" an art still more difficult than delightful. Yet I
doubt whether I wince at this hour any more than I winced on the
spot at hearing it quoted from this proprietor of the first of those
with which I effected an understanding that such a strain of pessimism
in the would-be picture of life had an odd, had even a ridiculous, air
on the part of an author with his mother's milk scarce yet dry on his
lips. It was to my amused W. D. H. that I owed this communication,
as I was to owe him ever such numberless invitations to partake of
his amusement; and I trace back to that with interest the first note
of the warning against not "ending happily" that was for the rest of
my literary life to be sounded in my ear with a good faith of which
the very terms failed to reach me intelligibly enough to correct my
apparent perversity. I labored always under the conviction that to
terminate a fond aesthetic effort in felicity had to be as much one's
obeyed law as to begin it and carry it on in the same; whereby how
could one be anything less than bewildered at the non-recognition
of one's inveterately plotted climax of expression and intensity? One
went so far as literally to claim that in a decent production—such as
one at least hoped any particular specimen of one's art to show for—
the terminal virtue, driven by the whole momentum gathered on the
way, *had* to be most expressional of one's subject, and thereby more
fortunately pointed than whatever should have gone before. I remem-

ber clinging to that measure of the point really made even in the tender dawn of the bewilderment I glance at and which I associate with the general precarious element in those first *Atlantic* efforts. It really won me to an anxious kindness for Mr. Fields that though finding me precociously dismal he yet indulgently suffered me—and this not the less for my always feeling that Howells, during a season his sub-editor, must more or less have intervened with a good result.

The great, the reconciling thing, however, was the easy medium, the generally teeming Fields atmosphere, out of which possibilities that ravished me increasingly sprang; though doubtless these may speak in the modern light quite preponderantly of the young observer's and devourer's irrepressible need to appreciate—as compared, I mean, with his need to *be* appreciated, and a due admixture of that recognized. I preserve doubtless imperfectly the old order of these successions, the thrill sometimes but blandly transmitted, sometimes directly snatched, the presented occasion and the rather ruefully missed, the apprehension that in such a circle—with centre and circumference, in Charles Street, coming well together despite the crowded, the verily crammed, space between them—the brush of aesthetic, of social, of cultural suggestion worked, when most lively, at the end of a long handle that had stretched all the way over from Europe. How it struck me as working, I remember well, on a certain afternoon when the great Swedish singer Christine Nielsen, then young and beautiful and glorious, was received among us—that is, when she stood between a pair of the windows of the Fields museum, to which she was for the moment the most actual recruit, and accepted the homage of extremely presented and fluttered persons, not one of whom could fail to be dazzled by her extraordinary combination of different kinds of lustre. Then there was the period of Charles Fechter, who had come over from London, whither he had originally come from Paris, to establish a theatre in Boston, where he was to establish it to no great purpose, alas! and who during the early brightness of his legend seemed to create for us on the same spot an absolute community of interests with the tremendously knowing dilettanti to whom he referred. He referred most of course to Dickens, who had directed him straight upon Charles Street under a benediction that was at first to do much for him, launch him violently and to admiration, even if he was before long, no doubt, to presume overmuch on its virtue.

Highly effective too, in this connection, while the first portents lasted, was the bustling virtue of the Fieldses—on that ground and on various others indeed directly communicated from Dickens's own, and infinitely promoting the delightful roused state under which we grasped at the aesthetic freshness of Fechter's Hamlet in particular. Didn't we react with the finest collective and perceptive intensity against the manner of our great and up to that time unquestioned exponent of the part, Edwin Booth?—who, however he might come into his own again after the Fechter flurry, never recovered real credit, it was interesting to note, for the tradition of his "head," his facial and physiognomic make-up, of a sudden quite luridly revealed as provincial, as formed even to suggest the powerful support rendered the Ophelia of *Pendennis*'s Miss Fotheringay. I remember, in fine, thinking that the emissary of Dickens and the fondling of the Fieldses, to express it freely, seemed to play over our classic, our livid ringletted image a sort of Scandinavian smoky torch, out of the lurid flicker of which it never fully emerged.

These are trivial and perhaps a bit tawdry illustrations; but there were plenty of finer accidents: projected assurances and encountered figures and snatched impressions, such as naturally make at present but a faded show, and yet not one of which has lost its distinctness for my own infatuated piety. I see now what an overcharged glory could attach to the fact that Anthony Trollope, in his habit as he lived, was at a given moment literally dining in Charles Street. I can do justice to the rich notability of my partaking of Sunday supper there in company with Mrs. Beecher Stowe, and making out to my satisfaction that if she had, of intensely local New England type as she struck me as being, not a little of the nonchalance of real renown, she "took in" circumjacent objects and more agitated presences with the true economy of genius. I even invest with the color of romance, or I did at the time, the bestowal on me, for temporary use, of the precursory pages of Matthew Arnold's *Essays in Criticism*, honorably smirched by the American compositor's fingers, from which the Boston edition of that volume, with the classicism of its future awaiting it, had just been set up. I can still recover the rapture with which, then suffering under the effects of a bad accident, I lay all day on a sofa in Ashburton Place and was somehow transported, as in a shining silvery dream, to London, to Oxford, to the French Academy, to Languedoc, to Brittany, to ancient Greece; all under the fingered spell of the little loose smutty London sheets. And I somehow even felt in my face the soft side wind of that "arranging" for punctualities of production of the great George Eliot, with whom our friends literally conversed, to the last credibility, every time they went to London, and, thanks to whose intimate confidence in them, doesn't it seem to me that I enjoyed the fragrant foretaste of *Middlemarch*?—roundabout which I patch together certain confused reminiscences of a weekly periodical, a younger and plainer sister of the *Atlantic*, its title now lost to me and the activity of which was all derivative, consisting as it did of bang-on-the-hour English first-fruits, "advance" felicities of the London press. This must all have meant an elated season during which, in the still prolonged absence of an international copyright law, the favor of early copy, the alertness of postal transmission, in consideration of the benefit of the quickened fee, was to make international harmony prevail. I retain but an inferential sense of it all, yet gilded again to memory by perusals of Trollope, of Wilkie Collins, of Charles Reade, of others of the then distinguished, quite beneath their immediate rejoicing eye and with double the amount of quality we had up to that time extracted oozing gratefully through their pores.

Mrs. Fields was to survive her husband for many years and was to flourish as a copious second volume—the connection licenses the free figure—of the work anciently issued. She had a further and further, a very long life, all of infinite goodness and grace, and, while ever insidiously referring to the past, could not help meeting the future at least half-way. And all her implications were gay, since no one so finely sentimental could be noted as so humorous; just as no feminine humor was perhaps ever so unmistakingly directed, and no state of amusement, amid quantities of reminiscence, perhaps ever so merciful. It was not that she could think no ill, but that she couldn't see others thinking it, much less doing it; which was quite compatible too with her being as little trapped by any presumptuous form of it as if she had had its measure to the last fineness. It became a case of great felicity; she was all the gentle referee and servant, the literary and social executor, so to speak, of a hundred ghosts, but the scroll of her vivid commission had never been rolled up, so that it hung there open to whatever more names and pleas might softly inscribe themselves. She kept her whole connection insistently modern, in the sense that all new recruits to it found themselves in concert with the charming old tone, and, only wanting to benefit by its authority, were much more affected by it than it was perhaps fortunately in certain cases affected by them. Beautiful the instance of an exquisite person for whom the mere grace of unimpaired duration, drawing out and out the grace implanted, established an importance that she never lifted so much as a finger to claim, and the manner of which was that, while people surrounded her, admiringly and tenderly, only to do in their own interest all the reminding, she was herself ever as little as possible caught in the more or less invidious act. It was they who preferred her possibilities of allusion to any aspect of the current jostle, and her sweetness under their pressure made her consentingly modern even while the very sound of the consent was as the voice of a time so much less strident.

My sense of all this later phase was able on occasion to renew itself, but perhaps never did so in happier fashion than when Mrs. Fields, revisiting England, as she continued to embrace every opportunity of doing, kindly traveled down to see me in the country, bringing with her a young friend of great talent whose prevailing presence in her life had come little by little to give it something like a new centre. To speak in a mere parenthesis of Miss Jewett, mistress of an art of fiction all her own, even though of a minor compass, and surpassed only by Hawthorne as producer of the most finished and penetrating of the numerous "short stories" that have the domestic life of New

England for their general and their doubtless somewhat lean subject, is to do myself, I feel, the violence of suppressing a chapter of appreciation that I should long since somewhere have found space for. Her admirable gift, that artistic sensibility in her which rivaled the rare personal, that sense for the finest kind of truthful rendering, the sober and tender note, the temperately touched, whether in the ironic or the pathetic, would have deserved some more pointed commemoration than judge her beautiful little quantum of achievement, her free and high, yet all so generously subdued character, a sort of elegance of humility or fine flame of modesty, with her remarkably distinguished outward stamp, to have called forth before the premature and over-darkened close of her young course of production. She had come to Mrs. Fields as an adoptive daughter, both a sharer and a sustainer, and nothing could more have warmed the ancient faith of their confessingly a bit disoriented countryman than the association of the elder and the younger lady in such an emphasized susceptibility. Their reach together was of the firmest and easiest, and I verily remember being struck with the stretch of wing that the spirit of Charles Street could bring off on finding them all fragrant of a recent immersion in the country life of France, where admiring friends had opened to them iridescent vistas that made it by comparison a charity they should show the least dazzle from my so much ruder display. I preserve at any rate the memory of a dazzle corresponding, or in other words of my gratitude for their ready apprehension of the greatness of big "composed" Sussex, which we explored together almost to extravagance—the lesson to my own sense all remaining that of how far the pure, the peculiarly pure, old Boston spirit, old even in these women of whom one was miraculously and the other familiarly young, could travel without a scrap of loss of its ancient immunity to set against its gain of vivacity.

There was vivacity of a new sort somehow in the fact that the elder of my visitors, the elder in mere calculable years, had come fairly to cultivate, as it struck me, a personal resemblance to the great George Eliot—and this but through the quite lawful art of causing a black lace mantilla to descend from her head and happily consort with a

droop of abundant hair, a formation of brow and a general fine be-
nignity: things that at once markedly recalled the countenance of Sir
Frederick Burton's admirable portrait of the author of *Romola* and
made it a charming anomaly that such remains of beauty should
match at all a plainness not to be blinked even under the play of Sir
Frederick's harmonizing crayon. Other amplified aspects of the whole
legend, as have called it, I was afterwards to see presented on its native
scene—whereby it comes back to me that Sarah Jewett's brave ghost
would resent my too roughly Bostonizing her: there hangs before me
such a picture of her right setting, the antique dignity—as antiquity
counts thereabouts—of a clear colonial house, in Maine, just over
the New Hampshire border, and a day spent amid the very richest
local revelations. These things were not so much of like as of equally
flushed complexion with two or three occasions of view, at the same
memorable time, of Mrs. Fields's happy alternative home on the shining Massachusetts shore, where I seem to catch in latest afternoon
light the quite final form of all the pleasant evidence. To say which,
however, is still considerably to foreshorten; since there supervenes
for me with force as the very last word, or the one conclusive for
myself at least, a haunted little feast as of ghosts, if not of skeletons,
at the banquet, with the image of that immemorial and inextinguishable lady Mrs. Julia Ward Howe, the most evidential and most eminent presence of them all, as she rises in her place, under the
extremity of appeal, to disclaim a little quaveringly, but ever so gal-
lantly, that "Battle-hymn of the Republic," which she had caused to
be chanted half a century before and still could accompany with a
real breadth of gesture, her great clap of hands and indication of the
complementary step, on the triumphant line,

Be swift my hands to welcome him, be jubilant my feet!

The geniality of this performance swept into our collective breast
again the whole matter of my record, which I thus commend to safe
spiritual keeping.

BIBLIOGRAPHICAL NOTES

THE ART OF FICTION

First published in *Longman's Magazine*, September 1884; reprinted in *Partial Portraits* (London and New York: Macmillan and Co., 1888). The lecture of the same title by Walter Besant (1836–1901), to which James's essay is a reply, was delivered at the Royal Institution on April 25, 1884; it is excerpted in Stephen Regan, *The Nineteenth Century Novel: A Critical Reader* (London and New York: Routledge, 2001).

MARY ELIZABETH BRADDON, *AURORA FLOYD*

Published in *The Nation*, November 9, 1865. Braddon (1835–1915) was best known for *Lady Audley's Secret* (1862), a best-selling sensation novel whose plot turns on bigamy. She published more than eighty novels and edited a series of popular British magazines, but never matched her early success.

CHARLES DICKENS, *OUR MUTUAL FRIEND*

Published in *The Nation*, December 21, 1865. Dickens (1812–1870) was the most enduringly popular of Victorian novelists. His other works include *The Pickwick Papers* (1836), *David Copperfield* (1849), *Bleak House* (1853), and *Great Expectations* (1860), among many others.

ELIZABETH CLEGHORN GASKELL, *WIVES AND DAUGHTERS*

Published in *The Nation*, February 22, 1866. Gaskell (1810–1865) was a Manchester-based English novelist, best known for *Mary Barton* (1848), *Cranford* (1853), and *North and South* (1855). *Wives and Daughters* was left unfinished by her unexpected death from a heart attack, but is now regarded as her masterpiece.

GEORGE ELIOT, *MIDDLEMARCH*

Published in *Galaxy*, March 1873. George Eliot is the pseudonym of Mary Ann Evans (1819–1880). *Middlemarch* is now regarded as the greatest of nineteenth-century English novels. George Eliot's other major works include *Adam Bede* (1859), *The Mill on the Floss* (1860), and *Daniel Deronda* (1876). Her pen name was necessitated by her union with G. H. Lewes, long separated from his wife but unable to obtain a divorce; the secret was soon discovered and Victorian society proved more forgiving of genius than expected.

THOMAS HARDY, *FAR FROM THE MADDING CROWD*

Published in *The Nation*, December 24, 1874. Hardy (1840–1928) was a Dorset-born novelist of rural life. This novel's title comes from Thomas Gray's "Elegy Written in a Country Churchyard" (1751). Hardy set his fiction in an imaginary region in the west of England that he called Wessex after an Anglo-Saxon kingdom. Other Wessex novels include *The Return of the Native* (1878), *The Mayor of Casterbridge* (1886), and *Tess of the D'Urbervilles* (1891). In 1898 Hardy abandoned fiction and spent the rest of his life writing many volumes of formally conservative but thematically daring poems.

ÉMILE ZOLA, *NANA*

Published in *Parisian*, February 26, 1880. Zola (1840–1902) was raised in Aix-en-Provence. His major work is a twenty-volume cycle of linked novels, the Rougon-Macquart series, that traces the fortunes of one extended family under France's Second Empire, showing the influence of both heredity and environment upon them. Zola's major works include *L'Assommoir* (1877), *Germinal* (1885), *L'Argent* (1891), and *La Débâcle* (1892). In 1898 he published an open letter headlined "*J'Accuse . . .* !" in which he attacked the anti-Semitism of the French political and military establishment over the wrongful conviction of Captain Alfred Dreyfus on false charges of espionage.

GEORGE SAND

First published in *Galaxy*, July 1877; reprinted in *French Poets and Novelists* (1878). George Sand (1804–1876), born Amantine Lucile Aurore Dupin, was known during her lifetime for her novels, her many love affairs, and her habit of wearing men's clothing in public, the better to move about the streets. Her lovers included Prosper Mérimée, Alfred de Musset, and Frédéric Chopin.

She was extremely prolific and widely popular but her work is now little read; the consensus is that her early novels *Indiana* (1832), *Lélia* (1833), and *Consuelo* (1842) are the strongest.

ANTHONY TROLLOPE

First published in *Century Magazine*, July 1883; reprinted in *Partial Portraits* (London and New York: Macmillan and Co., 1888). Anthony Trollope (1815–1882), a prolific English novelist, civil servant, and enthusiastic fox-hunter, was best known for two six-volume series of linked novels: the Barsetshire series focuses on the lives of clergymen in the English countryside, the Palliser novels on Parliamentary affairs. His best books include *Barchester Towers* (1857), *Phineas Finn* (1867), and *The Way We Live Now* (1875).

IVAN TURGÉNIEFF

First published in *The Atlantic Monthly*, January 1884; reprinted in *Partial Portraits* (London and New York: Macmillan and Co., 1888). Ivan Sergeyevich Turgenev (1818–1883) was a Russian landowner and novelist. The unsparing realism of *Sketches from a Sportsman's Album* (1852) contributed to his being sentenced to exile on his own estates, but its stories are often described as having helped bring about the abolition of serfdom in 1861. His other works include *Home of the Gentry* (1859), *Fathers and Sons* (1862), many other novels, and short stories.

THE LIFE OF GEORGE ELIOT

First published in *The Atlantic Monthly*, May 1885; reprinted in *Partial Portraits* (London and New York: Macmillan and Co., 1888). After the 1878 death of her common-law husband G. H. Lewes, George Eliot married the much younger John Cross, a banker who had served as the couple's financial adviser and surrogate son. Cross became her first biographer, publishing *George Eliot's life as related in her letters and journals*; the work was described by the Liberal prime minister William Ewart Gladstone as not a life but "a reticence, in three volumes."

EMERSON

A review of *A Memoir of Ralph Waldo Emerson*, by James Elliot Cabot, 2 vols. (Cambridge, MA: The Riverside Press, 1887). First published in *Macmillan's*

Magazine, December 1887; reprinted as "Emerson" in *Partial Portraits* (London and New York: Macmillan and Co., 1888). Emerson (1803–1882)—an American essayist, lecturer, and poet, one of the founders of the Transcendentalist movement, and a friend of James's father—trained as a minister. In 1832 he famously renounced his Boston pulpit. Works include *Nature* (1836), "The American Scholar" (1837), and *Essays: First and Second Series* (1841, 1844).

BROWNING IN WESTMINSTER ABBEY

First published in *The Speaker*, January 4, 1890; reprinted in *Essays in London and Elsewhere* (London: James R. Osgood, 1893). Robert Browning (1812–1889), an English poet best known for his dramatic monologues in *Men and Women* (1855) and *Dramatis Personae* (1864), lived in Florence with his wife, the poet Elizabeth Barrett Browning, until her death in 1861. Afterward in England, he and the much younger James became friends. *The Ring and the Book* (1868), a book-length poem about a seventeenth-century Italian murder, later was the subject of a 1912 essay by James. See also "The Private Life," James's 1893 short story, which attempts to capture the oddness this essay describes.

GUY DE MAUPASSANT

First published in *Fortnightly Review*, March 1888; reprinted in *Partial Portraits* (London and New York: Macmillan and Co., 1888). Maupassant (1850–1893), born near the Norman coastal town of Dieppe, was a family friend and protégé of Gustave Flaubert, at whose Paris apartment James met him in the winter of 1875–1876. He made his name with "Boule de Suif" (1880), a short story about the Franco-Prussian War. He wrote hundreds of stories, most of them first published in French newspapers such as *Le Figaro*; many are on sexual themes but some are forerunners of modern horror fiction, such as "Le Horla" (1887). His best-selling novels include *Bel-Ami* (1885) and *Pierre et Jean* (1888), but he published little after 1890, when he began to suffer from the complications of the syphilis that killed him.

THE FUTURE OF THE NOVEL

Published in *International Library of Famous Literature*, vol. XIV, edited by Richard Garnet (London: The Standard, 1899).

MATILDE SERAO

First published in *North American Review*, 1901; reprinted in *Notes on Novelists* (London: J. M. Dent and Sons, 1914). Serao (1856–1927) was a Greek-born novelist and journalist, the daughter of an Italian political exile who brought his family back to Italy in 1860; she grew up in Naples. With her husband, Edoardo Scarfoglio, she founded a short-lived newspaper in Rome, and then in 1892 *Il Mattino* in Naples, which is still one of southern Italy's leading newspapers. She wrote many novels and stories and was nominated several times for the Nobel Prize in Literature. James met her at a luncheon party in Rome in 1894 and described her in a letter as a "wonderful little burly Balzac in petticoats—full of Neapolitan life and sound and familiarity."

GUSTAVE FLAUBERT

First published as the introduction to *Madame Bovary* (London: Heinemann, 1902); reprinted in *Notes on Novelists* (London: J. M. Dent and Sons, 1914). Flaubert (1821–1880), born in Rouen, the son of a prominent doctor, spent almost his entire life there in a village a few miles outside of the city, with the exception of visits to Paris, where in later life he kept an apartment, and a trip to the Middle East (1849–1850). His novels include *Madame Bovary* (1856) and *A Sentimental Education* (1869); his letters are now often cited for their *dicta* about the novelist's craft and calling.

ÉMILE ZOLA

First published in *The Atlantic Monthly*, August 1903; reprinted in *Notes on Novelists* (London: J. M. Dent and Sons, 1914). See note on *Nana*, above.

THE LESSON OF BALZAC

First published in *The Atlantic Monthly*, August 1905; reprinted in *The Question of Our Speech, The Lesson of Balzac: Two Lectures* (Boston and New York: Houghton Mifflin and Company, 1905). Born in Tours, the extraordinarily prolific Honoré de Balzac (1799–1850) made his name with *Le Père Goriot* (1835), but he had already conceived the idea of what he called *La Comédie Humaine*, in which he used a set of continuing characters to illustrate the totality of French life, its philosophical ideas as well as its manners. Balzac invented the modern city as a subject for fiction, and many of his most popular novels explore the secrets of Parisian life, among them *The Wild Ass's Skin*

(1831), *Lost Illusions* (1843), and *Cousine Bette* (1846). But he also often wrote of the provinces, as in *Eugénie Grandet* (1833). He was addicted to coffee, always plagued by debt, and forever on the run from creditors.

THE TEMPEST

First published as the introduction to the play for *The Complete Works of William Shakespeare*, edited by Sidney Lee, vol. XVI (New York: George D. Sproul, 1907). William Shakespeare (1564–1616) probably wrote *The Tempest* in 1610–1611. It is thought to be one of the last plays for which he is the sole author, though he did afterward work in collaboration with others.

MR. AND MRS. JAMES T. FIELDS

Published in *The Atlantic Monthly*, July 1915. James T. Fields (1817–1881), a partner in the Boston publishing house of Ticknor and Fields, published Hawthorne and was the American publisher of many British writers, including Dickens. He was one of the founders of *The Atlantic Monthly*, which he edited from 1861 to 1871. In 1854 he married Annie Adams Fields (1834–1915), who in the 1890s and after wrote and edited several volumes about the New England writers she had known (Harriet Beecher Stowe, Celia Thaxter, among others). *Memories of a Hostess*, edited by M. A. de Wolfe Howe (Boston: The Atlantic Monthly Press, 1922), is a posthumous selection from her letters and diaries.

OTHER NEW YORK REVIEW CLASSICS

For a complete list of titles, visit www.nyrb.com.

J.R. ACKERLEY Hindoo Holiday
J.R. ACKERLEY My Dog Tulip
J.R. ACKERLEY My Father and Myself
J.R. ACKERLEY We Think the World of You
HENRY ADAMS The Jeffersonian Transformation
CÉLESTE ALBARET Monsieur Proust
DANTE ALIGHIERI The Inferno; translated by Ciaran Carson
DANTE ALIGHIERI Purgatorio; translated by D. M. Black
CLAUDE ANET Ariane, A Russian Girl
HANNAH ARENDT Rahel Varnhagen: The Life of a Jewish Woman
ROBERTO ARLT The Seven Madmen
OĞUZ ATAY Waiting for the Fear
DIANA ATHILL Don't Look at Me Like That
DIANA ATHILL Instead of a Letter
WILLIAM ATTAWAY Blood on the Forge
W.H. AUDEN (EDITOR) The Living Thoughts of Kierkegaard
W.H. AUDEN W. H. Auden's Book of Light Verse
ERICH AUERBACH Dante: Poet of the Secular World
DOROTHY BAKER Cassandra at the Wedding
DOROTHY BAKER Young Man with a Horn
J.A. BAKER The Peregrine
HONORÉ DE BALZAC The Lily in the Valley
HONORÉ DE BALZAC The Unknown Masterpiece *and* Gambara
POLINA BARSKOVA Living Pictures
MAX BEERBOHM The Prince of Minor Writers: The Selected Essays of Max Beerbohm
MAX BEERBOHM Seven Men
ROSALIND BELBEN The Limit
ALEXANDER BERKMAN Prison Memoirs of an Anarchist
GEORGES BERNANOS Mouchette
ADOLFO BIOY CASARES Asleep in the Sun
ADOLFO BIOY CASARES The Invention of Morel
CAROLINE BLACKWOOD Corrigan
CAROLINE BLACKWOOD Great Granny Webster
HENRI BOSCO The Child and the River
HENRI BOSCO Malicroix
MALCOLM BRALY On the Yard
JOHN HORNE BURNS The Gallery
ROBERT BURTON The Anatomy of Melancholy
DINO BUZZATI The Betwitched Bourgeois: Fifty Stories
DINO BUZZATI A Love Affair
DINO BUZZATI The Singularity
DINO BUZZATI The Stronghold
GIROLAMO CARDANO The Book of My Life
J.L. CARR A Month in the Country
CAMILO JOSÉ CELA The Hive
BLAISE CENDRARS Moravagine
EILEEN CHANG Written on Water
FRANÇOIS-RENÉ DE CHATEAUBRIAND Memoirs from Beyond the Grave, 1800–1815
UPAMANYU CHATTERJEE English, August: An Indian Story
AMIT CHAUDHURI Afternoon Raag
AMIT CHAUDHURI Freedom Song

AMIT CHAUDHURI A Strange and Sublime Address

NIRAD C. CHAUDHURI The Autobiography of an Unknown Indian

ANTON CHEKHOV Peasants and Other Stories

ANTON CHEKHOV The Prank: The Best of Young Chekhov

LUCILLE CLIFTON Generations: A Memoir

RICHARD COBB Paris and Elsewhere

RACHEL COHEN A Chance Meeting: American Encounters

COLETTE Chéri *and* The End of Chéri

COLETTE The Pure and the Impure

JOHN COLLIER Fancies and Goodnights

IVY COMPTON-BURNETT A House and Its Head

IVY COMPTON-BURNETT Manservant and Maidservant

BARBARA COMYNS The Vet's Daughter

HAROLD W. CRUSE The Crisis of the Negro Intellectual

E. E. CUMMINGS The Enormous Room

JÓZEF CZAPSKI Memories of Starobielsk: Essays Between Art and History

LORENZO DA PONTE Memoirs

ELIZABETH DAVID A Book of Mediterranean Food

ELIZABETH DAVID Summer Cooking

MARIA DERMOÛT The Ten Thousand Things

ANTONIO DI BENEDETTO The Silentiary

ANTONIO DI BENEDETTO The Suicides

HEIMITO VON DODERER The Strudlhof Steps

ARTHUR CONAN DOYLE The Exploits and Adventures of Brigadier Gerard

PIERRE DRIEU LA ROCHELLE The Fire Within

CHARLES DUFF A Handbook on Hanging

ELAINE DUNDY The Dud Avocado

ELAINE DUNDY The Old Man and Me

FERIT EDGÜ The Wounded Age *and* Eastern Tales

G.B. EDWARDS The Book of Ebenezer Le Page

EURIPIDES Grief Lessons: Four Plays; translated by Anne Carson

J.G. FARRELL The Siege of Krishnapur

J.G. FARRELL The Singapore Grip

J.G. FARRELL Troubles

KENNETH FEARING The Big Clock

KENNETH FEARING Clark Gifford's Body

ROSS FELD Guston in Time: Remembering Philip Guston

FÉLIX FÉNÉON Novels in Three Lines

BEPPE FENOGLIO A Private Affair

M.I. FINLEY The World of Odysseus

THOMAS FLANAGAN The Year of the French

GUSTAVE FLAUBERT The Letters of Gustave Flaubert

WILLIAM GADDIS The Letters of William Gaddis

WILLIAM GADDIS The Recognitions

MAVIS GALLANT The Uncollected Stories of Mavis Gallant

MAVIS GALLANT Varieties of Exile

JEAN GENET The Criminal Child: Selected Essays

JEAN GENET Prisoner of Love

NATALIA GINZBURG Family *and* Borghesia

JEAN GIONO The Open Road

JOHN GLASSCO Memoirs of Montparnasse

P.V. GLOB The Bog People: Iron-Age Man Preserved

EDMOND AND JULES DE GONCOURT Pages from the Goncourt Journals

EDWARD GOREY (EDITOR) The Haunted Looking Glass
A.C. GRAHAM Poems of the Late T'ang
WILLIAM LINDSAY GRESHAM Nightmare Alley
VASILY GROSSMAN The People Immortal
OAKLEY HALL Warlock
PATRICK HAMILTON The Slaves of Solitude
PATRICK HAMILTON Twenty Thousand Streets Under the Sky
PETER HANDKE Short Letter, Long Farewell
PETER HANDKE Slow Homecoming
MARTIN A. HANSEN The Liar
ELIZABETH HARDWICK Seduction and Betrayal
ELIZABETH HARDWICK Sleepless Nights
ELIZABETH HARDWICK The Uncollected Essays of Elizabeth Hardwick
L.P. HARTLEY Eustace and Hilda: A Trilogy
L.P. HARTLEY The Go-Between
NATHANIEL HAWTHORNE Twenty Days with Julian & Little Bunny by Papa
JANET HOBHOUSE The Furies
GERT HOFMANN Our Philosopher
HUGO VON HOFMANNSTHAL The Lord Chandos Letter
JAMES HOGG The Private Memoirs and Confessions of a Justified Sinner
RICHARD HOLMES Shelley: The Pursuit
ALISTAIR HORNE A Savage War of Peace: Algeria 1954–1962
WILLIAM DEAN HOWELLS Indian Summer
RICHARD HUGHES A High Wind in Jamaica
RICHARD HUGHES In Hazard
HENRY JAMES The Ivory Tower
HENRY JAMES The New York Stories of Henry James
HENRY JAMES The Other House
HENRY JAMES The Outcry
RANDALL JARRELL (EDITOR) Randall Jarrell's Book of Stories
DAVID JONES In Parenthesis
ERNST JÜNGER The Glass Bees
ERNST JÜNGER On the Marble Cliffs
FRIGYES KARINTHY A Journey Round My Skull
MOLLY KEANE Good Behaviour
HELEN KELLER The World I Live In
YASHAR KEMAL Memed, My Hawk
YASHAR KEMAL They Burn the Thistles
WALTER KEMPOWSKI An Ordinary Youth
MURRAY KEMPTON Part of Our Time: Some Ruins and Monuments of the Thirties
DAVID KIDD Peking Story
ROBERT KIRK The Secret Commonwealth of Elves, Fauns, and Fairies
ARUN KOLATKAR Jejuri
TÉTÉ-MICHEL KPOMASSIE An African in Greenland
GYULA KRÚDY Sunflower
PAUL LAFARGUE The Right to Be Lazy
PATRICK LEIGH FERMOR Between the Woods and the Water
PATRICK LEIGH FERMOR Mani: Travels in the Southern Peloponnese
PATRICK LEIGH FERMOR Roumeli: Travels in Northern Greece
PATRICK LEIGH FERMOR A Time of Gifts
PATRICK LEIGH FERMOR A Time to Keep Silence
D.B. WYNDHAM LEWIS AND CHARLES LEE (EDITORS) The Stuffed Owl
SIMON LEYS The Hall of Uselessness: Collected Essays

GEORG CHRISTOPH LICHTENBERG The Waste Books

JAKOV LIND Soul of Wood and Other Stories

H.P. LOVECRAFT AND OTHERS Shadows of Carcosa: Tales of Cosmic Horror

JANET MALCOLM In the Freud Archives

JEAN-PATRICK MANCHETTE The N'Gustro Affair

JEAN-PATRICK MANCHETTE Skeletons in the Closet

OSIP MANDELSTAM The Selected Poems of Osip Mandelstam

THOMAS MANN Reflections of a Nonpolitical Man

JAMES McCOURT Mawrdew Czgowchwz

JOHN McGAHERN The Pornographer

HENRI MICHAUX Miserable Miracle

JESSICA MITFORD Hons and Rebels

NANCY MITFORD Frederick the Great

NANCY MITFORD Madame de Pompadour

EUGENIO MONTALE Butterfly of Dinard

AUGUSTO MONTERROSO The Rest is Silence

ELSA MORANTE Lies and Sorcery

ALBERTO MORAVIA Agostino

ALBERTO MORAVIA Boredom

ALBERTO MORAVIA Contempt

JAN MORRIS Conundrum

JAN MORRIS Hav

ÁLVARO MUTIS The Adventures and Misadventures of Maqroll

L.H. MYERS The Root and the Flower

DARCY O'BRIEN A Way of Life, Like Any Other

YURI OLESHA Envy

IONA AND PETER OPIE The Lore and Language of Schoolchildren

MAXIM OSIPOV Kilometer 101

RUSSELL PAGE The Education of a Gardener

PIER PAOLO PASOLINI Boys Alive

PIER PAOLO PASOLINI Theorem

BORIS PASTERNAK, MARINA TSVETAYEVA, AND RAINER MARIA RILKE Letters, Summer 1926

KONSTANTIN PAUSTOVSKY The Story of a Life

CESARE PAVESE The Moon and the Bonfires

CESARE PAVESE The Selected Works of Cesare Pavese

DOUGLAS J. PENICK The Oceans of Cruelty: Twenty-Five Tales of a Corpse-Spirit, a Retelling

LUIGI PIRANDELLO The Late Mattia Pascal

ANDREY PLATONOV Chevengur

ANDREY PLATONOV Soul and Other Stories

J.F. POWERS Morte d'Urban

J.F. POWERS The Stories of J.F. Powers

J.F. POWERS Wheat That Springeth Green

MARCEL PROUST Swann's Way

ALEXANDER PUSHKIN Peter the Great's African: Experiments in Prose

RAYMOND QUENEAU The Skin of Dreams

RAYMOND QUENEAU We Always Treat Women Too Well

RAYMOND QUENEAU Witch Grass

RAYMOND RADIGUET Count d'Orgel's Ball

JEAN RENOIR Renoir, My Father

GREGOR VON REZZORI Memoirs of an Anti-Semite

FR. ROLFE Hadrian the Seventh

WILLIAM ROUGHEAD Classic Crimes

CONSTANCE ROURKE American Humor: A Study of the National Character

RUMI Gold; translated by Haleh Liza Gafori
FELIX SALTEN Bambi; or, Life in the Forest
JONATHAN SCHELL The Village of Ben Suc
GERSHOM SCHOLEM Walter Benjamin: The Story of a Friendship
DANIEL PAUL SCHREBER Memoirs of My Nervous Illness
JAMES SCHUYLER Alfred and Guinevere
JAMES SCHUYLER What's for Dinner?
LEONARDO SCIASCIA The Day of the Owl
LEONARDO SCIASCIA Equal Danger
LEONARDO SCIASCIA The Moro Affair
LEONARDO SCIASCIA To Each His Own
LEONARDO SCIASCIA The Wine-Dark Sea
VICTOR SEGALEN René Leys
ANNA SEGHERS The Dead Girls' Class Trip
VICTOR SERGE The Case of Comrade Tulayev
VICTOR SERGE Conquered City
VICTOR SERGE Last Times
VICTOR SERGE Memoirs of a Revolutionary
VICTOR SERGE Midnight in the Century
VICTOR SERGE Notebooks, 1936–1947
VICTOR SERGE Unforgiving Years
ELIZABETH SEWELL The Orphic Voice
ANTON SHAMMAS Arabesques
CHARLES SIMIC Dime-Store Alchemy: The Art of Joseph Cornell
CLAUDE SIMON The Flanders Road
MAY SINCLAIR Mary Olivier: A Life
TESS SLESINGER The Unpossessed
WILLIAM GARDNER SMITH The Stone Face
VLADIMIR SOROKIN Blue Lard
VLADIMIR SOROKIN Red Pyramid: Selected Stories
VLADIMIR SOROKIN Telluria
JEAN STAFFORD Boston Adventure
GEORGE R. STEWART Fire
GEORGE R. STEWART Storm
STENDHAL The Life of Henry Brulard
ADALBERT STIFTER Motley Stones
HOWARD STURGIS Belchamber
ITALO SVEVO As a Man Grows Older
ITALO SVEVO A Very Old Man
HARVEY SWADOS Nights in the Gardens of Brooklyn
A.J.A. SYMONS The Quest for Corvo
MAGDA SZABÓ The Fawn
SUSAN TAUBES Lament for Julia
ELIZABETH TAYLOR Mrs Palfrey at the Claremont
TEFFI Other Worlds: Peasants, Pilgrims, Spirits, Saints
TATYANA TOLSTAYA The Slynx
TATYANA TOLSTAYA White Walls: Collected Stories
EDWARD JOHN TRELAWNY Records of Shelley, Byron, and the Author
LIONEL TRILLING The Liberal Imagination
LIONEL TRILLING The Middle of the Journey
YŪKO TSUSHIMA Woman Running in the Mountains
IVAN TURGENEV Fathers and Children
IVAN TURGENEV Virgin Soil

LISA TUTTLE My Death

PAUL VALÉRY Monsieur Teste

RAMÓN DEL VALLE-INCLÁN Tyrant Banderas

JULES VALLÈS The Child

MARK VAN DOREN Shakespeare

CARL VAN VECHTEN The Tiger in the House

SALKA VIERTEL The Kindness of Strangers

ELIZABETH VON ARNIM The Enchanted April

EDWARD LEWIS WALLANT The Tenants of Moonbloom

ROBERT WALSER Berlin Stories

ROBERT WALSER Girlfriends, Ghosts, and Other Stories

ROBERT WALSER Jakob von Gunten

ROBERT WALSER Little Snow Landscape

ROBERT WALSER A Schoolboy's Diary and Other Stories

MICHAEL WALZER Political Action: A Practical Guide to Movement Politics

REX WARNER Men and Gods

SYLVIA TOWNSEND WARNER The Corner That Held Them

SYLVIA TOWNSEND WARNER Lolly Willowes

SYLVIA TOWNSEND WARNER Mr. Fortune

SYLVIA TOWNSEND WARNER Summer Will Show

ALEKSANDER WAT My Century

LYALL WATSON Heaven's Breath: A Natural History of the Wind

MAX WEBER Charisma and Disenchantment: The Vocation Lectures

C.V. WEDGWOOD The Thirty Years War

SIMONE WEIL On the Abolition of All Political Parties

SIMONE WEIL AND RACHEL BESPALOFF War and the Iliad

GLENWAY WESCOTT Apartment in Athens

GLENWAY WESCOTT The Pilgrim Hawk

REBECCA WEST The Fountain Overflows

EDITH WHARTON Ghosts: Selected and with a Preface by the Author

EDITH WHARTON The New York Stories of Edith Wharton

PATRICK WHITE Riders in the Chariot

T.H. WHITE The Goshawk

JOHN WILLIAMS Augustus

JOHN WILLIAMS Butcher's Crossing

JOHN WILLIAMS (EDITOR) English Renaissance Poetry: A Collection of Shorter Poems

JOHN WILLIAMS Nothing but the Night

JOHN WILLIAMS Stoner

HENRY WILLIAMSON Tarka the Otter

ANGUS WILSON Anglo-Saxon Attitudes

EDMUND WILSON Memoirs of Hecate County

RUDOLF AND MARGARET WITTKOWER Born Under Saturn

GEOFFREY WOLFF Black Sun

RICHARD WOLLHEIM Germs: A Memoir of Childhood

FRANCIS WYNDHAM The Complete Fiction

JOHN WYNDHAM Chocky

JOHN WYNDHAM The Chrysalids

XI XI Mourning a Breast

BÉLA ZOMBORY-MOLDOVÁN The Burning of the World: A Memoir of 1914

STEFAN ZWEIG Beware of Pity

STEFAN ZWEIG Chess Story

STEFAN ZWEIG Confusion

STEFAN ZWEIG Journey into the Past